W9-BXP-123

Age of Folly

Also by Lewis H. Lapham

The Agony of Mammon
Fortune's Child
Gag Rule
Hotel America
Imperial Masquerade
Lights, Camera, Democracy!
Money and Class in America
Pretensions to Empire
Theater of War
30 Satires
Waiting for the Barbarians
The Wish for Kings
With the Beatles

Age of Folly

*America Abandons
Its Democracy*

Lewis H. Lapham

VERSO
London • New York

First published by Verso 2016
© Lewis Lapham 2016
The essays comprising Part I appeared first in the pages of *Harper's Magazine* between 1990 and 2015; chapters 33 through 35 were published originally in *Lapham's Quarterly* between 2014 and 2016

All rights reserved

The moral rights of the author have been asserted

1 3 5 7 9 10 8 6 4 2

Verso
UK: 6 Meard Street, London W1F 0EG
US: 20 Jay Street, Suite 1010, Brooklyn, NY 11201
versobooks.com

Verso is the imprint of New Left Books

ISBN-13: 978-1-78478-711-0
ISBN-13: 978-1-78478-712-7 (UK EBK)
ISBN-13: 978-1-78478-713-4 (US EBK)

British Library Cataloguing in Publication Data
A catalogue record for this book is available from the British Library

Library of Congress Cataloging-in-Publication Data
A catalog record for this book is available from the Library of Congress

Typeset in Sabon by MJ & N Gavan, Truro, Cornwall
Printed in the US by Maple Press

For Lewis, Pierce, Theodora,
Ugo, Miranda, and Urbano.

Contents

CONTENTS

Preface

A frivolous society can acquire dramatic significance only through what its frivolity destroys.

—Edith Wharton

The voices of conscience in every sector of the opinion-making news media stand united this fall in their fear and loathing of Donald J. Trump, real estate mogul, reality TV star, Republican nominee for president of the United States. The viewing with alarm is non-partisan and heartfelt, but the dumbfounded question "How can such things be?" is well behind the times. Trump is undoubtedly a menace, but he isn't a surprise. His smug and gloating face is the face of the way things are and have been in Washington and Wall Street for the last quarter of a century.

The age of folly of which Trump is an exemplary embodiment spreads across the pages of this book from America's 1991 invasion of Iraq (reality TV show armed with self-glorifying high explosives and a nonsensical casus belli) to Trump in 2016 marching in triumph on the White House (self-glorifying photo op bursting star-spangled bombast in air). Over the course of the twenty-five years from point A to point B, America changes regimes; a weakened but still operational democracy gives way to stupefied, dysfunctional plutocracy.

The spectacle of a frivolous society seeking dramatic significance doesn't lend itself to the telling of an uplifting tale. For the ancient Greeks it served as a proof of Aristotle's hypothesis that forms of government follow one another in a sequence as certain as the changing of the seasons—monarchy dissolving into despotism, despotism overthrown by democracy, democracy degenerating into plutocracy, plutocracy prompting a return to monarchy. All government, according to Aristotle, is the means by which a privileged few arrange the distribution of property and law to the less fortunate many—an oligarchy, its life span dependent on the character of the men charged with the management of its moral, political and economic enterprise.

Oligarchies bear an unhappy resemblance to cheese. Sooner or later they turn rancid in the sun. Wealth accumulates, men decay, and a band of brothers that once might have aspired to forming a wise and just government acquires the texture of what Aristotle likened to that of the "prosperous fool"—a class of men so besotted by their faith in money "that they therefore imagine there is nothing it cannot buy." Afflicted with the illness diagnosed by the Greeks as *pleonexia*, the unbridled appetite for more—more laurel wreaths and naval victories, more banquets, dancing girls, and mirrors—the fatted calves forget why sovereign nations go to war or how it comes to pass that money doesn't grow on trees.

By 1990, America was showing vivid signs of the disease. President Ronald Reagan's dancing onto the White House stage in 1981 foretold the second coming of an American Gilded Age more selfish than the first; greed was good, money the hero with a thousand faces, the notion of such a thing as democratic self-government slipping from the mind of an electorate asking of its rulers what the rich ask of their servants—comfort us, be good to us, tell us what to do.

Democracy degrading into plutocracy was the work in progress when the unlooked-for collapse of the Berlin Wall in

November 1989 confronted the prosperous bourgeois statesmen in Washington with a problem undreamed of in their philosophy: What to do without the Russians. For half a century, as long as anybody inside Washington's Beltway bubble could remember, the Evil Soviet Empire—stupendous enemy, world class and operatic, menace for all seasons—had furnished nine American presidents with a just and noble *raison d'etat*, fattened America's gross domestic product on the seed of profligate defense spending, smothered the mutterings of American political dissent with the fear of nuclear annihilation.

A precious asset, the Communist ogre in the totalitarian snow, and in 1990 sorely missed. Absent the Cold War with the Russians, how then defend, honor, and protect the cash flow of the nation's military–industrial complex pumping air and iron into the conspicuous consumptions of the American dream? The government had on hand a war machine marvelous to behold and expensive to maintain—gun platforms of every conceivable caliber and throw-weight, aircraft, tanks, and naval vessels at all points of every compass, guidance systems endowed with the wisdom of angels and armed with the judgments of doom. But other than as a means of changing lead into gold, who could say what the thing was supposed to do? Where was the tactical or strategic objective, and to what end the patriotic call to arms?

In search of dramatic significance, President George H. W. Bush in 1991 sent the gunboats, the cameras, and the flags to the Persian Gulf; his historically illiterate adjutants at the Pentagon (among them Secretary of Defense Dick Cheney and Chairman of the Joint Chiefs of Staff Colin Powell), drafted a *Defense Strategy for the 1990s* appointing America Keeper of World Peace. As subsequently published in 1993, the policy paper envisioned an invincible military establishment capable of waging, simultaneously, major wars on two continents, while at the same time attending to the minor nuisances of terrorists here and there in the slums of the Middle East and bandits in the mountains of Afghanistan and the jungles of Colombia. The claim to the crown of world empire set forth the doctrines of "Forward Deterrence," "Anticipatory Self-Defense," and "Preemptive Strike," informed the lesser nations of the earth of their inferior and subsidiary status. Let any failed or upstart state even begin to think of challenging American supremacy, and America reserved the right to strangle the impudence at birth, bomb the peasants or the palace, block the flow of sympathy and bank credit, change the sheets in the brothels and the information ministries.

During the decade of the 1990s, the Pentagon's pitch for unlimited subsidy gathered the force of an obligation to rule and save the world. President Bill Clinton seconded the motion, approved and carried by a clear majority of the nation's self-glorifying media—conservative and neoconservative, liberal and neoliberal, literary and academic. How could it be otherwise? The Soviets had lost the Cold War, their weapons gone to rust, their economy in ruins, the statues of V. I. Lenin reduced to scrap. History was at an end, America "the single model of human progress." The American way was the only way, and if not America bestriding the narrow world like a Colossus, who else to lift the burden once borne on the back of Imperial Rome?

Reinforced by the fortunes accruing to the Silicon Valley marketers of virtual reality and by the high-rise speculation floating the Dow Jones Industrial Average across the frontier of a new millennium, the delusions of omnipotent omniscience bubbled upward to so condescending a height that in March 2001, six months before the destruction of the World Trade Center, *Time* magazine gave voice to what on Washington's think tank and cocktail party circuits had become a matter of simple truth and common knowledge:

> America is no mere international citizen. It is the dominant power in the world, more dominant than any since Rome. Accordingly, America is in the position to re-shape norms, alter expectations and create new realties. How? By unapologetic and implacable demonstrations of will.

The old Greeks also had a word, *hubris,* for the unbridled vanity that goeth before a fall, men tempted to play at being gods and drawn to the flame of their destruction on the wings of braggart moths. Thus President George W. Bush, prosperous fool, and braggart moth, on May 1, 2003, six weeks after launching a second American invasion of Iraq, stepping aboard the aircraft carrier *U.S.S. Abraham Lincoln* stationed close inshore the coast of California to pose for the news cameras under a banner headlined MISSION ACCOMPLISHED.

Wonderful news; magnificent photo-op. Boy wonder as deus ex machina in *Top Gun* navy fighter pilot costume. But what was the mission to which the banner headline referred? Not the winning of the war on terror, unwinnable because nobody wins wars against an unknown enemy and an abstract noun. Not the nondiscovery of Saddam Hussein's nonexistent weapons of mass destruction. Nothing so pedestrian. The accomplishment was the dramatic significance of the invasion as prime time television spectacle. Frivolity unbound. An act of folly more glorious than any since the Athenians in 415 B.C. sent a splendid and costly fleet of gilded triremes to its destruction in Sicily, and by so doing lost both the Peloponnesian war and the life of their democracy.

Like Bush the elder staging the made-for-reality TV show invasion of Iraq in 1991, Bush the younger in 2003 didn't make tiresome distinctions between reality and virtual reality. Neither did the masters and commanders at the Pentagon. With an army that hadn't fought a war in forty years—hadn't won a war in seventy years—they weren't in the business of securing a military objective. They were in the business of making war movies with live ammunition, directed at unarmed civilians; the fireworks displays overhead scenic Baghdad (like those overhead Hanoi, Panama, Grenada, Libya, and Belgrade) were show instead of tell, intended to gain status, not territory. Not to conquer the natives but to awaken them to the worship of America's divinity as advertised in *Time* magazine.

The invasion of Iraq was undertaken to demonstrate America's omnipotence; the ongoing turmoil throughout the Middle East testifies to its military failures and continues to downgrade the country's standing as moral precept and example. The damage done to America's reputation abroad is extensive, but not as extensive as the damage done to the American democracy at home, the missions accomplished over the last twenty-five years by the servants of a stupefied plutocracy—the bulk of the nation's wealth amassed by 10 percent of its population, class warfare waged by the increasingly selfish and frightened rich against the increasingly debt-burdened and angry poor, the democratic electing of an American president overruled by the Supreme Court, a national security apparatus herding the American citizenry into the shelters of heavy law enforcement and harmless speech, the 2008–09 devastation of the nation's wealth and credit, the public good systematically shuffled into the private purse, occupants of the White House pleased to hold themselves above the law, futile but unending foreign war, both houses of Congress reduced to a state of impotent paralysis, a political discourse made by a celebrity-besotted news media posing demagogues on selfie sticks.

An age of folly worthy of the name, its consequence the presence of Donald J. Trump, prosperous fool and braggart moth, on November's presidential ballot. The book in hand doesn't speculate on the outcome of the election; it offers an acquaintance with the past as a hedge against the despairing of the present. History doesn't save the day or provide a PowerPoint projection of a new and better world; it is the fund of energy and hope that makes possible the revolt against what G. K. Chesterton once called "the small and arrogant oligarchy of those who merely happen to be walking about."

What's been happening for the last twenty-five years stands camera ready and picture-perfect in this year's presidential campaign—Trump's frivolous magnificence walking about with Hillary Clinton's remorseless selfishness, Washington housewife celebrity bride and reality game show groom atop the wedding cake of a stupefied plutocracy. They make an ugly couple, the opinion polls showing them feared and loathed by a majority of the prospective electorate. The curtain coming down on an age of folly, revolt the work in progress on the part of an electorate no longer willing or able to afford it and therefore given the best chance in nearly two generations to recover its wits, possibly revive the American idea of democracy in a way that meets the terms and conditions of a century not likely to be remembered as America's own.

The notes and observations in Part I proceed in the order of their appearance, portraits of an age (1990–2015), making itself up as it goes along. They were written as monthly commentary for *Harper's Magazine*, intended to place in perspective the events marching across the stage of the news. The essays in Part II, all but one of them written as backstory introducing issues of *Lapham's Quarterly*, deploy an acquaintance with history as folly's antidote, teaching us that we have less reason to fear what might happen tomorrow than to beware what happened yesterday. Individuals deprived of memory lose track of where they've been or where they might be going; a nation denied knowledge of its past cannot make sense of its present or imagine its future. Construed as means instead of end, history teaches the art of democratic self-government, sustains the hope of individual liberty.

Part I

Folly

1990

1. Democracy in America?

The spirit of liberty is the spirit which is not too sure it is right.
—Judge Learned Hand

Over the course of the last eighteen months, no American politician worth his weight in patriotic sentiment has missed a chance to congratulate one of the lesser nations of the earth on its imitation of the American democracy. Invariably, the tone of the compliment is condescending. The politician presents himself as the smiling host who welcomes into the clean and well-lighted rooms of "the American way of life" the ragged and less fortunate guests, who—sadly and through no fault of their own—had wandered for so many years in darkness.

The orators haven't lacked edifying proofs and instances. First the Chinese students in Tiananmen Square, holding aloft a replica of the Statue of Liberty against the armies of repression. Next the German crowds dancing on the ruin of the Berlin Wall; then the apprentice democrats triumphant in Budapest and Warsaw and Prague; then President Mikhail Gorbachev in Washington, amiably recanting the Communist heresy to his new friend in the White House. And always the Americans, saying, in effect, "You see, we were right all along; we were right, and you were wrong, and if you know what's good for you, you will go forth and prosper in a bright new world under the light of an American moon."

At the end of last summer Ronald Reagan was in Berlin, conducting a seminar for the East Germans on the theory and practice of democracy; John Sununu, the White House chief of staff, was in Moscow showing the hierarchs in the Kremlin how to organize the paperwork of a democratic government; a synod of American journalists had gone off to Budapest to teach their Hungarian colleagues how to draft a First Amendment; in Washington the chief correspondent of the *New York Times* was celebrating the crisis in the Persian Gulf as great and glorious proof that the United States had regained its status as the world's first and foremost superpower, that all the dreary talk about American bankruptcy and decline was just so much sniveling, trendy rot.

I listen to the speeches and read the bulletins in the newspapers, and I marvel at my own capacity for the willing suspensions of disbelief. I find myself humming along with the self-congratulatory cant on *Nightline* and *Face the Nation* or beating four-quarter time with the jingoists' chorus in *Newsweek*, and I forget for the moment that we're talking about a country (the United States of America, a.k.a, "the light of hope and reason in a dark and discordant world") in which the spirit of democracy is fast becoming as defunct as the late Buffalo Bill. About a country in which most of the population doesn't take the trouble to vote and would gladly sell its constitutional birthright for a Florida condominium or another twenty days on the corporate expense account. About a country in which the president wages war after consultation with four or five privy councillors and doesn't inform either the Congress or the electorate (a.k.a. "the freest, happiest, and most enlightened people on earth") until the armada has sailed.

Although I know that Jefferson once said that it is never permissible "to despair of the commonwealth," I find myself wondering whether the American experiment with democracy may not have run its course. Not because of the malevolence or cunning of a foreign power (the Russians, the Japanese, the Colombian drug lords, Saddam Hussein) but because a majority of Americans apparently have come to think of democracy as a matter of consensus and parades, as if it were somehow easy, quiet, orderly, and safe. I keep running across people who speak fondly about what they imagine to be the comforts of autocracy, who long for the assurances of the proverbial man on the white horse likely to do something hard and puritanical about the moral relativism that has made a mess of the cities, the schools, and prime-time television.

If the American system of government at present seems so patently at odds with its constitutional hopes and purposes, it is not because the practice of democracy no longer serves the interests of the presiding oligarchy (which it never did), but because the promise of democracy no longer inspires or exalts the citizenry lucky enough to have been born under its star. It isn't so much that liberty stands at bay but, rather, that it has fallen into disuse, regarded as insufficient by both its enemies and its nominal friends. What is the use of free expression to people so frightened of the future that they prefer the comforts of the authoritative lie? Why insist on the guarantee of so many superfluous civil liberties when everybody already has enough trouble with the interest rates and foreign cars, with too much crime on the streets, too many Mexicans crossing the border, and never enough money to pay the bills? Why bother with the tiresome chore of self-government when the decisions of state can be assigned to the functionaries in Washington, who, if they can be trusted with nothing else, at least have the wit to pretend that they are infallible? President Bush struck the expected pose of omniscience in the course of the 1988 election campaign when he refused to answer a rude question about an American naval blunder in the Persian Gulf (the shooting down of an Iranian airliner) on the ground that he would "never apologize for the United States of America. I don't care what the facts are."

As recently as 1980 I knew a good many people who took a passionate interest in politics, who felt keenly what one of them described as "the ancient republican hostility" to the rule of the self-serving few. They knew the names of their elected representatives, and they were as well-informed on the topics of the day as any government spokesman paid to edit the news. By the end of the decade most of them had abandoned their political enthusiasm as if it were a youthful folly they no longer could afford—like hang gliding or writing neosymbolist verse.

Much of the reason for the shift in attitude I attribute to the exemplary cynicism of the Reagan Administration. Here was a government obsequious in its devotion to the purposes of a selfish oligarchy, a regime that cared nothing for the law and prospered for eight years by virtue of its willingness to cheat and steal and lie. And yet, despite its gross and frequent abuses of power, the country made no complaint. The Democratic Party (the nominal party of opposition) uttered not the slightest squeak of an objection. Except for a few journals of small circulation, neither did the media.

During the early years of the administration, even people who recognized the shoddiness of Reagan's motives thought that the country could stand a little encouragement—some gaudy tinsel and loud advertising, a lot of parades, and a steady supply of easy profits. The country had heard enough of Jimmy Carter's sermons, and it was sick of listening to prophecies of the American future that could be so easily confused with a coroner's report. In return for the illusion that the United States was still first in the world's rankings, the country indulged Reagan in his claptrap economic and geopolitical theories. For a few years it didn't seem to matter that the Laffer curve and the Strategic Defense Initiative had been imported from the land of Oz. What difference did it make as long as the Japanese were willing to lend money and Rambo was victorious in the movies?

But it turned out that the lies did make a difference—the lies and the Reagan relentless grasping of illegal and autocratic privilege. Congress offered itself for sale to the highest bidder, and the political action committees bought so many politicians of both denominations that it was no longer possible to tell the difference between a Republican and a Democrat: Both sides of the aisle owed their allegiance to the same sponsors. Nor was it possible to distinguish between the executive and the legislative functions of government. Any doubts on this score were dissolved in the midden of the Iran–Contra deals. President Reagan and his aides-de-camp on the National Security Council sold weapons to a terrorist regime in Iran in order to finance a terrorist revolt in Nicaragua. The scheme obliged them to make a mockery of the Constitution, dishonor their oaths of office, declare themselves above the law. They did so without a qualm, and the subsequent congressional investigation absolved them of their crimes and confirmed them in their contempt for the law and the American people. The principal conspirators were allowed to depart with no more than a reprimand.

It was this series of events—so obviously and complacently corrupt throughout the whole course of the narrative—that proved even more damaging to the American polity than the ruin of the economy. Justified by a timid Congress and excused by a compliant media, the Reagan Administration reduced the Constitution to a sheaf of commercial paper no more or less worthless than a promissory note signed by Donald Trump.

The defeat might be easier to bear if the politicians would quit mouthing the word "democracy." If they were to say instead, "Yes, we are a great nation because we obey the rule of the expedient lie" or, "Yes, believe in our power because we have gerrymandered our politics to serve the interests of wealth," I might find it easier to wave the flag and swell the unison of complacent applause.

But not "democracy." Maybe "plutocracy," or "oligarchy," or even "state capitalism," but not, please God, "a free nation under law" or, as a professor of government put it in an address to a crowd of newly naturalized citizens of Monticello, the "moral and political reasoning [that] is the republic's unique and priceless heritage."

What "moral and political reasoning"? Between which voices of conscience, and where would the heritage be exhibited to public view? On network television? In the U.S. Senate? In a high school auditorium in Detroit?

Saddam Hussein's invasion of Kuwait presented a fairly prominent occasion for a display of America's moral and political reasoning, but it was a spectacle that nobody wanted to see or hear. The national choir of newspaper columnists banged their cymbals and drums, shouting for the head of the monster of Baghdad. Loudly and without a single exception, the 535 members of Congress declared themselves loyal to the great American truth that had descended into the Arabian desert with the 82nd Airborne Division. The television networks introduced a parade of generals, all of them explicating the texts of glorious war. The few individuals who publicly questioned the wisdom of the president's policy instantly found themselves classified as subversives, spoilsports, ingrates, and sore thumbs.

The judgment is one with which I am familiar, probably because my own remarks on the state of American politics often have been attacked by more or less the same gang of angry nouns. With respect to the argument in progress, I can imagine the rejoinder pronounced by a self-satisfied gentleman in his middle forties, a reader of *Time* magazine and a friend of the American Enterprise Institute. He wears a three-piece suit and speaks slowly and patiently, as if to a foreigner or a prospective suicide. Having done well by the system, he begins by reminding me that I, too, have done well by the system and should show a decent respect for the blessings of property. His voice is as smug as his faith in the American political revelation ("not perfect, of course, but the best system on offer in an imperfect world"). His argument resolves into categorical statements, usually four, presented as facets of a flawless truth.

1.

The American government is formed by the rule of the ballot box. What other country trusts its destiny to so many free elections?

The statement is true to the extent that it describes a ritual, not a function, of government. Early last spring the Times Mirror Center for the People and the Press conducted a survey of the political attitudes prevailing among a random sampling of citizens between the ages of eighteen and twenty-nine. To nobody's surprise the survey discovered a generation that "knows less, cares less, votes less and is less critical of its leaders and institutions than young people in the past." The available statistics support the impression of widespread political apathy. In this month's congressional election it is expected that as many as 120 million Americans (two thirds of the eligible electorate) will not bother to vote.

The numbers suggest that maybe the people who don't vote have good and sufficient reasons for their abstentions. Vote for what and for whom? For a program of false promises and empty platitudes? For ambitious office-seekers distinguished chiefly by their talents for raising money? For a few rich men (i.e., the sixty or seventy senators possessing assets well in excess of $1 million) who can afford to buy a public office as if it were a beach house or a rubber duck?

Since the revision of the campaign finance laws in the late 1970s, most of the candidates don't even take the trouble to court the good opinion of the voters. They speak instead to the PACs, to the lobbyists who can fix the money for campaigns costing as much as $350,000 (for the House of Representatives) and $4 million (for the Senate). The rising cost of political ambition ensures the rising rate of incumbency (47 percent of the present United States Congress were in office in 1980, as opposed to 4 percent of the Supreme Soviet). The sponsors back the safe bets and receive the assurance of safe opinions. (As of last June 30, the incumbent senators up for reelection this month had collected $83.1 million for their campaigns, as opposed to $25.9 million raised on behalf of the insurgents.)

A democracy supposedly derives its strength and character from the diversity of its many voices, but the politicians in the Capitol speak with only one voice, which is the voice of the oligarchy that buys the airline tickets and the television images. Among the company of legislators in Washington or Albany or Sacramento I look in vain for a representation of my own interests or opinions, and I never hear the voice of the scientist, the writer, the athlete, the teacher, the plumber, the police officer, the farmer, the merchant. I hear instead the voice of only one kind of functionary: a full-time politician, nearly always a lawyer, who spends at least 80 percent of his time raising campaign funds and construes his function as that of a freight-forwarding agent redistributing the national income into venues convenient to his sponsors and friends.

Maybe it still can be said that the United States is a representative government in the theatrical sense of the word, but if I want to observe the workings of democracy I would be better advised to follow the debate in the Czech Parliament or the Soviet Congress of People's Deputies. The newly enfranchised politicians in Eastern Europe write their own speeches and delight in the passion of words that allows them to seize and shape the course of a new history and a new world. Unlike American voters, voters in the Soviet Union (repeat, the Soviet Union, Russia, the U.S.S.R., the "Evil Empire," the Communist prison, etc., etc.) enjoy the right to express the full range of their opinions at the polls. Instead of marking the ballot for a favored candidate, the Soviet voter crosses off the names of the politicians whom he has reason to distrust or despise. He can vote against all the candidates, even an incumbent standing unopposed. Because a Soviet politician must receive an absolute majority, the election isn't valid unless more than half of the electorate votes, which means that in Moscow or Leningrad the citizens can vote for "none of the above," and by doing so they can do what the voters in New York or Los Angeles cannot do—throw the thieves into the street.

2.

Democratic government is self-government, and in America the state is owned and operated by the citizens.

I admire the sentiment, and I am willing to believe that in the good old days before most of what was worth knowing about the mechanics of government disappeared under the seals of classified information, it was still conceivable that the business of the state could be conducted by amateurs. In the early years of the twentieth century, it was still possible for anybody passing by the White House to walk through the front door and expect a few words with the president. It's true that the promise of democracy is synonymous with the idea of the citizen. The enterprise requires the collaboration of everybody present, and it fails (or evolves into something else) unless enough people perceive their government as subject rather than object, as animate organism rather than automatic vending machine.

Such an antique or anthropomorphic understanding of politics no longer satisfies the wish to believe in kings or queens or fairy tales. Ask almost anybody in any street about the nature of American government, and he or she will describe it as something that belongs to somebody else, as a them, not an us. Only advanced students of political science remember how a caucus works, or what is written in the Constitution, or who paves the roads. The active presence of the citizen gives way to the passive absence of the consumer, and citizenship devolves into a function of economics. Every two or four or six years the politicians ask the voters whether they recognize themselves as better or worse off than they were the last time anybody asked. The question is only and always about money, never about the spirit of the laws or the cherished ideals that embody the history of the people. The commercial definition of democracy prompts the politicians to conceive of and advertise the republic as if it were a resort hotel. They promise the voters the rights and comforts owed to them by virtue of their status as America's guests. The subsidiary arguments amount to little more than complaints about the number, quality, and cost of the available services. The government (a.k.a. the hotel management) preserves its measure of trust in the exact degree that it satisfies the whims of its patrons and meets the public expectation of convenience and style at a fair price. A debased electorate asks of the state what the rich ask of their servants—i.e., "comfort us," "tell us what to do." The wish to be cared for replaces the will to act.

3.

*The American democracy guarantees the freedom of its people
and the honesty of its government with a system of checks and
balances; the division or separation of powers prevents the government from indulging the pleasures of despotism; the two-party
system ensures the enactment of just laws vigorously debated and
openly arrived at.*

It was precisely this principle that the Iran–Contra deals (the
trading of weapons for hostages as well as the subsequent reprieves
and exonerations) proved null and void. President Reagan usurped
the prerogatives of Congress, and Congress made no objection.
President Bush exercised the same option with respect to the expedition in the Persian Gulf, and again Congress made no objection,
not even when it was discovered that Saudi Arabia had offered
to hire the CIA to arrange the overthrow of Saddam Hussein.
For the last forty years it has been the practice of the American
government to wage a war at the will and discretion of the foreign-
policy apparat in Washington—without reference to the wishes or
opinions of the broad mass of the American people.

Dean Acheson, secretary of state in the Truman Administration,
understood as long ago as 1947 that if the government wished
to do as it pleased, then it would be necessary to come up with
a phrase, slogan, or article of faith that could serve as a pretext
for arbitrary decisions. He hit upon the word "nonpartisan."
Knowing that the American people might balk at the adventure
of the Cold War if they thought that the subject was open to discussion, he explained to his confederates in the State Department
that a militant American foreign policy had to be presented as a
"nonpartisan issue," that any and all domestic political quarreling
about the country's purposes "stopped at the water's edge."

"If we can make them believe that," Acheson said, "we're off
to the races."

Among the promoters of the national security state, the theory
of "nonpartisanship" was accorded the weight of biblical revelation, and for the next two generations it proved invaluable to

a succession of presidents bent on waging declared and unde-
clared wars in Korea, Vietnam, Guatemala, Grenada, Panama,
Cambodia, Lebanon, Nicaragua, and the Persian Gulf. President
John F. Kennedy elaborated the theory into a doctrine not unlike
the divine right of kings. At a press conference in May 1962,
Kennedy said, with sublime arrogance,

> Most of us are conditioned for many years to have a political
> viewpoint—Republican or Democratic, liberal, conservative, or
> moderate. The fact of the matter is that most of the problems ...
> that we now face are technical problems, are administrative prob-
> lems. They are very sophisticated judgments, which do not lend
> themselves to the great sort of passionate movements [that] have
> stirred this country so often in the past. [They] deal with questions
> which are now beyond the comprehension of most men.

To President Bush the word "nonpartisan" is the alpha and
omega of government by administrative decree: a word for all
seasons; a word that avoids the embarrassment of forthright political argument; a word with which to send the troops to Saudi
Arabia, postpone decisions on the budget, diffuse the blame for
the savings and loan swindle. The White House staff takes pride
in the techniques of what its operatives refer to as "conflict avoidance." Speaking to a writer for the *New Republic* in August, one
of Bush's senior press agents said, "We don't do [political] fighting
in this administration. We do bipartisan compromising."

But in a democracy everything is partisan. Democratic politics is about nothing else except being partisan. The American
dialectic assumes argument not only as the normal but as the
necessary condition of its continued existence. The structure of
the idea resembles a suspension bridge rather than a pyramid or
a mosque. Its strength depends on the balance struck between
countervailing forces, and the idea collapses unless the stresses
oppose one another with equal weight, unless enough people have
enough courage to sustain the argument between rich and poor,
the government and the governed, city and suburb, presidency and
Congress, capital and labor, matter and mind. It is precisely these

arguments (i.e., the very stuff and marrow of democracy) that the word "nonpartisan" seeks to annul. With reference to domestic political arguments, the word "consensus" serves the same purpose as the word "nonpartisan" does in the realm of foreign affairs: It is another sleight of hand that makes possible the perpetual avoidance of any question that might excite the democratic passions of a free people bent on governing themselves. The trick is to say as little as possible in a language so bland that the speaker no longer can be accused of harboring an unpleasant opinion. Adhere firmly to the safe cause and the popular sentiment. Talk about the flag or drugs or crime (never about race or class or justice) and follow the yellow brick road to the wonderful land of "consensus." In place of honest argument among consenting adults, the politicians substitute a lullaby for frightened children: the pretense that conflict doesn't really exist, that we have achieved the blessed state in which (because we are all American and therefore content) we no longer need politics. The mere mention of the word "politics" brings with it the odor of something low and rotten and mean.

Confronted with genuinely stubborn and irreconcilable differences (about revising the schedule of Social Security payments, say, or closing down a specific number of the nation's military bases), the politicians assign the difficulty to the law courts, or to a special prosecutor, or to a presidential commission. In line with its habitual cowardice, Congress this past September dispatched a few of its most pettifogging members to Andrews Air Force Base, where, behind closed doors, it was hoped they might construct the facade of an agreement on the budget.

For the better part of 200 years it was the particular genius of the American democracy to compromise its differences within the context of an open debate. For the most part (i.e., with the tragic exception of the Civil War), the society managed to assimilate and smooth out the edges of its antagonisms and by so doing to hold in check the violence bent on its destruction. The success of the enterprise derived from the rancor of the nation's loudmouthed politics—on the willingness of its citizens and their elected representatives to defend their interests, argue their case, and say what they meant. But if the politicians keep silent, and if the citizenry no longer cares to engage in what it regards as the distasteful business of debate, then the American dialectic cannot attain a synthesis or resolution. The democratic initiative passes to the demagogues in the streets, and the society falls prey to the ravening minorities in league with the extremists of all denominations who claim alliance with the higher consciousness and the absolute truth. The eloquence of Daniel Webster or Henry Clay degenerates into the muttering of Al Sharpton or David Duke.

The deliberate imprecision of the Constitution (sufficiently vague and spacious to allow the hope of a deal) gives way to rigid enumerations of privileges and rights. A democracy in sound working order presupposes a ground of tolerance, in Judge Learned Hand's phrase, "the spirit which is not too sure that it is right." I might think that the other fellow is wrong, but I do not think that he is therefore wicked. A democracy in decay acquires the pale and deadly cast of theocracy. Not only is the other fellow wrong (about abortion, obscenity, or the flag); he is also, by definition, an agent of the Antichrist.

4.

The Constitution presents the American people with as great a gift of civil liberties as ever has been granted by any government in the history of the world.

But liberty, like the habit of telling the truth, withers and decays unless it's put to use, and for the last ten years it seems as if the majority of Americans would rather not suffer the embarrassment of making a scene (in a public place) about so small a trifle as a civil right. With scarcely a murmur of objection, they fill out the official forms, answer the questions, submit to the compulsory urine or blood tests, and furnish information to the government, the insurance companies, and the police.

The Bush Administration cries up a war on drugs, and the public responds with a zeal for coercion that would have gladdened the hearts of the Puritan judges presiding over the Salem witch trials.

Of the respondents questioned by an *ABC/Washington Post* poll in September 1989, 55 percent supported mandatory drug testing for all Americans, 52 percent were willing to have their homes searched, and 83 percent favored reporting suspected drug users to the police, even if the suspects happened to be members of their own family. Politicians of both parties meet with sustained applause when they demand longer jail sentences and harsher laws as well as the right to invade almost everybody's privacy; to search, without a warrant, almost anybody's automobile or boat; to bend the rules of evidence, hire police spies, and attach (again without a warrant) the wires of electronic surveillance. Within the last five years the Supreme Court has granted increasingly autocratic powers to the police—permission (without probable cause) to stop, detain, and question a traveler passing through the nation's airports in whom the police can see a resemblance to a drug dealer; permission (again without probable cause) to search barns, stop motorists, inspect bank records, and tap phones.

The same Times Mirror survey that discovered a general indifference toward all things political also discovered that most of the respondents didn't care whether a fair percentage of the nation's politicians proved to be scoundrels and liars. Such was the nature of their task, and it was thought unfair to place on the political authorities the additional and excessive burden of too many harsh or pointed questions. "Let them," said one of the poor dupes of a respondent, "authoritate."

Democracy, of course, is never easy to define. The meaning of the word changes with the vagaries of time, place, and circumstance. The American democracy in 1990 is not what it was in 1890; democracy in France is not what it is in England or Norway or the United States. What remains more or less constant is a temperament or spirit of mind rather than a code of laws, a set of immutable virtues or a table of bureaucratic organization. The temperament is skeptical and contentious, and if democracy means anything at all (if it isn't what Gore Vidal called "the great American nonsense word" or what H. L. Mencken regarded as a synonym for the collective fear and prejudice of an ignorant mob), it means the freedom of thought and the perpetual expansion of the discovery that the world is not oneself. Freedom of thought brings the society the unwelcome news that it is in trouble. But because all societies, like all individuals, are always in trouble, the news doesn't cause them to perish. They die instead from the fear of thought—from the paralysis that accompanies the wish to make time stand still and punish the insolence of an Arab who makes a nuclear bomb or sells gasoline for more than twenty-five dollars a barrel.

Democracy allies itself with change and proceeds on the assumption that nobody knows enough, that nothing is final, that the old order (whether of men or institutions) will be carried off-stage every twenty years. The multiplicity of its voices and forms assumes a ceaseless making and remaking of laws and customs as well as equations and matinee idols. Democratic government is a purpose held in common, and if it can be understood as a field of temporary coalitions among people of different interests, skills, and generations, then everybody has need of everybody else. To the extent that democracy gives its citizens a chance to chase their own dreams, it gives itself the chance not only of discovering its multiple glories and triumphs but also of surviving its multiple follies and crimes.

1991

2. Brave New World

Saints should always be judged guilty until they are proved innocent.
—George Orwell

During the autumn advertising campaign meant to sell the American public on the prospect of war in Iraq, President George H. W. Bush dressed up his gunboat diplomacy in the slogans of conscience and the costume of what he was pleased to call "the new world order." First and foremost, he had it in mind to prove to the lesser nations of the earth that any misbehavior on their part (any sacking of cities or setting of commodity prices without express, written permission from Washington) would be promptly and severely punished. Never, he said, would Saddam Hussein be allowed to receive any reward, profit, acclaim, benefit, or honor for his trespass in the desert. No, sir, by no means, under no circumstances, not while the United States still had soldiers and bombs to send eastward out of Eden.

The president's righteousness waxed increasingly militant as the merely political or commercial reasons for war proved inadequate to the occasion. When the expedient arguments failed (the ones about the price of oil, the preservation of American jobs and the American way of life, the protection of Israel, the likelihood of nuclear war), Mr. Bush shifted his flag to the higher ground of the moral argument, the one about the American obligation to enforce the laws of God. Behold, he said, the villainy of Saddam Hussein, an evil man committing acts of "naked aggression" in what was once the innocent paradise of Kuwait. Know, O doubting world, that America stands willing to make the crooked straight and the rough places plain.

By October the president had tuned his rhetoric to the pitch of intransigent virtue announced by Saddam Hussein. Saddam was talking about "rivers of blood," about the will of Allah and a holy war against the foreign infidel. Mr. Bush was saying that "no price is too heavy to pay" to defend the standards of Christian behavior in a world already too densely populated with thugs. In late November, in an interview on CNN and still summoning the faithful to a twelfth-century crusade, Mr. Bush looked firmly into the television camera and asked what I'm afraid he thought was a shrewd and high-principled question: "When you rape, pillage, and plunder a neighbor, should you then ask the world, 'Hey, give me a little face'?"

The answer, regrettably, is yes. Of course you ask the world for a little face, not only for a little face but for as much face as can be had at the going rates. Why else did three American presidents persist in the devastation of Vietnam, at the price of 57,000 American dead, if not for the sake of what they defined as "America's credibility," "America's honor," "America's image in the world"? Why else did Mr. Bush invade Panama if not to prove that America's military prowess deserved the compliment of the world's fear and applause? Why else have we sent 400,000 troops to the Persian Gulf if not to outbid Saddam Hussein in the display of aggression?

I write these lines on January 17, the second day of Operation Desert Storm. Why else did Mr. Bush give the order to attack Iraq if not to ask of the world, "Hey, give me a little face"?

The phrasing of the president's question proclaimed his

allegiance to the old world order, the one governed by force and the show of force. The autumn's diplomatic maneuvers made it clear that the White House meant to restore what used to be called "Pax Americana."

Between August and January the United States paid handsome bribes for the votes of the Security Council at the United Nations but otherwise listened as inattentively to the counsel of its nominal allies as George Will might listen to the political views of the wine steward in an Argentine restaurant in Santa Monica. The alliance put together in the Persian Gulf, with whichever kings or kingdoms happened to be free on waivers from OPEC or the Arab League, might as easily have been arranged by the late John Foster Dulles.

Careless of the costs, knowing little or nothing of the languages, history, or cultural traditions of the Middle East, confident that the war with Iraq would be won in a matter of weeks if not days or even hours, the makers of American policy assumed (as did Saddam Hussein) that their own moral equations somehow were synonymous with the laws of nature and the will of God.

In opposition to the incessant moralisms broadcast from the White House, a fair number of people in Washington, both in Congress and in the national media, offered tentative sketches of a world order that might not have been so easily understood by Saladin or Godfrey of Bouillon. They argued for patience, for the efficacy of economic sanctions, for an army under the command of the United Nations, for a coalition comprising more or less equal interests, for the use of as little force as possible and then only as a defensive measure. They questioned the American capacity to balance the world on the scale of American justice or in the ledger of American commerce. From whom did we think we could borrow the money to pay for the imperial legions? Upon conquering the wicked city of Baghdad, whom did we hope to appoint to the office of proconsul?

The voices of doubt and restraint were lost in the din of the marching bands. Nobody in the Bush Administration made the slightest attempt to imagine a future that didn't look exactly like the past. Nobody wished to understand the historical origins of

Iraq's grievances, which have more to do with the British and Ottoman Empires than with the United States. Nobody wished to restrain the predatory oil pricing that suits our own convenience. Nobody said anything about taking down the expensive military arsenals that we have so profitably sold to so many aspiring despots. Nor did anybody say much of anything about a decent settlement of the Arab–Israeli dispute, about alternative fuels and the management of the world's energy resources, about redistributing the wealth of the Middle East in some way that might promote the chance of peace.

By trying to preserve the illusion of a balance of power along the lines set forth by Lord Palmerston or Kaiser Wilhelm, Mr. Bush and his nostalgic friends in Congress and the Pentagon seek to comfort themselves with the cheerful news that they live in an orderly and coherent world, or at least in a world in which order and coherence remain within the range of the heaviest artillery.

The old world order assumes a distinction between naked and fully clothed aggression. On Sunday afternoons in Mozambique and Guatemala, law-abiding families vanish as abruptly from sight as did the law-abiding citizens of Kuwait, but they leave so quietly and so often that they offer no affront to the harmony of nations. Through the autumn ad campaign crying up the prospect of war with Iraq, the Bush Administration made little mention of the thirty-three other wars currently in progress in the world. Nor did our media think to make the point that our own society assumes a norm of violence that would frighten all but the most remorseless Arab. No other modern nation, whether capitalist or socialist or Christian or Muslim, shares the American tolerance for crime. The indexes of murder and theft in the United States (i.e., aggression dressed in old sneakers as well as by Brooks Brothers and Bijan) dwarf the comparative statistics in England, Libya, France, Germany, and Iran. As with the old game of power politics, the rich man's aggression provokes less censure than the poor man's aggression, which suggests that Saddam's fault can be found not only with his tank captains but also with his tailor.

But the idea of a balance of power implies the existence of reasonably long-term interests and alliances, and in a world subject to sudden technological revolutions as well as to the bewildering movements of peoples, currencies, markets, oil spills, and fervent nationalisms, who can be sure that anything will remain the same from one week to the next? So many forces and allegiances have been let loose in the world, and the major powers find so many ways in which to combine and recombine that even so subtle a statesman as Metternich would have been hard-pressed to change last year's enemies into next year's friends. What would have become of his certainties about Germany or Russia or the Polish frontier?

The fear of an ambiguous future in the aftermath of the Cold War gives rise to the wish for simplifications and a safe return to the past. Often on seeing Mr. Bush threaten Saddam with the scourge of war, I thought that he might be trying to substitute a lesser fear for a greater one, as if he would rather confront Iraq, no matter how despotic or heavily armed, than confront a world dissolved into anarchy, a world in which any terrorist with a crackpot dream of heaven can stuff an atomic weapon into an old suitcase and hold for ransom the life of New York or Washington.

Americans tend to think of foreign affairs in terms of sporting events that allow for unambiguous results. Either the team wins or it loses; the game is over within a reasonable period of time, and everybody can go back to doing something else. Much to everyone's regret, and regardless of the outcome of this winter's war in the Gulf, the events of the next twenty years seem likely to make nonsense of the sporting analogies. Too many powers can make their anger known to the world (if not at conference tables, then by means of an assassination or the poisoning of a reservoir), and the chains of causation have become much longer and more democratic than those conceived of by the Congress of Vienna.

If tomorrow morning at ten o'clock Iraq renounced its belief in Allah and withdrew its armies from Kuwait, the crisis in the world would not resolve itself into a finale by Busby Berkeley and the chorus line at the American Enterprise Institute. If it isn't the Iraqis, then it will be the Syrians; if not the Syrians, then the Brazilians or the Lithuanians or the South Africans.

The pervasive intuitions of dread give rise to a confusion of feeling that makes it difficult to interpret such phrases as "the national interest" or to guess whether the voices prophesying war mean to signal an advance or a retreat. The presentiment of a terrible looming just over the horizon of the news seeps through the voices of people pleading for surcease and disengagement, who argue that the United States has wasted enough blood and treasure in the ill-conceived crusades of the past thirty years, that the country should retire to the fastnesses of its coasts and leave the rest of the world to its murdering corruption.

But where is it safe to hide? Odysseus could return from his wanderings to Ithaca, but the modern world doesn't provide the refuge of home islands. Who is not hostage to the interconnectedness of the AIDS virus and the radioactive wind?

Within the world's military headquarters I'm sure that innumerable officers have drawn contingency plans for all kinds of wars—wars against revolutions, proxy wars, diplomatic wars, wars in Yugoslavia and Korea, wars for oil and bauxite and grain, wars fought with conventional weapons, amphibious wars, air wars, ground wars, nuclear wars. But how large will these wars become, and how many people might have to be killed before the bugles sound the retreat? Nobody likes to discuss this question in public (as witness the recent silence in Congress about our probable casualties in the Persian Gulf) because it has become difficult to find either a sufficiently high-minded principle or an inescapable material interest on behalf of which 250 million people might think it glorious to sacrifice their children.

The vagueness is traditional. In August 1914 none of the Allied or Central powers could explain its reasons for going off to World War I. Four years later, after 10 million soldiers had died in the trenches, the governments in question still could not give a plausible reason for the killing. The best that anybody could do was to say that the war had been fought to end all wars, that its purpose had been to establish a "new world order" immune to the disease of power politics.

But who now expects the war in the Middle East to bring about a lasting peace or a better world? Who believes that the United

States would risk annihilation to preserve a free and independent Abu Dhabi or the sacred anomaly of Israel?

Whether expressed in the Aesopian language of diplomacy or in the deployment of navies, the rules of power politics fail to take into account the number of people in the world who judge they have more to gain by the risk of war than by the prospect of negotiation. Most of the world is hungry, armed, and not much impressed by the rules of diplomatic procedure set forth with such earnest longing in the editorial pages of the *New York Times*.

Of the nations now buying weapons in the international arms markets, the majority must be considered young, both in terms of their existence as states (of the 159 nations represented at the U.N., nearly half have come into being within the past thirty years) and in terms of the average age of their populations. In the industrialized West the average age of the inhabitants continues to rise; in the Third World the demographics go the other way.

The passions of transcendence seize on the young, and as more and more nations suffer the anxieties and enthusiasms of youth, they can be expected to confuse the purposes of government with the freedom of individuals. The doctrines of nationalism hold that certain nations emerge from the chaos of history as objects of divine favor; the states that interpret those doctrines with the fervor of youth presumably will conduct their foreign affairs as if they were affairs of the heart.

Since the end of World War II—probably since the end of World War I—the supposedly civilized nations of the world have been noticeably unsuccessful at transmitting to the next generation the public virtues of patience and self-restraint. They have distributed instead a more profitable line of private goods, among them visions of God and definitions of the higher truth, as well as cameras and transistor radios. Within the arenas of domestic American politics the romanticism of eager factions has dissolved the common interest into a multitude of special interests, all of them warring with one another for the available money and authority.

Over the next ten years I can imagine a comparable spectacle in the arena of international politics. Together with single-issue lobbies in Congress, I can conceive of single-issue nations dedicated to the proposition that their own flag, their own folk songs, and their own way of making fish soup constitutes a foreign policy. At the same time they will find themselves armed with weapons capable of inflicting vast Oedipal punishments on an older generation perceived to be obstructive and corrupt. Absent an imperial peace imposed on a recalcitrant world by parental fiat (a task for which the United States possesses a notable lack of talent), I find it hard to imagine a political order balanced by a squadron of gunboats.

The more prosperous and settled a nation, the more readily it tends to think of war as a regrettable accident; to nations less fortunate, the prospect of war presents itself as a possibly bountiful friend.

1992

3. Who and What Is American?

There may not be an American character, but there is the emotion of being American. It has many resemblances to the emotion of being Russian—that feeling of nostalgia for some undetermined future when man will have improved himself beyond recognition and when all will be well.

—V. S. Pritchett

Were I to believe what I read in the papers, I would find it easy to think that I no longer can identify myself simply as an American. The noun apparently means nothing unless it is dressed up with at least one modifying adjective. As a plain American I have neither voice nor authentic proofs of existence. I acquire a presence only as an old American, a female American, a white American, a rich American, a black American, a gay American, a poor American, a Native American, a dead American. The subordination of the noun to the adjectives makes a mockery of both the American premise and the democratic spirit, but it serves the purposes of the politicians as well as the news media, and throughout the rest of this election year I expect the political campaigns to pitch their tents and slogans on the frontiers of race and class. For every benign "us," the candidates will find a malignant "them"; for every neighboring "we" (no matter how eccentric or small in number), a distant and devouring "they." The strategies of division sell newspapers and summon votes, and to the man who would be king (or president, or governor), the popular hatred of government matters less than the atmosphere of resentment in which the people fear and distrust one another.

Democratic politics trades in only two markets—the market in expectation and the market in blame. A collapse in the former engenders a boom in the latter. Something goes wrong in the news —a bank swindle of genuinely spectacular size, a series of killings in Milwaukee, another disastrous assessment of the nation's schools—and suddenly the air is loud with questions about the paradox of the American character or the Puritan subtexts of the American soul. The questions arise from every quarter of the political compass—from English professors and political consultants as well as from actors, corporate vice presidents, and advertising salesmen—and the conversation is seldom polite. Too many of the people present no longer can pay the bills, and a stray remark about acid rain or a third-grade textbook can escalate within a matter of minutes into an exchange of insults. Somebody calls Jesse Helms a fascist, and somebody else says that he is sick and tired of paying ransom money to a lot of welfare criminals. People drink too much and stay too late, their voices choked with anecdote and rage, their lexicons of historical reference so passionately confused that both Jefferson and Lincoln find themselves doing thirty-second commercials for racial quotas, a capital gains tax, and the Persian Gulf War.

The failures in the nation's economy have marked up the prices for obvious villains, and if I had a talent for merchandising I would go into the business of making dolls (black dolls, white dolls, red-necked dolls, feminist dolls, congressional dolls) that each of the candidates could distribute at fundraising events with a supply of color-coordinated pins. Trying out their invective in the preseason campaigns, the politicians as early as last October were attributing the cause of all our sorrows to any faction, inter-est, or minority that could excite in its audiences the passions of a beloved prejudice. David Duke in Louisiana denounced the sub-sidized beggars (i.e., black people) who had robbed the state of its birthright. At a partisan theatrical staged by the Democratic Party in New Hampshire, Senator Tom Harkin reviled the con-spiracy of Republican money. President Bush went to Houston, Texas, to point a trembling and petulant finger at the United States Congress. If the country's domestic affairs had been left to him, the president said, everybody would be as prosperous and smug as Senator Phil Gramm, but the liberals in Congress (blind as mol-lusks and selfish as eels) had wrecked the voyage of boundless opportunity.

The politicians follow the trends, and apparently they have been told by their handlers to practice the arts of the demagogue. Certainly I cannot remember an election year in which the politi-cal discourse—among newspaper editorialists and the single-issue lobbies as well as the candidates—relied so unashamedly on pitting rich against poor, black against white, male against female, city against suburb, young against old. Every public event in New York—whether academic appointment, traffic delay, or homi-cide—lends itself to both a black and a white interpretation of the news. The arguments in the arenas of cultural opinion echo the same bitter refrain. The ceaseless quarrels about the canon of preferred texts (about Columbus the Bad and Columbus the Good, about the chosen company of the politically correct, about the ice people and the sun people) pick at the scab of the same questions. Who and what is an American? How and where do we find an identity that is something other than a fright mask? When using the collective national pronoun ("we the people," "we happy few"), whom do we invite into the "we" club?

Maybe the confusion is a corollary to the end of the Cold War. The image of the Soviet Union as monolithic evil held in place the image of the United States as monolithic virtue. Break the circuit of energy transferred between negative and positive poles, and the two empires dissolve into the waving of sectional or nation-alist flags. Lacking the reassurance of a foreign demon, we search our own neighborhoods for fiends of convincing malevolence and size.

The search is a boon for the bearers of false witness and the builders of prisons. Because it's so easy to dwell on our differences, even a child of nine can write a Sunday newspaper sermon about the centrifugal forces that drive the society apart. The more difficult and urgent questions have to do with the centripetal forces that bind us together. What traits of character or temperament do we hold in common? Why is it that I can meet a black man in a street or a Hispanic woman on a train and imagine that he and I, or she and I, share an allied hope and a joint purpose? That last question is as American as it is rhetorical, and a Belgian would think it the work of a dreaming imbecile.

What we share is a unified field of emotion, but if we mistake the sources of our energy and courage (i.e., if we think that our uniqueness as Americans rests with the adjectives instead of the noun), then we can be rounded up in categories and sold the slogan of the week and the fear of the month. Political campaigns deal in the commodity of votes, and from now until November I expect that all of them will divide the American promise into its lesser but more marketable properties. For reasons of their own convenience, the sponsors of political campaigns (Democratic, environmental, racial, Republican, sexual, or military–industrial) promote more or less the same false constructions of the American purpose and identity. As follows,

that the American achieves visible and specific meaning only by reason of his or her association with the political guilds of race, gender, age, ancestry, or social class.

The assumption is as elitist as the view that only a woman endowed with an income of $1 million a year can truly appreciate the beauty of money and the music of Cole Porter. Comparable theories of grace encourage the belief that only black people can know or teach black history, that no white man can play jazz piano, that blonds have a better time, and that Jews can't play basketball.

America was founded on precisely the opposite premise. We were always about becoming, not being; about the prospects for the future, not about the inheritance of the past. The man who rests his case on his color, like the woman who defines herself as a bright cloud of sensibility beyond the understanding of merely mortal men, makes a claim to special privilege not unlike the divine right of kings. The pretensions might buttress the cathedrals of our self-esteem, but they run counter to the lessons of our history.

We are a nation of parvenus, all bound to the hopes of tomorrow, or next week, or next year. John Quincy Adams put it plainly in a letter to a German correspondent in the 1820s who had written on behalf of several prospective émigrés to ask about the requirements for their success in the New World. "They must cast off the European skin, never to resume it," Adams said. "They must look forward to their posterity rather than backward to their ancestors."

We were always a mixed and piebald company, even on the seventeenth-century colonial seaboard, and we accepted our racial or cultural differences as the odds that we were obliged to overcome or correct. When John Charles Frémont (a.k.a. The Pathfinder) first descended into California from the East in 1843, he remarked on the polyglot character of the expedition accompanying him south into the San Joaquin Valley:

> Our cavalcade made a strange and grotesque appearance, and it was impossible to avoid reflecting upon our position and composition in this remote solitude … still forced on south by a desert on one hand and a mountain range on the other; guided by a civilized Indian, attended by two wild ones from the Sierra; a Chinook from the Columbia; and our own mixture of American, French, German—all armed; four or five languages heard at once; above a hundred horses and mules, half-wild; American, Spanish and Indian dresses and equipments intermingled—such was our composition.

The theme of metamorphosis recurs throughout the whole chronicle of American biography. Men and women start out in one place and end up in another, never quite knowing how they got there, perpetually expecting the unexpected, drifting across the ocean or the plains until they lodge against a marriage, a land deal, a public office, or a jail. Speaking to the improvised character of the American experience, Daniel Boorstin, the historian and former Librarian of Congress, also summed up the case against the arithmetic of the political pollsters' zip codes: "No prudent man dared to be too certain of exactly who he was or what he was about; everyone had to be prepared to become someone else. To be ready for such perilous transmigrations was to become an American."

That the American people aspire to become more nearly alike.

The hope is that of the ad salesman and the prison warden, but it has become depressingly familiar among the managers of political campaigns. Apparently they think that no matter how different the native songs and dances in different parts of the country, all the tribes and factions want the same beads, the same trinkets, the same prizes. As I listen to operatives from Washington talk about their prospects in the Iowa or New Hampshire primary, I understand that they have in mind the figure of a perfect or ideal American whom everybody in the country would wish to resemble if only everybody could afford to dress like the dummies in the windows of Bloomingdale's or Saks Fifth Avenue. The public opinion polls frame questions in the alphabet of name recognitions and standard brands. The simplicity of the results supports the belief that the American citizen or the American family can be construed as a product and that with only a little more time and a little more money for research and development, all of us will conform to the preferred images seen in a commercial for Miller beer.

The apologists for the theory of the uniform American success sometimes present the example of Abraham Lincoln, and as I listen to their sentimental after-dinner speeches about the poor country boy grown to greatness, I often wonder what they would say if they had met the man instead of the statue. Throughout most of his life Lincoln displayed the character of a man destined for failure—a man who drank too much and told too many jokes (most of them in bad taste), who was habitually late for meetings and always borrowing money, who never seized a business opportunity and missed his own wedding.

The spirit of liberty is never far from anarchy, and the ur-American is apt to look a good deal more like one of the contestants on *Let's Make a Deal* (i.e., somebody dressed like Madonna, or Wyatt Earp, or a giant iguana) than any of the yachtsmen standing around on the dock at Kennebunkport. If America is about nothing else, it is about the invention of the self. Because we have little use for history, and because we refuse the comforts of a society established on the blueprint of class privilege, we find ourselves set adrift at birth in an existential void, inheriting nothing except the obligation to construct a plausible self, to build a raft of identity on which (with a few grains of luck and a cheap bank loan) maybe we can float south to Memphis or the imaginary islands of the blessed. We set ourselves the tasks of making and remaking our destinies with whatever lumber we happen to find lying around on the banks of the Snake or Pecos River.

Who else is the American hero if not a wandering pilgrim who goes forth on a perpetual quest? Melville sent Ahab across the world's oceans in search of a fabulous beast, and Thoreau followed the unicorn of his conscience into the silence of the Maine woods. Between them they marked out the trail of American literature as well as the lines of speculation in American real estate. To a greater or a lesser extent, we are all confidence men, actors playing the characters of our own invention and hoping that the audience—fortunately consisting of impostors as fanciful or synthetic as ourselves—will accept the performance at par value and suspend the judgments of ridicule.

The settled peoples of the earth seldom recognize the American as both a chronic revolutionary and a born pilgrim. The American is always on the way to someplace else (i.e., toward some undetermined future in which all will be well), and when he meets a stranger on the road he begins at once to recite the summary of the story so far—his youth and early sorrows, the sequence of his exits and entrances, his last divorce and his next marriage, the point of his financial departure and the estimated time of his spiritual arrival, the bad news noted and accounted for, the good news still to come. Invariably it is a pilgrim's tale, and the narrator, being American, assumes that he is addressing a fellow pilgrim. He means to exchange notes and compare maps. His newfound companion might be bound toward a completely different dream of Eden (a boat marina in Naples, Florida, instead of a garden in Vermont; a career as a Broadway dancer as opposed to the vice presidency of the Wells Fargo bank), but the destination doesn't matter as much as the common hope of coming safely home to the land of the heart's desire. For the time being, and until something better turns up, we find ourselves embarked on the same voyage, gazing west into the same blue distance.

That the American people share a common code of moral behavior and subscribe to identical theories of the true, the good, and the beautiful.

Senator Jesse Helms would like to think so, and so would the enforcers of ideological discipline on the vocabulary of the doctrinaire left. The country swarms with people making rules about what we can say or read or study or smoke, and they imagine that we should be grateful for the moral guidelines (market-tested and government-inspected) imposed (for our own good) by a centralized bureau of temporal health and spiritual safety. The would-be reformers of the national character confuse the American sense of equality with the rule of conformity that governs a police state. It isn't that we believe that every American is as perceptive or as accomplished as any other, but we insist on the preservation of a decent and mutual respect across the lines of age, race, gender, and social class. No citizen is allowed to use another citizen as if he or she were a means to an end; no master can treat his servant as if he or she were only a servant; no government can deal with the governed as if they were nothing more than a mob of votes. The American loathing for the arrogant or self-important man follows from the belief that all present have bet their fortunes (some of them bigger than others, and some of them counterfeit or stolen) on the same hypothesis.

The American premise is an existential one, and our moral code is political, its object being to allow for the widest horizons of sight and the broadest range of expression. We protect the other person's liberty in the interest of protecting our own, and our virtues conform to the terms and conditions of an arduous and speculative journey. If we look into even so coarse a mirror as the one held up to us by the situation comedies on primetime television, we see that we value the companionable virtues—helpfulness, forgiveness, kindliness, and (above all) tolerance.

The passenger standing next to me at the rail might be balancing a parrot on his head, but that doesn't mean that he has invented a theory of the self any less implausible than the one I ordered from a department-store catalogue or assembled with the tag lines of a two-year college course on the great books of Western civilization. If the traveler at the port rail can balance a parrot on his head, then I can continue my discussion with Madame Bovary and Mr. Pickwick, and the two gentlemen standing aft of the rum barrels can get on with the business of rigging the price of rifles or barbed wire. The American equation rests on the habit of holding our fellow citizens in thoughtful regard not because they are exceptional (or famous, or beautiful, or rich) but simply because they are our fellow citizens. If we abandon the sense of mutual respect, we abandon the premise as well as the machinery of the American enterprise.

That the triumph of America corresponds to its prowess as a nation-state.

The pretension serves the purposes of the people who talk about "the national security" and "the vital interest of the American people" when what they mean is the power and privilege of government. The oligarchy resident in Washington assumes that all Americans own the same property instead of taking part in the same idea, that we share a joint geopolitical program instead of a common temperament and habit of mind. Even so faithful a servant of the monied interests as Daniel Webster understood the distinction: "The public happiness is to be the aggregate of individuals. Our system begins with the individual man."

The Constitution was made for the uses of the individual (an implement on the order of a plow, an ax, or a surveyor's plumb line), and the institutions of American government were meant to support the liberties of the people, not the ambitions of the state. Given any ambiguity about the order of priority or precedence, it was the law that had to give way to the citizen's freedom of thought and action, not the citizen's freedom of thought and action that had to give way to the law. The Bill of Rights stresses the distinction in the two final amendments, the ninth ("The enumeration in the Constitution, of certain rights, shall not be construed to deny or disparage others retained by the people") and the tenth ("The powers not delegated to the United States by the Constitution, nor prohibited by it to the States, are reserved to the States respectively, or to the people").

What joins the Americans one to another is not a common nationality, language, race, or ancestry (all of which testify to the burdens of the past) but rather their complicity in a shared work of the imagination. My love of country follows from my love of its freedoms, not from my pride in its fleets or its armies or its gross national product. Construed as a means and not an end, the Constitution stands as the premise for a narrative rather than a plan for an invasion or a monument. The narrative was always plural—not one story but many stories.

That it is easy to be an American.

I can understand why the politicians like to pretend that America is mostly about going shopping, but I never know why anybody believes the ad copy. Grant the existential terms and conditions of the American enterprise (i.e., that we are all bound to invent ourselves), and the position is both solitary and probably lost. I know a good many people who would rather be British or Nigerian or Swiss.

Lately I've been reading the accounts of the nineteenth-century adventurers and pioneers who traveled west from Missouri under circumstances almost always adverse. Most of them didn't find whatever it was they expected to find behind the next range of mountains or around the next bend in the river. They were looking for a garden in a country that was mostly desert, and the record of their passage is largely one of sorrow and failure. Travelers making their way across the Great Plains in the 1850s reported great numbers of dead horses and abandoned wagons on the trail, the echo of the hopes that so recently preceded them lingering in an empty chair or in the scent of flowers on a new grave.

Reading the diaries and letters, especially those of the women in the caravans, I think of the would-be settlers lost in an immense wilderness, looking into the mirrors of their loneliness and measuring their capacity for self-knowledge against the vastness of the wide and indifferent sky.

Too often we forget the proofs of our courage. If we wish to live in the state of freedom that allows us to make and think and build, then we must accustom ourselves to the shadows on the walls and the wind in trees. The climate of anxiety is the cost of doing business. Just as a monarchy places far fewer burdens on its subjects than a democracy places on its citizens, so also bigotry is easier than tolerance. When something goes wrong with the currency or the schools, it's always comforting to know that the faults can be easily found in something as obvious as a color, or a number, or the sound of a strange language. The multiple adjectives qualifying the American noun enrich the vocabulary of blame, and if the election year continues as it has begun I expect that by next summer we will discover that it is not only middle-aged Protestant males who have been making a wreck of the culture but also (operating secretly and sometimes in disguise) adolescent, sallow, Buddhist females.

Among all the American political virtues, candor is probably the one most necessary to the success of our mutual enterprise. Unless we try to tell each other the truth about what we know and think and see (i.e., the story so far as it appears to the travelers on the voyage out) we might as well amuse ourselves (for as long as somebody else allows us to do so) with fairy tales. The vitality of the American democracy always has rested on the capacity of its citizens to speak and think without cant. Addressing the topic of *The American Democrat*, James Fenimore Cooper argued in 1838 that the word "American" was synonymous with the habit of telling the truth:

> By candor we are not to understand trifling and uncalled for expositions of truth; but a sentiment that proves a conviction of the necessity of speaking truth, when speaking at all; a contempt for all designing evasions of our real opinions.
>
> In all the general concerns, the public has a right to be treated with candor. Without this manly and truly republican quality ... the institutions are converted into a stupendous fraud.

If we indulge ourselves with evasions and the pleasure of telling lies, we speak to our fears and our weaknesses instead of to our courage and our strength. We can speak plainly about our differences only if we know and value what we hold in common. Like the weather and third-rate journalism, bigotry in all its declensions is likely to be with us for a long time (certainly as long as the next hundred years), but unless we can draw distinctions and make jokes about our racial or cultural baggage, the work of our shared imagination must vanish in the mist of lies. The lies might win elections (or sell newspapers and economic theories), but they bind us to the theaters of wish and dream. If I must like or admire a fellow citizen for his or her costume of modifying adjectives (because he or she is black or gay or rich), then I might as well believe that the lost continent of Atlantis will rise next summer from the sea and that the Japanese will continue to make the payments—now and forever, world without end—on all our mortgages and battleships.

Among all the nations of the earth, America is the one that has come most triumphantly to terms with the mixtures of blood and caste, and maybe it is another of history's ironic jokes that we should wish to repudiate our talent for assimilation at precisely the moment in time when so many other nations in the world (in

Africa and Western Europe as well as the Soviet Union) look to the promise of the American example. The jumble of confused or mistaken identities that was the story of nineteenth-century America has become the story of a late twentieth-century world defined by a vast migration of peoples across seven continents and as many oceans. Why, then, do we lose confidence in ourselves and grow fearful of our mongrel freedoms?

The politician who would lift us to a more courageous understanding of ourselves might begin by saying that we are all, each and every one of us, as much at fault as anybody else, that no matter whom we blame for our troubles (whether George Bush, or Al Sharpton, or David Duke) or how pleasant the invective (racist, sexist, imperialist pig), we still have to rebuild our cities and revise our laws. We can do the work together, or we can stand around making strong statements about each other's clothes.

1993

4. Versailles on the Potomac

Should a man be appointed to a new post, praise of him pours forth, overflowing into courtyards and chapels, reaching the stair, the hall, the gallery, the whole of the royal apartment; one's quite submerged, one's overwhelmed by it. There are no two opinions on the man; envy and jealousy speak with the same voice as adulation; all are swept away by the torrent, which forces them to say what they think or don't think, of a man, and often to praise one whom they do not know. A man of wit, merit, or valor becomes, in one instant, a genius of the first rank, a hero, a demi-god.

—La Bruyère, *Characters*

Like the notables assembled under Louis XIV's roof at Versailles, official Washington divides the known world into only two parts. First there is Washington, and then there is everyplace else. The planes arriving and departing National Airport cross the only frontier of any consequence—the one between the inside and the outside—and all the truly momentous topics of conversation center on only one question, which is always and unfailingly the same: Who's in and who's out? The court might seem to be talking about something else—about war, or peace, or racial hatred, or the deficit—but the words serve a decorative or theatrical purpose, and they are meant to be admired for their polished surfaces, as if they were mirrors or gilded chairs. What's important is what happens in Washington. Yes, it might be interesting to know that the United States now must pay $292 billion a year in interest on the national debt, and, yes, the poor blacks in the slums of Los Angeles obviously have their reasons to riot, but their suffering is far away and in another country, and what matters is the way in which the story plays tomorrow morning at the White House or the Department of Defense. Who will come, and who will go? Who will occupy the office overlooking the lawn? Who will ride in the secretary's limousine, and who will carry the president's messages? Court ritual obliges all present to wear the masks of grave concern and utter the standard phrases of alarm ("America at the Crossroads," "The Crisis of the Cities"), but behind the facade of stately euphemism, the accomplished courtier learns to hide the far more urgent question: "What, please God, is going to happen to *me*?"

The masks come loose when the possession of the White House passes from one political party to the other and the would-be servants of the new world order parade their ambition in plain sight. The spectacle is marvelous to behold, and in the days and weeks following the election of Bill Clinton the news from Washington might as well have been extracted from an eighteenth-century book of court etiquette. On the Wednesday after the election the important columnists in town began making their bows and curtsies by comparing the new president with the young Jack Kennedy, and the more gracious members of the troupe professed to see rising from the mists of the Arkansas River the fabled towers of Camelot. Mo Sussman's Restaurant, much frequented by the city's principal careerists, added Arkansas Stew to its menu, and at the better markets in Georgetown the salesclerks murmured their appreciation of fried green tomatoes and sweet potato pie. The Securities Industry Association obligingly replaced its executive director, a Republican, with a Democrat who had known

Bill Clinton at Oxford. Similarly abrupt exits and entrances took place in the executive offices of Hill and Knowlton, a consortium of prominent influence peddlers, and at the American Bankers Association.

On Thursday afternoon, less than thirty-six hours after the polls closed in California, Jack Kent Cooke, the owner of the Washington Redskins, discovered that he was acquainted with a surprisingly large number of Democrats. An invitation to sit in his box at RFK Stadium counts as one of the most visible proofs of rank within the Washington nobility, and during the fat years of the Reagan triumph and the Bush succession the sixty-four seats were comfortably stuffed with personages as grand as former attorney general Edwin Meese, columnist George Will, and businessman Robert Mosbacher. But on that Thursday, in answer to a question from a correspondent for the *New York Times*, Mr. Cooke remembered that time passes and fashions change: "I'm a Republican, but strangely I have a great many Democrat friends. Dodd. Brzezinski. Greenspan—he's of indeterminate lineage. Sam Donaldson—what's he? Gene McCarthy and George McGovern."

The reporter asked if Mr. Cooke knew of any football friends among President Clinton's circle of dependents and admirers. "'You must understand,' Mr. Cooke said. 'The box is not used to ingratiate myself with the administration. Please quote me precisely on that. I invite people who are good company, happy, cheerful, good-humored people who love football.'"

Over the first weekend of the new revelation, the publications that provide the court with topics of conversation—the *Times* and the *Washington Post* as well as *Time* and the *New Republic*— began rearranging the furniture in the drawing rooms of power. Previously resplendent figures much praised for their infallible judgment—among them James Baker, the once-upon-a-time secretary of state—were seen in the light of the democratic dawn as shabby impostors, as far behind the times as President Bush's collection of old tennis balls and the baseball glove that he had brought with him from the playing fields at Yale. Together with the work of revision, the court gazettes published the first in a long series of ornamental opinion pieces—from former ambassadors and deputy secretaries of state, directors of policy institutes, eager Harvard professors, and economists in exile—meant to prove their authors deserving of an appointment to Paris or the National Security Council. Other voices in other rooms proclaimed their love of the environment and their interest in the saxophone, and at Wonder Graphics Picture Framing on Vermont Avenue, the owner of the store beheld a vision of prosperity: "'Everyone's going to have to hang up new pictures in their offices,' [he] said. 'They're going to be putting up new Clinton–Gore glad-handing pictures. They're going to need framing, and we do a very nice job.'"

The talented courtier possesses what Plutarch called "the soul of an acrobat"—that is, a man who discovers very early in his career that if he can learn to lick one boot he can learn to lick the boots of a regiment—and through the month of November, as the dance of grace and favor became both more desperate and more refined, I noticed that people long associated with Republican causes, with supply-side economics and weekends shooting quail in the company of Senators Simpson and Gramm, presented themselves as voices of bipartisan conscience. Robert Strauss, the Washington lobbyist whom President Bush had appointed ambassador to Russia, appeared on network television to say that he once had been chairman of the Democratic National Committee and that he had voted, out of conviction and with a whole heart, for Bill Clinton.

Even in New York the conversations often veered off into the niceties of Washington protocol. One morning over breakfast at the Regency Hotel with a government lawyer whom I had last seen in the twilight of the Carter Administration, I was surprised to find myself talking about the Roman emperor Marcus Aurelius. The lawyer ordinarily didn't concern herself with events to which she couldn't attach living witnesses as well as a handsome fee, and I remembered her once telling me that history was the refuge of men who were afraid of the world. It wasn't until we had come to the end of the emperor's reign—his stoicism, his persecution of Christians, his bestowal of the empire on Commodus—that she informed me of Clinton's fondness for the late emperor's *Meditations*. She had been invited to a dinner given by one of

Clinton's advisers, and she wished to make a subtle reference—as if derived from long reflection rather than a quick briefing—to the emperor's noble melancholy.

Three days later, in conversation with a professor of biochemistry at Yale, I was asked to speak for twenty minutes about the significance of environmentalist Chico Mendes and Secretary of State Cordell Hull. The professor had heard that photographs of those two individuals were to be seen on the walls of Al Gore's office in the Senate (together with photographs of conservationist Rachel Carson and Soviet poet and novelist Yevgeny Yevtushenko), and if he could connect the metaphysical dots between the four names, then maybe when he went to Washington in a week's time to apply for a post at the Environmental Protection Agency, he might know what else to say after he had made his ritual devotions to the Manchurian tiger and the Japanese crane.

As long ago as 1831, passing through Cincinnati and Nashville, Alexis de Tocqueville was surprised by the virulence of what he called "the courtier spirit" among the supposedly plain and democratic Americans. He had thought that the citizens of the new democracy would prove to be homespun and roughhewn people, direct in their actions and forthright in their address. He hadn't expected to find them so well schooled in the arts of servility. True, they didn't dress as well or as expensively as the ladies and gentlemen in France; their conversation wasn't as refined, and neither were their manners, but they possessed a native talent for ingratiating themselves with anybody and everybody who could do them a favor or grant them a privilege. The effect was often comic—dandies in broadcloth instead of silk brocade, loud in their brag and fantastic in their gestures, bowing and scraping to one another while standing up to their ankles in the muddy street of a wooden town on the edge of a savage wilderness.

After considering the paradox for some years, Tocqueville concluded that in a monarchy the courtier spirit was less pervasive and less damaging than it was in a democracy. Even the most arrogant of kings seldom had the gall to speak in the name of the public interest. Louis XIV couldn't impose a military conscription, and he always had considerable trouble with the levying of taxes.

The king's interest was clearly his own. But a democracy claims to serve the interest of the sovereign people, and so the officials who write and administer the laws can claim to act on behalf of anything that they can classify as the common good. The presumption allows for a more expansive abrogation of power than the divine right of kings, and because the figure of the prince in a democracy appears in so many different forms and disguises—as politician, network executive, corporate chairman, town clerk, foundation hierarch, and Washington columnist—the anxious sycophant is constantly bowing and smiling in eight or nine directions, forever turning, like a compass needle or a weather vane, into the glare of new money. A democracy transforms the relatively few favors in the monarch's gift—sinecure, benefice, or patent royal—into the vast cornucopia of patronage distributed under the nominally egalitarian rubrics of tax exemption, defense contract, publication, milk subsidy, tenure, government office.

Numerous writers over the last four hundred years have attempted to describe or define the courtier spirit, and on reading the news from Washington last autumn, I thought not only of Tocqueville but also of Denis Diderot's satirical dialogue *Rameau's Nephew*. The text takes the form of a conversation set in a café in Paris in 1761, and the author presents himself in the character of a moral philosopher (very dignified, very grave) engaged in an antic dispute with Jean-François Rameau, a musician and music teacher who prides himself on his talents as scoundrel, rogue, flatterer, hanger-on, opportunist, hypocrite. The two men talk during the hour before a performance of the opera near the Palais Royal, Rameau berating himself for having committed the stupidity of telling his patron the truth and so having lost his place at his patron's table. He is a wonderfully comic figure, given to sudden and fanciful gesture, often interrupting himself to mime the stance and character of somebody whom he wishes to mock. At one point he performs the beggar's pantomime, the dance that he defines as the perfect expression of the courtier spirit and describes as follows:

Then smiling as he [Rameau's nephew] did so, he began impersonating the admiring man, the supplicating man, the complaisant man, right foot forward, left foot behind, back bent, head up, looking fixedly into somebody else's eyes, lips parted, arms held out toward something, waiting for a command, receiving it, off like an arrow, back again with it done, reporting it. He is attentive to everything, picks up what has been dropped, adjusts a pillow or puts a stool under someone's feet, holds a saucer, pushes forward a chair, opens a door, shuts a window, pulls curtains, keeps his eyes on the master and mistress, stands motionless, arms at his side and legs straight, listening, trying to read people's expressions.

At the court of Louis XIV in seventeenth-century France, people occupied themselves with the work of making small distinctions—those greeted at the door, those offered armchairs, those deemed worthy of being seen off in their coaches. In official Washington in late twentieth-century America, the court occupies itself with similar distinctions—those granted government cars, those awarded parking spaces at National Airport, those invited to sit in Jack Kent Cooke's box at RFK Stadium. Against the sum of such tremendous trifles, the questions of yesterday's riot or tomorrow's debt beat as heavily as the wings of moths.

1993

5. Show and Tell

The formula "Two and two make five" is not without its attractions.
—Dostoevsky

The Clinton Administration apparently means to define itself as a television program instead of a government, and although I admire what I take to be the theme of the show—restoring belief in the American promise—I don't know how it can please both its sponsors and its intended audience. The difficulty follows from the need to protect the interests of oligarchy (i.e., the people who put up the campaign money) and at the same time sustain the illusion of popular sovereignty among an electorate hoping for proofs through the night that our flag is still there.

The events attending President Clinton's inaugural might as well have been chosen as demonstrations of an untenable political theorem. Obliged to reward his patrons and comfort his fans, the president provided the former with the gifts of office and the latter with ritual songs and dances. On Capitol Hill the Congress went about the business of confirming the president's nominees to the Cabinet—most of them corporate lawyers, several of them patently unqualified or inept, all of them loyal servants of the status quo that as a candidate the president had so often decried as timid, self-serving, and corrupt.

More or less simultaneously, the president appeared as the friend of the common man in the series of tableaux vivants staged against the backdrops of Washington's best-known monuments— Bill Clinton at Monticello, departing for the Capitol under the aegis of Thomas Jefferson, and riding through the landscape of the Civil War in a bus bearing the license plate HOPE 1; Bill Clinton by candlelight, approaching the Lincoln Memorial on foot; Bill Clinton ringing a replica of the Liberty Bell; Bill Clinton listening, transfixed, to Diana Ross sing "We Are the World" and to ten saxophonists play Elvis Presley's "Heartbreak Hotel"; Bill Clinton in tears at the Capital Centre, accepting the badges and emblems of democratic sentiment at the hands of Barbra Streisand and Michael Jackson; Bill Clinton swearing the oath of office in the presence of Maya Angelou, who read an ode to the multicultural text ("the Asian, the Hispanic, the Jew/The African, the Native American, the Sioux ... the Gay, the Straight, the Preacher/ the privileged, the homeless, the Teacher") of the American soul.

The juxtaposition of the two series of events—the one on Capitol Hill confirming the rule of entrenched privilege, the other a spectacle made for the hired help—established the plot lines and introduced the principal characters of the Democratic sequel to the Ronald Reagan show. The extravagant sum of money spent on the inaugural pageant ($17 million provided by the nation's leading business corporations) expressed the degree to which the nation's possessing classes were worried about the resentment still at large in the public opinion polls. President Clinton clearly delights in the character of amiable television host, as he was glad to demonstrate at a televised "town meeting" in suburban Detroit in early February, but the audience is not apt to be as easily amused as it was in 1980, and the new star of political television lacks Mr. Reagan's talent for looking presidential. To see him give a speech, or watch his wife ascend the steps of the Capitol, was to be reminded not of Thomas Jefferson or an act of Congress, not even of a documentary series produced by PBS, but of *Donahue* and *Designing Women*.

An election-year script obliges the candidate to campaign on the promise of social and economic change, as no friend of the corporate lobbyists and the status quo. Following the accepted practice, candidate Clinton from time to time had presented himself as a tribune of the people pledged to cleanse Washington of "the rich and special interests" that for twelve years of Republican misrule had robbed the American people of their tax money and their constitutional birthright. At the same time and sometimes in the same speech, he described himself as "pro-business and pro-labor," "for economic growth and for protecting the environment," "for affirmative action but against quotas," "for legal abortions but also for making abortion as rare as possible." His opinions were those that his audiences wished to hear, and never once did I hear him venture the word "justice," presumably on the grounds that it might be mistaken, like "liberty" (a word he also avoided), for a criticism of his corporate sponsors.

The speeches were letter-perfect, but when it came time to name his Cabinet and define his government, Mr. Clinton lost his hustler's touch for the political shell game. In place of the diverse and unorthodox team of American talent that he had so often promised, he substituted the familiar trick of labels and tokens ("the Hispanic … the African … the Gay, the Straight, the Preacher, the privileged … the Teacher"), and instead of appointing at least a few citizens remarkable for their courage and independence of mind (i.e., the kind of people who might lend verisimilitude to the impression of change), the president assembled a company of functionaries burdened with an average term of service in Washington of thirteen years. The principal figures in his Cabinet—Warren Christopher, the secretary of state; Les Aspin, the secretary of defense; Lloyd Bentsen, the secretary of the treasury—were men grown bleak and pale in the dim basements of politics-as-usual. For twenty-one years as a congressman from Wisconsin, and as chairman of the House Armed Services Committee, Secretary Aspin diligently forwarded the freight of the defense industry. During his 1990 congressional campaign, each of the nation's ten largest military contractors returned the favor with appreciative contributions. As the senior senator from Texas and the chairman of the Senate Finance Committee, Secretary Bentsen consistently supported the banking and insurance lobbies, voting in favor of each of President Reagan's major tax bills. As a corporate lawyer in Los Angeles and deputy secretary of state in the Carter Administration, Secretary Christopher earned a reputation for his discreet silence, a man known and relied upon for his unwillingness to offend the consensus of opinion seated at the expensive end of the conference table.

Similar traits of mind and character distinguished almost the whole company of the new Cabinet. As a prominent Washington lobbyist, Ronald H. Brown, the secretary of commerce, counted among his clients "Baby Doc" Duvalier, the former Haitian tyrant, as well as the government of Japan. On being raised to federal office, he was so gauche as to demand exemption from the customary rules of pecuniary decency, and it didn't occur to him to discourage the organization of a gala dinner party in his honor that was to have been staged (three days before President Clinton's inaugural) by a quorum of grateful business corporations, among them J. C. Penney, Anheuser-Busch, Sony Music Entertainment, and Pepsico. Robert E. Rubin, the former cochairman of Goldman, Sachs & Company whom President Clinton named chairman of the National Economic Council, was equally careless of appearances. On his way to Washington from New York, he sent letters to as many as 1,000 corporate clients (foreign and domestic), assuring them that both he and his firm "look forward to continuing to work with you in my new capacity."

With only a few modest or senior exceptions, the collective tone of voice of the new Cabinet was that of the acquisitive and self-satisfied child of the 1980s. Unlike the privy councillors appointed by President Bush, most of whom enjoyed the status conferred by inherited wealth, President Clinton's surrogates derived their presumption of privilege from their institutional provenience, not by right of birth but by right of the academic degrees bestowed by Harvard, Oxford, and Yale Law School. The seals and stamps embossed on their résumés certified their standing as newly minted members of the nation's ruling oligarchy. Like their contemporaries in Hollywood and on Wall Street, they had proved themselves equal to the tasks of self-promotion and adept at the arts of getting rich. Almost without exception they were people whose moral reasoning conformed to the circular design fashionable among the adherents of both presidents Reagan and George H. W. Bush—what is good is rich and successful; what is rich and successful is good; I am rich and successful, therefore I am good, and so is my car and my theory of the just society. If the servants of the Reagan and Bush Administrations wished to divide the country into an equestrian and a plebeian class, they at least were content to give up the ornaments of conscience in exchange for the house in Virginia. The friends of Bill Clinton apparently want it all—everything in both column A and column B, the Zen garden and the BMW as well as the three-masted schooner and the friendship of rap musicians.

The too blatant contradiction in terms both embarrassed and frightened the Washington news media, who had thought that Mr. Clinton knew how to stage the play of appearances as adroitly as President Reagan. Certainly as a candidate he had understood that people who would wear the masks of populism must be careful to avoid the shows of vanity. The news media didn't object to the hypocrisy, which is as necessary to Washington as tap water, but they were troubled by the style of the hypocrisy, which was either twenty years out of date or five years ahead of its time. It was this latter possibility that compounded their embarrassment with the trace elements of fear. What if the Clinton Administration was about nothing else except the projection of images? A collage of symbols made only for television? The president during his first few days in office toyed with a number of substantive political issues (campaign finance reform and the rescue of the Haitian refugees) as if they were as light as balsa wood or as transparent as a studio photographer's gauze. The feeling of weightlessness corresponded to what was apparently the president's utter lack of conviction. Even President Reagan entertained at least two genuine beliefs (the Nicaraguan Contras were good; high taxes were bad), and three or four of President Bush's opinions held their shape from one week to the next.

But Mr. Clinton apparently believes in nothing except the presentation of self. His rhetoric suits the uses of television because it can be cut into any convenient length (twelve seconds, thirty seconds, five minutes, forty minutes) and because it employs the diction of group therapy. Like the evangelist or faith healer, he delivers the good news in a language empty of existential context or historical reference. Politics is never about who has the power to do what to whom but always (as Mr. Clinton said on the night of his election on the steps of the governor's mansion in Little Rock and again when explaining to Congress the need for economic sacrifice) about the clash of giant abstractions—about "a fight between hope and fear, a fight between division and unity, a fight between blame and taking responsibility ... and may God bless America."

By seeming to say everything, the president manages to say nothing. He defines himself as a man desperately eager to please, and the voraciousness of his appetite—for more friends, more speeches, more food and drink, more time onstage, more hands to shake, more hugs—suggests the emptiness of a soul that knows itself only by the names of what it seizes or consumes. At the television gala presented in his honor the night before the inauguration, he couldn't prevent himself from mouthing the lyrics while Barbra Streisand sang "Evergreen." The cameras drifted away from Streisand—as Mr. Clinton knew they must—and found the tear-stained face of the new president, devouring the words as if they were made of sugar or chocolate. His infant's dream of all-embracing celebrity would have been well understood by President William Howard Taft, who once was astonished to discover himself traveling on a train with Mary Pickford and Francis X. Bushman, the silent-screen stars who were then the wonder of the age. When he saw how the actress was mobbed by eager crowds at the station, he summoned Bushman into his presence and confessed that he envied him the adoration of the public. "All the people love you," he said to the actor, "and I can't have even the love of half the people."

Moved by a comparable feeling of melancholy and boundless desire, President Clinton at the televised town meeting in Detroit began by saying that after only three weeks in the White House he had learned "how easy it is for the president to get out of touch." He roamed across the soundstage like a starved animal, feeding on the questions from the audience as if they were the stuff of life and breath.

To the extent that the rule of love supersedes the rule of law, self-government becomes representative in the theatrical rather than the constitutional sense of the word, and democracy defines itself in the language of advertising. By that line of reasoning, the Clinton Administration might prove to be best understood as a ceaseless campaign or a never-ending talk show. At a White House press conference in the not-too-distant future, I wouldn't be surprised to see the president interrupt the discussion—about jobs or Bosnia or the debt—and turn graciously to the camera to announce a commercial break. I can imagine him saying, "Don't go away, we'll be right back," but as his smile dissolves into an advertisement for Bud Light, I can also imagine myself wondering what the show is about and why democracy at the end deteriorates into a child's game of show and tell.

1995

6. Reactionary Chic

The 104th Congress assembled in Washington on January 4 amid a dark murmur of sworn oaths about rescuing the captive spirit of American success from the dungeons of big government. As I listened to the right-wing radio broadcasters sending their furious signals from their newly installed transmitters in the basement of the Capitol, I was struck by the resemblance between this season's Republican revolution and the old countercultural rebellion of thirty years ago. Once again the partisans of a romantic anti-politics intended a guerrilla raid on the wicked cities of death and time. Although nobody described the mission in precisely those words, the exuberant cheers welcoming Newt Gingrich to the Speaker's chair in the House of Representatives (loud cries of "Newt!" "Newt!" "Newt!") swelled with high purpose and zealous intent, the applause rising to the pitch of enthusiasm appropriate to the arrival of a hero or a saint. Here at last was the purifying wind from the South, the politician who had been touring the country both before and after the November election preaching the gospel of revolt, sacker of shibboleths and government spending programs come to lead the American people out of the deserts of the welfare state.

Under the circumstances and given the fierce expectations gathered on the Republican side of the aisle, Gingrich's inaugural address as speaker of the House was surprisingly and uncharacteristically mild. Pronouncing the occasion "historic," he put aside for the moment his familiar persona as arrogant bully and humbly introduced himself as an adopted child and a common man. He expressed his approval of Franklin D. Roosevelt's social conscience and Benjamin Franklin's faith in God, and generously distributed the alms of his compassion to people who were poor and black as well as to people who were white and rich. The "most painful problems" abroad in the land he identified as "moral problems," and toward the end of his speech he began to talk about bringing the United States more nearly in line with the kingdom of Heaven.

The speech was at once pious and sly, and although I suspect that some of the talk show hosts in the basement were disappointed by its noncombative tone and because nobody was handing out weapons as well as platitudes, the Republican majority received it with gusts of tumultuous applause (more cries of "Newt!" "Newt!" "Newt!"), and quite a few of the members looked as if they stood ready to carry the Speaker on their shoulders to the White House or the Air and Space Museum.[1]

Like so much else about the Republican risorgimento, the political passion was attached to a preferred image rather than a plain or ambiguous fact, not to the Gingrich who had just delivered a conciliatory speech but to the Gingrich renowned for being nasty and brutish and short—the militant Gingrich blessed with

---

[1]   Peggy Noonan both captured and embodied the fervent spirit of the occasion in an editorial published in the *Wall Street Journal* under the headline "Bliss to Be Alive." Saying that she had been present at the glorious moment when Representative Gingrich "became a great man," she observed that "now and then history turns electric. Last week it was wonderful to see the current light up this town." She heard in Gingrich's speech the trumpet of deliverance—"the authentic sound of post-Reagan conservatism ... the authentic sound of the next ten years."

a boll weevil's appetite for destruction who had ordered a skull of *Tyrannosaurus rex* as an ornament for his new office in the Longworth building.

It was the scornful Gingrich who had come to stand during his sixteen years in Congress as the shared symbol of resentment binding together the several parties of the disaffected right—the Catholic conservatives with the Jewish neoconservatives, the libertarians with the authoritarians, Pat Robertson's Christian Coalition with the disciples of white nationalist David Duke. Clearly a man for all grievances, Gingrich summed up (in his person as well as in his lectures on the decline and fall of American civilization) the whole of the conservative objection that since the dawn of the Reagan Revolution in the early 1980s has comprised the course of required reading at the Heritage Foundation and the American Enterprise Institute. Over the last fifteen years I probably have read two or three thousand variations of the complaint— editorials in the *Wall Street Journal*, articles in *Commentary* and *The New Criterion*, the speeches of William Bennett and the columns of George Will, the soliloquies of Rush Limbaugh, the books in the line of frowning succession, from Allan Bloom's *The Closing of the American Mind* through George Gilder's *Wealth and Poverty*, Dinesh D'Souza's *Illiberal Education*, and Charles Murray's *Losing Ground*—but when I delete the repetitions and piece together what remains of a coherent narrative, the entire sum of the great suburban remonstrance fits within the span of a short fairy tale:

> Once upon a time, before the awful misfortunes of the 1960s, America was a theme park constructed by nonunion labor along the lines of the Garden of Eden. But then something terrible happened, and a plague of guitarists descended upon the land. Spawned by the sexual confusions of the amoral news media, spores of Marxist ideology blew around in the wind, multiplied the powers of government, and impregnated the English departments at the Ivy League universities, which then gave birth to the monster of deconstruction that devoured the arts of learning. Pretty soon the trout began to die in Wyoming, and the next thing that anybody

knew the nation's elementary schools had been debased, too many favors were being granted to women and blacks, federal bureaucrats were smothering capitalist entrepreneurs with the pillows of government regulation, prime-time television was broadcasting continuous footage from Sodom and Gomorrah, and the noble edifice of Western civilization had collapsed into the rubble of feminist prose.

The story somehow made more sense when set against the operatic backdrop of the Cold War, possibly because the familiar stage design called to mind the first act of *The Nutcracker Suite* when the toy soldier does battle with the army of horrific mice. The evil Soviet Empire furnished the book and lyrics for the election campaigns of both presidents Reagan and Bush, and for a few years it was possible to imagine that the fungus blighting the apple trees in the American orchard had something to do with the weather on the totalitarian steppe. The sudden tearing down of the Berlin Wall took everybody by surprise—the director of the CIA as well as the editors at *National Review*—and the tellers of the tale found themselves in pressing need of other antagonists to take the place of the grim but harmless ogre. The departure of the Russian trolls prompted a casting call for prospective bogeymen and likely villains. The Japanese couldn't play the part because they were lending the United States too much money; the Colombian drug lords were too few and too well connected in Miami; Panamanian military dictator Manuel Noriega and Iraqi president Saddam Hussein failed the audition; the Arab oil cartel was broke; and the Chinese were busy making shirts for Ralph Lauren.

In the absence of enemies abroad, the protectors of the American dream began looking for inward signs of moral weakness rather than outward shows of military force; instead of examining the dossiers of foreign tyrants, they searched the local newspapers for flaws in the American character, and the surveillance satellites overhead Leipzig and Sevastopol were reassigned stations over metropolitan Detroit and the back lots of Hollywood studios. Within a matter of months the authorities rounded up as suspects a motley crowd of specific individuals and general categories of subversive behavior and opinion—black male adolescents as well as leftist English professors, multiculturalists of all descriptions, the liberal news media, the 1960s, the government in Washington, welfare mothers, homosexuals, drug criminals, performance artists, illegal immigrants. Some enemies of the state were easier to identify than others, but in all instances the tellers of the tale relied on images seen in dreams or on the network news rather than on the lessons of their own experience.

Believing themselves under assault from what they took to be the hostile forces of history, the heirs and servants of American oligarchy chose to cast themselves as rebels against "the system," as revolutionary idealists at odds with a world they never made. The pose was as ludicrous as it was familiar. Here were the people who owned most of what was worth owning in the country (the banks and business corporations as well as the television networks and most of the members of Congress) pretending that they were victims of a conspiracy raised against them by the institutions that they themselves controlled. What was even more extraordinary was the general likeness between their own revolutionary pretensions and the posturing of the 1960s counterculture that they so often and so loudly denounced. Although I had made occasional notes over a number of years about the similarities between the two camps of *soi-disant* revolutionaries, it wasn't until last October 19, during the course of a publisher's lunch at the Harvard Club in New York, that I fully appreciated the extent to which the reactionary chic of the 1990s mimics the set of 1960s attitudes memorialized by Tom Wolfe in the phrase "radical chic."

Sponsored by the Manhattan Institute (a think tank that funds rightist political theory) and meant to welcome the arrival of a new work of neoconservative doctrine (*Dictatorship of Virtue* by Richard Bernstein), the lunch attracted a crowd of fifty individuals who for the most part were affiliated with publications and charitable foundations (among them *Forbes*, *Commentary*, and the John M. Olin Foundation) known for their allegiance to the miracle of finance capitalism. The intellectual tide last fall was running strongly in favor of more prisons and higher interest rates, and the mood in the dining room was smiling and complacent. The Democrats clearly were on their way to defeat in the November elections; President Clinton had been brought up on charges of sexual harassment by Paula Jones; Newt Gingrich was marching through Georgia with "The Battle Hymn of the Republic" and the terrible swift swords of Christian vengeance. Even more to the point, two other works allied with Bernstein's tract (Charles Murray and the late Richard Herrnstein's *The Bell Curve* and William Henry's *In Defense of Elitism*) already had reached the season's bestseller lists, which was good news because the authors of both works, like Bernstein, affirmed the great truth so dear to the hearts of almost everybody in the room—that is, that the American upper middle class was a dwindling minority besieged by enemies at all points of the moral and intellectual compass, and thus deserving (like other aggrieved citizens) of protection and special privilege.[2]

Introduced as "the John Keats of the *New York Times*," Bernstein, earnest and ingratiating and safe, set forth the thesis of his book as an ominous comparison between late twentieth-century America and the moment of the *dérapage* in late eighteenth-century France when the enlightened idealism that had inspired the immortal "Declaration of the Rights of Man" began to degenerate into the Terror forced upon a hapless people by the guillotine and the Committee of Public Safety. He was addressing his remarks to people as little threatened by the circumstances he described as the Wednesday matinee audience at *Les Misérables*, but all present were thrilled beyond words to know that they too were living in stirring times, that the barbarians once again were at the gates, and that, when one really got to thinking about it,

---

2 Before attending the lunch I had taken the precaution of reading the book. Bernstein's complete list of enemies appears on page 230: "the penetration of the new sensibility into the elite institutions, in the universities, the press, the liberal churches, the foundations, the schools, and show business, on PBS and '*Murphy Brown*,' at Harvard and Dallas Baptist University, on editorial boards and op-ed pages, at the Ford Foundation and the Rockefeller Brothers Fund, the National Education Association, the American Society of Newspaper Editors, the National Council of Churches, and the Pew Charitable Trusts."

new anchorman Sam Donaldson and film studio executive David Geffen were just as awful as Danton and Robespierre.

Listening to Bernstein talk about "the tyranny of the left" crushing the universities under the iron heel of "moralistic liberalism," I understood that I was revisiting a make-believe time and place not unlike the one that used to be known as the Age of Aquarius. The wording of the manifestos might have changed (William Bennett's "Empower America" in place of Huey Newton's "Power to the people"), and so might have the age and social standing of the malcontents (Howard Stern and Rush Limbaugh sitting in for Lenny Bruce and Abbie Hoffman at the drums of a politically incorrect comedy), but the habits of mind remained all but identical, and so did the air of self-righteousness and the settled conviction that virtue is a trait inherited at birth. Thirty years ago it was "the conservative establishment" that was at fault, a conspiracy largely composed of university professors, government bureaucrats, and network television executives who couldn't play guitar and trembled at the sound of Dylan's harmonica. Now it is "the liberal establishment" that is at fault, a conspiracy largely composed of university professors, government bureaucrats, and network television executives who can't quote freely from *The Federalist* and tremble before the wisdom of Alvin Toffler and Arianna Huffington.[3]

---

3 Arianna Huffington's New Age meditations, *The Fourth Instinct*, appear on Representative Gingrich's unofficial list of recommended reading; the official list, the one he hands out to stray visitors wandering through the halls of the Capitol, comprises the following texts: the *Declaration of Independence*, 1776; *The Federalist*, 1788; *Democracy in America*, by Alexis de Tocqueville, 1835–40; *The Effective Executive*, by Peter F. Drucker (Harper & Row, 1966; reissued by Harper Business, 1993); *Washington: The Indispensable Man*, by James T. Flexner (Little, Brown, 1974; reissued 1994); *Leadership and the Computer*, by Mary E. Boone (Prima Publishing, 1991; reissued 1994); *Creating a New Civilization: The Politics of the Third Wave*, by Alvin and Heidi Toffler (with a foreword by Gingrich and published by the Progress and Freedom Foundation, 1994); *Working Without a Net: How to Survive and Thrive in Today's High Risk Business World*, by Morris R. Shechtman (Prentice Hall, 1994).

Once I began to draw the parallels between the radical Sixties left and the reactionary Nineties right (between Bernstein's grandiose moment of *dérapage* and the "Days of Rage" announced by Weather Underground leaders Mark Rudd and Bernadine Dohrn), I found myself making a longer list of the sentiments and tactics common to both bands of guerrillas gathered in the mountains of what the Chicago Seven liked to call "the Higher Consciousness":

1. The definition of the United States as a nation betrayed (in the 1960s by the government and the defense industries, in the 1990s by the government and the news media).
2. The revolution proclaimed in the name of the dispossessed (identified in 1965 as the urban and Appalachian poor, in 1995 as "the forgotten American middle class").
3. The demonization of the ordinary functions of government (the Pentagon in 1965, the IRS in 1995).
4. The salvation of private individuals taking precedence over the restoration of public institutions ("personal awareness" in the 1960s, "personal responsibility" in the 1990s).
5. Romantic arcadianism (Carlos Castaneda and *The Whole Earth Catalog* replaced by the L. L. Bean catalogue and the visionary prophecies of George Gilder).
6. The revolution announced by people believing themselves entitled to more than they already possess (the children of oligarchy in 1965, the servants of oligarchy in 1995).
7. The delight in military analogies (the 1960s Weathermen, quoting Chairman Mao: "Political power grows out of the barrel of a gun"; Ralph Reed speaking on behalf of the 1990s Christian Coalition: "If you reveal your location, all it does is allow your opponent to improve his artillery bearings …").
8. The insurgents allied with the auxiliary forces of religion (in the 1960s with William Sloane Coffin and the antiwar protest, in the 1990s with Pat Robertson and the anti-abortion protest).
9. The radio as the voice of revolution (FM music stations in the 1960s, AM talk stations in the 1990s).

The countercultural insurgents of the 1960s were forever demanding "Freedom now," by which they meant the freedom from constraint, the freedom to do as they pleased, the freedom to go wandering through a world in which the prettiest girls belonged to the well-connected, the adventurous, and the strong. What else is the promise of the new Republican risorgimento if not the dream of politics lost and American pastoralism regained, of the freedom to go plundering through a world in which the best-looking real estate belongs to the well-connected, the adventurous, and the strong? In the 1990s sequel, Cobb County, Georgia, displaces the Woodstock nation as the railhead of crusade, and the locus of the earthly paradise moves from a commune in the White Mountains to a gated community in Tucson or Palm Springs, but the paying of income tax is still a crime against conscience and a sin against nature. If the flower children believed they owed nothing to the Republic except an encore of "Blowin' in the Wind," their middle-aged avatars believe they owe nothing to the Republic except a demonstration of their golf swings.

Like the 1960s radical left, the 1990s reactionary right declares its principled opposition to the passage of time (the manifestos written by children who never wanted to grow up revised by parents who never want to grow old), but despite everybody's best efforts and the wonders of modern cosmetics, days pass and things change. After the age of forty, clean shirts and station wagons seem more in line with what America is all about than long hair and motorcycles. The rebellious impulse might remain as strong as it once was, and so might the anarchic turn of phrase, but the terms of what in the 1960s were known as "nonnegotiable demands" now tend to express the certainties of the established order and the doctrines of the bottom line. The partisans of the conservative cause retain their faith in the romance of natural man, but having learned to appreciate the wisdom of Adam Smith, they recant their loyalty to Rousseau and announce a program of liberating capitalism instead of liberating consciousness. In the Republican remake of Jack Kerouac's *On the Road*, the rebellious pilgrims travel west as an embassy of computer salesmen, and instead of looking for Judy Collins in the hotel bar, they order up *Romancing Sarah* from the hotel library of adult films.

But to whom do they then direct their protests, and what names do they put on their placards and cast like stones into the teeth of time? How do they organize the sullen draft of their hastily recruited enemies into coherent legions and simple slogans?

As so often in moments of rhetorical crisis, it was the belligerent Gingrich who answered the questions with the phrase "discredited liberal establishment," which connoted both the absence of virtue and the presence of a monolith not unlike the old Soviet Union. Understood as a conspiracy of dunces, the "discredited liberal establishment" could be held responsible for all the mistakes that had been made with the planning of the American Eden. It was the "discredited liberal establishment" that opened the Pandora's box out of which sprang the three evil spirits that wrecked the economic and spiritual environment.

The Welfare State

To hear the story told on the fairways of the nation's better golf courses, the American welfare state is a foreign country that resembles Rwanda or Chiapas, Mexico. Although administered as a protectorate by the U.S. government and supplied with an ungodly sum of money, the metaphysical terrain is so harsh, and the moral climate so poor, that we can never rescue the place, and we would all be better off if we just withdrew our army of Harvard sociologists and let the local rulers sign a treaty with the Baptist Church. If the line of argument is familiar, it is because it so closely parallels the argument advanced by the radical Sixties left in opposition to the Vietnam War. Why continue to underwrite an expensive and futile expedition doomed to certain failure?

The blurring of the distinctions between crime and race and moral behavior plays to the prejudice of an audience eager to believe the worst that can be said of people whom they would rather not know, and to the extent that the word "poor" can be made to serve as a synonym for "black," the big-city slums become alien nations on the wrong side of the cultural and economic frontiers. Gingrich is especially skillful at conveying his point in the unspoken subtext, and during last year's election campaign he often summarized the nation's troubles in a single sentence made to the measure of the six o'clock news: "It is impossible to maintain civilization with twelve-year-olds having babies, fifteen-year-olds killing each other, seventeen-year-olds dying of AIDS, and eighteen-year-olds receiving diplomas they cannot read."

What he had in mind (and what his audiences knew he had in mind) was the desolation of Harlem or East Los Angeles. Taking a similar approach in his inaugural remarks as Speaker of the House, Gingrich only once used the word "black"—in reference to the Black Caucus. He talked about little children found in Dumpsters, or thrown off the roofs of Chicago housing projects, or buried at the age of eleven with their teddy bears, but he avoided mentioning the race of the deceased. Instead of saying that their suffering might be alleviated by the acts of government (or that maybe the mechanics of finance capitalism had something to do with the buried teddy bears), he remanded the obligation to Christian charity and appealed to his fellow politicians to take heed of the parable of the good Samaritan.

The referral is standard procedure among the apologists for the Republican right. William Bennett, author of the best-selling compendium of uplifting anecdote *The Book of Virtues*, seldom misses an opportunity to suggest that the moral pestilence in the society rises like fog in the urban slums: "During the last three decades a lot has gone wrong in America. Our society is far more violent and vulgar than it used to be. We have experienced enormous increases in violent crime, out-of-wedlock births, abortions, divorces, suicides, child abuse and welfare dependency. The answer to much of what ails us is spiritual and moral regeneration."

Applying the same kind of sophism to the questions of intelligence, Murray and Herrnstein's book *The Bell Curve* argues that the excessive number of crimes committed by black people, as well as their poverty and lack of employment, can be attributed, more or less directly, to their low I.Q. ratings. The pseudoscientific speculation adds a few more brush strokes to the standard portrait of black people as synonyms for catastrophe. The image deletes the greater part of the black presence in the country—the rise of the black middle class over the last thirty years, the successes achieved under the rules of affirmative action, the real ratios between impoverished white and black people (two white to one black), the dramatis personae appearing in television situation comedies, the complexion of the United States Army—but it is an image that serves the plotlines of a bedtime story about the wages of sin.[4] As conditions in the slums deteriorate, which they inevitably must as a consequence of their designation as enemy countries, the slums come to look just the way they are supposed to look in the suburban imagination. The burned-out buildings and the number of dead in the streets support the notion that crimes allied with poverty can be classified as individual moral problems rather than a common political problem. At long last and with a clear conscience, the governing and possessing classes can comfort themselves with the thought that poor people deserve what they get, that their misery is nobody's fault but their own. The bleak prospect confirms the Republican faith in prisons and serves as an excuse for imposing de facto martial law on a citizenry construed as a dangerous rabble. Even the sunniest neoconservative optimisms carry the threat of stern punishment, and the tone of the intolerant scold that appears in the speeches of Gingrich and Bennett (as well as in those of Irving Kristol, Charles Krauthammer, and Michael Novak) has been most succinctly expressed by *Washington Times* columnist Cal Thomas: "If we will not be constrained from within by the power of God, we must be constrained from without by the power of the State, acting as God's agent."

---

4   In the proposal submitted to prospective publishers of *The Bell Curve*, Murray didn't mince words about the bigotry that he meant to confirm and sustain. "[There are] a huge number of well-meaning whites who fear that they are closet racists, and this book tells them they are not. It's going to make them feel better about things they already think but do not know how to say."

The Liberal News Media

Among the partisans of the populist and suburban right, no article of faith is more devoutly held than the one about the feral cynicism of the metropolitan news media. Although nobody at the mall ever can remember seeing a journalist who didn't look like the boy or girl next door, the crowd sitting around the tables in the food court likes to think that the news comes to them from sallow-faced leftists who cut up the wholesome American moral fabric into patches of socialist propaganda and strips of pornographic film.

The supposition bears comparison to Jane Fonda's belief in the innocence of Ho Chi Minh. The manufacture and sale of the nation's news is the work of very large, very rich, and very timid corporations—the Washington Post Co., Fox Broadcasting, and Turner Network Television. The managers of the commercial television networks, like the publishers of large and prosperous newspapers, define news as anything that turns a profit, no matter how indecent the photograph or how inane the speeches, and they seldom take chances with any line of thought that fails to agree with what their audiences wish to see and hear.

The *Wall Street Journal*, probably the most widely read newspaper in the country, heavily favors the conservative side on any and all questions of public policy, and both the *Washington Post* and the *New York Times* fortify their op-ed pages with columnists who strongly defend the established order—William Safire and A. M. Rosenthal in the *Times*, Charles Krauthammer, George Will, and Richard Harwood in the *Post*. The vast bulk of the nation's talk-radio shows (commanding roughly 80 percent of the audience) reflect a conservative bias, and so do all but one or two of the television talk shows that deal with political topics on PBS, CNN, and CNBC.

Among the smaller journals of opinion, the presiding sentiment is even more bluntly conservative, a state of affairs that didn't come to pass by accident. As long ago as 1972, the corporations began to worry about the number of long-haired hippies attending Grateful Dead concerts and George McGovern rallies, and a cadre of rightist philanthropic foundations (among them Olin, Smith Richardson, Lilly, and Scaife) set about the task of cornering the market in ideas. The allegiance to their preferred worldview as well as to their financial patronage shapes the socioeconomic debate presented in the pages of the *National Review*, *Commentary*, *Chronicles of Culture*, the *American Spectator*, *National Interest*, the *New Criterion*, the *Public Interest*, and *Policy Review*. On the nation's lecture circuit the voices of conscience that attract the biggest crowds and command the highest fees (George Will, Gordon Liddy, Safire) all speak for one or another of the parties of the right. Augmenting the instruments of the nominally secular media, the chorus of religious broadcasts and pamphlets (among them Pat Robertson's *700 Club* and the publications under the direction of the Reverend Sun Myung Moon), as well as the direct-mail propaganda mills run by right-wing polemicists on the order of Richard Viguerie, envelops the country in a continuous din of stereophonic conservative sound.

As proof of the absurdity implicit in the complaint about the liberal news media, I can think of no better demonstration than the one offered by Rush Limbaugh to the C-Span cameras in mid-December of last year at the Radisson Hotel in Baltimore. Ripe with self-congratulation and glistening under the lights like a Las Vegas lounge comic, Limbaugh appeared as the principal banquet speaker before an audience of newly elected Republican congress-men attending a three-day conference organized by the Heritage Foundation and meant to acquaint them with their tasks as saviors of the Republic. Eager and young and as freshly scrubbed as a cohort of college fraternity pledges, they laughed on cue at Limbaugh's snig-gering jokes about President Clinton, condoms, and mushy-headed liberals. Limbaugh told them that in Washington they would find themselves surrounded on all sides by enemies, by newspaper col-umnists and anchorpersons as treacherous as Cokie Roberts, who would cajole them with flattery and then betray them for the price of a cheap headline. "You are going to be hated," Limbaugh said. "Remember that you are targets. Remain hostile."

After twelve years of the administrations of presidents Reagan and Bush, and two years of the neo-Republican presidency of

Bill Clinton, the notion of Washington as a city somehow hostile to political conservatives of any kind was as preposterous as Limbaugh's posing as a victim of liberal tyranny and persecution. The spectacle of his overstuffed pretension brought to mind the sight of Norman Mailer on various occasions in the late 1960s in New York and Washington presenting himself as a victim of fascist censorship and repression before a crowd of self-proclaimed freedom fighters wearing stylish ammunition belts from Saks Fifth Avenue. Like Mailer, Limbaugh was a best-selling author who knew how to provide copy to the credulous news media—two toy revolutionaries playing the part of Caliban, adjusting the grimace of their fright masks to reflect the seasonal fear of the prosperous middle class. During the same week that Limbaugh exhorted the faithful in Baltimore to defy the foul fiend of the liberal press, he was appearing as celebrity shill in television advertisements for the *New York Times*.

The Marble Ruin of American Civilization

The last of the dearly beloved tales told around the campfires of the reactionary right is the one about the once-sacred temples of American art and political philosophy turned into pornographic movie theaters by the same crew of guitarists and literary critics that poisoned the pure streams of Republican economic thought. The story has so many variants and inflections that it is hard to fix the precise tone of indignation (sometimes choleric, sometimes wistful or smug), but it invariably entails the assigning of subversive motives to the universities, the Hollywood movie companies, the popular music business, the publishing industry, the Broadway stage, and the aforesaid liberal news media. Although the bad news sometimes takes grandiose forms—Irving Kristol informing the guests at conservative banquets that rock and roll music presents a greater threat to Western civilization than world Communism—for the most part it comes down to a complaint about a cheapened sense of aesthetics and school curricula debased by trendy (i.e., leftist) political alloys. Instead of reading

Chaucer, students read the works of minor African poets; instead of going to see Shakespeare's plays, they gape at the sins of the flesh paraded through the courtyard of *Melrose Place*.

Again, as with so many of the other excited announcements emanating from the press offices of the right, the facts of the matter have been suborned by the preferred image. The mournful defenders of classical learning and Renaissance humanism ignore the point that the United States makes business its culture and its culture a business. Art is what sells, and education is what draws a paying crowd. Americans go to school to improve their lot, to study the arts of getting ahead in the world, to acquire the keys to the commercial kingdom stocked with the material blessings that constitute our society's highest and most heavenly rewards. The objectives conform to the popular as opposed to the privileged understanding of democracy. As Americans, we make the heroic attempt to educate all our citizens, to provide as many people with as many opportunities as possible, to do for our children what we couldn't do for ourselves. Because the schools serve a political idea (as opposed to an intellectual idea), they cannot afford to make invidious comparisons between the smart kids and the dumb kids, between the kids who read Montaigne's essays and those who read Spider-Man comics; contrary to the failing report cards issued by people like Allan Bloom, it isn't necessary to know much about the liberal arts to make a success of an American life. Children learn by example as well as by precept, and they have only to look at Times Square and Disneyland, or consider the triumphs of Michael Jackson or Michael Jordan, to know that society bestows its rewards on the talent for figuring a market, not on a knowledge of Thucydides.

Nor is the popular culture by any means as immoral as it is dreamed of in the philosophy of the academic deans on the neoconservative and Christian right. As measured by its lists of best-selling books and long-running Broadway plays, as well as by its successful television comedies, sporting events, and popular songs, the American cultural enterprise (in 1995 as in 1895) is as irremediably conservative as it is relentlessly sentimental. During any Sunday's playing of the Top 40, the rap songs and heavy-metal rhythms show up at the bottom of the list, but as the countdown proceeds upward toward a kindly and forgiving providence, the music turns increasingly sweet and melodic. The lyrics almost always affirm the wisdom of a Rod McKuen poem or a speech by Peggy Noonan—love will last forever; our love will never die; you are the only one; my love for you is like a thousand points of light. The same moral teaching informs ninety-eight of every hundred situation comedies that last more than three weeks on prime-time television. To watch *Home Improvement* or *The Simpsons* is to know that virtue triumphs, that love conquers all, and that in this best-of-all-possible American worlds, victory is always close at hand and children never starve.

In which of the country's leading newspapers does the editorial page defend adultery as a civil liberty or advance the social program of the Marquis de Sade? A study published last October by the National Opinion Research Center at the University of Chicago showed the American people to be astonishingly monogamous, and the moral attitudes governing the rules of sexual conduct at most of the nation's universities more nearly resemble the ones in effect in Victorian England than those on display in ancient Babylon or late eighteenth-century France. Notwithstanding the proliferation of peep shows made for cable television, we remain a deeply conservative, almost prudish, people, and sex, like art, most fetchingly presents itself as commercial advertisement (to hustle the business or move the product), not as an invitation to a waltz.[5]

When listening to people describe the marble ruin of American civilization (as if it were something seen in a Piranesi drawing or a Louisiana mangrove swamp), I'm always struck by the lack of a historical sense on the part of the tellers of the tale. Lately, I've been gathering research material for a book that touches upon the American condition in the eighteenth and nineteenth centuries, and it's fair to say that the university curricula were always

---

5 The BBC produces two variants of the television drawing-room comedies that venture upon sexual subjects—an unexpurgated version for the British audience and a bowdlerized version for export to the more easily offended American market.

debased and the natives always restless. The incidence of crime in New York City in the 1870s or on the Texas frontier in the 1840s defined itself as a statistical ratio surpassing the percentages now being reported by the FBI. The divorce rates in colonial America exceeded those of the present day, and in 1905 the immigrant swarm on Manhattan's Lower East Side measured its density at 1,000 people per acre, a ratio that dwarfed the crowding in the slums of Bombay. On no less of an authority than that of Jonathan Edwards, God abandoned the American forest in the winter of 1719, and throughout most of the nineteenth century, prior to the advent of the media circus and Clint Eastwood movies, Americans attended public hangings and the freak shows mounted by impresarios on the order of P. T. Barnum.

At the presumably higher elevations of culture, the air was always thick with Christian piety and bourgeois sentiment. Herman Melville was condemned to obscurity, Mark Twain was obliged to present himself as an amiable clown, and Edith Wharton, together with Henry James and Ezra Pound, left for Europe. The joke about the marble ruin is that American civilization never was much of a match for Periclean Greece. When the tellers of the sad Republican tale agree to take questions on the subject (reluctantly and usually in a hurry to leave the lecture hall), it turns out that the lost culture for which they grieve is the culture best expressed by the sensibility of the 1950s, the musical comedies of Rodgers and Hammerstein, the history of the world as told by Disney and Time Life, the list of great books that everybody owns but nobody has read.

Hoisted up by the cranes of populist bombast to the platforms of great expectation, the newly enskied 104th Congress confronts an ancient problem in socioeconomics—how does a wealthy and increasingly nervous plutocracy preserve its privileges while at the same time maintaining its reputation as an oppressed minority and a noble cause? The answer is never easy, but the *soi-disant* anarchists of the 1990s reactionary right come poorly equipped for the task of making good on their promises. Just as the mock insurgents of the 1960s staged their masques and dances against a backdrop of cardboard scenery, the rebels of the 1990s shape their morality play from images they have seen on television and abstractions they have discovered in books written by their friends and former economics professors. Their delight in theory and ignorance of history saps them of the strength to answer their own call to arms.

What they have in hand is a dissenting rhetoric best suited to cries from the wilderness, a feeling for nostalgia, a faith in the claptrap futurism of Alvin and Heidi Toffler, the dubious economic theory inherited from the early days of the Reagan revolution, and an instinct for repression. Although convenient to pop quizzes and the nightly television news, the syllabus of glib answers bears comparison to the secrets of the universe packaged for sale in the supermarket press, and it isn't likely to prepare the class for the midterm examination. The electorate last fall was saying something about its fear and uneasiness, about jobs being sent overseas and the future (their own and that of their children) beginning to look like the receding objects seen through the wrong end of a telescope. For the last ten or fifteen years, the parties of the right have managed to convert the emotions rooted in economic anxiety into the polio tics of cultural anxiety, substituting the questions of moral conduct and deportment (the marble ruin, the heathen poor) for the more intractable ones about the division of the national spoils.

But the act is getting harder to perform, and the audience in the first ten rows has begun to figure out the trick with the coins and the scarves. Let the interest rate continue to rise, and who will applaud the futurist cant ("Parallel Transformations!" "Paradigms!" "Quality Management!") so dear to the heart of Speaker Gingrich? Let the chimera of a balanced budget drift off into the haze of what Washington calls "the out years," and people might begin to notice the difference between the big print and the small print in the Contract With America.

The paragraphs in large print postulate a return to an imaginary time and place in which the work of government could be performed by a volunteer fire department—a few hardy fellows cleaning up the village green after a winter storm, a benign judge adjudicating the occasional land dispute or divorce proceeding, a friendly county official awarding the rights of way for five hundred miles of railroad track in Kansas. The provisions in small print grant the propertied classes the freedom to acquire more property—a freedom expressed, among other ways, in the form of capital gains tax breaks in the amount of $25 billion a year—and for everybody else, more police and more sermons.

Whether dressed up as a radical or reactionary chic, the striking of revolutionary poses doesn't fit very well with necessarily bureaucratic forms of government. Norman Mailer once ran for the office of mayor of New York City, and I expect that he was glad to lose the election. Maybe I underestimate the talents of the 104th Congress, and maybe the new season's band of guerrillas will figure out a way to play at revolution without the slightest risk of damage to their automobiles or their bond portfolios. But I admit that I am curious to see Speaker Gingrich presenting his formulation of "New Hope!" "New Dialogue!" "New Access!" to a crowd of bankrupt farmers, or expounding for the benefit of five hundred unemployed textile-machine operators the theory of limitless wealth revealed to Adam Smith and Pitt the Younger in the workshop of the Napoleonic Wars. And if for some reason the mood in the hall should turn ugly, I can imagine the Speaker losing his temper and reverting to type as Gingrich the belligerent, sacker of shibboleths, and I like to think of him defying the storm of insults, shouting into the microphones, calling down on the heads of his enemies the terrible maxims of Voltaire, reminding them that the comfort of the rich rests upon an abundant supply of the poor.

1996

7. Lights, Camera, Democracy!

The poor have been rebels but they never have been anarchists; they have more interest than anyone else in there being some decent government; the poor man really has a stake in the country. The rich man hasn't; he can go away to New Guinea in a yacht. The poor have sometimes objected to being governed badly; the rich have always objected to being governed at all.

—G. K. Chesterton

As long ago as last June, well before the first rain of balloons fell on either of the summer's nominating conventions, it was hard to find a public-spirited citizen anywhere in New York who wasn't dissatisfied with the prospect of the November presidential election. No matter what the venue of the conversation—an editorial in the *New York Post*, a scholarly conference at New York University, a cocktail reception on Central Park West—the standard complaint relied on one or all of the following points:

1. Both candidates were paltry politicians.
2. Nobody was seriously discussing the serious issues.
3. The amoral news media subvert the hope of reason.
4. The country was being asked to vote for television commercials.

The dismal observations have become by now as much a matter of polite convention as remarks about the weather, and having listened to the requiem at the tomb of American politics for at least twenty years, I know when to regret the passing of Teddy Roosevelt, when to mention other crimes against democracy that the speaker might have overlooked, and when to stare wistfully off into the historical past or glance sadly down at the marinated shrimp. But this year I ran across a more irritable tone in the voices of mourning, and on the Monday before the Fourth of July I was taken unawares by a sudden silence at a dinner party on East Sixty-fourth Street. Apparently I had missed one of the antiphonal responses, and both the woman on my left (a partner at Salomon Brothers) and the man sitting opposite (a network television correspondent) were waiting for my contribution to the sum of the nation's sorrow. I couldn't remember whether they had been finding fault with the Unabomber or Senator Alfonse D'Amato, but on the assumption that what was wanted was something politely apocalyptic, I said that if things kept going the way they were going, then we might as well assign the management of the country's politics to the Disney Company. The woman frowned, and the man impatiently tapped the table with his salad fork. They reminded me that we were talking about the most awesome office in the free world, about the fate of nations and the destiny of mankind, and that the topic was not one that invited levity. Anxious to avoid another mistake, I listened to the rest of the evening's conversation a good deal more closely than usual, wondering why the company was so skittish.

To most of the forty-odd people in the room—among them two or three Wall Street lawyers, several journalists, a Washington lobbyist, a television producer in town from Los Angeles, at least four investment bankers, the owner of a recently formed company supplying racetrack results to the Internet, and the proprietor of a resort island off the coast of North Carolina—the result of the November election was a matter of little consequence. Both candidates were as sound as J. P. Morgan or Ronald Reagan in their belief that money was good for the rich and bad for the poor, and what else was it important to know? Most everybody present was in the business of managing the world's traffic in expensive images—rendered as Hollywood movies and programs of political reform as well as stock-market symbols and Italian silk—and because the traffic was international, they found themselves more at ease with their economic peers in London, or Tokyo, or Berlin, than with their poorer fellow citizens encountered, preferably at a safe distance, in the streets of Miami, or Chicago.

Nor were most of the guests much interested in the mechanics (as opposed to the theatrics) of American politics or much worried about the future prospects of the American Commonwealth. It was a fairly safe guess that few of them could name their congressman or deputy mayor and an even-money bet that several of them had shifted their principal financial assets to Switzerland or Grand Cayman. They could afford to think that the difference between a Republican and Democratic administration was the difference between a marginally higher or lower tax rate and the number of invitations likely to be extended by the organizers of Washington policy conferences. Were Dole to be elected, the banker seated under the Picasso drawing might become a cabinet official; if Clinton remained in office, the television producer might be appointed to a presidential commission meant to study (and be appalled by) the quality of American education; in either event, one or two of the journalists might find themselves transformed into deputy secretaries of state. Otherwise the election would come and go without noticeable effect, the summer's campaign rhetoric as promptly forgotten as Newt Gingrich's Contract with America or the evening's carrot soup.

Why then the attitudes of grave foreboding? Why not simply enjoy the comedy of the nominating conventions and take comfort in the accumulating profits in the stock market? The questions stayed in mind during the somber discussions of Clinton's failures as a statesman and Republican senator Robert Dole's failures as an actor, and by the time the caterers served the lemon sorbet I understood that the criticisms of the year's political entertainment· encompassed two sets of concerns, one of them about the style of the performance, and the other, more troublesome but less clearly expressed, about its lack of meaning. Although few of the people at dinner believed in the practice of democratic self-government, they deemed the belief necessary to the maintenance of public order. Too general a loss of faith in the symbols of democracy might lead to rioting in the streets, and it was therefore incumbent upon the managers of Democracyland to make a good show of flags and speeches and counting votes. But the guests also wished to think of themselves as patriots instead of exiles; worried about their own degrees of separation from what was once a familiar plot, they were reluctant to concede that the American political system grants parallel sovereignty to both a permanent and a provisional government and that it is always a mistake to let them be seen as different entities.

The permanent government is the secular oligarchy (a.k.a. the 20 percent of the population holding 93 percent of the nation's wealth) that runs the corporations and the banks; owns and operates the news and entertainment media; administers the universities; controls the philanthropic foundations, the policy institutes, the casinos, and the sports arenas; hires the country's politicians; and sets the terms and conditions under which the citizens can exercise their rights—God-given but increasingly expensive—to life, liberty, and the pursuit of happiness. Obedient to the rule of men, not laws, the upper servants of the permanent government, among them most of the members of Congress and the majority of the news media's talking heads, enjoy their economic freedoms by way of compensation for the loss of their political liberties, the right to freely purchase in exchange for the right to freely speak.

The provisional government is the spiritual democracy that comes and goes on the trend of a political season and oversees the production of pageants. It exemplifies the nation's moral aspirations, protects the citizenry from unworthy or unholy desires, and devotes itself to the mending of the American soul. The tribunes of the people mount the hustings to give voice to as many of the nation's conflicting ideals as can be recruited under the banners of freedom and fitted into the time allowed, ideals so at odds with one another that the American creed rests on the rock of contradiction—a self-righteously Christian country that supports the world's largest market for pornography and cocaine; a nation of prophets and real estate developers that defines the wilderness as both spiritual retreat and cash advance; the pacifist outcries against the evils of the weapons industry offset by the patriotic demand for an invincible army; a land of rugged individualists quick to seek the safety of decision by committee.

Positing a rule of laws instead of men, the provisional government must live within the cage of high-minded principle, addressing its remarks to the imaginary figure known as the informed citizen or the thinking man, a superior being who detests superficial reasoning and quack remedies, never looks at *Playboy*, remembers the lessons of history, trusts Bill Moyers, worries about political repression in Liberia, and reads (and knows himself improved by) the op-ed page of the *Wall Street Journal*.

The quadrennial presidential election is the most solemn of the festivals staged by the provisional government, and the prolonged series of ceremonies—the ceaseless round of public opinion polls, the muster of earnest newspaper editorials, the candidates riding the parade floats of the Washington talk shows—belong to the same order of events as the songs and dances performed at a Zuni corn harvest. The delegates gather to invest the next president of the United States with the magical prowess of a kachina doll, embodying the country's ancestral truths and meant to be exhibited in hotel ballrooms and baseball parks. Bustling with images salvaged from the costume trunks of American history, the amplified voices of conscience ascend the pulpits of liberty to proclaim their faith in nobody knows exactly what, but something that has to do with a noble spirit, a just society, and America the beautiful. As always, the language is abstract, the speakers being careful to avoid overly specific reference to campaign finance reform or the depletion of the Social Security trust fund (questions best left to the sounder judgment of the permanent government) and directing their passion to the telling of parables—about character, thrift, integrity, family values, individual initiative, points of light. The intention is to make a loud and joyful noise in which the contradictions inherent in the American creed will vanish in a cloud of balloons or march triumphantly out of the convention hall with one of the high school bands.

What troubled the dinner guests on East Sixty-fourth Street was the lack of *gravitas* in this year's staging of the America Is a Democracy Festival. Neither candidate took naturally to wearing the masks of bountiful renewal. The grotesque inadequacies of Clinton and Dole offended people accustomed to seeing Pavarotti in *Tosca* and Michael Jordan in Madison Square Garden. Here they were in the front row of American success, and the stumbling performance of the prayer for rain was an insult to both their intelligence and wealth. The television correspondent mentioned the summer's competing attractions, among them the Olympic Games in Atlanta, and asked indignantly why, if America was still the richest and most powerful country on earth, it couldn't stage a better minstrel show.

Other voices at other tables extended the range of complaint to the lack of principled people in Washington and the loss of civility in the films of Oliver Stone. The unanimous tone of nervous irritation suggested that the guests had begun to worry about what might happen to their own privileged estate if it became too apparent that the agendas of the permanent and provisional governments had as little to do with each other as the bond market and the phases of the moon. Over the last four or five years, entirely too many people (envious and irresponsible people) had been talking about the widening gulf between the fortunes of the rich and the misfortunes of the poor. The fact was certainly plain enough, but what if it should become too widely accepted as proof that the premise of an egalitarian democracy was as extinct as the Dusky Seaside Sparrow?[1]

---

1 The standard set of observations attributes the increasing distances between rich and poor to the policies of the Reagan and Bush Administrations, but the trend has become even more evident under the auspices of the Clinton Administration. Supported in large part by the

The company at dinner had noticed that something was amiss in the engine room of freedom. They could tell by looking at the crowds in the streets, and by the airport and restaurant signs they saw printed in Korean or Spanish, that the United States was tending toward the multiracial and multilingual society described by literary academics as anti-democratic and portrayed on advertising posters as the United Colors of Benetton. The newly enfiefed minorities might respect the same rules of commercial enterprise, but who was to say that they would agree to belong to the same political enterprise? Anybody could open a grocery store or operate a fleet of taxicabs, but it was something else entirely to know the words of the Marine Hymn and the "Ballad of Buffalo Bill." The division of the country into separate provinces of feeling (some of them as large as Louis Farrakhan's Nation of Islam, others as militant as the Freemen lately confined to quarters in Jordan, Montana) made it increasingly difficult to bind together what was once the American polity with a common narrative. It was getting harder and harder to pump up the parade balloons with the willing suspensions of disbelief, which was why the news media were sending 15,000 correspondents of various magnitudes to the summer nominating conventions, why the networks already had granted free time to both candidates in October, why the campaigning season never ends. If the American Commonwealth was nowhere to be found among the strip malls between Boston and San Diego (a wilderness in which the squares of safe suburban lawns begin to seem as isolated from one another as the fortified stockades on the old Indian frontier), maybe it could be simulated on television—not only with the convention broadcasts and the pious commentary of David Brinkley but also in the exemplary displays of egalitarian good fellowship presented by *Seinfeld* and *Murphy Brown*.

---

steady rise in the stock market (up 61 percent in the last three years), the share of the nation's income going to the wealthiest 5 percent of the population increased from 18.6 percent in 1992 to 20 percent in 1993 to 21.1 percent in 1994. Within the last eighteen months, roughly one million men between the ages of twenty-five and fifty-five (i.e., in their prime working years) disappeared from the labor force.

Reminded of the media's ceaseless advertisement for a democratic reality, I understood that the evening's lament was also part of the necessary ritual. The guests might as well have been shaking cornstalks and beating feathered drums. As statements of fact, none of the points of complaint about the November election made any sense. Few of the people present had any use for politicians who weren't paltry, for the perfectly good reason that nonpaltry politicians disturbed the status quo. Nor did they wish to engage in serious discussion of any issues that might seriously inhibit the sovereignty of money. The country was being asked to vote for television commercials because only in the happy, far-off land of television commercials could the American democracy still be seen to exist. But understood as ritual chant, the remarks at dinner sustained the nostalgic remembrance of time past. The company might object, in Chesterton's phrase, "to being governed at all," but nobody was eager to sail away, at least not yet, to New Guinea or Barbados on a yacht, and if the political small talk was more obsessive than in years past, louder in volume and grimmer in tone, possibly it was because the citizens on East Sixty-fourth Street—as superstitious as the new media they habitually reviled and as stateless as the oligarchy of which they were a part—were making the noises of democracy to ward off the fell spirit of a future to which they couldn't give an American name.

2001

8. The Dimpled Chad

When I die—if I die—I want to be buried in Louisiana so I can stay active in politics.

—Earl K. Long

Until the 2000 presidential election ran afoul of events in Florida in the early morning of November 8, the interested parties had managed to keep the politics out of the politics—behind the rope lines, off the podium, out of the camera shots and the conversation. For nearly twelve months the Republican and Democratic campaigns had assumed that in place of politics—a word they associated with "partisan ugliness" and "angry name-calling"— they could substitute handsomely framed photo opportunities and winsomely edited television commercials. Why not? Who would care?

The country apparently was at ease with itself, enjoying its prosperity and content with its toys; no wars loomed on a distant horizon, and the presumed apathy of a supposedly ignorant electorate suggested a general preference for a government so securely checked and balanced that it could do nothing that might upset the golden applecart of the Dow Jones Industrial Average.

What was wanted was a president conveniently impotent, and the requirement favored the qualities of Texas governor George W. Bush and Vice President Al Gore—two ornamental sons of the American plutocracy bearing well-known national brand names and with as little difference between them as Pepsi and Coke, both capable of cameo appearances on *Oprah* and well enough schooled in the art of foraging for money to know where to stand and when to crawl.

If neither candidate commanded a broad or popular following among the American people, what difference did it make? The trend of the times over the last twenty years has reduced the figure of the president of the United States from a leading to a support-ing role, and either the governor or the vice president would pass muster as the corporate spokesman for America the Beautiful. Maybe they weren't as good at making the pitch as either Ronald Reagan or Bill Clinton, but at least they could memorize a script, hit their marks, know their place; and because each of them so often found it necessary to say that he was his own man, even the dullest voter would be encouraged to understand that he wasn't. Surely the country was safe enough and rich enough to afford the luxury of two gentlemen from Verona or the Ivy League so amiably lacking in conviction that their words could be relied upon to mean as little as possible.

Any other year and the modest sets of accomplishment might have proved sufficient. Neither candidate fell off a bandstand or a parade float; the vice president discovered the secret of studio makeup, the governor learned how to pronounce the name Slobodan Milošević, and over the course of the summer cam-paigns they obligingly displayed their talents as character actors in the various personae of visiting clergyman, bedside compan-ion, and late-night talk-show clown. Drawn by the gravitational force of the opinion polls to the still center of amiable consensus (i.e., the great good American place where nothing changes and everybody gets rich), both candidates cheerfully avoided most of the topics apt to excite controversy, and with regard to the standard operating procedures of the oil, banking, and telecommunications monopolies they were as silent as the ball washers at a country-club golf tournament. Resolute in their opposition to breast cancer, forthright in their commitment to dignity and leadership, uncompromising in their support of better days, bluer skies, and secure retirement, they were always glad to pose for Kodak moments on an aircraft carrier or a kindergarten chair. Most important, they put to rest any lingering suspicions that they might be interested in politics as an experiment with anything dangerous or new.

Not a brilliant campaign, but adequate to its purpose, and one that under ordinary circumstances would have resolved itself into the customary victory celebration (many balloons, joyful applause) and the corollary concession speech (scattered tears, noble melancholy). By the time the polls opened on Election Day the prospect of a vote "too close to call" presented the news media with a better show than anybody had thought possible after the summer nominating conventions. The television anchorpersons inflated the sporting analogies as soon as the polls closed on the East Coast—Tom Brokaw promising his viewers a wild and thrilling rollercoaster ride through the theme park of American history; Dan Rather announcing a contest "hot enough to peel house paint."

During the first few hours of the nationwide count of the election returns, the mood in the broadcast booths remained upbeat and sunny. For two weeks the studio people had been promoting the drama of narrow margins on the assumption that they were hyping an otherwise mediocre story about two second-tier celebrities, and they didn't draw too careful a distinction between democracy as a system of government and democracy as a form of entertainment. ("Here we all are in Democracyland, folks! Stay tuned! Don't go away! We'll be right back with Cokie and Jeff and Rutherford B. Hayes!") Accustomed to believing themselves the creators of the character of the American president (whether the role happens to be played by Michael Douglas on HBO, Richard Nixon on the History Channel, Bill Clinton on C-Span, or Harrison Ford on Cinemax), the news and entertainment media had seen the summer campaigns as an audition for a four-year gig in the Oval Office. The White House set by now has become as familiar as Jerry Seinfeld's apartment or the booth on *Monday Night Football*, and the political analysts know where to look for the Marine helicopter and the portrait of George Washington. When obliged to drum up interest in national affairs, they ask questions not much different from those of the film critics. How will next season's situation comedy differ from the undignified burlesque of the Bill Clinton show? Is it an action movie or sentimental melodrama along the lines of NBC's *The West Wing*? How many women in the cast, and is the national security adviser insane?

Which was more or less the tone of the complacent commentary on MSNBC and at CNN headquarters in Atlanta until something began to go wrong with the news from Florida. Nobody knew who was making what kind of mistakes—some difficulties, apparently, with missing ballots, faulty voting machines, confused pensioners—but by 3:00 A.M. it had begun to look as if the election wasn't going to follow the studio scripts, and after having twice awarded the prize of Florida's electoral votes and the presidency to the wrong candidate, the anchorpersons in the broadcast booths were showing a marked resemblance to aquarium fish. Their mouths were opening and closing; they were floating around in their state-of-the-art habitat, the red-and-blue maps as colorful as tiny coral reefs, but when they peered into the glass wall of the camera, it was as if they were wondering what had happened to the Caribbean Sea.

Astonishingly, and for the first time in twelve months, the election news was about something other than Al Gore's hairstyle or George Bush's English springer spaniel. Few of the people in the broadcast studios were old enough to remember ever having seen such a thing as democracy—the living organism as opposed to the old paintings and the marble statues—and judging by the startled expressions in their faces, they didn't like the look of it. It hadn't been circumcised, and probably it was criminal.

By noon on Wednesday the politics were back in the politics, pushing through the rope lines and crowding into the camera shots. The election still being in doubt, the interested parties were off message and out of costume, and for the next several days the country was granted what John Adams knew to be the most precious right of a free people—"an indisputable, unalienable, indefeasible, divine right to that most dreaded and envied kind of knowledge, I mean of the characters and conduct of their rulers."

Although compressed into a brief time period, the impromptu course in civics was comprehensive, and if I don't have the space to mention all the points in the syllabus, two of them seemed especially instructive.

The Candidates

Revealed as popped balloons and empty boasts. Without a script neither the vice president nor the governor knew what to say, and as the days passed their wax images melted in the sun. The fine phrases (about "leadership," "restoring honor and dignity to the White House," "fighting for working families," "compassionate conservatism," etc., etc.) went missing in action. The two gentlemen from Verona elected to hide. Governor Bush retreated to his Texas ranch to pose for photographs in what he hoped was a presidential sort of way, among the props of a jury-rigged White House Map Room. During the campaign he had acknowledged his dependence on the advice of his father's senior bagmen (he knew their telephone numbers and promised to get in touch if something important came up), and when confronted with the possible loss of the election in Florida, he sent James A. Baker III, his father's former secretary of state, to fix the judge.

The vice president retired into a cloud of piety. Not having Colin Powell for a prop, he appeared briefly for the cameras with a football that maybe once had been tossed around a Virginia lawn by Jack or Bobby Kennedy. Like the governor, the vice president sought to convey an air of Olympian calm, as indifferent as Zeus to the struggles of merely mortal men and so devoted to democracy's holy cause that he didn't wish to win the presidency "by a few votes cast in error." He went on to say that he was sure Governor Bush, that great and loyal American, would take the same view of the matter, and the gorgeous sweetness of his hypocrisy was a wonder to behold.

The Electorate

By no means as apathetic as it is customarily supposed by the Washington gentry and their attendant pundits, who conceive of democratic self-government as an heirloom or a trust fund, a theatrical trunk in which to find the costumes of an imaginary and risk-free past rather than as a blueprint and a source of energy with which to build a new and therefore dangerous future.

Once the politics were in plain sight, out from behind the screen of the soft-focus television commercials and the Hallmark greeting-card chatter of the Sunday talk-show crowd, a very large number of people expressed a keen and well-informed interest in the proceedings. They knew what they were looking at, and they knew also that "partisan ugliness" is the bone and marrow of democracy.

All at once and without cue cards, the liveliness of the political debate was a match for the barroom discussions of a World Series or a Super Bowl. High school students who a week earlier would have been hard-pressed to name three American presidents, living or dead, suddenly were talking, and talking knowledgeably, about the Electoral College, the Fourteenth Amendment, and the prior-arrest records of select Florida politicians. Every news organization, daily paper as well as the radio and cable-television networks, reported audiences four and six times as large as those that had attended the O. J. Simpson trial or the funeral of Princess Di. Although various important persons, most of them government officials, stepped up to a microphone to suggest that one of the candidates graciously resign (for the sake of a democracy so fragile that it might get broken if somebody tried to take it out of the museum), the guests on the Leno and Letterman shows (more representative of the broader spectrum of American opinion) were asking one another why the Bush and Gore campaigns had forgotten to register the graveyard vote.

All present on both sides of the argument filed amicus curiae briefs in favor of high-minded sentiment (for the good of the country, on behalf of the Constitution), but in the context of a real argument taking place in real time with a real consequence in the offing, it wasn't hard to notice that the most selfless principle was usually the one that served the most selfish motive. Thus Republican congressman Connie Mack, affronted by the spectacle of Democrats actually trying to win the election—"They're politicizing the political process." Or Governor Bush's man Baker, pompous and indignant, complaining about "mischief" and "human error" as if politics ever had consisted of anything else.

Ordinary citizens took the points more quickly than the legal and academic authorities delivering sermons from the pulpit of an op-ed page, and the more interesting commentary tended to show up on a newspaper letters page rather than on the network news broadcasts. Here were the American people, for the most part good-natured and patient, working their way around the lies to the harder and better questions that had been ignored or suppressed by the managers of the brightly packaged presidential campaigns. Who gets to say when the voting stops? To whom do we assign political sovereignty—to the polls or the courts? If the latter jurisdiction, then to a federal or a state court? Maybe it isn't such a good idea to form a government so securely checked and balanced that it becomes both harmless and inert? Maybe the country is neither rich enough nor safe enough to afford the weakness of two playpen politicians who don't know how to either win or steal an election?

Judging by what I could see or infer from the all-but-continuous television transmissions from Florida, the local political people (state senators, trial judges, members of county canvassing boards) were more seriously committed to the idea of democracy than were the Washington grandees extending the courtesy of a dissembling press conference. Unexpectedly, and against the grain of my own sarcasm, I was as moved as I was impressed by the sight of the precinct workers holding paper ballots up to the light, looking to see whether the chad was dimpled or bulged, hanging by two threads or three. The tactical circumstance obligated the Republican strategists to scorn them for their "shenanigans" and to mock them for their innocence. Mere human beings, said Mr. Baker and Mr. Bush, imperfect and subjective, incapable of meeting the uniform standards of a machine. The assertion served its expedient purpose, but the condescension missed the point. Democracy isn't made by a machine; it is made with the wit and courage of citizens willing to undertake, for low pay and no credit, a tedious and time-consuming search for a straight answer in a little square of perforated light.

As of this present writing the election remains in doubt, and it's not inconceivable that the next president of the United States will be named by the Supreme Court or the House of Representatives. But if nobody can guess what happens next, we know from the lesson chalked up on the tote boards in Florida that we live in an energetic democracy that at least gives us a sporting chance at an inventive future—whether we rig it with persuasive speeches, artful lawsuits, or a dimpled chad.

2001

9. Civics Lesson

[A free people has] an unalienable, indefeasible, divine right to that most dreaded and envied kind of knowledge, I mean of the characters and conduct of their rulers.

—John Adams

During the month when the presidential election was still a work in progress, the television footage from Washington and Tallahassee provided hourly updates of Adams's "most dreaded and envied kind of knowledge," and for nearly forty days and forty nights we had a chance to see what we mean by the phrases "the rule of law" and "democratic self-government." Opinions differed as to whether the course of instruction was worth the harm done to our notion of free and fair elections, and for many years to come I expect to be reading books explaining how and why it came to pass that the Supreme Court appointed George W. Bush to the office of president.

Authors in liberal jurisdictions undoubtedly will cite passages from the Florida civics lesson as the premise for treatises on the fall of the American empire or the ruin of the American republic. Apostles of the conservative revelation conceivably will cite the same testimony as preface to five-volume histories of America's moral reawakening. My own view is more haphazard and less apocalyptic—a sequence of preliminary observations rather than the components of a theory or a conclusion.

When the Florida ballot on November 8 failed to find in favor of either candidate, the news media swarmed to the occasion with so many cameras and talking heads that the shape of the Story was as quickly lost as that of a dead buffalo under a veil of shrieking crows. At every hour of the day and night the all but ceaseless commentary tended to obscure rather than illuminate the text, and I knew that I was likely to forget what I was being told unless I kept a fairly extensive set of notes. I didn't follow all the lines of all the legal maneuvers. Every motion filed by both parties to the dispute proceeded from the assumption that if all the votes cast in Florida somehow could be accurately counted, Vice President Al Gore probably would win the election, and I was content to stipulate what was attested to by the lack of argument on the point. Why else did the Republicans seek to stop, impede, indefinitely postpone, any revisiting of the ballots? They never tired of accusing the Democrats of trying to steal the election ("chad molesters!" "Commanders in Thief!"), but it was their own behavior that was more obviously suspect, hurrying to get the votes across the border and out of state before somebody searched their luggage.

Mostly I was interested in traits of character, and on reviewing my own brief I notice that I weighted the emphasis toward the furious confusion in the minds of the Republicans-who-would-be-king. I could understand their wanting to carry Mr. Bush in triumph to the White House (as if he were the family silver or a baseball signed by Babe Ruth), and I could appreciate their sense of urgency and haste. But why were they always enraged? They controlled almost all of the political machinery in Florida (the legislature, the governor's office, the state government, the Cuban diaspora), and yet they imagined themselves unfairly persecuted by a jealous god and wicked trolls. What was it to which they believed themselves entitled, and how did they arrive at the certain knowledge of their own virtue?

I never came up with clear answers to the questions, but now that the country has been placed in the care of Mr. Bush's tutors, I expect that I'll be returning to them at frequent intervals over the next four years, and if I'm at a loss to understand a point of national policy—why we're at war with China, or what happened to the forests in Oregon—I can recall the sight of James A. Baker III on the evening of November 21, angrily informing a press conference in Tallahassee that the Florida Supreme Court had committed what he construed to be the crime of lese majesty. The court had handed down a decision of which Mr. Baker disapproved—to permit the recounting, by hand, of undervoted ballots in three Florida counties—and therefore, in Mr. Baker's view, the decision was null and void. A ruling by "judicial fiat," he said; insolent and not to be endured. The expression in his face—pinched, vengeful, and mean—I could assign to a choleric temperament or a display of tactical emotion on the part of a clever bully. What surprised me was the strength of his conviction. The man apparently believed what he was saying, a rich lawyer inveighing against the rule of law, inciting the Florida legislature to overturn (by a fiat more to Mr. Baker's liking) the judgment of the court. Watching him read his statement, I understood that he conceived of the law as a nuisance, an idiot tangle of "legalistic language," superfluous and tiresome, that mostly served as a recourse for people too poor or too weak to buy what they wished or do as they pleased.

What frightened Mr. Baker was the prospect of the country's democratic institutions falling into the hands of the wrong people —that is, anybody unpersuaded by the holy writ of orthodox Republicanism—and so he perceived the uses of political power as primarily defensive. The laws were forms of crowd control, meant to inhibit, punish, and restrict. Like Dick Cheney (saying dismissively to an impertinent newspaper reporter, "You've had your question"), or Katherine Harris, the Florida secretary of state (refusing to accept the revised tally from Palm Beach County because the paperwork was ninety minutes late), or the Supreme Court justices (silencing the presumptuous continuation of the

Florida election by a 5–4 vote), the custodians of the Republican conscience interpreted the power of government not as creative agency or constructive force but as the power to suppress and deny—the power of the customs official, the traffic judge, the police sergeant.

The great truth proclaimed through clenched teeth by Mr. Baker in Tallahassee guided the Republican operatives in Florida to a strategy summed up in the phrase "Unless we win, it's illegal." Quick to impugn the character and motives of their opponents, they seldom missed the chance for malicious slander. A court that ruled in favor of Governor Bush was a court deserving of compliance and respect; a court that ruled otherwise was a treasonous court, renegade and corrupt. As with the courts, so also with judges, town clerks, members of county canvassing boards. Citizens allied with Governor Bush or the prima facie righteousness of the Republican cause deserved the name of "patriot." Democrats were "partisan hacks," by definition crooked and self-serving, slum-dwelling perps accustomed to stealing elections and cars.

I don't think I'm misreading the record. The feverish rhetoric shows up in my notes both as paraphrase and direct quotation, incessantly repeated throughout the month of November by Republican politicians in Washington and Florida. If it wasn't Mr. Baker broadly hinting at likely instances of theft and fraud, then it was Congressman Tom DeLay or Senator Trent Lott threatening "unelected judges" with charges of conspiracy. Even Governor Bush, frowning darkly in far-off Texas, was prompted to say that he didn't think it was right (no sir, not right at all) for an election to be "usurped."

The voices of Republican alarm in the print and television media upgraded the rhetoric to the pitch of near hysteria. *The Wall Street Journal*'s lead editorial accused the Democrats of attempting a "coup d'état." Excited columnists elsewhere on the page likened Al Gore to Adolf Hitler and Al Capone; every Democratic legal argument was "preposterous" or "illegitimate," every filing of a motion on Mr. Gore's behalf "an unfolding miscarriage of justice." When Jesse Jackson addressed a crowd in Palm Beach

County, the paper discerned the threat of an organized putsch by rabble-rousing thugs. When a mob of Republican Party functionaries (several of them hired by Congressman DeLay) staged a riot in Miami-Dade County, the paper saw a quorum of true and loyal Americans standing up for free speech and the rights of man.

National Review on December 4 published the confession of Jay Nordlinger, one of its New York editors, who had taken a temporary leave of absence to write speeches for the Bush campaign and who had suffered dreadful torment on election night in Austin. Nordlinger told the story of how he had gone to bed "full of fear" and grim foreboding, certain that he would awaken to the news of Mr. Gore's accession to the White House. He knew that something bad was bound to happen because Democrats were born cheats and instinctive liars and therefore "better at politics than we are ... better at fraud," unscrupulous people "ten feet tall," just like the Russians during the Cold War.

Equally distraught writers marked up other pages in the magazine with the entire catechism of Republican fear and loathing. A columnist by the name of Mark Steyn found the goodness of the American heart in the inland states colored red on November's electoral map; the color blue indicated the "debauched dystopias" on the nation's coastlines "that the rest of us can visit for wild weekends every now and again before returning to our homes in solid, enduring, conservative ... America." Puzzled and disturbed by the unexpectedly large number of voters who had preferred the Democratic candidate, Steyn asked himself the question, "Who *are* these people?" and fortunately discovered, much to his relief, that most of them were misfits, criminals, and foreigners—"aliens Al Gore strong-armed the Immigration and Naturalization Service into hustling through the naturalization process without background checks," also the friends of Al Sharpton and Alec Baldwin, senile pensioners rounded up from nursing homes, "gay scoutmasters," and "partial-birth-abortion fetishists," "the Palm Beach chapter of Jews for Buchanan."

The poisonous language dribbling out of the mouths of people who as recently as last summer had been talking about restoring "civility" to the American political discussion somehow seemed to me less surprising than the paranoid romance from which the plaintiffs apparently derived the casus belli for their imbecile remonstrance. They tell themselves a fairy tale, engaged in deadly combat with they know not what:

> The Vice President of the United States receives a plurality of the popular vote, and the Republican fantasts portray him as a jack-booted tyrant seizing a Latin American army or a Bulgarian radio station.
>
> The Clinton Administration for eight years bestows on the country's corporate clients the blessings of the China Trade Bill, repeal of the Glass-Steagall Act, low-cost labor, high stock-market prices, lenient interpretation of the anti-trust laws, [and] reduced welfare payments to the poor, and in the minds of Rupert Murdoch's editorial writers the Clinton Administration is a sinister cabal sacking the temple of Mammon.
>
> The nation enjoys the comforts of a timid and predominantly conservative news media (the four television networks and most of the cable channels, Time Warner, *USA Today*, nine often radio talk stations, etc., etc.), and on the foreheads of Kewpie-doll anchorpersons earning upward of $2 million a year the fierce polemicists at The Heritage Foundation stamp the labels "Leftwing!" "Liberal!" "Anarchist!"

Maybe I was laboring under an unexamined bias, but I didn't find the same sort of stupidity on the Democratic side of the dispute. Not that the Democrats didn't reserve their constitutional right to unctuous statement, rank hypocrisy, and bitter diatribe. Whenever possible they presented their own interest as a synonym for "the will of the people," and certainly they were as swift as the Republicans to reverse their prior positions with respect to states' rights and the authority of the courts, but they seemed to know the difference between what was said and what was meant. More at ease in the company of their own cynicism, they didn't mistake their opponents for the friends of Darth Vadar or senior consultants to the Antichrist. Yes, politics was about the grasp for power, sometimes by any means available and often not a pretty sight, but where else did one find the weapons contract or the milk subsidy if not in the legislative game of three-card monte?

The Republican visionaries frown on ambiguity—as subjective and imperfect as a dimpled chad—and, like the long-lost legions of the 1960s counterculture, they imagine themselves bearers of a higher truth at odds with a world they never made. They belong to the party of transcendence, captivated by the beauty of ideological abstraction and contemptuous of low-born historical fact, always being confronted by monsters and apparitions instead of by the ordinary interests and desires of other human beings. The political zealots of the 1960s tended to appear on the ideological left, allied with the promise of a utopian future. The Republican Risorgimento of the 1980s relocated the good news in the memory of an arcadian American past where John Wayne and Ronald Reagan rode together at the head of the wagon trains moving west into the California sunset. The scouts and trail bosses who served as Reagan's economic, spiritual, and foreign-policy advisers (many of them now attached to President Bush the Younger) haven't brooked the insult of a new idea in twenty years, which possibly is why I could never match the frenzied Republican commentary with the discussion of the election among people who weren't speaking to a camera.

Remarking on the turn of events in Florida over the span of five weeks with a fairly large number of people in New York and Washington (on the telephone, at dinner parties and subway stops, waiting in line at an airport or a movie theater), I seldom came across the rancorous tones of voice that showed up in the news media. Unless bound to party doctrine or the hope of appointment in a Bush or a Gore Administration, the respondents stood willing to grant either candidate unclouded title to the White House. For the most part they saw the dispute as a political quarrel rather than as a constitutional crisis, and they didn't much care which of the two sides won the game of capture the flag. Their good humor I sometimes could attribute to their fair-mindedness and forbearance, at other times to a lack of interest in what's become of a national politics given over to politicians who fancy themselves as born-again aristocrats and biblical prophets. When listening to

Trent Lott or reading the *Wall Street Journal*, I was reminded of Kenneth Starr looking for a scarlet letter somewhere on the person of Monica Lewinsky and the road-show Savonarolas in Congress crying down the wrath of Heaven on President Clinton's penis.

But then I remembered what I'd seen on the morning of December 9 at the public library in Tallahassee—judges and county officials doing their best to come up with an honest count and a fair judgment of the ballots ignored by a machine. They were keeping faith with the idea of the country's democratic institutions in the hands of a democratic people, and although mocked by Mr. Baker and ordered by the Supreme Court to cease and desist, they sifted through the boxes of computer cards as deliberately as if they were examining a mortgage contract, and I was proud of what I took to be their impartiality and seriousness of intent.

If my bias had been dormant on the morning of November 8, by December 12, when the Supreme Court ushered Mr. Bush into the White House, I could recognize it not as a preference for Al Gore and the Democrats but as opposition to the parties of transcendence and a fear of fools armed with the bright swords of shining ideology.

2001

10. Bolt from the Blue

As our case is new, so we must think anew, and act anew. We must disenthrall ourselves, and then we shall save our country.

—Abraham Lincoln

The offices of *Harper's Magazine* occupy the eleventh floor of a nineteenth-century commercial building in lower Manhattan, east of Greenwich Village and just over a mile north of the wreckage that was once the World Trade Center. On the morning of September 11, I had come to work earlier than usual, at eight instead of ten, to write my November column on a screening of HBO's *Band of Brothers* that I'd seen the previous Thursday evening at the Council on Foreign Relations. Produced by Steven Spielberg and Tom Hanks as a ten-part television series, the film was being billed as the season's newest and most exciting portrait of America the Invincible. Against the grain of the reviews ("shatteringly emotional," "awe-inspiring," "never to be forgotten"), I'd seen the film not as drama but as agitprop, and I was trying to discover my reasons for the opinion when I was surprised by the sound of what I guessed to be an explosion. A distant but heavy sound, not one that I could place or remember having heard before; not a car bomb, probably not a subway tunnel. Maybe a factory in Brooklyn.

No further developments making themselves immediately audible, I returned to my recollection of the scene at the Council's handsome town house on Park Avenue and Sixty-eighth Street and to the presence of the historian Stephen Ambrose seated center stage during the discussion period, his tie sporting the pattern of the American flag, retelling the heroic tale of the D-Day landings on the beaches of Normandy in June 1944. My notes indicated that a young woman in the after-dinner audience, an Army captain on the faculty at West Point, had asked Ambrose to speak to the secret of leadership, but before I could find the scrap of paper on which I had written down the answer (something about ancient Greeks on the plains of Troy), it occurred to me that I was listening to sirens—ambulances and fire trucks, many of them close by, none of them on the way to Brooklyn. I also noticed that although it was nearly ten o'clock, nobody else was in the office. The only television set on the premises wasn't receiving signals from the major networks, and not until I'd learned to look through the haze of static on one of the cable channels did I discover the pictures of the World Trade Center's twin towers, both of them burning.

Soon afterward other editors began to arrive in the office, their faces empty of expression, their voices dull and thin. They spoke of having seen the second explosion from a subway train on the Manhattan Bridge, of the black shroud of smoke sprawling across the bright blue September sky, of a strange scent in the air, of bewildered crowds walking aimlessly north on Broadway. Somebody managed to bring the television broadcasts into clearer focus, and over the course of the next half hour, unable to look or turn away, saying nothing that wasn't trite ("surreal," "like a movie"), we watched the towers crumble and fall. For the rest of Tuesday we followed the news bulletins and tried to make sense of the story line. The networks played and replayed the montage of horrific images, soon familiar but always seen as if for the first time, never losing the force of a sudden and sickening blow, and I don't expect that I'll ever be rid of the sight of the United Airlines Flight 175 out of Boston coming straight at the south tower, or that of men and women, seemingly no bigger than dolls, dropping away from the windows of the north tower's upper floors, or the whirlwind of gray smoke, coiled and malevolent, devouring the light in Vesey Street.

Through the whole of Tuesday afternoon and evening the nation's leaders came before the television cameras burdened with rage and grief but at a loss to say much else except that what had happened was "unbelievable" and that the world never again would be the same. By nightfall President George W. Bush had returned from Florida to Washington, his arrival delayed by nervous hesitations at Air Force bases in Louisiana and Nebraska, and at 8:30 P.M., twelve hours after the first explosion, he addressed the American people with a not very convincing show of resolve:

"These acts of mass murder," he said, "were intended to frighten our nation into chaos and retreat. But they have failed. Our country is strong."

The message was somewhat at odds with the facts. The losses had been immense, far more terrible than anybody could have foreseen and well beyond anybody's capacity to measure or count. The country might be strong but it was badly frightened, and the chaos was unmistakable—roughly 3,000 dead in Manhattan, another 200 dead in the shambles at the Pentagon, all airline travel suspended, White House secretaries running for their lives, a frantic sealing off of the country's nuclear power stations as well as Mount Rushmore, Disneyland, and the Liberty Bell, the New York Stock Exchange out of commission and the city's primary mayoral election postponed, telephone communications down across large sectors of the Northeast, Major League Baseball games canceled, the Capitol evacuated and most government offices in Washington closed until further notice, the military services placed on high alert.

If the president's rhetoric didn't quite meet the circumstances, neither did it account for the energy transfers—negative as well as positive—made possible by the several technological revolutions of the last thirty years, and as I listened to him speak I couldn't escape the feeling that he was reading a script not unlike the one that carried Spielberg's "band of brothers" to victory in Germany in the spring of 1945.

Wednesday's newspapers confirmed the impression. I didn't read all the reports or listen to all the television commentaries, but most of the ones that I did see and hear presented the catastrophe in the context of World War II—mobilizing the infantry and maneuvering the aircraft carriers, drawing the comparison to Pearl Harbor and declaring another day of infamy, calling out the dogs of war:

Robert Kagan, in the *Washington Post*: "Congress, in fact, should immediately declare war. It does not have to name a country."

Steve Dunleavy in the *New York Post*: "The response to this unimaginable 21st century Pearl Harbor should be as simple as it is swift—kill the bastards ... Train assassins ... Hire mercenaries ... As for cities or countries that host these worms, bomb them into basketball courts."

Richard Brookhiser in the *New York Observer*: "The response to such a stroke cannot be legal or diplomatic—the international equivalent of mediation, or Judge Judy. This is what we have a military for. Let's not build any more atomic bombs until we use the ones we have."

As the week passed and the full extent of the damage became increasingly apparent, the widening salients of fear (of a third or fourth attack, possibly with a nuclear or biological weapon) amplified the tone of defiance. Thousands of American flags appeared in the streets, also in store windows and flying from the fenders of cars; the television networks hardened the tag lines promoting their news programs ("America Under Attack" changed to "America's New War" and "America Rising"), and the anchorpeople abandoned the poses of objective impartiality that might be construed as unpatriotic. The Army called up the reserves; Air Force fighter planes patrolled the skies over New York and Washington; a choir of congressional voices gathered on the steps of the Capitol to bear witness to our sorrow and sing "God Bless America."

President Bush declared the country at war against terrorism, not only against the individuals responsible for Tuesday's attacks but also against any country that provided them with encouragement and a headquarters tent. Between Wednesday and Saturday he made brief but firm appearances on various home fronts (with Billy Graham at the National Cathedral in Washington, among firemen and rescue workers in lower Manhattan, with his senior advisers at Camp David), and gradually he escalated the rhetorical terms of engagement—from "The First War of the Twenty-first Century" to "A New War" to the "Monumental Struggle of Good Versus Evil."[1]

Every now and then I came across somebody on television or in the newspapers saying that bold military action was not likely to put a stop to terrorism—that it was, in fact, bound to make matters worse—but the voices arguing for restraint were for the most part shouted down by the partisans of the old World War II script. Speaking for what by Sunday had become the majority opinion, Kagan on Wednesday in the *Washington Post* had urged the country to respond to "an attack far more awful than Pearl Harbor" with "the same moral clarity and courage" brought into the field by the "Greatest Generation." The fatuousness of his sentiment—"There's no need for nostalgia now ... The question is whether this generation of Americans is made of the same stuff"—clarified the reasons for my objection to *Band of Brothers* and for my disgust with the attitudes of smug self-congratulation that the screening of the film had evoked from the audience at the Council on Foreign Relations.

Everybody had been so pleased with themselves, nearly 200 guests notable for their wealth and corporate rank (presidents of

---

1 On Friday, September 14, Congress granted the president the right to "use all necessary and appropriate force against those nations, organizations, or persons he determines planned, authorized, committed, or aided the terrorist attacks." Passed unanimously by the Senate, the resolution was opposed in the House of Representatives by one dissenting vote, from Barbara J. Lee (D., California), who said that military action could not guarantee the safety of the country and that "as we act, let us not become the evil we deplore."

banks and insurance companies, managers of media syndicates, high-ranking military officers, partners of Wall Street law firms, senior journalists) come to reaffirm their belief in the doctrine of American exceptionalism, and the whole of the evening's program had buttressed the mood of smiling self-congratulation. First a sequence of scenes from the movie, which follows the advance of a single company of the 101st Airborne Division on their perilous journey from the landing in Normandy to the crossing of the Rhine. The soft cinematography and lack of a plot reduces the effect to that of an advertisement or a recruiting poster, the soldiers in Easy Company indistinguishable not only from each other but also from a troop of young men outfitted with military accessories in a Ralph Lauren catalogue. During the after-dinner discussion, the tone of the questions suggested the flattering murmur of department-store buyers interested in the marketing strategy for an upscale men's cologne.

Several guests had heard rumors about the current generation of recruits succumbing to the temptations of cynicism and drugs, and Ambrose was at pains to assure them that the American Army had recovered from its wounds in Vietnam (no more whining complaint from Bob Dylan's harmonica), up to the task of defending Greenwich, Connecticut, and the Chase Manhattan Bank, glad to pay the price of glory. As the author of the best-selling book on which the film was based, Ambrose said that he'd been touring it around the country on a literary lecture circuit and that he often was asked whether the kids born after 1980 were capable of "doing another D-Day."

"My answer is you're damn right they could," Ambrose said. "They're the children of democracy ... American kids are brought up to know the difference between right and wrong."

Although everybody was heartened by the news, nobody was surprised. How could it be otherwise? America had saved Western civilization in 1945, defeated Hitler and the monstrous Japanese, conceived the Marshall Plan, distributed the gifts of trade, industry, and lofty sentiment to the lesser nations of the earth. A supremacy wonderful to behold, and it was good to know (while making one's way out to the limousines standing at attention on East Sixty-eighth Street) not only that America was beyond reproach but also that one could live so comfortably (now and forever, world without end) on the trust fund of liberty established on Omaha Beach and Guadalcanal. The Greatest Generation deserved a vote of thanks. Not only from their direct descendants but also from all the people everywhere in the world who wished they were just like us, embracing the same values, shopping for the same prizes, endorsing the same definitions of the good and happy life. Fortunately for the peace and safety of mankind, our triumph was complete; we were the world's only superpower and therefore (once again, a nod of thanks to the Greatest Generation) invulnerable.

My memory of the evening in the sky-booth seats of the American establishment undoubtedly has been darkened by the irony of its counterpoint to the devastation, five days later, of the Trade Center and the Pentagon, but I don't think I misrepresent the character of its easy arrogance and witless boast. I do know that I was frightened by the exhibition of what the ancient Greeks (the ones whom Ambrose left on the plains of Troy) would have recognized as the dangerous form of pride they defined as hubris. Here were people well-placed within the hierarchies of American business and government, captivated by the iconography of the Pax Americana but incapable of imagining, or unwilling to acknowledge, a world other than the one they had inherited from John Wayne and Ronald Reagan and Stephen Spielberg, a world in which America was not only inevitably victorious but also universally loved, its motives always pure, its principles always just, and its soldiers always welcomed by pretty French girls bearing flowers. The complacence of the American ruling class was nothing new under the sun and by no means an unfamiliar sight, but seldom had I seen it so sleek and fat, and I remember that I was anxious to get quickly away from a would-be statesman in the brokerage business telling me that we had been lucky, really privileged, to see so grand a television show.

Cherished illusions don't die as easily as Israeli or Palestinian children torn to pieces by a truck bomb, and in the aftermath of even so spectacular a calamity as the one visited upon New York and Washington on the morning of September 11, the majority of the television voices continued to say that what they had seen was "unbelievable." But why unbelievable? Do the merchants of the global economy not read their own sales promotions? For the last ten years the apostles of technological change have been telling the customers about the ways in which the new systems of communication confer the godlike powers of government and the freedom of nation-states upon solitary individuals seated in front of a computer in San Jose. The commercial imagery depicts a Mongolian yak herder talking on a cell phone to a fisherman in Tahiti; the ad copy reads, "We're all inter-connected," or, "Invent your own world." Do we suppose that the message doesn't translate into Urdu, that only graduates of Harvard understand the wonders of globalization (among them techniques of money-laundering and electronic encryption), or that the uses of the Internet remain beyond the grasp of Arab street people last seen as background noise in *The English Patient*?

Whoever organized the attack on the United States clearly understood not only the arcana of postmodern finance capitalism but also the idiom of the American news and entertainment media. The pictures of the World Trade Center collapsing in ruins ("shatteringly emotional," "awe-inspiring," "never to be forgotten") were made to the model of a Hollywood disaster film; not a senseless act but cost-efficient and highly leveraged, the arrival of the second plane timed to the expectation of the arriving cameras, the production values akin to those of *Independence Day* and *Air Force One* rather than *Band of Brothers*.

Why then "unbelievable," and from whom do we suppose the terrorists learned to appreciate the value of high explosives as a vivid form of speech if not from our own experiments with the genre in Iraq, Serbia, and Vietnam? Robert McNamara, the American secretary of defense in the summer of 1965, explicitly defined the bombing raids that eventually murdered upwards of 2 million civilians north of Saigon as a means of communication. Bombs were metaphors meant to win the North Vietnamese to a recognition of America's inevitable victory (also to an appreciation of its goodness and freedom-loving purpose), and American planes dropped what came to be known to the staff officers in the Pentagon as "bomb-o-grams." The NATO alliance adopted a similar approach to the bombardment of Belgrade in March 1999; the targets, both military and civilian, were chosen for rhetorical rather than tactical reasons, the destruction intended to persuade Slobodan Milošević to please read the notes being sent to him in the overly polite language of diplomacy. Again in Iraq, in 1991, we imposed harsh economic sanctions on the country in order to send a stern message to Saddam Hussein, and when Madeleine Albright, then the American secretary of state, was asked in an interview on *60 Minutes* whether she had considered the resulting death of 500,000 Iraqi children (of malnutrition and disease), she said, "We think the price is worth it."

I don't wish to argue the rights and wrongs of American foreign policy, but how do we find it incredible that other people might not have noticed the planes in the sky or the corpses in the street? No fewer than 62 million civilians died in the twentieth century's wars (as opposed to 43 million military personnel), buried in mud or sand or broken stones in all seasons and every quarter of the globe—in London and Paris as well as in Sarajevo and Baghdad. Why not New York and Washington?

Nor have we been inattentive to the problem of motive. By choosing to support oppressive governments in the Middle East (in Saudi Arabia and Israel as well as in the United Arab Emirates, and, when it suited our purposes, in Iraq), we give people reason to think of America not as the land of the free and the home of the brave—a democratic republic to which they might attach their own hopes of political freedom and economic growth—but as a corpulent empire content to place the administration of its justice in the hands of brutal surrogates. The perception might be wrongheaded and perverse, failing to account for the prompt deliveries of McDonald's cheeseburgers and Arnold Schwarzenegger movies, but the mistake is an easy one to make in Jiddah when having one's right hand cut off for the crime of petty theft or being sentenced to a punishment of 400 lashes for failing to heed a call to prayer.

Almost as soon as the Trade Towers fell down, a loud caucus of commentators and politicians began to complain about the criminal incompetence of our intelligence agencies. We should have known. Where was the CIA? Why no timely warning or preemptive arrest? Who had neglected to alert James Bond or Bruce Willis?

The questions missed the point. We had suffered not from a lack of data but from a failure of imagination. Accustomed to the unilateral privilege of writing the world's blockbuster geopolitical scripts, hiring the cast and paying for the special effects, the Washington studio executives seldom take the trouble to look at the movie from the point of view of an audience that might be having trouble with the subtitles. Why bother? Let them eat popcorn and look at the pictures. It isn't only that we don't learn the languages[2]—we don't remember history. Obliged to issue a statement to the cameras while traveling to Washington on September 11, President Bush began by saying, "Freedom itself was attacked this morning by a faceless coward." Two days later he was talking about mindless hatred and unfathomable evil.

But it wasn't freedom that had been attacked; an abstract rather than a proper noun, freedom is as safe as love or justice from the effects of burning kerosene and collapsing steel. Nor were the attackers faceless or their hatred mindless. The networks were proud to show their photo album of Osama bin Laden (romantic bandit once associated with the CIA), and it wasn't difficult to find university professors prepared to discuss the reasons why at least some of the Arabs in the Middle East might have nurtured a long and bitter grievance against the American presence in Israel and the Persian Gulf.

The history lesson was too hard to set to the music of trumpets and drums, and most of the media voices (politicians, generals, anchorpersons) chose to place the attack in the self-referential context of the great American shopping mall. Obviously the

---

2 Five days after the September 11 attack, Mike Wallace interviewed two senior officials formerly charged with directing the CIA's intelligence operations in the Middle East and Afghanistan. Neither of them spoke fluent Arabic, Pashto, or Dari. Similarly, during the entire twelve years of the Vietnam War, only one American university offered graduate instruction in the Vietnamese language.

terrorists wanted everything in all the suburban show windows, wanted to drive a Lexus, own a beach house in East Hampton, wear an Armani suit. Unhappily, they couldn't afford the prices because, in the phrase of one of the experts on CBS, "They hadn't done too well in the modern world." Thus their envy and resentment. An expression of childish rage or a proof of possession by the Devil. Nothing to do with history or politics, let alone a philosophical objection or a legitimate argument against a global economic order, largely denominated in American money, that decides what other people shall produce, what they will be paid for their labor, how they live, and when they die. Reading the few commentators attempting to parse the theory of Islamic jihad, I was reminded of the anarchist movement in late nineteenth-century Europe and of Barbara Tuchman's chapter on the topic in *The Proud Tower*, an aptly titled book about another age of wealth and ease rudely awakened from its dream of moral sovereignty. Utopian in their thinking and certainly not crazy, the anarchist prophets, among them Mikhail Bakunin, Pierre Proudhon, and Prince Peter Kropotkin, defined all government (under any name, in any form) as a synonym for slavery, the laws (in any form, under any name) "cobwebs for the rich and chains of steel for the poor."[3] They sought to destroy the systems in place (the secular consumer society then known, more simply, as the bourgeoisie) with what they called "the propaganda of the deed." The assassins,

---

3   Proudhon's excoriation of government prefigures the proclamations of the Islamic jihad as well as those of Timothy McVeigh and the Unabomber:

To be governed is to be watched, inspected, spied on, regulated, indoctrinated, preached at, controlled, ruled, censored, by persons who have neither wisdom nor virtue. It is every action and transaction to be registered, stamped, taxed, patented, licensed, assessed, measured, reprimanded, corrected, frustrated. Under pretext of the public good it is to be exploited, monopolized, embezzled, robbed and then, at the least protest or word of complaint, to be fined, harassed, vilified, beaten up, bludgeoned, disarmed, judged, condemned, imprisoned, shot, garroted, deported, sold, betrayed, swindled, deceived, outraged, dishonored.

usually Latins or Slavs, threw their bombs at kings and opera houses (the symbolic targets of the day), and although they were invariably seized soon afterward by the army or the police, they went defiantly to death, fierce zealots (not mindless, not faceless, not cowards) carrying their passion to the scaffold or the guillotine, willing to sacrifice their lives on what they called "the altar of the Idea."[4]

The nineteenth-century enemies of the Gilded Age, like the contemporary believers in the Islamic jihad, had no political program in mind, no interest in labor reform or the redistributions of wealth. On behalf of what they thought was revealed truth, they wished to make an apocalyptic statement, to annihilate "mankind's tormentors," whom Bakunin listed as "priests, monarchs, statesmen, soldiers, officials, financiers, capitalists, moneylenders, lawyers"—a.k.a. each and every member of the Council on Foreign Relations, myself among them, no matter how blameless our individual consciences or how generous our contributions to the Public Broadcasting System.

No sum of historical justification can excuse the attack on the World Trade Center and the Pentagon, but neither can we excuse our own arrogance behind the screens of shock and disbelief. Enthralled by an old script, we didn't see the planes coming because we didn't think we had to look.

---

4   Six heads of state were assassinated in the name of anarchism in the twenty years prior to 1914. Tuchman writes, "They were President Carnot of France in 1894, Premier Canovas of Spain in 1897, Empress Elizabeth of Austria in 1898, King Humbert of Italy in 1900, President McKinley of the United States in 1901, and another Premier of Spain, Canalejas, in 1912."

2001

11. *Res Publica*

There is nothing stable in the world; uproar's your only music.

—John Keats

Throughout the month of October the fire continued to burn in the ruin of lower Manhattan, and the numerous politicians who came to look upon the face of apocalyptic destruction never failed to see, somewhere behind the veil of rancid and still-drifting smoke, an American phoenix rising from the ashes. None of them pretended to a close acquaintance with the miraculous bird, but the metaphor was never far from their thought when they spoke of a renewed sense of national unity and purpose, of democracy regained and liberty reborn, of the American spirit, eagle-feathered and indomitable, shining with the promise of a new day's dawn.

Given the ground on which the speakers stood (a makeshift cemetery in which 3,000 of their fellow citizens lay buried under 1.2 million tons of fallen concrete and twisted steel), it was impossible to doubt the truth of their emotion or the honesty of their intent. What was more difficult to judge was the portrait of the future they had in mind. Almost as soon as they had said that America never again would be the same, they began to talk about the restoration—of the familiar and heroic past, making good the losses of September 11 with quicker-witted intelligence agents, heavier artillery, more patriotic displays of consumer confidence in all the nation's better stores. If the fine words didn't amount to much when weighed for the content of their thought or meaning, possibly it was because the destruction of the World Trade Center also obliterated most of the supporting theory that for the last twenty years had buttressed the American claim to an advanced state of economic and political enlightenment. As construed by the household sophists in the Reagan Administration and endorsed by their successors in the Bush and Clinton Administrations, the intellectual foundation for the country's wealth and happiness rested on four pillars of imperishable wisdom:

1. Big government is by inclination Marxist, by definition wasteful and incompetent, a conspiracy of fools indifferent to the welfare of the common man. The best government is no government. The agencies of big government stand as acronyms for overbearing bureaucracy, as synonyms for poverty, indolence, and disease.

2. Global capitalism is the eighth wonder of the world, a light unto the nations and the answer to everybody's prayers. Nothing must interfere with its sacred mysteries and omniscient judgment.

3. The art of politics (embarrassingly human and therefore corrupt) is subordinate to the science of economics (reassuringly abstract and therefore perfect). What need of political principle or philosophy when it is the money markets that set policy, pay the troops, distribute alms? What need of statesmen, much less politicians, when it isn't really necessary to know their names or remember what they say?

4. History is at an end. The new world economic order vanquished the last of the skeptics by refuting the fallacy of Soviet Communism. Having reached the final stopping place on the road to ideological perfection, mankind no longer need

trouble itself with any new political ideas. Francis Fukuyama, an author much admired by the *Wall Street Journal*, summed up the proposition in a sentence deemed sublime, "For our purposes, it matters very little what strange thoughts occur to people in Albania or Burkina Faso."

All four pillars of imperishable wisdom perished on the morning of September 11, reduced within an hour to the incoherence of the rubble in Liberty Street. By noon even the truest of true believers knew that they had been telling themselves a fairy tale. If not to big government, then where else did the friends of laissez-faire economics look for the rescue of their finances and the saving of their lives; if not the agencies of big government, who then brought the ambulances from as far away as Albany or sent the firemen into the doomed buildings with no promise of a finder's fee? It wasn't the free market that hijacked the airplanes and cross-promoted them into bombs, or Adam Smith's invisible hand that cut the throats of the pilots on what they thought was a flight to Los Angeles. History apparently was still a work in progress, the strange thoughts grown in the basements of Tirana possibly closer to the geopolitical spirit of the times than the familiar platitudes handed around the conference tables at the American Enterprise Institute.

By nightfall the revelation was complete, and during the weeks since September 11 the rush into the shelters of big government has come to resemble the crowding of sinners into the tent of a prairie evangelist. The corporate lobbyists make daily pilgrimages to Washington in search of federal subsidy; the Air Force bombs Afghanistan; the White House and the State Department revise the terms of our diplomacy with Russia, Pakistan, Saudi Arabia, Israel, and China; the FBI sets up our defences against the airborne spores of anthrax; and the once-gaudy advertisements for what was variously billed as the globalist hegemony and the new world economic order begin to look like faded circus posters peeling from a roadside billboard in eastern Tennessee. Every morning's paper and every evening's television broadcast punch a new hole in the old story, and it turns out that public service on behalf of the common good (as recently as last August thought no longer fashionable or pertinent) retains at least the memory of an honorable meaning. Mayor Rudolph Giuliani in New York gives voice to the city's courage, and among an electorate formerly presumed decadent the discovery of such a thing as an American Commonwealth finds expression not only in the show of flags but also in the myriad voluntary acts of citizenship—unpaid rescue workers clearing the wreckage in lower Manhattan, $850 million in emergency funds contributed by individuals as well as corporations, the news media accepting substantial loss of advertising revenue in order to provide more time and space for the discovery of maybe necessary information, a generous upwelling of tolerance and compassion among people of different colors, their regard for one another grounded in the recognition that the modifying adjectives (black, gay, white, native, etc.) matter less than the noun "American."

By the end of October it had been generally understood that America no longer enjoyed a special arrangement with Providence, preserved by the virtue of its inhabitants and the grace of its geography from the provocations of death, chance, kings, and desperate men. Confronted with determined enemies (many of them still unknown, some of them armed with appalling weapons), the nation stood exposed, like other nations, to the insults of outrageous fortune. The awareness of the predicament (on the part of both the politicians at the microphones and the voters in the streets) conceivably could lead to a reconstitution of the American idea, but the finding of the phoenix in the ashes presupposes a debate rising from an intellectual structure a good deal sturdier than the one lost in the wreckage of the World Trade Center. I imagine the argument falling along the division between the people who would continue the American experiment and those who think that the experiment has gone far enough, and if I can't frame all the questions that might well be asked, I can think of at least a few.

How high a price do we set on the head of freedom? If we delete another few paragraphs from the Bill of Rights (for our own protection, of course, in the interest of peace, prosperity, and carefree summer vacations), what do we ask of the state in return for our silence in court? Do we wish to remain citizens of a republic, or do we prefer the forms of participatory fascism in which the genial man on horseback assures us that repression is good for the soul? With what secular faith do we match the zeal of militant Islam and combat the enmity of the impoverished peoples of the earth to whom the choice between war and peace presents itself as a choice of no significance? How to define the American democracy as a *res publica* for which we might willingly give up our lives? (Our own lives, not the lives of foreign legions.) And of what does the *res publica* consist?

None of the questions lead to certain answers, but if we don't ask them of ourselves I don't know how we can expect to rediscover the American idea in a world unknown to Jefferson. Assume a conversation at least as long as the war that President Bush forecasts for the mountains of Afghanistan, and we might begin by strengthening the habit of dissent and improving our powers of observation. The barbarism in Washington doesn't dress itself in the costumes of the Taliban; it wears instead the smooth-shaven smile of a Senate resolution sold to the highest bidder—for the drilling of the Arctic oil fields or the lifting from the rich the burden of the capital-gains tax, for bigger defense budgets, reduced medical insurance, enhanced surveillance, grotesque monopoly. If we took more of an interest in the making of our foreign policy, usually for the profit of our corporate overlords rather than for the safety of the American people, maybe we would know why, when bringing the lamp of liberty to the darker places of the earth, the United States invariably chooses for its allies the despots who operate their countries on the model of a prison or a jail. We might even wonder why, ten years ago during the denouement of the Gulf War, George Bush the elder chose to leave an army in Saudi Arabia. Did we mean to protect our supply of cheap oil, or were we providing the Saudi ruling family with household troops to preserve them from a revolutionary uprising led by malcontents as clever as Osama bin Laden?

If we mean to project abroad the force of the *res publica* made glorious by the death of American teenagers and Muslim holy men, we might want to consider taking better care of our own domestic commonwealth. For the last twenty years we've let fall into disrepair nearly all of the public infrastructure—roads, water systems, schools, power plants, bridges, hospitals, broadcast frequencies —that provides the country with a foundation for its common enterprise. The privatization of the nation's public resources has enriched the investors fortunate enough to profit from the changes of venue, but at what cost to our sense of general well-being? The lopsided division of the country into the factions of the hapless many and the privileged few has allowed our faith in the republic to degenerate from the strength of a conviction into the weakness of a sentiment. By discounting what the brokers classify as "nonmarket values," we're left with a body politic defined not as the union of its collective energies and hopes but as an aggregate of loosely affiliated selfish interests (ethnic, regional, commercial, sexual), armed with their own manifestos, loyal to their own agendas, secure in the compounds of their own languages.

Any argument about the direction of the American future becomes an argument between the past and present tense. Let us hope that it proves to be both angry and fierce. The friends of the status quo (both houses of Congress, most of the national news media, the Hollywood patriots, and a legion of corporate spokespersons) already have made it clear that they prefer as little discussion as possible. They regard domestic political dissent as immoral and, in time of war, treasonous. They believe it their duty to invest President Bush not only with the powers of a monarch but also with the attribute of wisdom. Put out more flags, post more guards, distribute the pillows of cant. Maybe two or three years from now, when all the terrorists have been rounded up and the Trade Center towers replaced with a golden statue of Mammon, the time will come to talk of politics. In the meanwhile, my children, while waiting for that far-off happy day, follow directions, submit to the surveillance, look at the nice pictures brought to you by the Pentagon, know that your rulers are wise.

So sayeth Trent Lott and *Time* magazine, and the admonition seems to me as feckless as the theory that supported last summer's pillars of imperishable wisdom. The country at the moment stands in need of as many questions as anybody can think to ask. Rightly understood, democracy is an uproar—nothing quiet, orderly, or safe—and among all the American political virtues, candor is probably the one most necessary to the success of our shared enterprise; unless we try to tell one another the truth about what we know and think and see, we might as well amuse ourselves (for as long as somebody else allows us to do so) with Steven Spielberg movies.

12. American Jihad

War is the health of the state.

—Randolph Bourne

Fascism should more properly be called corporatism, since it is the merger of state and corporate power.

—Benito Mussolini

Three months ago I thought we'd been given a chance for a conversation about the future of the American political idea, the attacks on the Pentagon and the World Trade Center providing an impressive occasion for timely remarks on the topics of our foreign and domestic policy as well as an opportunity to ask what we mean by the phrases "public service," "common good," "civic interest." The newspapers were reporting daily proofs of selfless citizenship, not only on the part of the volunteers clearing the wreckage in lower Manhattan but also on the part of people everywhere else in the country giving of their money and effort to whatever need was nearest at hand, and I expected something of the same public-spiritedness to find a voice in the Congress, in the major news media, possibly on the television talk shows—informed argument about why and how America had come to be perceived as a dissolute empire; instructive doubts cast on the supposed omniscience of the global capital markets; sustained questioning of the way in which we divide the country's wealth; a distinction drawn between the ambitions of the American national security state and the collective well-being of the American citizenry.

By December I knew that I'd been barking at the moon. The conversation maybe had a chance of taking place in magazines of small circulation, or possibly somewhere in the distant reaches of C-SPAN (at two A.M., on the stage of a college auditorium in Wabash, Indiana), but not in the chambers of Congress, not under the circus tents of the big-time news and entertainment media, not, except by special permission and then only with a word of apology, on network television.

Ted Koppel struck the preferred note of caution on November 2 when introducing his *Nightline* audience to Arundhati Roy, an Indian novelist and a critic of the American bombing of Afghanistan: "Some of you, many of you, are not going to like what you hear tonight. You don't have to listen. But if you do, you should know that dissent sometimes comes in strange packages."

It wasn't clear whether Koppel was referring to Ms. Roy's opinions or to her sari, but at least he had the wit to know that she wasn't coming to the program with a press release from the Boeing Company. Most of the other security guards deciding what could and could not be seen on camera explained the absence of talking heads critical of the American "War on Terrorism" by saying that they couldn't find any credible experts inclined to make an argument both seditious and absurd. Thus Erik Sorenson, president of MSNBC, telling a reporter from the *New York Times* that apart from the raving of a few Hollywood celebrities there wasn't enough dissent in the country "to warrant coverage." Or Peter Beinart, editor of the *New Republic*, outraged by the noise of protest in the streets: "This nation is now at war. And in such an environment, domestic political dissent is immoral without a prior statement of national solidarity, a choosing of sides."

In other words, as President Bush had become fond of saying to United Nations ambassadors and foreign heads of state, "Either you are with us, or you're with the terrorists."

As a means of quieting the distemper of the press, nothing works as well as the anodyne of war. Caught up in the memory of a tale told by Homer or Rudyard Kipling, the keepers of the nation's conscience gladly smother the peepings of dissent and quickly learn to stuff a sock into the mouth of an impiety. Show them a cruise missile or a map, and they become more ferocious than the generals. The scouts for the Sunday talk shows might have found it difficult to recruit skeptics, but they didn't have any trouble enlisting fuglemen to blow the trumpets of imperial advance—Tom Brokaw, impatiently wanting to know why the Army wasn't deploying ground troops, "in division-size force" somewhere south of Kabul; Dick Morris on Fox News, urging the Pentagon to boldly extend Civilization's War Against Barbarism by occupying Libya and invading Iraq.

The eagerness to enlarge the theater of military operations—a strategy endorsed not only by the regimental commanders at Fox News but also by Newt Gingrich, Henry Kissinger, and Senator John McCain—seemed as senseless as the elevation of Osama bin Laden to a world figure on the scale of Fidel Castro or Charles de Gaulle, but by the end of October I'd begun to understand that the heavily armored media commentary fortified a broadcast studio and went well with flags, the rhetoric made of the same red, white, and blue bunting that decorates the speeches of President Bush— "We go forward to defend freedom and all that is good and just in the world," "We value the right to speak our minds," "Our ultimate victory is assured." The viewing audience isn't expected to know what the words mean; we're supposed to listen to them in the way one listens to a military band playing "Stars and Stripes Forever" on the Washington Mall, or to Ray Charles singing "God Bless America" in a World Series baseball park.

Language degraded into the currency of propaganda doesn't lend itself to conversations about the future course of the American political idea, and if in September I thought that the destruction of the World Trade Center and the Pentagon might teach us something about our own history as well as furnishing us with an English translation of the Arabic word for "student," it was because I'd neglected to ask where the profit was to be found in a cloud of black smoke rising from the ruin of lower Manhattan. Where was the silver lining, and where the blessings in disguise? *Qui bono?*, the oldest of the old maxims once learned in a high school Latin class. To what end, and in whose interest, do we astonish the world with the magnificence of "Operation Enduring Freedom"?

The attacks on the buildings in Virginia and New York were abominable and unprovoked, inflicting an as yet unspecified sum of damage and an as yet incalculable measure of grief, but they didn't constitute an act of war. By choosing to define them as such, we invested a gang of murderous criminals with the sovereignty of a nation-state (or, better yet, with the authority of a world-encircling religion) and declared war on both an unknown enemy and an abstract noun. Like an Arab jihad against capitalism, the American jihad against terrorism cannot be won or lost; nor does it ever end. We might as well be sending the 101st Airborne Division to conquer lust, annihilate greed, capture the sin of pride. The careless use of language is an error that works to the advantage of the American political, military, and industrial interests that prefer the oligarchic and corporatist forms of government to those of a democracy.

Absent the excitements of a foreign war, in what domestic political accident might we not have lost the wooden figurehead of President George Bush? Six months ago we were looking at a man so obviously in the service of the plutocracy that he could have been mistaken for a lawn jockey in the parking lot of a Houston golf club or a prize fish mounted on the wall of a Jacksonville bank. Having signed the law awarding $1.4 trillion of tax relief to the country's richest individuals, he'd reimbursed the people who had paid his ticket to the White House, but the smiling pose of "compassionate conservatism" was becoming hard to hold amidst the gradual recognition of both its fraudulence and rigidity. The economy was in trouble, the Senate had lost its Republican majority, the president's approval ratings were sliding into recession, and too many people still were wondering about the sleights-of-hand that won the electoral vote in Florida. All in all, not a promising outlook for a politician who had been told, and so believed, that the running of a government was no different than the management of a corporation.

On September 11, like Pinocchio brushed with the good fairy's wand on old Gepetto's shelf of toys, the wooden figurehead turned into flesh and blood. A great leader had been born, within a month compared (by David Broder in the *Washington Post*) to Abraham Lincoln. Suddenly we were looking at a man resplendent on the gilded throne of power, his clichéd speeches revealed as "Churchillian" in the bright new morning of a war that Secretary of Defense Donald Rumsfeld guessed might last as long as forty years.

Which was, of course, good news for the defense industries and the military establishment. The Senate wasn't slow to take the point, voting, unanimously and without debate on October 2, to fund a $60 billion missile-defense system that to the best of nearly everybody's knowledge can't hit its celestial targets and offers no defense against the deadly weapons (smallpox virus, dynamite stuffed into a barrel of nuclear waste) likely to be delivered in rented trucks. But why bother with cowardly and disloyal argument? The nation is at war; civilization trembles in the balance, and what true American stoops to haggle over the price of freedom?

If the Senate cannot bring itself to question a proposition as false as the missile-defense system, then what may we not expect in the months of crisis yet to come? The Navy will want bigger aircraft carriers, the Air Force another four hundred planes, the Army a set of tanks equipped with electronics so sophisticated that they can set up the targeting coordinates for each of the Koran's ninety-nine names for God.

Senator Carl Levin (D., Mich.), chairman of the Armed Services Committee, attributed the lack of debate about the missiles to the need for "unity" when America was under siege; similar flows of sentiment stifled the asking of rude questions about the war's long-term aims and short-term costs. The Democratic members in both houses of Congress as silent as the chairs; no memorable speech or hint of eloquence; nothing but an obedient show of hands and the hushed thumping of rubber stamps.

Addressing a joint session of Congress on the evening of September 20, the president congratulated the assembled politicians for their bravery in a time of trouble, thanking them "for what you have already done, and for what we will do together." Fortunately for the friends of good government, the patriotic news media have quarantined the tone of irony for the duration of the campaign against the world's "evildoers"; otherwise the president's speech might have evoked not only a round of brisk applause but also a gust of appreciative laughter. What the Congress had been doing (in concert with the White House and the federal regulatory agencies and brazen with the pretense of assisting the war effort) was looting the country's public interest on behalf of its well-placed private interests—the Interior Department relieved of its power to veto mining projects on public lands; the pharmaceutical companies negotiating the right to sell their drugs at the customary high prices in the event of a biological or biochemical catastrophe; the insurance industry collectively seeking a $10 billion deductible; best of all, the economic "stimulus package" passed on October 24 by the House of Representatives in the amount of $101 billion, the bulk of the stimulant administered to wealthy individuals and corporations.

Asked about the apparent senselessness of the repeal of the corporate alternative minimum tax, Dick Armey (R., Tex.), the House majority leader, justified the gifts ($1.4 billion to IBM, $833 million to General Motors, $671 million to General Electric, etc.) by saying, "This country is in the middle of a war. Now is not the time to provoke spending confrontations with our Commander-in-Chief." In answer to a related question as to why the $15 billion soothing of economic wounds suffered by the airline industry didn't allot any money, none whatsoever, to the 150,000 airline workers who had lost their jobs in September, Armey observed that any help extended to such people "is not commensurate with the American spirit."

Who but a decadent Arab could have thought otherwise? Like

Senator Levin, Congressman Armey understood that in time of war the United States can't afford the distraction of petty domestic politics. The promise of prescription-drug benefits for the elderly will have to wait; so will nearly everything else that most people associate with the words "national security"—repair of the nation's roads and schools and the prospect of decent health care for the 43 million citizens who can't afford to buy it at the going rate.

The country's corporate overlords don't associate the phrase "national security" with the health and well-being of the American public; they define the term as a means of acquiring wealth and as a reason for directing the country's diplomacy toward policies that return a handsome profit—the bombing of caves in the Hindu Kush preferred to the building of houses in St. Louis or Detroit. The work goes more smoothly when conducted in an atmosphere of constant dread, and how better to magnify that dread than by declaring a war against terrorism? Enemies on every hand and all of them unseen; nothing safe, not even a postcard from a maiden aunt. Happy to be of service and proud to protect the American people not only from bearded strangers but also from themselves, the Congress in September hurried to the task of forging legal shackles and restraints, also to the broadening of the government's police powers and the further destruction of the Bill of Rights. By the end of October the president had signed the USA PATRIOT Act, 342 pages of small print that hardly anybody in the Senate or the House of Representatives took the trouble to read but which nevertheless—permitted the attorney general to expand telephone and Internet surveillance, extend the reach of wiretaps, open financial and medical records to searches for suspicious behavior and criminal intent. Two weeks later he signed an emergency order (conceding that it set aside "the principles of law and the rules of evidence") allowing him to remand to a military tribunal any foreign national about whom he had "reason to believe" a rumor of cohabitation with a terrorist organization, a nihilist author, or an anarchist idea. The FBI in the meantime was rounding up legal immigrants of Middle Eastern descent (5,000 of them as of November 15) to inquire about their connections to

Saladin and the Third Crusade. Although the corporatist distaste for the Constitution is nothing new (cf., the deliberate weakening of the First, Fourth, and Sixth Amendments over the last twenty years), the guarantee of an always present danger extends the government's prerogative to enforce whatever rule of law happens to prove convenient to the rule of money.

On November 11 in Atlanta, standing in front of a photomontage of heroic New York City firemen, President Bush told his audience that the nation "faces a threat to our freedoms, and the stakes could not be higher." What he said was true, but not in the way that he intended. We have more to fear from the fatwas issued in Washington than from those drifting across the deserts of Central Asia. The agents of Al Qaeda might wreck our buildings and disrupt our commerce, maybe even manage to kill a number of our fellow citizens, but we do ourselves far greater harm if we pawn our civil rights and consign the safekeeping of our liberties to Mullah John Ashcroft and the mujahedeen in the hospitality tents of American crusade.

2002

13. Mythography

Our world has sprouted a weird concept of security and a warped sense of morality. Weapons are sheltered like treasures and children are exposed to incineration.

—Bertrand Russell

For the last four months the curators of the national news media have done their patriotic best to muffle objections to our worldwide crusade against terrorism, the editors of important newspapers removing contraband opinion from the manuscripts of known polemicists, the producers of network talk shows softening the criticisms of American foreign policy for fear that they otherwise might be seen as displays of weak-mindedness if not as proofs of treason. I don't wonder why the watchers at the gate of freedom might want to keep a sharp lookout for suspicious substances at a time when some of them had received anthrax in the mail, but I didn't think that we were well on the way to a ministry of state propaganda until I came across "Defending Civilization," a guide to the preferred forms of free speech issued last November in Washington by the American Council of Trustees and Alumni.

Knowing little else about the organization except what could be inferred from the writings of the conservative and neoconservative ideologues prominently identified as its leading lights (among them Lynne V. Cheney, the vice president's wife and a fellow of the American Enterprise Institute; Martin Peretz, chairman of the *New Republic*; Irving Kristol, coeditor of *The Public Interest*; and William Bennett, editor of *The Book of Virtues*), I took it as a given that the document would read like a sermon preached against the wickedness of the 1960s and the great darkness brought down upon the nation's universities by the werewolves of the intellectual left. It's an old sermon, discredited by the facts but still much beloved by the parties of the right, and I was prepared for the ritual scourgings of Eros, multiculturalism, and modernity. I expected cant; I didn't expect the bringing of what amounted to a charge of sedition against any university or scholar therein failing to pledge allegiance to the sovereign wisdom of President George W. Bush. I've had occasion to read a good deal of fourth-rate agitprop over the last thirty years, but I don't remember an argument as disgraceful as the one advanced by the American Council of Trustees and Alumni under the rubric of "academic freedom, quality and accountability"; if to no other purpose than that of appreciating its unctuousness and dishonesty, I think it worth the trouble of a brief review.

Proceeding from the assumption that the nation's universities—all the nation's universities—wander in a desert of ignorance, the report sets out to show that all of these universities failed to respond to the provocation of September 11 with a proper degree of "anger, patriotism, and support of military intervention." Right-thinking people everywhere else in the country were quick to recognize evil when they saw it, prompt in their exhibition of American flags, wholehearted in their rallying to the cause of virtue. "Not so in academe." Most university professors succumbed to "moral relativism"; "Some even pointed accusatory fingers," not at the terrorists but at their fellow Americans. So monstrous was the betrayal that "the message of much of academe was clear: BLAME AMERICA FIRST."

Although careful to make its curtsy to "the robust exchange of ideas" so "essential to a free society," the report makes little effort to conceal the stench of its intolerance. America's universities had proved themselves "distinctly equivocal" in their response to the nation's sorrow, and it was important to remember—"never more so than in these unsettling times"—that "Academic freedom does not mean freedom from criticism."

As evidence for its grotesque assertions, the report offers a list of 115 subversive remarks culled from college newspapers, or overheard on university campuses by the Council's vigilant informants, during the fifty-one days between September 14 and November 4. The following citations can be taken as representative of the sentiments deemed traitorous or un-American:

"We have to learn to use courage for peace instead of war."—Professor of Religious Studies, Pomona College

"[I]ntolerance breeds hate, hate breeds violence and violence breeds death, destruction and heartache."—Student, University of Oklahoma

"[We should] build bridges and relationships, not simply bombs and walls."—Speaker at Harvard Law School

"Our grief is not a cry for war."—Poster at New York University

I wish I thought the Council's paranoia confined to a small company of reclusive minutemen, outfitted with hunting rifles, and gathered around a campfire in Idaho or Montana. Unhappily, I suspect that the report accurately reflects the attitudes widely distributed among the upper servants of government and the news media, consistent with the judgments of Attorney General John Ashcroft, at one with the 90 percent approval rating accorded to the diplomacy of President Bush.

Words pressed into the service of propaganda lose the name and form of meaning, a point of which I was reminded when, at about the same time I encountered the Washington tract, I happened to read *The Psychology of War*, a study of the ways in which human beings adjust their interpretations of reality in order to recognize the mass murder of other human beings as glorious adventure and noble enterprise. First published in 1992 but fortunately brought back into print this year by Helios Press, the book, written by Lawrence LeShan, draws a distinction between the "sensory" and the "mythic" perceptions of war. Let war become too much of a felt experience, as close at hand as the putrid smell of rotting flesh or the presence of a newly headless corpse seated in a nearby chair, and most people tend to forget to sing patriotic songs. Much better for everybody's morale if the war takes place in a galaxy far, far away, in the mountains of high-sounding abstraction where only the enemy dies.

LeShan observes that governments wishing to produce success-ful, award-winning wars must be sure to reserve the right to what Hollywood film directors know as the final cut. Governments that fail to do so (allowing control of the script to escape into the hands of imperfectly indoctrinated journalists) give up the chance of transposing the war into the realm of myth (there to take its heroic place with World Wars I and II), and they're apt to lose both the viewing public and the next election. The critical and commercial failure of the wars in Korea and Vietnam demon-strated both the unwillingness of the American people to regard themselves as imperialists and their distaste for wars conducted in the sensory theaters of operation.

It's never easy to stage a mythic war, particularly a war in which, by definition, the civilian population becomes the primary target, and as if to illustrate the difficulties confronted by the apostles of never-ending crusade, New Line Cinema on December 19 of last year positioned the opening of *The Lord of the Rings* to compete for the Christmas box office against the Pentagon's production of "The Fall of Kandahar," then in its second month of national and international release. Despite certain similarities (President Bush as wholesome a protagonist as Frodo Baggins, the landscape of Afghanistan as desolate as Gorgoroth and Nurn), the government documentary suffered by comparison with the Hollywood romance—the cinematography not as good and the pacing embarrassingly slow; too many pointless repetitions; the characters ineptly named (Rumsfeld and Rice instead of Aragorn, Galadriel, and Gimli, the dwarf); no elves, too few mithril coats, not nearly enough Ringwraiths or wizards.

Lacking symbols of good and evil as formidable as the Dark Lord of Mordor and Gandalf the Grey, the studio executives in Washington rely on the genies in the bottles of technology and the telling of the story in the language of a fairy tale. Fortunately for the safety of the republic, the capacity of our defense industries cannot be matched by any country in the world—not now, probably not ever before in the history of mankind. Making weapons is what we know how to do best, the supreme achievement of late twentieth-century American civilization. To this blessed work we assign our finest intellect and the largest share of our treasure, and in the magnificence of an aircraft carrier or a cruise missile we find our moral and aesthetic equivalent of the Sistine ceiling and Chartres Cathedral.

But if the government need not worry about a shortage of special effects—the Pentagon's laser-guided bombs as stealthy in approach and as deadly in result as one of J. R. R. Tolkien's Nazgûls—the mythologizing of the plot requires the collaboration of a news media eager to bring urgent bulletins, every hour on the hour, from the frontiers of dread. The Pentagon provided the illustrations and nursery rhyme texts, and if the dispatches from the few reporters actually on the ground in Kabul or Mazar-i-Sharif tended to present the Taliban as ragged fugitives—lightly armed, often barefoot, their cause lost without a fight—the editors in Washington and New York strengthened the adjectives, brushed out the footage of dogs devouring dead bodies on the road to Kunduz, dressed up the headlines with "monsters" and "diabolical henchmen" overseeing "a web of hate." Geraldo Rivera went off to the Khyber Pass with a pistol in his luggage, informing his viewers on FOX News that he would consider killing Osama bin Laden if the chance presented itself somewhere on the snowy heights of Tora Bora.

When temporarily at a loss for melodrama, the news media applied to government officials for grim predictions or to university professors for dire warnings. Important members of Congress could be relied upon to demand the immediate subjugation of Iraq, various historians obligingly mentioned "the clash of civilizations" and an Arab host gathered on the plain of Armageddon under the glittering banners of militant Islam. Never mind that as of the first week in December the djinns of Al Qaeda were still nowhere to be found, and that what little could be seen of their abandoned crevices and holes suggested the improbability of their resemblance either to the Variags of Khand or to Suleiman the Just.

Failing to drum up a threat from an informed congressional or academic source, the authors of the daily allegory appealed to weapons experts and to theorists fluent in the jargon of Cold War realpolitik. Several such authorities took part in a roundtable discussion published as a special Thanksgiving issue of *The National Interest*, a journal that lists Henry Kissinger as cochairman of its editorial board, and on reading the transcript I remember thinking that the dialogue sounded like the muttering of orcs in the last chapters of *The Lord of the Rings*. Somebody said that the time had come to "flip" Iran (presumably from a low-growth theocracy to a high-yield democracy), and Dimitri Simes, president of the Nixon Center, said no, this wasn't the moment for flipping. It was the moment to consider dropping a nuclear bomb on Afghanistan—not for any strategic or tactical purpose but for the "very strong demonstration effect" that the explosion was likely to make on the rulers of Iran, Iraq, Syria, Libya, and Lebanon. He thought that altering the terrain of Central Asia might persuade Saddam Hussein to obey the instructions of the United Nations, and when asked by a fellow discussant whether he knew that he was talking about the obliteration of an unknown number of miscellaneous Afghans, Simes observed that the NATO victory in Serbia was not won against the Serbian military "but because we were effective against the Serbian civilian infrastructure."

Once placed within the context of the mythical reality, even the most fantastic notions of omnipotence acquire the semblance of everyday sense, which maybe explains why, during the months after the fall of the Twin Towers, both Osama bin Laden and Vice President Dick Cheney were hiding in caves. Also why President

Bush suddenly seemed a more forceful figure, transported between one day and the next into a more vivid interpretation of events, as certain as the agents of Al Qaeda that the world divided into "the camp of the faithful and the camp of the infidels." The president had come home to Hobbiton in the land of a Tolkien romance, a much happier and more comfortable place to live than the world of death and time. So elsewhere in Washington, grateful politicians found themselves possessed of an answer to every question, the fog of doubt and ambiguity chased into Mirkwood by the sun of transcendence and the sound of bugles. Glad of the chance to describe the contest between good and evil in terms as simpleminded as those cherished by its enemies, the American government was offering a $25 million reward for the death or capture of Osama (an advance of $22.5 million over the price of the fatwa posted on the head of Salman Rushdie by the Ayatollah Khomeini) and the American Council of Trustees and Alumni was handing around a report that brought to mind the rule books discovered in the wreckage of the Taliban's Ministry for the Promotion of Virtue and the Prevention of Vice.

All in all, at least for the time being, not an entirely unsatisfactory set of circumstances from the point of view of the Washington political and intelligence establishments anxious to shore up their authority in the aftermath of a calamity that revealed the magnitude of their stupidity and incompetence. The attack was an attack on American foreign policy, which, for the last thirty years, has allied itself, both at home and abroad, with despotism and the weapons trade, a policy conducted by and for a relatively small cadre of selfish interests unrepresentative of (and unaccountable to) the American people as a whole.

Probably because I'm used to reading the letters to the editor of *Harper's Magazine*, I incline to give the American people credit for a higher quotient of intelligence and a greater store of idealism than their supervisors in Washington think they want or deserve, and I suspect that if given a voice in the arrangement of the nation's foreign affairs they would endorse the policies (similar to those once put forward by Franklin D. Roosevelt) that reflected a concern for human rights, international law, nuclear disarmament, and freedom from both the colonial and neocolonial forms of economic monopoly. But the American people don't have a voice at the table, especially not now, not during what the media and the government aggressively promote as "a time of war." On numerous occasions last fall the Justice Department placed the country on high alert against an imminent terrorist attack (if not on the Sears Tower or the Golden Gate Bridge, then somewhere in Las Vegas or Miami); it wasn't that anybody knew how or where to forestall such an attack, but rather that the merchants of never-ending crusade wished to enlarge their arsenals of fear and maintain the credulity of the American public at combat strength. Because the civilian population finds itself drafted into service as the target of opportunity for terrorists armed with asymmetric weapons, we're being asked to believe that we're opposed by Morgoth and the Corsairs of Umbar rather than by an incoherent diaspora of desperate human beings, most of them illiterate and many of them children, reduced to expressing their resentment in the impoverished vocabularies of violence. Best not to see our enemies as they are; better to go quietly into the caves of myth thoughtfully prepared by our news media and our schools, there to find, praise be to Allah, our comfort, our salvation, and our glory.

2002

14. Spoils of War

Perpetual peace is a dream, and not even a beautiful dream, and War is an integral part of God's ordering of the universe. In War, man's noblest virtues come into play: courage and renunciation, fidelity to duty and a readiness for sacrifice that does not stop short of offering up Life itself. Without War the world would become swamped in materialism.

—Gen. Helmuth von Moltke

It's been nearly six months since the destruction of the World Trade Center, and we still haven't come to the end of listening to people say that the world is forever changed. On and off the record, whether privately at dinner or blowing through the trumpets of the media, our leading voices of alarmed opinion (politicians, syndicated columnists, retired generals) agree that America can't go home again and that nothing will ever be the same. Before September 11 the world was one thing; after September 11, the world is something else. Impossible to depict or describe, of course, but the transformation so unprecedented and complete as to require new maps and geopolitical surveys, new sets of emotion and states of mind.

The grave announcements invite an equally grave response, but although I usually can manage a solemn nod or worried frown, I'm never sure that I know what it is that I'm being asked to notice or why I can't find in myself the symptoms of an altered sensibility. Apparently the changes don't apply to the kingdom of day-to-day event. The Enron Corporation dissolves in a bankruptcy almost as spectacular as the collapse of the World Trade Center (a market capitalization of $63 billion reduced in nine months to worthless paper), but nobody pokes around in the rubble for a world-changing paradigm; nor does anybody mention radical theories of aesthetics or startling discoveries in the sciences. No miracles being reported elsewhere in the society, I assume that the important talk about "asymmetric reality" and "multilateral chaos" pertains to "the new kind of war" that President George W. Bush has loosed upon all the world's evildoers. It is Osama bin Laden who has rearranged the universe, Osama and his network of elusive assassins holding for ransom not only the Eiffel Tower, Mount Rushmore, and Buckingham Palace but also the beating heart of Western civilization. Madness stalks the earth, and except for Vice President Dick Cheney, none of us is safe.

But if that is the awful truth that divides the world of September 10 from the world of September 12, I'm at a loss to know why it deserves the name of news. Unless I'm badly mistaken or cruelly misinformed, madness has been stalking the earth ever since an American B-29 dropped an atomic bomb on Hiroshima on the day in August 1945 that Buckminster Fuller marked on his calendar as "the day that humanity started taking its final exam." I was ten years old in 1945, too young to understand the remark even if I'd known that Fuller had said it; by the time I was twenty I'd read enough of the literature to know that a radioactive Armageddon doesn't extend the option of any good places to hide, and ever since the Cuban missile crisis in October 1962 I've understood that I belong to an endangered species, never more than thirty minutes away from an appointment with extinction.

To be held hostage to the fear of a nuclear weapon brought into Manhattan on a truck doesn't seem to me much different than being held hostage to the fear of a nuclear weapon delivered to the same address by a Soviet submarine seventy miles east of Nantucket. The late Robert Benchley put the proposition about as plainly as it can be put on an examination paper that he failed to pass at Harvard in 1912. Asked to frame the legal dispute over fishing rights on the Grand Banks from both the American and British points of view, Benchley began his answer by saying that he never understood the American argument, never cared to know where England stood, but that he would like to consider the problem from the points of view of the fish. The statement of purpose introduced a dialogue in which a flounder and a cod take up the question as to whether it is better to be roasted in Liverpool, boiled in Boston, or sautéed in Paris.

In several speeches since September 11, President Bush has insisted that "terrorism is terrorism," its character always and everywhere the same, absolute and indivisible, not subject to extenuating circumstance or further explanation: Presumably he refers to terrorist acts staged by independent theater companies, not to the ones sponsored by nation-states. When wrapped up in the ribbons of patriotic slogan, terrorism becomes a show of diplomatic resolve or a lesson in democracy, the prerogative of governments apportioning its distribution to Cambodian peasants, dissident Soviet intellectuals, Israeli disco dancers, Chechen rebels, Palestinian refugees, Iraqi schoolchildren, Guatemalan coffee trees. Except as a form of terrorism, how else do we describe the doctrine of Mutual Assured Destruction that for the last fifty years has trapped the civilian populations of the earth in nets similar to the one in which Benchley's fish found themselves discussing the finer points of British and French cuisine? The doctrine evolved during the prolonged Cold War with the Soviet Union, the diplomatists on both sides of the Iron Curtain entrusting the peace and prosperity of mankind (also the light of reason and the rule of law) to what was bluntly recognized at summit conferences as "the balance of terror"—you kill everybody here, and we kill everybody there; together we preserve humanity by threatening to obliterate it. Citizens inclined to think the arrangement somehow disquieting or oppressive remained free to discuss the finer points of difference between the Russian and the American flag.

If I can understand why the managers of the state monopoly regard the privatization of terror as unwarranted poaching of their market, as a prospective consumer presented with variant packagings of the product I find the same instruction on the labels. Fear the unknown, reflect upon the transience of flounders, pay the ransom or the tax bill, pray for deliverance. The message is by no means new. The miraculous births of Fat Man and Little Boy in Los Alamos in 1945 pressed the fire of Heaven into the service of a religion (jury-rigged and hastily revealed) founded on the gospels of extortion. Powers once assigned to God passed into the hands of physicists and the manufacturers of intercontinental ballistic missiles; what had been human became divine, the idols of man's own nuclear invention raised up to stand as both agent and symbol of the Day of Judgment.

Historians still argue about whether the arms race was inevitable; some say that it was not, that if President Harry Truman in 1949 had heeded the advice of some of the wisest and most well-informed men in the country (among them Robert Oppenheimer and James Conant) he wouldn't have ordered the development of the hydrogen bomb, and if that program hadn't gone forward, the Russians might not have felt compelled to build their own towers of hideous strength. The Soviet Union at the end of World War II possessed few or none of the assets attributed to it by American intelligence operatives, and Stalin conceivably might have welcomed an excuse to forgo the making of weapons (at a cost that the Communist workers' paradise could ill afford) meant to be seen and not heard.

But if I don't know what was being said in Moscow in 1949, I do know that in Washington the managers of American foreign policy cherished the dream of omnipotence cued to a memorandum that George Kennan in the winter of the preceding year circulated within the State Department:

We have about 50 percent of the world's wealth, but only 6.3 percent of its population ... In this situation we cannot fail to be the object of envy and resentment. Our real task in the coming period is to devise a pattern of relationships which will permit us to maintain this position of disparity without positive detriment to our national security. To do so we will have to dispense with all sentimentality and day-dreaming.

The preferred patterns of relationship presupposed an American realpolitik strong-mindedly turned away from what Kennan regarded as "unreal objectives such as human rights, the raising of living standards, and democratization"; back home in Washington the interested parties (political, military, and economic) bent willingly to the task of replacing the antiquated American republic, modest in ambition and democratic in spirit, with the glory of a nation-state increasingly grand in scale and luxurious in its taste for hegemony. The imperial project flourished under both Democratic and Republican administrations, and over time it achieved the preferred pattern of relationships that Winston Churchill ascribed to the English government in office in 1904, at the moment when Britain reached its zenith as an empire on which the sun never set:

> A party of great vested interests, banded together in a formidable confederation; corruption at home, aggression to cover it up abroad ... sentiment by the bucketful; patriotism and imperialism by the imperial pint; the open hand at the public exchequer; the open door at the public house; dear food for the millions, cheap labour for the millionaire.

Fattened on the seed of open-handed military spending ($17 trillion dollars since 1950) and grazing in the pastures of easy credit and certain profit, the confederation of vested interests that President Eisenhower once identified as "the military–industrial complex" brought forth an armed colossus the likes of which the world had never seen—weapons of every conceivable caliber and size, 2 million men under arms on five continents and eight seas and oceans, a vast armada of naval vessels, light and heavy aircraft, command vehicles and communications satellites, guidance systems as infallible as the Pope, tracking devices blessed with the judgment of a recording angel.

The rich displays of armament bear comparison to religious statuary. No matter what the specific function of the weapons, as attack submarines or high-altitude gun platforms, they stand as symbols representative of the divinity (absolute, unfathomable, unseen but always present) implicit in the cloud of nuclear unknowing. For as long as I can remember I've heard debriefing officers in Washington say that the end of the world is near at hand, and I've been told to prepare for "the year of maximum danger" in 1954, 1962, 1968, 1974, 1983, and 1991. Possibly because the sounding of the final trumpet has been so often postponed, I no longer take the gentlemen at their word. The Navy lieutenant stands in front of a lovingly illuminated map overlay, pointing with an elongated baton to fleets and regiments and force levels, and I remember that the wealth and worldly power of the medieval Catholic Church depended upon its cornering of the market in terror. The lieutenant taps his pointer lightly on a crescent of aircraft carriers or a delicately shaded square of parachute brigades, and I think of the Jesuit art historian, soft-footed and subtle, who once conducted me on a tour of the Vatican, directing my attention to jeweled boxes and silver altarpieces, to ivory crosses inlaid with gold and lapis lazuli.

Critics of the military establishment tend to divide into two camps, those who object to the cost of its maintenance and those who complain of its incompetence. Neither caucus lacks reasons for its unhappiness, one of them classifying as extravagant waste the $200 billion contract awarded as recently as last October to Lockheed Martin for 3,000 F-35 Joint Strike Fighters, the second of them mentioning the loss of the war in Vietnam, the failure to rescue the Shah's Iran or conquer Saddam Hussein's Iraq. True enough and no doubt sad to say, but the critics allied with both the liberal and conservative schools of opinion usually manage to miss the point, failing to appreciate the military establishment's dual nature as successful business enterprise and reformed church. How well or how poorly the combined services perform their combat missions matters less than their capacity to generate cash and to sustain the images of omnipotence. Wars, whether won or lost, and the rumors of war, whether true or false, increase the budget allocations, stimulate the economy, clear the weapons inventory, and add to the stockpile of fear that guarantees a steady demand for security and promotes a decent respect for authority.

The country has been more or less continuously at war for sixty years, and we can't leave home without it: Otherwise we might not remember that we're the good guys or what would be playing at the movies. During the prosperous decade of the 1990s, the American public showed disturbing signs of weakness, too many people forgetting that without war they were apt to get lost in General von Moltke's "swamps of materialism." The breaking down of the Berlin Wall had brought an end to the skirmish with the Russians, the stock market was going nowhere but up, and the louche example being set by President Clinton in the White House (overweight, emotionally indulgent, morally slack) was bad for children and the weapons business. It wasn't that the American people no longer approved the uses of terrorism as a means of astute crisis management (in romantic Baghdad or picturesque Kosovo) or as a form of light entertainment (as video game, newspaper headline, and Hollywood plot device), but they had gotten into the habit of thinking that it was a product made exclusively for export.

At Washington policy conferences two and three years before the attack on the Pentagon and the World Trade Center, at least three of the four experts seated on the dais could be counted upon to say that nothing good would come of the American future unless and until the American people awakened to the fact that the world was a far more dangerous place than was dreamed of in the philosophy of Jerry Seinfeld and the World Wildlife Fund. I haven't spoken to any of the panelists since September 11, but I wouldn't be surprised to hear them say that although the attacks were abominable, a criminal outrage, and certainly a lot more destructive than might reasonably have been expected, sometimes people needed harsh reminders to recall them to the banners of noble virtue under which von Moltke's German army invaded Belgium in 1914 and massacred every man, woman, and child in the city of Dinant.

As for the critics who complain that President Bush has been sending ambiguous signals to the American people, once again I think they miss the point. They see a contradiction in the fact that one day he appears on television to say that we confront a future darkened by scenes of unimaginable horror and then, at the next day's press conference, tells everybody not to worry, to remain calm but stay alert, to keep up the strength of their buying in the nearest retail outlet.

Understood as a religious instead of a secular form of communication, the ritual makes liturgical sense. The president first ascends to the pulpit in the persona of the grim but righteous prophet, setting before the congregation a fiery vision of Hell, and then, in the bright sunlight on the steps of the church, he appears as the amiable vicar bidding his flock a kindly and reassuring farewell. Between the sermon and the benediction, a choir of media voices sings hymns of thanksgiving and anthems of praise, and men in uniform pass the collection plate.

2002

15. Road to Babylon

Misgovernment is of four kinds, often in combination. They are: 1) tyranny or oppression, of which history provides so many well-known examples that they do not need citing; 2) excessive ambition, such as Athens' attempted conquest of Sicily in the Peloponnesian War, Phillip II's of England via the Armada, Germany's twice-attempted rule of Europe by a self-conceived master race, Japan's bid for an empire of Asia; 3) incompetence or decadence, as in the case of the late Roman empire, the last Romanovs and the last imperial dynasty of China; and finally 4) folly or perversity.

—Barbara W. Tuchman

When President George W. Bush in his January State of the Union address pronounced the sentence of doom on Saddam Hussein ("America will do what is necessary to ensure our nation's security … I will not wait on events, while dangers gather"), I assumed that he was striking at a target of rhetorical convenience. The war on terrorism was not going as well as planned (Osama bin Laden still at large, Afghanistan not yet transformed into a Connecticut suburb, bombs exploding every seven or eight days on a bus in Israel), and who better than the tyrant of Baghdad to stand surrogate for all the world's evildoers? The man was undoubtedly a villain, a brutal psychopath who murdered children and poisoned village wells, stored biological weapons in hospitals, subjected his enemies to unspeakable torture, and imprisoned his friends in the cages of perpetual fear. Not a nice fellow. Who would not be glad to learn that he had retired from politics or died in a traffic accident? If Mr. Bush chose to express his disapproval in what he called "the language of right and wrong," who was I to deny him his demagogue's right to issue harebrained threats?

The opinion was not widely shared in New York among people possessed of an historical memory (i.e., by individuals who remembered the CIA's staging of "the glorious march to Havana" in the spring of 1961, or the "light at the end of the tunnel" so often seen by General William C. Westmoreland in the forests of Vietnam), but I held to it throughout the spring and early summer even as Mr. Bush mounted the flag-draped rostra at West Point and the Virginia Military Institute to threaten with the wrath of eagles far-off men of "mad ambitions," declaring null and void "the Cold War doctrines of deterrence and containment," championing the cause of "forward-looking and resolute ... preemptive action." When asked by worried friends and acquaintances whether the president was borrowing his geopolitical theory from the diaries of Joseph Stalin and Adolf Hitler, I assured them that the president didn't have the patience to read more than two or three pages of a Tom Clancy novel. True, the National Security Council was staffed by think-tank ideologues, and yes, some of the policy analysts strolling through the corridors of the White House imagined themselves wearing the uniform of the Bengal Lancers, but no, not even the Bush Administration was so stupid as to take up arms against a figment of its own imagination.

By the second week in August I understood that my assumptions were poorly placed. The spectacle of the American government making preparations for an invasion of Iraq suggested that maybe the Bush Administration was, in fact, stupid enough to call down air strikes on the last four paragraphs of one of the Pentagon's apocalyptic briefing papers. The president was hopping boldly out of golf carts in Texas and Maine to tell the traveling White House press corps that "regime change" was coming soon to downtown Baghdad; in appreciation of the president's enthusiasm and by way of reinforcing his credibility, the Defense Department was supplying the newspapers with documents supposedly top secret that sketched out tactical solutions to the problem of blitzkrieg. (The documents balanced the advantages of a simultaneous attack from three directions against the surprise of a swift commando raid, requisitions for 300,000 troops compared to those for only 80,000, something grandiloquent and imperial along the lines of the Japanese attack on Pearl Harbor as opposed to something stylish and postmodern with parachutes, two divisions of light infantry, and a diffusion of Turkish auxiliaries.) Senator Joseph Biden (D., Del.), chairman of the Senate Foreign Relations Committee, told a television news camera on August 4 that "there probably will be a war with Iraq. The only question is, is it alone, is it with others, and how long and how costly will it be?" On August 9 a delegation of Iraqi malcontents arrived in Washington to pledge their support of any overthrow of Saddam Hussein that the U.S. Army cared to pay for and arrange. Vice President Dick Cheney spoke to them by video conference from a mountain in Wyoming, reaffirming America's commitment to the principle of regime removal, and Donald Rumsfeld, the secretary of defense, bucked up their spirits with the smiling hope of freedom not far over the military horizon: "Wouldn't it be a wonderful thing if Iraq were similar to Afghanistan, if a bad regime was thrown out, people were liberated, food could come in, borders could be opened, repression could stop, prisons could be opened? I mean, it would be fabulous."

Fabulous for whom? The secretary didn't say; presumably he wasn't referring to the many thousands of people (American soldiers as well as Iraqi civilians) unlucky enough to be killed during the festivities, but none of the Washington correspondents asked why Afghanistan was such a wonderful tourist destination, or when and how it had come to pass that the bandits precariously enthroned in the palace at Kabul exemplified the goodness of free and democratic government. Nor did anybody spoil the upbeat mood of the secretary's press conference with moral or legal questions. Against every precedent in international law, in violation of the United Nations Charter, and without consent of the American Congress, the Bush Administration was proposing to sack a heathen city that had done it no demonstrable harm, and the news media were by and large happy to welcome the event with obedient commentary supportive of the belief that if America allowed Saddam to acquire weapons of mass destruction we would suffer consequences frightful to contemplate and terrible to behold. The lead editorial in *The Economist* on August 3 summed up the consensus of leading opinion in two sentences: "The honest choices now are to give up and give in, or to remove Mr. Hussein before he gets his bomb. Painful as it is, our vote is for war."

Give up to whom? Give in to what? The government didn't stoop to answer simpleminded questions; neither did the grand viziers of the print and broadcast media, who preferred to discuss the complexities of the logistics rather than the purpose of a policy apparently directed at nothing else except the fear of the future, that always dark and dangerous place, where, in five years or maybe ten, something bad is bound to happen. Competing television networks scheduled different time slots for the Pentagon's forthcoming fireworks display—before and after November's congressional election, in early January when the weather around Baghdad improved, next April because the Air Force needed six months to replenish its inventory of precision bombs. Competing newspaper columnists advanced competing adjectives to characterize the "extreme danger" presented to "the entire civilized world," but none of them offered evidence proving that Saddam possessed weapons likely to harm anybody who didn't happen to be living in Iraq; important military authorities appeared on the Sunday-morning talk shows to endorse policies of "forward deterrence" and "anticipatory self-defense," but none of them could think of a good reason why Saddam would make the mistake of attacking the United States; the Senate Foreign Relations Committee on July 31 and August 1 conducted hearings on the question of Iraq and learned that its expert witnesses couldn't say for certain whether they knew what they were talking about. The few shards of undisputed fact collected over two days of testimony suggested that Saddam doesn't sponsor Al Qaeda (or any of the other terrorist brigades that have asked him for money and explosives over the last eleven years), that the Iraqi army, never formidable, is less dangerous now than when it was routed in the four days of the Gulf War, the Iraqi Air Force of no consequence, the civilian economy too impoverished to support the reconstruction of the nuclear weapons program dismantled by the United Nations Special Commission between 1991 and 1998, and Saddam himself best understood as a small-time thug apt to deploy chemical or biological weapons (if he possesses chemical or biological weapons) only as a last and cowardly defense of his own person.

A government that must hold Senate hearings to discover whether it has a reason to go to war is a government that doesn't know the meaning of war. The inanity of the circumstance accounted for the mock-heroic tone of President Bush's golf-cart communiqués ("I call upon all nations to do everything they can to stop these terrorist killers. Thank you. Now watch this drive") as well as for the sublime complacence of the innumerable spokesmen testifying to the certainties of America's virtue, truth, justice, and power. Consistent with the latter set of assumptions, two of the statements presented to Senator Biden's committee invite lengthy quotation because they speak to the character of a government in the state of decadence. Thus, the heroics of Lieutenant General Thomas McInerney (retired), former assistant vice chief of staff of the U.S. Air Force:

> Thank you for this special opportunity to discuss a war of liberation to remove Saddam's regime from Iraq.
>
> I will not dwell on the merits of why he should be removed. Suffice it to say we must preempt threats such as those posed by Saddam Hussein ...
>
> I will now focus on the way to do it very expeditiously and with minimum loss of life in both the coalition forces, the Iraqi military and people themselves, and at the same time maintain a relatively

small footprint in the region ... Our immediate objective will be the following: help Iraqi people liberate Iraq and remove Saddam Hussein and his regime, eliminate weapons of mass destruction and production facilities, complete military operations as soon as possible, protect economic infrastructure targets, identify and terminate terrorism connections, establish an interim government as soon as possible. Our longer term objectives will be to bring a democratic government to Iraq using our post–World War II experiences with Germany, Japan, and Italy that will influence the region significantly.

Now I would like to broadly discuss the combined campaign to achieve these objectives using what I will call blitz warfare to simplify the discussion. Blitz warfare is an intensive 24-hour, seven days a week precision aircentric campaign supported by fast moving ground forces composed of a mixture of heavy, light, airborne, amphibious, special, covert operations working with opposition forces that all use effects-based base operations for their target set and correlate their timing of forces for a devastating violent impact ...

Using the Global Strike Task Force and Naval Strike Forces composed of over 1,000 land- and sea-based aircraft plus a wide array of air and sea launch Cruise missiles, this will be the most massive precision air campaign in history, achieving rapid dominance in the first 72 hours of combat ... [A]ll the Iraqi military forces will be told through the opposition forces in our information operations campaign that they have two choices: either help us change regime leadership and build the democracy, or be destroyed. In addition, commanders and men in weapons of mass destruction forces will be told that they will be tried as war criminals if they use their weapons against coalition forces or other nations.

I can understand the general being sensitive to the question of who is, and who is not, a war criminal. On the same day that he was fitting the First Amendment principle of free speech to the requirement of his information operations campaign (help us build democracy or be destroyed), the United States was demanding immunity from any and all judgments of the International Criminal Court that might find American soldiers guilty of crimes against humanity, which, given the collateral damage soon to be inflicted on the civilian population of Iraq, was a precaution both necessary and wise.

Other points in the general's testimony didn't seem as nicely judged. How does it happen that the "most massive precision air campaign in history" leaves but "a relatively small footprint in the region"? Even if one discounts the devastation of Baghdad as a minor and scarcely noticeable loss, what is to prevent the conflagration likely to erupt in the nearby countries of Saudi Arabia, Syria, and Iran once the U.S. Air Force has lit up the entire Muslim world with the purifying fires of civil and religious war? Who prevents Ariel Sharon from upgrading with nuclear weapons the Israeli program of "preemptive assassination," and, in the relatively sizable footprint of an oil price marked up to $50 or $70 a barrel, what happens to the economies of London, Paris, and New York?

The general revealed his plan for waste removal on the first day of the committee hearings, and on the second day Caspar Weinberger, a secretary of defense during the Reagan Administration, matched the general's notion of swift military victory in the desert with an equally fatuous theory of instant political rehabilitation. Observing that in Washington it was always easy to find excuses for inaction, Weinberger reminded the senators of the miraculous American descent on the Caribbean island of Grenada in April 1983:

> We went into Grenada with more troops than everybody thought we needed. And we had a very successful operation. And prevented the kidnapping and detention of American students. And we got out. And we got out in something under a month. And a couple of months after that, there was a free election. And we have not been back.

Not having kept up with events on Grenada, I have no reason to doubt Weinberger's happy news, and I'm sure that if Fidel

Castro were to send another invisible flotilla of gunboats, the U.S. Navy would defend the island against another invisible horde of savage Marxists. Elsewhere in the world, the record of American diplomatic achievement over the last thirty years doesn't inspire a similar degree of confidence. We're good with slogans, but we don't have much talent for fostering the construction of exemplary democracies; we tend to betray our allies, dishonor our treaties, and avoid the waging of difficult or extensive wars. Count through the list of foreign adventures since our hurried departure from Vietnam in April 1975, and we proceed, in random and unseemly sequence, to the exit from Iran and the flight from Lebanon, the pointless assault on Panama, the shutting down of the Gulf War without decisive victory, the abandonment of the Kurds in northern Iraq, the escape from Somalia, the refusal to intrude upon the killing in Rwanda or the Balkans. Drawn to despots whom we hire to represent our freedom-loving commercial interests (Diem, the Shah of Shahs, Somoza, Thieu, Marcos, Jonas Savimbi, Noriega, Saddam Hussein, King Fahd, Arafat, Mobutu Sese Seko, Ariel Sharon), we pretend that our new ally stands as a pillar of democracy in one or another of the world's poorer latitudes, and for however many years the arrangement lasts we send F-16s and messages of humanitarian concern. But then something goes amiss with the band music or the tin mines; the despot's palace guard doesn't know how to fire the machine guns, or fires them at the wrong people, and the prime minister's brother appropriates the traffic in cocaine. We decide that our virtue has been compromised, or that we no longer can afford the cost of the parliament, and we leave by helicopter from the roof of the embassy. The incoherence of our current policy in the Middle East (Saudi Arabia perceived by the Pentagon as our mortal enemy and by the White House as our dearest friend, President Bush committed on Tuesday to the establishment of a Palestinian state, on Thursday to the everlasting kingdom of Zion) suggests that the Washington travel agents have begun considering various estimated times of departure on the assumption that if we can run another "very successful operation" in and out "in something under a month," maybe Oliver North can get everybody to the roof of an embassy to watch the free election.

Fortunately for the republic, both Lieutenant General McInerney and Mr. Weinberger have retired from government service; not so fortunately, they retain the habit of mind that has guided the making of American diplomatic and military policy for the last thirty years. As stupefied as Dick Cheney or Donald Rumsfeld by the romance of imperial power, they speak from within a dream as old as the walls of Troy, and watching them bestow the favor of their prophecies on the Senate committee (to divine Saddam's plans, Senator Biden had said, "is like reading the entrails of goats"), it occurred to me that maybe the time had come to reread Thucydides' *History of the Peloponnesian War*. Much of the story I'd long forgotten, but I remembered that Athens corrupted its democracy and brought about the ruin of its empire by foolishly attempting the conquest of Sicily, and when I found the relevant chapters (the debate in the Athenian assembly prior to sending a fleet westward into the Ionian Sea), it was as if I were reading the front page of that morning's *New York Times* or the Pentagon's *Defense Planning Guidance*.

Athens in the winter of 415 B.C. stands alone as the preeminent hegemon of Greece. Sparta for the moment has lost its appetite for war, and the Athenians wish to extend their sovereignty over what was then the whole of the known world, not only as far as Sicily but also beyond Carthage to the Pillars of Hercules. Sophists sit around in the wrestling schools sketching with sticks in the sand the map of the Libyan coastline; old men in wine shops babble of victories promised by Egyptian oracles. Ambassadors arrive from Sicily in late March with news of trouble and a request for military assistance. The city of Syracuse threatens to seize the Athenian colony of Segesta, and how can the heirs of noble Pericles stomach so brazen an insult to their pride? What if the Syracusans took it into their heads to attack the glory of Athens?

Uproar and loud shouts of defiance. The impetuous Alcibiades presents the case for "forward deterrence" and "anticipatory self-defense," saying that it is in the nature of Athens to do great deeds. As certain as Lieutenant General McInerney of the city's military power, he assures the assembly that Syracuse is easy prey, weak and badly governed.

One does not only defend oneself against a superior power when one is attacked; one rakes measures in advance to prevent the attack materializing. And it is not possible for us to calculate, like housekeepers, exactly how much empire we want to have.

More uproar. Louder shouts of defiance. The Athenians know as little about Sicily as Senator Biden knows about Iraq ("For the most part ignorant of the size of the island and of the numbers of its inhabitants," says Thucydides, "they did not realize that they were taking on a war of almost the same magnitude as their war against the Peloponnesians"), but they are not the kind of men who stoop to count a crowd of mere barbarians.

Prudent Nicias thinks the Athenians too reckless in their enthusiasm. Like Alcibiades a general, but older and not as eager in his ambition, Nicias raises doubts similar to the ones released in the newspapers during the third week of August by several senior Republican statesmen (among them House Majority Leader Dick Armey and Brent Scowcroft, a former national security adviser) clearly worried both by President Bush's simplistic notions of geopolitics and by the absence of allies, either Arab or European, willing to join the American march on Baghdad. They employed a modern vocabulary, but they could have borrowed the substance of their advice from the speech that Thucydides assigns to Nicias:

In going to Sicily you are leaving many enemies behind you, and you apparently want to make new ones there and have them also on your hands ... [E]ven if we did conquer the Sicilians, there are so many of them and they live so far off that it would be very difficult to govern them. It is senseless to go against people who, even if conquered, could not be controlled, while failure would leave us much worse off than we were before we made the attempt ... [T]he next best thing is to make a demonstration of our power and then, after a short time, go away again. We all know that what is most admired is what is farthest off and least liable to have its reputation put to the test ... The right thing is that we should spend our new gains at home and on ourselves instead of on these exiles who are begging for assistance and whose interest it is to tell lies and make us believe them, who have nothing to contribute themselves except speeches, who leave all the danger to others and, if they are successful, will not be properly grateful, while if they fail in any way they will involve their friends in their own ruin.

The argument fails to make an impression. So excessive is the enthusiasm of the majority, says Thucydides, "that the few who actually were opposed to the expedition were afraid of being thought unpatriotic if they voted against it, and therefore kept quiet." The assembly declares for war, and over the next several months Athens musters an invasion fleet conforming to the current Pentagon doctrine of "overwhelming force" (134 triremes, expensively gilded; impressive numbers of archers, slingers, and javelin throwers; merchant vessels stocked with soothsayers and cavalry horses), and on a sunny day in July 415 B.C., trumpets blow, priests pour wine into golden bowls, and "by far the most costly and splendid" expedition "ever sent out by a single city" sails to its appointment with destruction.

During the last weeks of August 2002, it was hard to miss the newspaper reports of a splendid and costly American force gathering in the Middle East—merchant vessels putting to sea loaded with armored vehicles, helicopters, large stores of ammunition; the air base at Qatar upgraded with a runway convenient to heavy bombers and equipped with tents capable of housing 3,800 troops; a premium of $2 a barrel added to the price of Arabian oil to meet any sudden shift of supply or demand. Speaking to a battery of press cameras in Crawford, Texas, President Bush said that yes, he was aware of questions about the wisdom of invading Iraq (the doubts expressed both by members of his own party and, increasingly, in various alarmed sectors of the national news media), and yes, he would "listen very carefully" to what other people had to say, but no, he didn't think it necessary to complicate the decision with too much extraneous discussion. "America needs to know," he said, "I'll be making up my mind based upon the latest intelligence and how best to protect our own country plus our friends and allies."

Unwilling to expose "the latest intelligence" to the vulgar, democratic light of day, the president reserves the right to do what he, and he alone ("forward-looking and resolute," as brave as Alcibiades, disinclined to "wait on events, while dangers gather"), deems just. Taken together with the proven incompetence of the American intelligence agencies and the delusions of military grandeur cherished by the secretary of defense, the president's belated assurance that he would "continue to consult" ("When I say I'm a patient man, I mean I'm a patient man ... ") sounded both grudging and false. He had been shaking the fist of war at Iraq for two years, talking up the prospect of "regime change" to audiences both foreign and domestic, and how could the noble heir to the throne of Teddy Roosevelt retreat from his promise of retribution frightful to contemplate and terrible to behold?

The question was framed not by the president himself but by several Washington operatives closely allied with the administration and currently serving on the Pentagon's Defense Review Board. James Schlesinger, former secretary of defense, spoke for the jingoist majority: "Given all we have said as a leading world power about the necessity of regime change in Iraq means that our credibility would be badly damaged if that regime change did not take place."

The ancient Greeks at least had a prize in view—the harbors of Sicily and the wealth of Carthage; the Bush Administration erases the distinction between the reasons of state and the uses of publicity, and if we invade Iraq apparently we'll be doing so to make credible the president's boyish and theatrical saber-rattling with a blurb from the U.S. Air Force.

As a form of misgovernment that satisfies all the definitions set forth at the head of this essay in the epigraph borrowed from Barbara Tuchman's book *The March of Folly*, I can think of none more disastrous than the failure to distinguish fiction from fact, to substitute for the waging of war the making of war movies. Mark Twain remarked on the stupidity in 1905 during the American occupation of the Philippines. Objecting to the fraudulent piety of statesmen who don't know what they're saying, Twain wrote a story, "The War Prayer," in which an "aged stranger" enters a church where the congregation has been listening to a heroic sermon about the glory to be won in battle by young patriots armed with the love of God. Motioning the startled minister to stand aside, the aged stranger improvises a bitter peroration that makes clear the true meaning of the prayer:

O Lord our God, help us to tear their soldiers to bloody shreds with our shells; help us to cover their smiling fields with the pale forms of their patriot dead; help us to drown the thunder of the guns with the shrieks of their wounded, writhing in pain; help us to lay waste their humble homes with a hurricane of fire: help us to wring the hearts of their unoffending widows with unavailing grief; help us to turn them out roofless with their little children to wander unfriended the wastes of their desolated land in rags and hunger and thirst, sports of the sun flames of summer and the icy winds of winter, broken in spirit, worn with travail, imploring Thee for the refuge of the grave and denied it—for our sakes who adore Thee, Lord, blast their hopes, blight their lives, protract their bitter pilgrimage, make heavy their steps, water their way with their tears, stain the white snow with the blood of their wounded feet! We ask it, in the spirit of love, of Him Who is the Source of Love, and Who is the ever-faithful refuge and friend of all that are sore beset and seek His aid with humble and contrite hearts. Amen.

The story didn't see the light of print until 1923, thirteen years after Twain's death. The editors to whom he tendered the manuscript thought it "unsuitable" for publication at a moment of high and patriotic feeling.

2002

16. Hail Caesar!

Allow the President to invade a neighboring nation, whenever he shall deem it necessary to repel an invasion ... and you allow him to make war at pleasure. ... If, to-day, he should choose to say he thinks it necessary to invade Canada, to prevent the British from invading us, how could you stop him? You may say to him, "I see no probability of the British invading us," but he would say to you, "Be silent: I see it, if you don't."
—Abraham Lincoln

After the pretense of a debate that lasted less than a week, Congress on October 11 invested President George W. Bush with the power to order an American invasion of Iraq whenever it occurred to him to do so, for whatever reason he might deem glorious or convenient. Akin to the ancient Roman practice of enthroning a dictator at moments of severe crisis, the joint resolution was hurried into law by servile majorities in both a Senate (77–23) and a House of Representatives (296–133) much relieved to escape the chore—tiresome, unpopular, time-consuming, poorly paid—of republican self-government. The sergeants-at-arms didn't take the trouble to dress up the occasion with a slaughter of sacrificial goats or the presentation of a bull to Apollo, but the subtext of the vote could be understood as a submissive prayer:

> Our President is a Great General; he will blast Saddam Hussein and rescue us from doom. To achieve this extraordinary mission he needs extraordinary powers, so extraordinary that they don't exist in law. The barbarians are at the gates, but our general is all-knowing, and he sees what we cannot. Great is Caesar; God must be with him.

I don't know whether Diane Sawyer appeared on camera to release a fluttering of doves, but the prophets in the temples of the institutional news media didn't forget the business with the mirrors and the smoke. Following the scripts pre-positioned by the White House and the Pentagon, the chorus of solemn editorial voices interpreted the policy of preemptive bombing, precision-guided and courteously brief, as a form of compassionate conservatism. It wasn't that America would go willingly to war, but neither could it allow the forces of nuclear darkness to gather in the palaces of Baghdad. War was never easy and not to be lightly undertaken, but catastrophe loomed on both the far and near horizons, and who could doubt that Saddam must be destroyed? Not Citigroup or ExxonMobil; not the *New York Times*, CBS, the *Washington Post*, NBC, the *Wall Street Journal*, Fox News, or *USA Today*.

A few objections showed up on the margins of consensus—in political journals of modest circulation, the Saturday op-ed pages and National Public Radio, among a scattering of guests on cable television—but none of them were loud enough to disabuse the parade marshals in Washington of their fond assumption that the votes in Congress fairly represented the electorate's faith in God's will and Caesar's sword.

The news analysts cited the corroborating testimony of the opinion polls—a 70 percent approval rating for President Bush, 60 percent in favor of sending the Army to exterminate Saddam—but in New York during the months of September and October I could find little trace or sign of the militant spirit presumably eager to pat the dog of war. Not once in six weeks did I come across anybody who thought that the president had made a coherent argument in favor of an invasion of Iraq. Whether at lunch with film producers in Greenwich Village or at dinner among investment bankers overlooking Central Park, the commentary on the president's repeated attempts at explanation invariably descended into sarcasm. Who could take seriously the reasoning of a man armed with so few facts—no proof of Saddam's connection to Al Qaeda, no indication that Iraq threatens the United States (or even the nearby states of Jordan, Saudi Arabia, and Iran), no evidence that Saddam possesses weapons of mass destruction, the presidential indictment based on surveillance photographs too secret to be seen, on old stories of past atrocities and the premise that America "did not ask for this present challenge, but we accept it"?

The last statement, drawn from the president's speech in Cincinnati on October 7, prompted a civil rights lawyer the next morning at breakfast to mockery. "To whom does the man think he's talking?" she said. "To people so stupid that they can't see through the window of his lies? A Republican administration promotes a foreign war to hide the mess of its domestic politics, and the president asks us to believe that we're being attacked by Joseph Stalin?"

The lady voiced a New York opinion, and I accepted it as such. Given my long confinement in the city's spheres of literary influence, I don't know many people who admire President Bush or who feel anything but loathing for the reactionary scholars who teach him lessons in geography. In New York I expect to hear Bush compared to Little Lord Fauntleroy or Bernie Ebbers, and I take it for granted that nearly everybody else in the conversation shares my own low regard for the corporate-management theory that informs the making of American foreign policy.

What I didn't expect was the fierce opposition to the Iraqi adventure that I encountered elsewhere in the country. Traveling in California in September and October, and then in Oregon, Connecticut, and Virginia, I sought out fellow citizens unmarked by the stigmata of effete, liberal intellectualism—an aerospace engineer on the plane to Portland, a quorum of computer programmers in Hartford, two retired admirals on a golf course in San Diego, various unpublished social critics met with in hotel coffee shops and airport bars. It was as if I hadn't left New York. Never once did I find myself in the company of people who approved the Pentagon's strategies of "forward deterrence" and "anticipatory self-defense." The general opinion of President Bush wavered between the phrases "toy soldier" and "dangerous fool." A woman in San Francisco, a lifelong Republican who once had run a campaign headquarters for Governor Ronald Reagan, wondered whether the president had become stupefied by his desire for revenge. "I hear him say of Saddam that 'he tried to kill my Dad,' and I start to think that maybe I learn more about the White House from *The Sopranos* than from *The West Wing*." The aerospace engineer observed that many of the allegations brought against Saddam (possession of nuclear weapons, harboring terrorists, etc.) also would be charged to the account of the United States. "If we preemptively bomb other countries whenever we think we smell a rat," he said, "how can we not expect an increase in both the number and the violence of the attacks on us? Scrap the hope of international law, and all you've got left is the old news that might makes right; the strong do as they please, the weak do as they're told. Wonderful for military contractors; not so good for everybody else."

The more senior of the two admirals made a similar point. As a student of both the Spanish and the Austro-Hungarian empires, he had noticed that warrior kings invariably impoverish their people while pretending concern for their safety, and on the tee at the twelfth hole he remembered a maxim that had been impressed upon him at the Naval War College by a lecturer quoting the historian A. J. P. Taylor: "Though the object of being a Great Power is to be able to fight a Great War, the only way of remaining a Great Power is not to fight one."

Other voices in the wilderness asked questions that seldom make their way past the velvet rope at ABC News or the headwaiters at *Time* magazine—"Why must the security of every other nation in the world be subordinated to the comfort of the United States?" "I thought we learned from our mistake in Vietnam that we're no good at the mechanics of regime change?" "If Bush means what he says about a war on terrorism, why doesn't he begin by disarming the Arab and Israeli terrorists in Jerusalem and the Gaza Strip?"

Neither the candor nor the intelligence of the discussions beyond the perimeter of Washington reached the floor of what the media falsely advertised as the "debate" in Congress. "Appearance of debate" would have come closer to the mark, a theme-park performance, paltry in its substance, unctuous and condescending in its tone. A few forthright speeches proved exceptions to the rule of cowardice, and I was glad of the chance to hear Nancy Pelosi (D., Calif.) in the House as well as Robert Byrd (D., W.Va.) in the Senate. Pelosi counted the costs to the American economy of an unnecessary war waged to pay the bill for the administration's incompetent diplomacy; Byrd declaimed against both the ignoble scurrying to dispose of the question of Iraq ("Haste is blind and improvident, Mr. President, blind and improvident") and the betrayal of the Constitution ("What a shame. Fie upon the Congress"), and it was among his remarks that I found the apposite quotation at the head of this essay, Lincoln in 1848 writing a letter to William Herndon to explain his opposition to the Mexican–American War.

Most of what else I could hear or read of the speech making on Capitol Hill consisted of threadbare propaganda or rank hypocrisy. The time taken up with quibbling over the syntax and punctuation of the "Authorization for the Use of Military Force Against Iraq" rescued all present from the embarrassment of having to talk about the abdication of their legislative authority to the whim of a lying president. Nobody questioned the corruption of language that elevated random acts of criminal violence to the declaration of World War III; nor did anybody concede the brutal truth that no power on earth—not the CIA, the United States Marines, the Department of Homeland Security; not God or Yale or Caesar—can hold the United States harmless against the risk or fear of death.

Instead of arguing with one another, the politicians read prepared statements into the C-SPAN cameras, striking handsome poses, producing certificates of their moral character and worth, expressing their "deep concern" for human suffering and their "profound awareness" of the distinction between war and peace, before bowing to the knee of circumstance and to what for six months they had known would prove to be the will of the majority.

The question is why. Why the lack of courage on the part of our elected representatives, and why the hurry, as Tom Daschle, the Senate majority leader, put it on *Meet the Press* on October 6, "to move on"? Move on to where? President Bush had served Congress with notice of its irrelevance, and who would want to annoy the man by making a rude noise? Not Senator Daschle, not any loyal and patriotic public servant glad to escape the unpleasantness of speaking truth to power. Better to move on, quietly and as soon as possible, to a campaign rally in South Dakota, where a senator could count on a show of respect (also a round of applause and an apple pie) from voters grateful for a defense contract, a farm subsidy, or a dam.

The Sunday-morning talk shows rounded up the usual suspects to provide the usual set of dismal answers as to why so many prominent Democrats (among them Senators Hillary Clinton, John Kerry, and Diane Feinstein) deserted both the army of their constituents and the flags of their convictions—the polls showing strong flows of patriotic sentiment, the Republicans suborned by the White House and the Democrats worried about the positioning of their images in the autumn election campaigns, political partisanship feckless and unseemly in a time of trouble, the president in need of loud congressional support in order to extort an effectively punitive resolution from the U.N. Security Council.

Few or none of the assertions could match the weight of the follow-up questions. If the poll results published under the newspaper headline on page one showed 60 percent of the respondents supporting an invasion of Iraq, the further analysis of the numbers continued on page thirty-four showed the support to be tentative and ambivalent—37 percent unless the invasion was undertaken at the behest of the United Nations and in concert with numerous allies; not even a bare majority persuaded that Saddam presents a more imminent threat to the United States than the agents of Al Qaeda, 40 percent believing that President Bush's rush to war follows from motives having less to do with the security of the United States than with the security of his administration's hold on power—that is, a shell game not unlike the one with which Saddam entertains the people of Iraq.

Nor did the voters seem to be in a mood to punish displays of principle or conscience. During the three days after his speech to Congress, Senator Byrd received 18,000 telephone calls and more than 50,000 letters and emails approving of what he'd said; demonstrations protesting a war in Iraq made their way onto college campuses and into Central Park (25,000 people assembled on the East Meadow on October 6).

If the Sunday talk show wisdom didn't answer to the facts, why then the silence of the lambs? Possibly because the Congress represents the constituency of the frightened rich—not the will or the spirit of what was once a democratic republic but the interest of a scared and selfish oligarchy anxious to preserve its comforts in the impregnable vaults of military empire. The grotesque maldistribution of the country's wealth over the last thirty years has brought forth a class system fully outfitted with the traditional accessories of complacence, stupidity, and pride. People supported by incomes of $10 or $15 million a year not only mount a different style of living than those available to an income of $50,000 or even $150,000 a year, they acquire different habits of mind. They are reluctant to think for themselves, afraid of the future, careful to expatriate their profits in offshore tax havens, disinclined to trust a new hairdresser or a new idea, grateful for the security of gated residential protectorates, reassured by reactionary political theorists who say that history is at an end and that if events should threaten to prove otherwise (angry mobs rising in Third World slums to beg a chance at freedom or demand a piece of the action) America will send an army to exterminate the brutes.

Not an inspiring set of attitudes, but representative of the social class that owns our news media, staffs the White House, and pays for our elections. If neither the Republicans nor the Democrats have stumbled upon a forceful or generous political idea since 1968, it's because the widening distance between the American citizenry and the American elites obliges the candidates of both parties to go for money to the same body of comfortable opinion (the few hundred thousand individuals, interest groups, or corporations that contribute more than $1,000 to any single campaign) content to think that the idealism implicit in what Benjamin Franklin recognized as the American experiment has run its course, served its purpose, gone far enough. Whether sporting lapel pins in the shape of elephants or donkeys, the members of Congress dance to the tune of the same big but nervous money, the differences in their political views reduced to a choice between the grilled or potted shrimp.

It's conceivable that we might soon see a change in the program. The American citizenry isn't as dumb as the American elites condescendingly like to think and believe, and if it can be generally understood that an ill-conceived war with Iraq comes to us courtesy of the same feeblemindedness that set up the Enron and WorldCom swindles, we might learn to elect politicians who speak to our courage and intelligence rather than to our weakness and fear.

2003

17. Light in the Window

You may not be interested in war, but war is interested in you.
—Leon Trotsky

As a promotional venue for any season's collection of worthy thoughts and tasteful sentiments, the Sunday *New York Times Magazine* commands the authority of the show windows at Bergdorf Goodman. Of the moment and with the trend, the editors arrange the sociopolitical merchandise in ways meant to attract discriminating shoppers in the markets of received opinion—well-informed and right-thinking people, competently educated and decently affluent, alive to the similarities in the works of Versace and Matisse, fond of animals and the several shades of beige. Although the editors occasionally make space for ideas a trifle too advanced for some of their less sophisticated readers in Oklahoma or eastern Queens, they don't take chances with the big-ticket items or with what they judge to be the consensus of uptown money and downtown style.

Which is why, on first glancing at the no-nonsense cover lines for the issue of January 5—"The American Empire (Get Used to It)"—I knew that I was in the presence of an important fashion statement. The United States Army (very with it, very now) was on its way to an invasion of Iraq, there to exhibit a modish line of summer weapons at the military equivalent of a runway show, and the *Times* had gone to the trouble of furnishing a helpful program note: what to watch for, when to applaud, how to think about this year's new and exciting look in geopolitics. Michael Ignatieff, a brand-name foreign-policy intellectual recruited from the faculty of Harvard University, matched the assertive tone of his lead article to the red, white, and blue block lettering (not fussy, very bold) of the magazine's cover art:

> Americans are required, even when they are unwilling to do so, to include Europeans in the governance of their evolving imperial project. The Americans essentially dictate Europe's place in this new grand design. The United States is multilateral when it wants to be, unilateral when it must be; and it enforces a new division of labor in which America does the fighting, the French, British and Germans do the police patrols in the border zones and the Dutch, Swiss and Scandinavians provide the humanitarian aid.

An editor's note identified Ignatieff as the director of the Carr Center at the Kennedy School of Government, also as a teacher of "human rights" well versed in the syllabus of the world's sorrow. A man of sense and sensibility who had spent a lot of time "walking around" in the "frontier zones of the new American empire" in Bosnia, Kosovo, and Afghanistan, and who knew, as he himself said, that it wasn't enough to draw "the big picture" on the wall of a classroom in Cambridge, that one really must "get out of Harvard Yard" if one wants to "get really close to the intimate, tragic detail of it all."

And what did he learn, the professor, from his poking around in Afghan tents and Balkan graves? If nothing else, how to write sententious and vacant prose, most of it indistinguishable from the ad copy for an Armani scarf or a Ferragamo shoe. Too much direct quotation from the professor's text might be mistaken for unkindness, and I enter three of his *obiter dicta* into the record only because they fairly represent the attitudes currently in vogue among the marketers of the country's preferred wisdom:

> Imperial powers do not have the luxury of timidity, for timidity is not prudence; it is a confession of weakness.

> [The United States] remain[s] a nation in which flag, sacrifice and martial honor are central to national identity.

> The question, then, is not whether America is too powerful but whether it is powerful enough. Does it have what it takes to be grandmaster of what Colin Powell has called the chessboard of the world's most inflammable region?

If Ignatieff doesn't for a moment doubt that America has what it takes to play chess with Genghis Khan or Darius the Great, neither does he say anything that hasn't been said, repeatedly over the last nine months, by the cadre of Washington propagandists, both Democrat and Republican, writing for the policy journals that supply the government with its think-tank thoughts and Sunday-morning media phrases—America, the world's unrivaled hegemon, an empire in fact if not in name, its sovereign power the only hope for less fortunate nations groping toward the light of free markets and liberal democracy. Be not timid, do not flinch. Shoulder the burden of civilization and its discontents. Lift from the continents of Africa and Asia the weight of despotic evildoers. Know that if America does the fighting, other people will do the dying. Learn to appreciate the refined elegance (conceptually minimalist, gracefully postmodern) of high-altitude precision bombing.

When delivered by one of the rabid polemicists allied with Lockheed Martin, Fox News, or the Baptist church, the same message usually comes with a tactical objective in view—the seizure of the Iraqi oil fields, the destruction of Hugo Chávez, the safety of Israel. Ignatieff imparts to it an air of languid abstraction, not wanting to disturb anybody with the "intimate, tragic detail of it all." He briefly raises the question of terminology (America as democratic republic, America as military empire), but then he goes on to say that it doesn't make much difference how America chooses to see itself. The words don't matter. The country is what it is, so rich and powerful and good that it can't help but do what is just and right and true.

Never having met Ignatieff or read his books, I don't know how he defines his politics, or whether he construes himself as a liberal, a conservative, a lapsed Marxist, or a reconstructed Tory. After making my way through the 7,000 words of his article for the *Times*, I still couldn't guess who were his enemies and who were his friends, and it occurred to me that much the same can be said about most of the government officials and high-end journalists whose commentaries have decorated the display windows of the national news media for the better part of the last twenty years. They strike poses and adopt attitudes, pleased to imagine that politics amount to little else except the staging of *tableaux vivants*, the crowd scenes and the musical accompaniment matched with the PowerPoints in the season's polling data. The reliance on theatrical effects long ago destroyed the credibility of the voices of conscience associated with liberal causes and the Democratic Party. Too many nominally left-wing defenders of the realm couldn't disguise their loyalty to the right-wing Mouton Rothschild, their rhetorical tours de force (on behalf of racial equality, social justice, freedom of expression) too laughably at odds with their views of the sea from a sundeck in East Hampton. A similar fate befell the apostles of the conservative truth soon after the election of Ronald Reagan. The actor arrived in Washington under the impression that he had been hired to make a movie, and it was only a matter of months before the claque of his apologists in the news media began to think of aircraft carriers as set decorations.

Reading Ignatieff I was reminded of a dinner-table conversation in Washington in the mid-1980s at which an authoritative syndicated columnist explained that he was "depressed" by "the quality of the regime" in Nicaragua. Judging only by the tone of his voice, I might have guessed that he was talking about a second-rate wine or a Caribbean resort hotel gone to seed and no longer fit to welcome golf tournaments. He wasn't concerned about Nicaragua's capacity to harm the United States; the army was small and ill equipped, the mineral assets not worth the cost of a first-class embassy. Nor did the columnist think the governing junta particularly adept at exploiting "the virus of Marxist revolution." What troubled him was the "indecorousness of the regime." Nicaragua was in bad taste.

In the similarly detached context of a Fifth Avenue cocktail party on the Tuesday after the publication of Ignatieff's article, I listened to two political correspondents, one from *Vanity Fair* and the other from *Newsweek*, analyze the differences between the Democratic and Republican attitudes toward the liberation of Iraq. The important question was aesthetic, not geopolitical; not whether Saddam Hussein deserved to die a coward's death (the fact so obvious that it didn't bear discussion), but how to accessorize the coverage of the assault on Baghdad, whether it was best to present it as a crusade ordered by God or as a hostile corporate takeover arranged by a consortium of Texas oil companies. The first option indicated a heartland sensibility, the second an instinct perversely urban.

I mention the conversation because, like the brass-band promotion of Ignatieff's article in the *New York Times Magazine*, it speaks to the insouciance with which so many people party to the formulation of our public argument regard the current recasting of the country's laws. The government in Washington makes no secret of its wish to eliminate the freedoms of speech, thought, and movement synonymous with the workings of a democratic republic, and where is the senator or syndicated columnist who gives voice to an intelligible objection? To the civilian populations of Basra or Islamabad it might not make much difference whether the United States styles itself hegemon or republic—the bombs fall from the same clouds, the buildings collapse into the same ruins, and who doesn't know that an F-16 by any other name is still an F-16? For the residents of Philadelphia and Colorado Springs, however, the words should matter; despite Ignatieff's bland assurances to the contrary, so should their supporting connotations. A government that becomes accustomed to thinking of itself as an empire falls easily into the habit of issuing imperial decrees and soon acquires the characteristics that Secretary of State Colin Powell last February attributed to a failed state, "unrepresentative of its people ... rife with corruption," blighted by "a lack of transparency," thinking that "it can achieve a position on the world stage through development of weapons of mass destruction that will turn out to be fool's gold ... " The secretary was speaking of North Korea and Iraq; he might as well have been talking about Vice President Dick Cheney's vision of a reconfigured United States.

If not as a concerted effort to restrict the liberties of the American people, how else does one describe the Republican agenda now in motion in the nation's capital? Backed by the specious promise of imminent economic recovery and secured by the guarantee of never-ending war, the legislative measures mobilized by the White House and the Congress suggest that what the Bush Administration has in mind is not the defense of the American citizenry against a foreign enemy but the protection of the American oligarchy from the American democracy. In every instance, and no matter what the issue immediately at hand, the bias is the same—more laws limiting the rights of individuals, fewer laws restraining the rights of property:

1. The systematic transfer of the nation's wealth from the union of the poor to the confederacy of the rich. President Bush's new plan to exclude from taxation all corporate dividends received by individuals, at the same time lowering the income-tax rates previously scheduled to take effect between now and 2009, assigns the bulk of the refund (64 percent) to the wealthiest 5 percent of the nation's taxpayers, more than half of the award to people earning at least $200,000 a year, a quarter of it to people earning more than $1 million a year.
2. The easing of environmental regulations on the energy industries in New England.
3. The opening of the national forests in the Pacific Northwest and the Arctic National Wildlife Refuge to further expropriation by the oil, gas, mining, and timber industries.
4. The persistent issuing of health-insurance regulations intended

to subvert and eventually overturn the 1973 Supreme Court ruling, *Roe* v. *Wade*, that recognized a woman's freedom to decide whether or not she will give birth to a child.

5. The reinforcing of the monopolies held by the big media syndicates on the country's systems of communication.

6. Outfitting the banks and credit-card agencies with the privilege to sell to the highest bidders any or all of the personal data acquired from their customers.

7. The broad expansion of the government's police powers under the USA PATRIOT and Homeland Security acts, the Justice Department reserving to itself the right to tap anybody's phone and open everybody's mail.

8. A series of bills in Congress meant to reduce the nation's health-care costs by denying medical services to people too poor to pay for the upkeep of the insurance companies.

9. The nomination to the federal appeals courts of judges apt to find legal precedents in the pages of the Bible rather than in the Constitution.

As if wishing to leave nobody in doubt about the political bias now afoot in Washington, President Bush took the trouble to juxtapose his endorsement of affirmative action for the rich (the speech to the Economic Club of Chicago on January 7 favoring the removal of all taxes paid on corporate dividends) with his objection to affirmative action for the poor (his remarks from the White House on January 15 finding fault with the admissions policies at the University of Michigan). The interval of a week between the two announcements was brief enough to impress the lesson upon a national television audience known for its short attention span, but among most of the upscale journalists in New York (of the moment, with the trend) the point was by and large ignored. The best and most tasteful opinion doesn't countenance the notion of class warfare. President Bush rejects even the suggestion of such a thing as wrongheaded and maybe treasonous, partisan agitprop distributed by envious Democrats and would-be demagogues. His indignant tabling of the proposition, in a speech on January 9 at a Virginia company that produces American flags, was strongly seconded by the right-thinking managers of the nation's better media boutiques, who regard the subject as preposterously *démodé*—threadbare cant found in the attic of the 1960s with the rest of the sensibility (go-go boots, *Sgt. Pepper*, Woodstock, Vietnam) that embodied the failed hopes of a discredited decade.

The media take pride in their exquisite collections of historical certainty, and so, being persuaded that class war invariably manifests itself as an uprising of the angry poor against the greedy rich (pitchforks, sansculottes, the guillotine), and having seen the reassuring photographs of both Teddy and Franklin Roosevelt, they also know that all American politicians are, by definition, gregarious and open-hearted people, industrious, well meaning, occasionally eccentric but always friendly, sometimes caught, unwillingly and through no fault of their own, in the webs of corrupt circumstance. Armed with combat-hardened anecdotes excerpted from the writings of Tom Clancy and the late Stephen Ambrose, our high-toned window dressers like to imagine that politics are about the more or less attractive arrangement of words, not about who gets to do what to whom, at what price, and for how long. Their gift for clever decoration serves the interest of the oligarchy currently at home in Washington (more frightened of the freedom of the American people than of the tyranny of Saddam Hussein), and obscures the fact of a war waged by the angry rich against what they perceive to be the legions of the greedy poor.

2003

18. Cause for Dissent

The dissenter is every human being at those moments of his life when he resigns momentarily from the herd and thinks for himself.
—Archibald MacLeish

As a director of the government's ministry of propaganda during World War II, Archibald MacLeish knew that dissent seldom walks on stage to the sound of warm and welcoming applause. As a poet and later the librarian of Congress, he also knew that liberty has ambitious enemies and that the survival of the American democracy depends less on the size of its armies than on the capacity of its individual citizens to rely, if only momentarily, on the strength of their own thought. We can't know what we're about, or whether we're telling ourselves too many lies, unless we can see or hear one another think out loud. Tyranny never has much trouble drumming up the smiles of prompt agreement, but a democracy stands in need of as many questions as its citizens can ask of their own stupidity and fear. Voiced in the first-person singular and synonymous with the courage of a mind that a former editor of *Harper's*

Magazine once described as "unorganized, unrecognized, unorthodox and unterrified," dissent is what rescues the democracy from a slow death behind closed doors.

Unpopular during even the happiest of stock-market booms, in time of war dissent attracts the attention of the police. The parade marshals regard any wandering away from the line of march as unpatriotic and disloyal; the unlicensed forms of speech come to be confused with treason and registered as crimes, and in the skyboxes of the news media august personages reaffirm America's long-standing alliance with God and the Statue of Liberty. Counting through the list of the country's exemplary virtues—a just cause, an invincible air force, a noble truth—they find no reasons for dissent. On the threshold of a war in Iraq, I can think of seven:

1. Agitprop

I don't know how else to characterize the Bush Administration's effort to convince the public of the need for an immediate American assault on the land of Mordor. Whether expressed in the language of religious exorcism by President Bush in his annual message to Congress or chopped into nourishing sound bites by National Security Adviser Condoleezza Rice for the fans of CNN's *Larry King Live*, the government's relentless ad campaign rests on the principle announced nearly a year ago by Secretary of Defense Donald Rumsfeld at a press conference in Brussels. Asked by a crowd of European journalists for proof of the assertion that weapons of mass destruction confronted the United States with a clear and present danger, Rumsfeld said, "The absence of evidence is not evidence of absence."

Secretary of State Colin Powell didn't come up with a substantially different explanation in early February when he presented the United Nations Security Council with a slide show meant to serve as a trailer for the forthcoming action movie soon to be filmed in the deserts of Mesopotamia. The surveillance photographs of Iraqi trucks demanded the kind of arcane exposition that New York art critics attach to exhibitions of abstract painting. By way of adding drama to the performance, Powell held up a vial of white powder (meant to be seen as anthrax but probably closer in its chemistry to granulated sugar) and rolled tape of two satellite telephone intercepts of Iraqi military officers screaming at one another in Arabic, but he didn't provide an answer to the question: Why does America attack Iraq when Iraq hasn't attacked America? In lieu of demonstrable provocations Mr. Powell offered disturbing signs and evil portents, and when the voice of Osama bin Laden turned up a week later on an audiotape broadcast from Qatar, the secretary seized upon the occasion to discover a "partnership" between Al Qaeda and the government of Iraq. No such conclusion could be drawn from even a careless reading of the transcript, but to Mr. Powell the sending of a message (any message) proved that Osama bin Laden and Saddam Hussein somehow had morphed into the same enemy.

The secretary's PowerPoint slides didn't add to the sum of a convincing argument, but then neither did the advertising copy for the Spanish–American War or the sales promotions for the war in Vietnam, and if the agitprop failed to persuade the French, Russian, or Chinese representatives to the Security Council, it was more than good enough for the emissaries from the major American news media. Our television networks and large-circulation newspapers trade in the same commodity. They identify themselves as instruments of the American government rather than as witnesses beholden to the American people, and they bring to their work the talents and the haircuts of expensive corporate lobbyists. All but unanimous in their infatuation with President Bush (a Churchillian figure, sometimes Lincolnesque), they've been packing their safari hats ever since the navy sent the carriers to the Persian Gulf. In Secretary Powell's remarks to the U.N. the editors of the *Wall Street Journal* discovered echoes of Talleyrand and Metternich.

2. "We refuse to live in fear"

President Bush presented the statement to an audience in Cincinnati on October 7, and of all lies told by the government's faith healers and gun salesmen, I know of none as cowardly. Where else does the Bush Administration ask the American people to live except in fear? On what other ground does it justify its deconstruction of the nation's civil liberties?

Ever since the September 11 attacks on New York and Washington, no week has passed in which the government has failed to issue warnings of a sequel. Sometimes it's the director of the FBI, sometimes the attorney general or an unnamed source in the CIA or the Department of Homeland Security, but always it's the same message: suspect your neighbor and watch the sky; buy duct tape, avoid the Washington Monument, hide the children.

Let too many citizens begin to ask impertinent questions about the shambles of the federal budget or the disappearance of a forest in Montana and the government sends another law-enforcement officer to a microphone with a story about a missing tube of aluminum or a newly discovered nerve gas.

3. Somnambulism

Washington these days suffers no shortage of visionary geopoliticians touting the wonders of an American empire imposing, by act of conscience and force of arms, peace on earth and good will toward men. The prophets enjoy the patronage of power, some of them White House privy counselors, others advisers to the Pentagon, all of them utopian anarchists. They envision a slum-clearance project for the whole of the Islamic Middle East, Iraq the first in a series of model democracies soon to be erected in Syria, Iran, Libya, Egypt, and Saudi Arabia, and when reading their articles in the policy journals, I remember a remark I once came across in a novelist's description of four Marxist assassins seated at a cafe table in Paris in the 1920s: "They believe everything they can prove, and they can prove everything they believe."

The Bush Administration employs a good many ideologues afflicted with a similarly messianic turn of mind and who take for granted the stupefaction of an electorate too lazy to open its mail. Assuming a general state of political somnambulism not much different from their own, the authors of the government's press releases count on an audience that thinks of politics as trivial entertainment. The supposition isn't entirely wrong.

The successful operation of a democracy relies on acts of government by no means easy to perform, and for the last twenty years we have been unwilling to do the work. Choosing to believe that the public good comes to us at the discretion of private wealth, all politicians therefore as interchangeable as hotel bartenders, we don't bother to vote, don't read through the list of budget appropriations, content ourselves with the opinions advertised on prime-time television by talk-show guests holding up little vials of important news—sometimes anthrax, usually sugar. Our prosperity finances the habits of indolence. We leave the small print for the lawyers to clean and maybe press, and in place of an energetic politics we get by with nostalgic sentiment and the public-spirited postcards sent by PBS—elections a cascade of balloons, liberty a trust fund, and America the land in which the money never dies.

4. The Insolence of Office

In a recent and best-selling book, *Bush at War*, Bob Woodward presents a portrait of the president so flattering that had it been rendered in oil on canvas, the curator of the White House art collection might wish to hang it in the Blue Room. One of the bon mots that Woodward attributes to his subject could as easily have been attributed to Louis XIV: "That's the interesting thing about being the President. Maybe somebody needs to explain to me why they say something, but I don't feel like I owe anybody an explanation."

The administration's senior ministers share that view. Often petulant and openly contemptuous of opinions not their own, they listen to opposing argument with impatience and disdain.

At the United Nations last winter, when the French and German statesmen raised pointed questions about both the necessity and the timing of a police raid on Iraq, Mr. Rumsfeld received the skepticism as an insult. France and Germany, he said, spoke for an "old Europe" long ago reduced to a harmless tourist attraction—France a country famous for its vanity and pride; Germany stubborn and wrongheaded.

5. Negligence

The destruction of the World Trade Center evoked an immense surge of pro-American feeling everywhere in the world—in Cairo and Amman as well as in London and Paris. Within the brief span of nineteen months our government has managed to squander almost the whole of the asset. Mocked by its failure to find Osama bin Laden, the Bush Administration has bullied our allies, scorned the United Nations, subverted the principle of international law, recruited an angry host of new enemies, and exchanged the hard currency of our inherent idealism for the counterfeit coin of a hairbrained cynicism.

In return for what? A "regime change" in Afghanistan. The horsedrawn and all but helpless Taliban put to rout at a cost of more than $15 billion, Kabul remanded to the custody of a freedomloving warlord, and tranquility along the border of Pakistan achieved with a $1 billion bribe paid to the military dictatorship of General Pervez Musharraf.

6. Barbed Wire

Unable to erect a secure perimeter around the whole life and landscape of a free society, the government bureaus of public safety solve the technical problems by seeing to it that the society becomes less free. The USA PATRIOT Act has been reinforced so many times since it was first passed by Congress in October 2001 that by now the country's law-enforcement agencies have been equipped with as many powers as they choose to exercise—random search, unwarranted seizure, arbitrary arrest.

Every month brings with it some new proof of the frightened and punitive states of mind that inform the imposition of additional rules, more efficient procedures, further restrictions. My notes from the last week in January through the second week in February mention the dropping of a blue curtain over a tapestry of Pablo Picasso's *Guernica* outside the Security Council chambers (to spare Secretary Powell from the embarrassment of having to pose for photographs in front of a work of art depicting the horrors of war), Laura Bush canceling a poetry symposium at the White House when told that one or more of the poets might read an antiwar poem, the New York Police Department forbidding an antiwar march in front of the United Nations, a consortium of scientific journals (among them *Nature* and *The New England Journal of Medicine*) agreeing to censor any articles that might compromise national security, and then, most unequivocally, in January the Department of Transportation proposing to establish a system of records classifying any and all commercial airline passengers as suspected terrorists and thus subject to background investigations that might otherwise require a court order.

7. Sloth

The question most often asked of the American mission to Iraq can be reduced to two words: "Why now?" I've listened to numerous explanations—the weather, America's credibility at stake, Saddam about to poison Israel's reservoirs—but I suspect that the best answer is the simplest. War is easier than peace. The government elects to punish an enemy it perceives as weak because it's easier to send the aircraft carriers to the Persian Gulf than to attempt the harder task of making an American society not so wretchedly defaced by its hungry children, its crowded prisons, and its corporate thieves.

The Bush Administration owes its existence to our apathy and sloth; if we have allowed the American political argument to degenerate into mindless catchphrase and the fifteen-second sound bite, how can we not expect our government to think in the same language, to depend for its authority on the easy and patriotic lie, and whenever it doesn't know what else to do, to arrest mysterious strangers and bomb Iraq?

2003

19. Shock and Awe

If we go back to the beginning we shall always find that ignorance and fear have created gods; fancy, enthusiasm, or deceit has adorned or disfigured them; weakness worships them; credulity preserves them in life; custom regards them and tyranny supports them in order to make the blindness of men serve its own ends.

—Baron d'Holbach

When President Bush appeared in the White House on the evening of March 6 to announce the imminent scourging of Iraq, it was a wonder that he didn't speak in tongues. His topic was geopolitical, but his message was religious, the blank expression engraved on his face disquietingly similar to the thousand-yard stare of the true believer gazing into the mirror of eternity. Reading first from a prophetic text, and then, for the better part of an hour, answering questions from the assembled scribes and pharisees, the president bore witness to a revelation mounted on four pillars of holy wrath:

1. America allies itself with Christ and goes to war to rid the world of evil.
2. Iraq is Sodom, or possibly Gomorrah.
3. Saddam is the Devil's pawn.
4. Any nation that refuses to join the "coalition of the willing" deserves to perish in the deserts of disbelief.

The president knows himself allied with the thrones of Christian virtue, and from the mouths of his biographers the adoring phrases pour forth as if from Solomon's well of living waters, perfumed with myrrh and frankincense: "steely, eye-of-the-storm serenity," "casting his mission and that of the country in the grand vision of God's master plan," "humble leader of a great country," "impervious to doubt," "brother in Christ." Left to his own or his speechwriters' devices in front of an open microphone, the president seldom misses a chance to restate the good news in the language of the Bible:

> The liberty we prize is not America's gift to the world, it is God's gift to humanity.

> We do not claim to know all the ways of Providence, yet we can trust in them, placing our confidence in the loving God behind all of life, and all of history.

> Events aren't moved by blind change and chance ... [but] by the hand of a just and faithful God.

> The crew of the shuttle *Columbia* did not return safely to earth. Yet we can pray that all are safely home.

> We will export death and violence to the four corners of the earth in defense of our great nation.

I don't doubt that somewhere on a road in Texas or a pond in Maine, the president beheld a great light, but I find as little sense in what he says as I find in the rustling of leaves or the pattering of rain. The failure in translation I attribute to my early education, which was entirely secular in its character and curriculum. On hearing my first Sunday sermon, at the age of thirteen in the white and gold chapel of a New England boarding school, I responded with the firm applause that I'd been taught was owed to a commencement or a campaign speech. Brought up to admire the founders of the American republic as men defined by the energy of their intellect and the courage of their experiments, for the last fifty years I've been content to regard the bows that politicians make to an altar or a cross as a courtesy that reason pays to superstition. The candidate has come in search of votes, and he doesn't wish to slight the native handicrafts or walk in the wrong direction around the totem poles.

President Ronald Reagan's wearing of religion on his sleeve I could understand as a compliment to the choir, but the sight of President George Bush shaking the fist of righteousness at the Four Horsemen of the Apocalypse doesn't bring to mind the political theory of James Madison; I think instead of Jonathan Edwards preaching a furious sermon to a congregation of sinners in colonial Massachusetts ("The bow of God's wrath is bent, and the arrow made ready on the string, and justice bends the arrow at your heart ..."), or possibly of Al-Hajjaj, who assumed the governorship of Baghdad in the year 694, and greeted the inhabitants with a message meant to administer shock and inspire awe: "O people of Iraq ... by God, I shall strip you like bark, I shall truss you like a bundle of twigs, I shall beat you like stray camels ... By God, what I promise, I fulfill; what I purpose, I accomplish; what I measure, I cut off."

The makers of America's liberties were discoverers of new plants and new stars, delighting in what Thomas Jefferson called "the inimitable freedom of the human mind," bringing to their studies of science and philosophy the excitement of explorers mapping the headwaters of the Missouri River or measuring the transit of Venus—Benjamin Franklin (author, printer, inventor, statesman), William Bartram (botanist), Thomas Paine (essayist, engineer), Benjamin Rush (physician, chemist), Thomas Jefferson (author, architect, diplomat, agronomist). They didn't have much use for priests, and they insisted on the separation of church and state, not because they feared the power of the state to harm religion but because they feared, more sensibly, the power of religion to harm the state. Mindful of the religious wars in Europe, of the St. Bartholomew's Day Massacre, the fires of the Catholic Inquisition, and the blood-soaked cross of the medieval Crusades, Jefferson associated the power of religion with a tyranny that "has been severely felt by mankind, and has filled the history of ten or twelve centuries with too many atrocities not to merit a proscription from meddling with government."

Tirelessly curious about all things great and small, the inventors of the American idea pursued what they took to be the proper study of mankind in as many spheres of reference as they could crowd into a Philadelphia library company or a Boston philosophical society, always with the hope of constructing a government on the blueprint of universal reason despite, again in Voltaire's words, "all the passions which struggle against it; despite the tyrants who wish to drown it in blood; despite the imposters who would employ superstition to bring it to naught."

President Bush speaks for an earlier period in American history, from a pulpit in the Puritan forest before it received the gift of books. If his biographers can be trusted, we now have in the White House a president so secure in his belief that the course of human events rests in "the hand of a just and faithful God" that he counts his ignorance as a virtue and regards his lack of curiosity as a sign of moral strength. A similarly primitive way of thinking (fearful, intolerant, fond of magic) darkens the mind of the shamans drawing up the Pentagon's plans for the conquest of evil and accounts for the punitive reign of virtue currently being imposed upon the American body politic by the Justice Department, the Congress, and the Supreme Court. The collective retreat into the mist of a simplified past speaks to the exhaustion of the mentality that framed the Constitution and for two centuries carried forward the American experiment with freedom. Our Washington geopoliticians like to imagine their war on terrorism as "a clash of civilizations." They flatter themselves with the high-toned noun; what they have incompetently in hand is a clash of superstitions.

2003

20. The Demonstration Effect

All you have to do is to tell them that they are being attacked, and denounce the pacifists for lack of patriotism and exposing the country to danger. It works the same in every country.

—Hermann Göring

If by Easter Sunday the purification of Iraq was still a work in progress—Saddam Hussein nowhere to be found, sporadic gunfire lingering in the streets of Basra and Mosul, a new government not yet seated on its prayer rugs—in Washington the flags were blooming on the bandstands, and the heralds of American empire were crying up the news of great and glorious victory. Our forces under the command of General Tommy Franks had destroyed the semblance of an Iraqi army, rescued the oil fields of Kirkuk, chased an evil tyrant from his throne, cleansed the Tigris Valley of an unsanitary regime. Priced at a cost of $60 billion and 129 American lives (forty-five of them lost in accidents), the month's work lifted President George W. Bush to a 70 percent approval rating in the opinion polls, the friends and officers of his administration everywhere attended by congratulatory nods and the gifts of loyal applause. Important newspaper columnists pointed proudly to the "highwater mark" of America's "resurgent power"; elevated sources at the White House declared themselves well pleased with "the demonstration effect" of a military maneuver that "opens all sorts of new opportunities for us."

As to the nature of the new opportunities and the use of precision-guided bombs as an inspirational sales technique, I don't doubt that over the next few months we can expect the publication of numerous manuals (political, military, and geostrategic) reflecting on the lessons learned in the deserts of Mesopotamia. Because the teaching almost certainly will be expressed in government-inspected prose, I have undertaken to reduce the syllabus to its principal points of interest.

The moral splendor of American empire can be made to stand on a pedestal of lies

During the months prior to the bombing of Baghdad on March 19, every government spokesman in Washington likened Saddam Hussein to Adolf Hitler or Joseph Stalin, a villain "stifling the world," his powers all but supernatural and thus presenting an immediate and terrible danger not only to the peoples of Saudi Arabia, Israel, and Kuwait but also to every man, woman, and child in the United States. Saddam was said to be hiding nuclear weapons, allied with the terrorist networks of Al Qaeda, and complicit in the events of September 11, plotting monstrous but unspecified attacks (if not tomorrow or next week, then two or four or six months hence), extending the reach of his murderous regime across the whole of Central Asia and the Middle East, certain to oppose any attempts at punishment with vengeful clouds of poison gas.

The first week of invasion proved every assertion false. In place of Hitler or Stalin, the American armies found the remnants of a dictator more accurately compared to a psychopathic prison warden, a brutal but almost comic figure, so enslaved to the dream of his omnipotence that he apparently had trusted the defense of his kingdom to histrionic press releases and gigantic portraits of himself armed with a shotgun and a porkpie hat.

No Iraqi shock troops appeared in the field against the American infantry divisions; no Iraqi aircraft presumed to leave the ground; no allied combat unit met with, much less knew where to find, the fabled weapons of mass destruction. The desultory shows of resistance at the river crossings constituted ragged skirmish lines of young men for the most part barefoot and lightly armed, so many of them out of uniform that it wasn't worth the trouble to distinguish between the civilian and the military dead.

The weakness of the Iraqi target made ridiculous Washington's propaganda poster of Saddam as the second coming of Adolf Hitler, and the useful lesson to be learned presented itself on April Fool's Day. Here was the American army in the sinister landscape of Iraq, equipped to fight the Battle of Normandy or El-Alamein but conducting a police action in the manner of the Israeli assassination teams hunting down Palestinian terrorists in the rubble of the Gaza Strip. Would it be possible to hide in plain sight the false pretext of Operation Iraqi Freedom? The Bush Administration answered the question with its customary mendacious aplomb, simply by changing the mission statement. The American army had not come to Iraq to remove the totalitarian menace threatening all of Western civilization—absolutely not; the American army had come briefly eastward out of Eden to "liberate" the long-suffering Iraqi people from the misery inflicted upon them by an evildoer with the bad habit of cutting out their tongues. One excuse for war was as good as any other.

The American news media can be relied upon to sell the spectacle and leave the story to the government

The news transmissions from the fog of war were as relentless as the bombing raids on Baghdad: incessant, deafening, blind to the hope of a coherent narrative. The twenty-four-hour montage on the cable channels resembled the dream sequences of a commercial for men's cologne, the misinformation and the disinformation deftly intercut with the frontline first impressions, the images so quickly revised, repeated, updated, cross-promoted, or shifted to another camera angle—mortar rounds entering stage left, an artillery barrage exiting stage right, two- and three-star generals parading to and fro on Tom Brokaw's reviewing stand, the correspondent aboard an aircraft carrier handing the microphone across a split screen to the correspondent in a Bradley fighting vehicle—that before the invasion was two days north of Umm Qasr the accelerated data stream was as impenetrable as the sandstorm descending on the 3rd Infantry Division's auxiliary helicopters.

The demonstration effects multiplied the news media's enthusiasm for their assignment to Camp Adventure, and they did their best to tell a tale worthy of Stephen Ambrose or Rudyard Kipling. Journalists on duty at the Pentagon characterized the assault as a magnificent achievement, one of the most extraordinary military campaigns ever conducted in the history of the world; reporters traveling with the troops discovered comparisons to the glory of World War II—the tanks in the desert reminding them of Generals George Patton and Erwin Rommel, the siege of Basra analogous to the defense of Stalingrad. The hyperbole never quite squared with the discernible facts. Every day's news cycle began with rumors of appalling danger on both the near and far horizon (the Iraqi Republican Guard entrenched in a grove of palm trees, a battalion of Arab martyrs infiltrating the Syrian border, "heavy fighting," "pockets of resistance," etc.), but by the time the reporters reached the scene of rumored slaughter, the proofs of its occurrence were nowhere to be found. A few wrecked or burning trucks, the flashes of a distant explosion, once or twice an Iraqi corpse, but never any American casualties, no Republican Guard, no Arab martyrs or enemy artillery. The media made up the loss of awe-inspiring sights by starting the clock on another news cycle (more to come, don't go away) or by lending ballast to the photo opportunities. The pulling down of Saddam's statue on April 9 achieved parity with the crumbling of the Berlin

Wall, even though the event took place in an all-but-empty plaza cordoned off by a perimeter of U.S. Marines, in the presence of maybe 150 pro-American Iraqis, half of them imported by the Pentagon several days earlier from London. The careful framing of the camera shots sustained the illusion of an immense and wildly cheering crowd.

When temporarily short of footage incoming from Iraq, the television networks in Washington and New York dressed up their screens with American flags and courageous anchorpersons pledging allegiance to "America's Bravest." MSNBC decorated its primary set with a portrait of President Bush—the studio equivalent of a loyalty oath. Erik Sorenson, the executive in charge of the network, was proud to say that the press had no business asking ugly or discourteous questions. "After September 11 the country wants more optimism and benefit of the doubt ... It's about being positive as opposed to being negative."

At Fox News the talking heads transformed their jingoistic fervor into an article of totalitarian faith, speaking directly to any scoundrels who might have wandered into the viewing audience with the dissenting notion that the war was not a war and therefore unnecessary as well as wrong—"You were sickening then, you are sickening now," "leftist stooges," "absolutely committing sedition, or treason." The *New York Times* added a further proof of the media's subservience to the government when, on April 21, one of its reporters filed a dispatch (dictated by American army officers and before publication submitted to their approval) announcing the discovery of Saddam's illegal chemical weapons by an unnamed Iraqi scientist, seen at an unspecified distance, wearing a baseball cap and pointing to an unknown object buried in the sand. The reporter wasn't allowed to speak to the man, but the paper printed her account on page one, below a headline suggesting that the Bush Administration finally had found the long sought and much hoped for casus belli of its splendid little war.

Package the imperialist agenda as instructive entertainment, and the American public will come to know and love the product

The fireworks display over old, romantic Baghdad inspired heroic feats of merchandising not only on the part of the Pentagon and White House briefing officers but also among the manufacturers of cigars and women's underwear. The excitement prompted a flurry of applications for the trademark "Shock and Awe"; together with the cigars and women's underwear the list of products included teddy bears, bubble-making wands, dollhouse furnishings, ski boots, mouse pads, smoking jackets, yo-yos, and inflatable bathtub toys.

Concerns about the possible squeamishness of the prime-time audience when exposed to scenes of horror proved to be unwarranted and overblown. The computer animations of the weapons systems and the tactical movements looked like video games, the "virtual views" of the topography like the golf-course graphics deployed to illustrate the perils of the PGA Tour.

On the first day of hostilities President Bush cautioned the country's senior news executives against publishing photographs of dead Iraqi civilians. As events moved forward and the home audience registered its approval of a new and improved form of reality TV, it was understood that foreign dead counted merely as unpaid extras briefly available to the producers of the nightly news to stand around in front of the machine-gun bullets and fuel the fireballs. By April 12 the American public had shown sufficient bravery in the face of a foreign enemy that the *New York Times* didn't think it imprudent to publish a handsome color photograph of dead Iraqi children thrown like spoiled vegetables into a refrigerated truck.

But if the pictures didn't present a problem, one still had to be careful with the words. As a matter of well-known and long-established principle, imperialist powers shoot and kill only for the good of the people shot down, but the policy usually requires some sort of upbeat euphemism ("the training of backward peoples" in the art of "democratic self-government," the building of a "free and flourishing" Sumatra or Iraq) with which to ease the minds of the women and children in the room. The producers of The March on Baghdad took the necessary precautions. The killing of Iraqis, both military and civilian, was softened to "attriting" or "degrading" resources; when it was noticed that in Arabic the word "fedayeen" means "those who sacrifice themselves for a cause," our official spokesmen substituted "terrorist death squads"; the looting of the Iraqi National Museum and the burning of the country's National Library were ascribed to the joys of "freedom." Nothing to do with our Navy's cruise missiles, of course, and in no way the fault of our Army units that had been asked to protect both buildings, and with them the 12,000-year history of a civilization that prior to the arrival of General Franks had survived the conquests of the Emperor Heraclius, Suleiman the Magnificent, and Genghis Khan. Secretary of Defense Donald Rumsfeld scowled at the suggestion that somehow the destruction could have been prevented, possibly in the same way that American troops preserved the Oil Ministry. "Freedom's untidy," he said, "and free people are free to make mistakes and commit crimes and do bad things."

So are military empires free to seize "all sorts of new opportunities" opened to them by "demonstration effects" similar to the ones brought by an Athenian army to the island of Melos in the summer of 416 B.C. Having first butchered the Melian military commanders, the Athenians presented the citizens of the town with the choice of abandoning their loyalty to Sparta or accepting the sentence of death.

"As practical men," said the Athenian heralds, "you know and we know that the question of justice arises only between parties equal in strength, and the strong do what they can, and the weak submit."

The corporate managers of the Bush Administration lack the concision of the Attic style, but they didn't find it hard to appreciate the ancient moral of the tale. The high-tech gladiatorial show in the Iraqi coliseum had served as a test market not only for the Pentagon's new and exciting inventory of weapons but also for the premise of American military empire—set the proper tone, established the necessary precedent, opened the road to the grandeur that was Rome. The absence of objection on the part of the American public and the American news media suggested that the truth didn't matter, that motive was irrelevant, that the Bush Administration was free to do as it pleased.

Heartened by the message not likely to be lost on either the voters in next year's presidential election or America's enemies both east and west of Suez, various staff officers attached to the White House, its supporting neoconservative think tanks, and the Pentagon expressed varying degrees of satisfaction. Secretary of State Colin Powell threatened Syria, telling a press conference that Syria would have to change its ways, but, no, "no war plan right now." Vice President Dick Cheney admonished Germany and France, indicating that neither country could expect oil or construction contracts from a new jurisdiction in Iraq, saying that "perhaps, time will help in terms of improving their outlook."

Ken Adelman, a member of the Pentagon's Defense Policy Board, hoped that the conquest of Baghdad "emboldens leaders to drastic, not measured, approaches," but it was left to Michael Ledeen, resident scholar in the Freedom Chair at the American Enterprise Institute, to place the great victory in its clearest perspective. "Every ten years or so, the United States needs to pick up some crappy little country and throw it against the wall, just to show the world we mean business."

2004

21. Dar al-Harb

Men never do evil so fully and so happily as when they do it for conscience's sake.

—Pascal

During the two and a half years since the terrorist attacks on New York and Washington, the country's book publishers have poured forth a steady flow of propaganda recruiting the American citizenry to never-ending war against all the world's evildoers. The edifying tracts come in two coinages—those that praise America the Beautiful (virtuous and just, forever innocent and pure in heart) and those that magnify the threat posed by sinister enemies as numberless as the names for grief—nuclear weapons in the hands of North Korean generals and Pakistani bicyclists, smallpox virus hidden in the luggage or on the person of a gentleman from Bolivia, Arab fanatics spawning in the sewers of the once-romantic Middle East. The sales pitch can be inferred from a short but representative list of titles—*Taking America Back*; *Why We Fight*; *Ripples of Battle*; *An Autumn of War*; *A Heart, a Cross, and a Flag.* I can't pretend to having read more than a few of the hundred-odd books made to the design specifications of a Pentagon press release, but judging by those of which I've read at least enough to appreciate the author's command of the false but stouthearted syllogism, the attempt at persuasion appears to have shifted from the secular to the religious lines of argument.

The books published during the first twelve months of the country's introduction to the concept of its own mortality stated the problem as one open to solution with the instrument of reason, possibly also with some knowledge of history and a passing acquaintance with the socioeconomic circumstances confronted by a majority of most of the world's peoples, Asian, African, and Latin American as well as Muslim. The writing wasn't distinguished, but at least it could be said that the discussion was taking place in the vernacular languages of the world. The more recent books borrow their inspiration from the verses of the Bible and the suras of the Koran. The authors who decry the sins committed by Americans in America (cynicism, homosexuality, believing what they read in the *New York Times*) adopt the rhetoric of Jonathan Edwards cleansing the souls of the unfaithful in the seventeenth-century wilderness of Puritan New England; the authors who preach holy crusade against the foreign infidel in modern-day Jerusalem and Damascus issue fatwas in the manner of Osama bin Laden.

To the latter company of vengeful imams we now can add the names of David Frum, a former speechwriter for President George W. Bush, and Richard Perle, member and former chairman of the Defense Policy Board within the U.S. Department of Defense. Their jointly assembled "manual for victory" (*An End to Evil: How to Win the War on Terror*) reached the bookstores in early January and was promptly boosted onto the bestseller list because of the authors' elevated rank within the intellectual apparat that supplies the Bush Administration with its delusions of moral grandeur. Attached to the White House staff in 2002, Frum brightened that year's State of the Union Address with the phrase "axis of evil"; in 2003 he published *The Right Man*, a hagiography portraying President Bush as a man impervious to doubt, casting his mission and that of his country in the grand vision of God's master plan. Perle has served as an apostle of hard-line power politics since the early 1980s: an assistant secretary of defense in the Reagan Administration, closely associated with the troop of visionary ideologues currently directing the course of our militant foreign policy, a resident fellow, together with Frum, of the American Enterprise Institute.

The result of their collaboration is an ugly harangue that if translated into Arabic and reconfigured with a few changes of word and emphasis (the objects of fear and loathing identified as America and Israel in place of Saudi Arabia and the United Nations) might serve as a lesson taught to a class of eager jihad-ists at a madrasa in Kandahar. The book's title testifies both to the absurdity of its premise and the ignorance of its authors. Evil is a story to which not even Billy Graham can write an end; nor can the 101st Airborne Division set up a secure perimeter around the sin of pride. The War on Terror is a war against an abstract noun, as unwinnable as the wars on hunger, drugs, crime, and human nature, and were it not for the authors' involvement with the affairs of state (informed sources, highly placed, presumably knowing why and whereof they speak), the entire press run of their book might be more usefully transformed into a shipment of paper hats.

But ours is an age in which hijacked airliners and preci-sion-guided cruise missiles follow flight paths dreamed of in the minds of men like mullahs Omar, Frum, and Perle, and some of the prospective casualties (most of them civilian) might care to read at least a brief summary of the work in hand. As with all forms of propaganda, the prose style doesn't warrant extensive quotation, but I don't do the authors a disservice by reducing their message to a series of divine commandments. Like Mohammed bringing the word of Allah to the widow Khadija and the well Zem-Zem, they aspire to a tone of voice appropriate to a book of Revelation.

The War on Terror—"Has only just begun." "There is no middle way for Americans: It is victory or holocaust."

The United States—"The greatest of all great powers in world history."

Militant Islam—Vast horde of Arabs, possibly numbering in the millions, bent on world domination. They intend to "fasten unthinking, unquestioning slavery" on the mind of Western civilization. As insatiable in their thirst for blood as Adolf Hitler and Joseph Stalin.

The CIA and the FBI—Staffed by "faint-hearted" types who lack "the nerve for the fight."

The State Department—"An obstacle to victory." Controlled by "complacent" functionaries who seek "to reconcile the irreconcilable, to negotiate the unnegotiable, and to appease the unappeasable."

The United Nations—"Not an entirely useless organization," but one that does more harm than good. It "regularly broadcasts a spectacle as dishonest and morally deadening as a Stalinist show trial, a televised ritual of condemnation that enflames hatreds and sustains quarrels that might otherwise fade away." The United States doesn't require the U.N.'s permission to attack any country in which George Bush, like Teddy Roosevelt before him, notices "a general loosening of the ties of civilized society."

The Middle East—"Fetid swamp" crawling with "venomous vermin." America must cast the whole of it into a purifying fire. "The toughest line is the safest line."

The American Occupation of Iraq—A triumph. Another six months, and nobody will be able to tell the difference between Baghdad and Orlando.

Saudi Arabia—Headquarters tent of militant Islam. "The Saudis qualify for their own membership in the Axis of Evil." Must be purged of ideological infection.

Arabs Resident in Palestine—Must learn "to swallow their defeat." They have as little chance of territorial restoration as the Oglala Sioux who once drifted through the valley of the Little Bighorn.

Israel—Land of heroes, light unto the gentiles. "Everything that liberal Europeans think a state should not be: proudly nationalist, supremely confident, willing and able to use force to defend itself—alone if need be."

Iran—"The regime must go."

Critics of America's War on Terror—Cowards, "softliners," "Clintonites," "defeatists," pillars of salt.

Germany—"Fair-weather friend." An ally no longer to be trusted.

France—An unfriendly power that "gleefully smashed up an alliance [NATO] that had kept the peace of the world for half a century." Jealous and resentful of America's greatness and goodness of heart. Europe must be forced "to choose between Paris and Washington."

Nondemocratic Governments—America not obliged to honor their pretensions. "It's not always in our power to do anything about such criminals, nor is it always in our interests, but when it is in our power and our interests we should toss dictators aside with no more compunction than a police sharpshooter feels when he downs a hostage-taker."

Dark Places of the Earth—Any city, town, desert, parliament, or shopping mall where "terrorists skulk and hide." Among the countries eligible for some form of instructive intervention, the authors list Lebanon, Sierra Leone, Colombia, Venezuela, Paraguay, Brazil, Zimbabwe, Syria, Yemen, Somalia, northern Nigeria.

National Identification Card—Necessary precaution. All Americans must learn to inform on one another, to admire the vigilant citizen "who *does his or her part*." "A free society is not an un-policed society. A free society is a self-policed society."

American Civilian Population—Must be prepared to accept losses. The protection of American citizens not as important as the killing of Satanic Muslims. The authors cite General George Patton: "Nobody ever won a war by caring for his wounded. He won by making the other poor SOB care for *his* wounded."

In their setting forth of the reforms that must soon descend on Saudi Arabia (on pain of swift punishment if the reforms don't come soon enough), Mullah Frum and Mufti Perle complain of the puritanical clerics in that country who "preach hate-filled sermons, teach the most frightful lies, and disseminate the deadliest conspiracy theories," who claim the authority of God for exhorting the faithful to acts of "cruelty and evil." They describe themselves. Their book summons all loyal and true Americans to the glory of jihad, and as an indication of the sort of thing they have in mind they rely on the wisdom of Sheikh Yousuf al-Qaradawi, dean of Islamic studies at the University of Qatar and an admirer of the terrorist bombings in Jerusalem and Tel Aviv. The two Washington ayatollahs mean to damn the sheikh, not to praise him, but when they quote his interpretation of Dar al-Harb (the Domain of Disbelief) they define the concept that they have made their own. The sheikh put it as plainly as possible to a crowd of Western journalists in Stockholm in the summer of 2003: "It has been determined by Islamic law that the blood and property of people of Dar al-Harb (i.e., non-Muslims) is not protected. Because they fight against and are hostile toward the Muslims, they annulled the protection of his blood and his property."

Nor did the sheikh draw an unnecessarily fine distinction (defeatist, appeasing, faint-hearted) between the military and civilian targets of jihad. A good Christian is a dead Christian. "In modern war," so said the sheikh, "all of society, with all its classes and ethnic groups, is mobilized to participate in the war, to aid its continuation, and to provide it with the material and human fuel required for it to assure the victory of the state fighting its enemies.

Every citizen in society must take upon himself a role in the effort to provide for the battle. The entire domestic front, including professionals, laborers, and industrialists, stands behind the fighting army, even if it does not bear arms."

The Bush Administration's senior geopoliticians, among them Tom Ridge at the Department of Homeland Security and Donald Rumsfeld at the Pentagon, give weekly press conferences at which they make more or less the same speech—our Army in Iraq bringing the great truths of democracy and global capitalism to the Domain of Disbelief, our civilian population girded for battle at security checkpoints on every major highway, at every airport, river crossing, and bus and subway stop. Last year on Christmas Eve the FBI issued a bulletin advising 18,000 of the country's law-enforcement agencies to watch out for people carrying almanacs—works that answer to the uses of the intellect rather than to the joys of superstition. Almanacs, said the FBI, can be used by terrorists "to assist with target selection and preoperational planning." Because almanacs contain information, often accompanied by photographs and maps, about waterways, bridges, dams, reservoirs, tunnels, buildings, and roads, anyone carrying such a thing might be a terrorist or a friend of a terrorist. It was suggested that police officers approach with caution all almanacs "annotated in suspicious ways."

Never having heard the angry teaching in a madrasa or a mosque, I can't make a close or fair comparison to the briefing papers passed around the conference tables at the American Enterprise Institute, but if what I've been told is true (that the sermons depend for their effect on the expression of high-pitched rage) then I don't know how the language differs from that of Mufti Frum and Mullah Perle. Their truths are absolute, their verbs invariably violent—"destroy," "smash," "purge," "deny," "punish," "cut off," "stomp." Provide them with a beard, a turban, and a copy of the Koran, and I expect that they wouldn't have much trouble stoning to death a woman discovered in adultery with a cameraman from CBS News.

Set aside the question as to whether *An End to Evil* proceeds from a cynical motive (the authors fully aware of the lies told to promote a fanciful dream of paradise), and we're still left with a frightening display of ignorance that doesn't augur well for the future of the American Republic. In place of reasoned argument, we have Stone Age incantation, the sense or knowledge of history grotesquely distorted in the fun-house mirrors of ideological certainty, the observations of two respected and supposedly well-informed civil servants framed in a vocabulary as primitive as the one that informs the radio broadcasts of Rush Limbaugh, the television commentary of Sean Hannity and Bill O'Reilly, and the novels of Tim LaHaye and Saddam Hussein.

Historians who study the rise and fall of nations mark the downward turn at the point when the rulers of the state begin to lose faith in the merely human institutions that embody a society's courage of mind and rule of law. They place their trust in miracles and look for their salvation to charlatans who come to comfort them with stories about the end of evil. When the Turks sacked Constantinople in 1453, they found 10,000 people in the church of Santa Sophia, earnestly praying for deliverance in a sanctuary made sweet with the smell of incense and stale with the scent of fear. Authors Frum and Perle trade in the same commodities.

2004

22. Propaganda Mill

When in all our history, has anyone with ideas so bizarre, so archaic, so self-confounding, so remote from the basic American consensus, ever got so far?

—Richard Hofstadter

Trundled into Madison Square Garden in August 2004 for the Republican nominating convention, President George W. Bush affirmed the great truths preached from the pulpits of Fox News and the *Wall Street Journal*—government the problem, not the solution, the free market the answer to every maiden's prayer—and in the press gallery listening to the rattle of the rhetorical brass and tin I found myself asking the same question that Richard Hofstadter had asked of the 1964 Republican convention in San Francisco that nominated as its candidate Barry Goldwater, Senator from Arizona, declaring the American government the enemy of the American people.

The "basic American consensus" in 1964 was firmly liberal in character and feeling, assured of a clear majority in both chambers of Congress as well as a sympathetic hearing in the print and broadcast press. Even the National Association of Manufacturers was still aligned with the generous impulse of Franklin Roosevelt's New Deal, accepting of the proposition, as were the churches and the universities, "that government must do for people what people cannot do for themselves."[1]

And yet, seemingly out of nowhere and suddenly at the rostrum of the Cow Palace, here was Goldwater, cowboy-hatted herald of enlightened selfishness portraying government not as a guarantor of the country's freedoms but as syndicate of quasi-Communist bureaucrats poisoning the wells of commercial enterprise with "centralized planning, red tape, rules without responsibility, and regimentation without recourse." A band played *America the Beautiful,* and in a high-noon glare of klieg light the convention delegates beheld a militant captain of capitalist jihad ("extremism in the defense of liberty is no vice"), known to favor the doctrines of forward deterrence and preemptive strike ("let's lob a nuclear bomb into the men's room at the Kremlin"), believing that poverty was proof of bad character ("lazy, dole-happy people who want to feed on the fruits of somebody else's labor"), convinced that Mammon was another name for God.

The star-spangled oratory didn't draw much of a crowd on the autumn campaign trail. The electorate in 1964 wasn't interested in the threat of an apocalyptic future or the comforts of an imaginary past, and Goldwater's reactionary vision in the desert faded into the sunset of the November election won by Lyndon Johnson with 61 percent of the popular vote. The suburban sheriffs on their palomino ponies withdrew to Scottsdale and Pasadena in the orderly and inoffensive manner of the Mongol hordes retiring from the gates of thirteenth-century Vienna.

---

1 With regard to the designation "liberal," the economist John K. Galbraith said in 1964, "Almost everyone now so describes himself." Lionel Trilling, the literary critic, observed in 1950 that "in the United States at this time, liberalism is not only the dominant but even the sole intellectual tradition." He went on to say that "there are no conservative or reactionary ideas in general circulation," merely "irritable mental gestures which seek to resemble ideas."

Departed but not disbanded. As the basic American consensus has shifted over the last forty years from a liberal to a conservative bias, so also the Senator from Arizona has come to be seen as a prophet in the western wilderness, apostle of the rich man's dream of Heaven that placed Ronald Reagan in the White House in 1980 and provides the G. W. Bush Administration with the sound and fury of both its domestic and foreign policy. Hofstadter didn't stay to answer the question as to how a set of ideas both archaic and bizarre made its way into the center ring of the American political circus of 1964, but forty years later, seated among the balloons and paper elephants in New York's Madison Square Garden, I was at least able to make an informed guess as to how the Ayn Rand fairy tale made its way from that day to this.

About the workings of the right-wing propaganda mills in Washington and New York I knew enough to know that the numbing of America's political senses didn't happen by mistake, but it wasn't until I met Rob Stein, formerly a senior adviser to the chairman of the Democratic National Committee, that I came to fully appreciate the nature and the extent of the re-education program undertaken in the early 1970s by a cadre of ultraconservative and self-mythologizing millionaires bent on rescuing the country from the hideous grasp of Satanic liberalism. To a small group of Democratic activists meeting in New York City in late February, Stein had brought thirty-eight charts diagramming the organizational structure of the Republican "Message Machine," an octopuslike network of open and hidden microphones that he described as "perhaps the most potent, independent institutionalized apparatus ever assembled in a democracy to promote one belief system."

It was an impressive presentation, in large part because Stein didn't refer to anybody as a villain, never mentioned the word "conspiracy." A lawyer who also managed a private equity investment fund—that is, a man unintimidated by spreadsheets and indifferent to the seductions of the pious left—Stein didn't begrudge the manufacturers of corporatist agitprop the successful distribution of their product in the national markets for the portentous catch-phrase and the camera-ready slogan. Having devoted several months to his search through the available documents, he was content to let the facts speak for themselves—fifty funding agencies of different dimensions and varying degrees of ideological fervor, nominally philanthropic but zealous in their common hatred of the liberal enemy, disbursing the collective sum of roughly $3 billion over a period of thirty years for the fabrication of "irritable mental gestures which seek to resemble ideas."

The effort had taken many forms—the publication of expensively purchased and cleverly promoted tracts (Milton Friedman's *Free to Choose*, Charles Murray's *Losing Ground*, Samuel Huntington's *The Clash of Civilizations*), a steady flow of newsletters from more than 100 captive printing presses (among them those at the Heritage Foundation, Accuracy in the Media, the American Enterprise Institute, and the Center for the Study of Popular Culture), generous distributions of academic programs and visiting professorships (to Harvard, Yale, and Stanford universities), the passing along of sound-bite slanders (to Bill O'Reilly and Matt Drudge), the formulation of newspaper op-ed pieces (for the *San Antonio Light* and the *Pittsburgh Post-Gazette* as well as for the *Sacramento Bee* and the *Washington Times*). The prolonged siege of words had proved so successful in its result that on nearly every question of foreign or domestic policy in this year's presidential campaign, the frame and terms of the debate might as well have been assembled in Taiwan by Chinese child labor working from patterns furnished by the authors of ExxonMobil's annual report.

No small task and no mean feat, and as I watched Stein's diagrams take detailed form on a computer screen (the directorates of the Leadership Institute and Capital Research Center all but identical with that of The Philanthropy Roundtable, Richard Mellon Scaife's money dispatched to the Federalist Society as well as to *The American Spectator*), I was surprised to see so many familiar names—publications to which I'd contributed articles, individuals with whom I was acquainted—and I understood that Stein's story was one that I could corroborate, not with supplementary charts or footnotes but on the evidence of my own memory and observation.

The provenience of the Message Machine Stein traced to the recognition on the part of the country's corporate gentry in the late
1960s that they lacked the intellectual means to comprehend, much
less quell or combat, the social and political turmoil then engulfing
the whole of American society. If I had missed Goldwater's foretelling of an apocalyptic future in the Cow Palace, I remembered
my own encounter with the fear and trembling of what was still
known as "The Establishment," four years later and 100 miles to
the north at the July encampment of San Francisco's Bohemian
Club. Over a period of three weeks every summer, the 600-odd
members of the club, most of them expensive ornaments of the
American haute bourgeoisie, invite an equal number of similarly
fortunate guests to spend as many days as their corporate cal-
endars permit within a grove of handsome redwood trees, there
to listen to the birdsong, interest one another in various business
opportunities, and exchange misgivings about the restlessness of
the deutschmark and the yen.

In the summer of 1968 the misgivings were indistinguishable
from panic. Martin Luther King had been assassinated; so had
Robert Kennedy, and everywhere that anybody looked the country's institutional infrastructure, also its laws, customs, best-loved
truths, and fairy tales, seemed to be collapsing into anarchy and
chaos—black people rioting in the streets of Los Angeles and
Detroit, American soldiers killing their officers in Vietnam, long-
haired hippies stoned on drugs or drowned in the bathtubs of Bel
Air, short-haired feminists playing with explosives instead of dolls,
the Scottsdale and Pasadena sheriffs' posses preparing their palomino ponies to stand firm in the face of an urban mob.

Historians revisiting in tranquility the alarums and excursions
of the Age of Aquarius know that Revolution Now was neither
imminent nor likely—the economy was too prosperous, the
violent gestures of rebellion contained within too small a demo-
graphic, mostly rich kids who could afford the flowers and the
go-go boots—but in the hearts of the corporate chieftains wandering among the redwood trees in the Bohemian Grove in July 1968,
the fear was palpable and genuine. The croquet lawn seemed to
be sliding away beneath their feet, and although they knew they

were in trouble, they didn't know why. Ideas apparently mattered, and words were maybe more important than they had guessed; unfortunately, they didn't have any. The American property-holding classes tend to be embarrassingly ill at ease with concepts that don't translate promptly into money, and the beacons of conservative light shining through the liberal fog of the late 1960s didn't come up to the number of clubs in Arnold Palmer's golf bag. The company of the commercial faithful gathered on the banks of California's Russian River could look for succor to Goldwater's autobiography, *The Conscience of a Conservative*, to William F. Buckley's editorials in *National Review*, to the novels of Ayn Rand. Otherwise they were as helpless as unarmed sheepherders surrounded by a Comanche war party on the old Oklahoma frontier before the coming of the railroad and the six-gun.

The hope of their salvation found its voice in a 5,000-word manifesto written by Lewis Powell, a Richmond corporation lawyer, that was circulated in August 1971 by the United States Chamber of Commerce under the heading *Confidential Memorandum; Attack on the American Free Enterprise System*. Soon to be appointed to the Supreme Court, lawyer Powell was a man well known and much respected by the country's business community; within the legal profession he was regarded as a prophet. His heavy word of warning fell upon the legions of reaction with the force of Holy Scripture: "Survival of what we call the free enterprise system," he said, "lies in organization, in careful long-range planning and implementation, in consistency of action over an indefinite period of years, in the scale of financing available only through joint effort, and in the political power available only through united action and national organizations."

The venture capital for the task at hand was provided by a small sewing circle of rich philanthropists—Richard Mellon Scaife in Pittsburgh, Lynde and Harry Bradley in Milwaukee, John Olin in New York City, the Smith Richardson family in North Carolina, Joseph Coors in Denver, David and Charles Koch in Wichita. They entertained visions of an America restored to the safety of its mythological past—small towns like those seen in prints by Currier and Ives, cheerful factory workers whistling while they worked,

politicians as wise as Abraham Lincoln and as brave as Teddy
Roosevelt, benevolent millionaires presenting Christmas turkeys
to deserving elevator operators, the sins of the flesh deported to
Mexico or France. Suspicious of any fact that they hadn't known
before the age of six, the wealthy saviors of the Republic also
possessed large reserves of paranoia, and if the world was going
rapidly to rot (as any fool could plainly see), the fault was to be
found in everything and anything tainted with a stamp of liberal
origin—the news media and the universities, income taxes, Warren
Beatty, transfer payments to the undeserving poor, restraints of
trade, Jane Fonda, low interest rates, civil liberties for unapprecia-
tive minorities, movies made in Poland, public schools.[2]

Although small in comparison with the sums distributed by the
Ford and Rockefeller foundations, the money was ideologically
sound, and it was put to work leveraging additional contributions
(from corporations as well as from other like-minded foundations), acquiring radio stations, newspapers, and journals of
opinion, and bankrolling intellectual sweatshops for the making
of political and socioeconomic theory. Joseph Coors established
The Heritage Foundation with an initial gift of $250,000 in 1973,
the sum augmented over the next few years with $900,000 from
Richard Scaife; the American Enterprise Institute was revived and
fortified in the late seventies with $6 million from the Howard
Pew Freedom Trust; the Cato Institute was set up by the Koch
family in 1977 with a gift of $500,000. If in 1971 the friends of
American free enterprise could turn for comfort to no more than
seven not very competent sources of inspiration, by the end of
the decade they could look to eight additional installations committed to "joint effort" and "united action."[3] The senior officers

---

2   The various philanthropic foundations under the control of the
six families possess assets estimated in 2001 at $1.7 billion. Harry
Bradley was an early and enthusiastic member of the John Birch
Society; Koch Industries in the winter of 2000 agreed to pay $30
million to settle claims related to 300 oil spills from its pipelines in
six states; it was the largest civil fine ever imposed on a private U.S.
company under any federal environmental law.

3   Paul Weyrich, the first director of The Heritage Foundation, has

of the Fortune 500 companies meanwhile organized the Business Roundtable, providing it by 1979 with a rich endowment for the hiring of resident scholars loyal in their opposition to the tax and antitrust laws.

The quickening construction of Santa's workshops outside the walls of government and the academy resulted in the increased production of pamphlets, histories, monographs, and background briefings intended to bring about the ruin of the liberal idea in all of its institutionalized forms—the demonization of the liberal press, the disparagement of liberal sentiment, the destruction of liberal education—and by the time Ronald Reagan arrived in triumph at the White House in 1980 the assembly lines were operating at full capacity. Well in advance of inauguration day the Christmas elves had churned out so much paper that had they been told to do so, they could have shredded it into tickertape and welcomed the new cowboy-hatted herald of enlightened selfishness with a parade like none other ever before seen by man or beast. Unshredded, the paper was the stuff of dreams from which was made Mandate for Leadership, the "bible" presented by The Heritage Foundation to Mr. Reagan in the first days of his presidency with the thought that he might want to follow its architectural design for an America free at last from "the tyranny of the Left," rescued from the dungeons of "liberal fascism," once again a theme park built by nonunion labor along the lines of Walt Disney's gardens of synthetic Eden.

Signs of the newly minted intellectual dispensation began showing up in the offices of *Harper's Magazine* in 1973, the manuscripts invariably taking the form of critiques of one or another of the absurdities then making an appearance before the Washington congressional committees or touring the New York literary scene with Susan Sontag and Norman Mailer. Over a period of several years the magazine published articles and essays by authors later to become well-known apologists for the conservative creed,

---

often been described by his admirers as "the Lenin of social conservatism." Seldom was he at a loss for a military analogy: "If your enemy has weapons systems working and is killing you with them, you'd better have weapons systems of your own."

among them George Gilder, Michael Novak, William Tucker, and Philip Terzian; if their writing in the early seventies was remarkable both for its clarity and wit, it was because they chose topics of opportunity that were easy to find and hard to miss.

The liberal consensus hadn't survived the loss of the Vietnam War. The subsequently sharp reduction of the country's moral and economic resources was made grimly apparent by the impeachment of Richard Nixon and the price of Arab oil, and it came to be understood that Roosevelt's New Deal was no longer on offer. Acting on generous impulse and sustained by the presumption of limitless wealth, the American people had enacted legislation reflecting their best hopes for racial equality and social justice (a.k.a. Lyndon Johnson's "Great Society"), but any further efforts at transformation clearly were going to cost a great deal more money than the voters were prepared to spend. Also a good deal more thought than the country's liberal-minded intelligentsia were willing to attempt or eager to provide. The universities chose to amuse themselves with the crossword puzzles of French literary theory, and in the New York media salons the standard-bearers of America's political conscience were content to rest upon what they took to be their laurels, getting by with the striking of noble poses (as friends of the earth or the Dalai Lama) and the expression of worthy emotions (on behalf of persecuted fur seals and oppressed women). The energies once contained within the nucleus of a potent idea escaped into the excitements of the style incorporated under the rubrics of Radical Chic, and the messengers bringing the good news of conservative reaction moved their gospel-singing tent show into an all but deserted public square.

Their chief talents were those of the pedant and the critic, not those of the creative imagination, but they well understood the art of merchandising and the science of cross-promotion, and in the mid-1970s anybody wishing to appreciate the character and purpose of the emerging conservative putsch could find no better informant than Irving Kristol, then a leading columnist for the *Wall Street Journal*, the author of well-received books (*On the Democratic Idea in America* and *Two Cheers for Capitalism*), trusted counselor and adjunct sage at the annual meetings of the Business Roundtable. As a youth in the late 1930s, at a time when literary name and reputation accrued to the accounts of the self-styled revolutionary left, Kristol had proclaimed himself a disciple of Leon Trotsky, but then the rimes changed, the winds of fortune shifting from east to west, and after a stint as a CIA asset in the 1950s, he had carried his pens and papers into winter quarters on the comfortably upholstered bourgeois right.

On first meeting the gentleman at a literary dinner in New York's Century Club, I remember that I was as much taken by the ease and grace of his manner as I was impressed by his obvious intelligence. A man blessed with a sense of humor, his temperament and tone of mind more nearly resembling that of a sophisticated dealer in art and antiques than that of an academic scold, he praised *Harper's Magazine* for its publication of Tom Wolfe's satirical pieces and for the prominence that it had given to the essays of Senator Daniel Patrick Moynihan, and I was flattered by his inclination to regard me as an editor-of-promise who might be recruited to the conservative cause, presumably as an agent in place behind enemy lines. The American system of free enterprise, he said, was being attacked by the very people whom it most enriched—by the pampered children of privilege disturbing the peace of the Ivy League universities, doing lines of cocaine in Manhattan discotheques, making decadent movies in Hollywood—and the time had come to put an end to their dangerous and self-indulgent nonsense. Nobody under the age of thirty knew what anything cost, and even the senior faculty at Princeton had forgotten that it was none other than the great Winston Churchill who had said, "Cultured people are merely the glittering scum which floats upon the deep river of production."

In the course of our introductory conversation Kristol not only referred me to other old masters whom I might wish to reread (among them Plutarch, Gibbon, and Edmund Burke); he also explained something of his technique as an intellectual entrepreneur. Despite the warning cries raised by a few prescient millionaires far from the fashionable strongholds of the effeminate east, the full membership of the American oligarchy still wasn't alive to the threat of cultural insurrection, and in order to awaken the management to a proper sense of its dire peril, Kristol had been traveling the circuit of the country's corporate board-rooms, soliciting contributions given in memory of Friedrich von Hayek, encouraging the automobile companies to withdraw their advertising budgets from any media outlet that declined to echo their social and political prejudices.

"Why empower your enemies?" he said. "Why throw pearls to swine?"[4]

Although I didn't accept Kristol's invitation to what he called the "intellectual counterrevolution," I often ran across him during the next few years at various symposia addressed to the collapse of the nation's moral values, and I never failed to enjoy his company or his conversation. Among all the propagandists pointing out the conservative path to glory, Kristol seemed to me the brightest and the best, and I don't wonder that he eventually became one of the four or five principal shop stewards overseeing the labors of the Republican message machine.

It was at Kristol's suggestion that I met a number of the fund-rais-ing people associated with the conservative program of political correctness, among them Michael Joyce, executive director of the Olin Foundation in the late seventies. We once traveled together on a plane returning to New York from a conference that Joyce had organized for a college in Michigan, and somewhere over eastern Ohio he asked whether I might want to edit a new journal of

---

4 Henry Ford II expressed a similar thought on resigning as a trustee of the Ford Foundation in late 1976. Giving vent to his con-fusion, annoyance, and dismay, he took the trouble to write a letter to the staff of the foundation, reminding them that they were associ-ated with "a creature of capitalism." Conceding that the word might seem "shocking" to many of the people employed in the vineyards of philanthropy, Mr. Ford proceeded to his defense of the old ways and old order:

"I'm not playing the role of the hard-headed tycoon who thinks all philanthropoids are Socialists and all university professors are Communists. I'm just suggesting to the trustees and the staff that the system that makes the foundation possible very probably is worth preserving."

cultural opinion meant to rebut and confound the ravings of *The New York Review of Books*. The proposition wasn't one in which I was interested, but the terms of the offer—an annual salary of $200,000, to be paid for life even in the event of my resignation or early retirement—spoke to the seriousness of the rightist intent to corner and control the national market in ideas.[5]

The work went more smoothly as soon as the Reagan Administration had settled itself in Washington around the fountains and reflecting pools of federal patronage. Another nine right-thinking foundations established offices within a short distance of Capitol Hill or the Hay-Adams Hotel (most prominent among them the Federalist Society and the Center for Individual Rights); more corporations sent more money; prices improved for ideological piecework (as much as $100,000 a year for some of the brand-name scholars at Heritage and American Enterprise Institute), and eager converts to the various sects of the conservative faith were as thick upon the ground as maple leaves in autumn. By the end of Reagan's second term the propaganda mills were spending $100 million a year on the manufacture and sale of their product, invigorated by the sense that once again it was morning in America and redoubling their efforts to transform their large store of irritable mental gestures into brightly packaged policy objectives—tort reform, school vouchers, less government, lower taxes, elimination of the labor unions, bigger military budgets, higher interest rates, reduced environmental regulation, privatization of social security, down-sized Medicaid and Medicare, more prisons, better surveillance, stricter law enforcement.

If production increased at a more handsome pace than might have been dreamed of by Richard Scaife or hoped for by Irving Kristol, it was because the project had been blessed by Almighty

---

5   The proposed journal appeared in 1982 as The New Criterion, promoted as a "staunch defender" of high culture, "an articulate scourge of artistic mediocrity and intellectual mendacity wherever they are found." Joyce later took over direction of the Bradley Foundation, where he proved to be as deft as Weyrich and Kristol at what the movement conservatives liked to call the wondrous alchemy of turning intellect into influence.

God. The Christian right had come into the corporate fold in the late 1970s. Abandoning the alliance formed with the conscience of the liberal left during the Great Depression (the years of sorrow and travail when money was not yet another name for Jesus), the merchants of spiritual salvation had come to see that their interests coincided with those of the insurance companies and the banks. The American equestrian classes were welcome to believe that slack-jawed dope addicts had fomented the cultural insurrection of the 1960s; Jerry Falwell knew that it had been the work of Satan. Together with Paul Weyrich at The Heritage Foundation, Falwell sponsored the formation of the Moral Majority in 1979, at about the same time and in much the same spirit that Pat Robertson, the Christian televangelist, sent his congregation a fund-raising letter saying that feminists encourage women to "leave their husbands, kill their children, practice witchcraft, destroy capitalism and become lesbians." Before Ronald Reagan was elected to a second term the city of God signed a nonaggression pact with the temple of Mammon, their combined forces waging what came to be known as "The Culture War."

For a few years I continued to attend convocations sponsored by the steadily proliferating agencies of the messianic right, but although the discussions were held in increasingly opulent settings —the hotel accommodations more luxurious, the food better, with views of the mountains as well as the sea—by 1985 I could no longer stomach either the sanctimony or the cant. With the coming to power of the Reagan Administration most of the people on the podium or the tennis court were safely enclosed within the perimeters of orthodox opinion and government largesse, and yet they persisted in casting themselves as rebels against "the system," revolutionary idealists being hunted down like dogs by a vicious and still active liberal prosecution. The pose was as ludicrous as it was false. The leftist impulse had been dead for ten years, ever since the right-wing Democrats in Congress had sold out the liberal portfolio of President Jimmy Carter and revised the campaign-finance laws to suit the convenience of their corporate patrons. Nor did the news media present an obstacle. By 1985 the *Wall Street Journal* had become the newspaper of record most widely read by the people who made the decisions about the country's economic policy; the leading editorialists in the *New York Times* (A. M. Rosenthal, William Safire) as well as in the *Washington Post* (George Will, Richard Harwood, Meg Greenfield) ably defended the interests of the status quo; the vast bulk of the nation's radio talk shows (reaching roughly 80 percent of the audience) reflected a conservative bias, as did all but one or two of the television talk shows permitted to engage political topics on PBS. In the pages of the smaller journals of opinion (such as *National Review, Commentary,* the *American Spectator,* the *National Interest,* the *New Criterion,* the *Public Interest, Policy Review*), the intellectual décor, much of it paid for by the Olin and Scaife foundations, was matched to the late-Victorian tastes of Rudyard Kipling and J. P. Morgan. The voices of conscience that attracted the biggest crowds on the nation's lecture circuit were those that spoke for one or another of the parties of the right, and together with the chorus of religious broadcasts and pamphlets (among them Pat Robertson's 700 Club and the publications under the direction of Jerry Falwell and the Reverend Sun Myung Moon), they enveloped the country in an all but continuous din of stereophonic, right-wing sound.

The facts seldom intruded upon the meditations of the company seated poolside at the conferences and symposia convened to bemoan America's fall from grace, and I found it increasingly depressing to listen to prerecorded truths dribble from the mouths of writers once willing to risk thinking for themselves. Having exchanged intellectual curiosity for ideological certainty, they had forfeited their powers of observation as well as their senses of humor; no longer courageous enough to concede the possibility of error or enjoy the play of the imagination, they took an interest only in those ideas that could be made to bear the weight of solemn doctrine, and they cried up the horrors of the culture war because their employers needed an alibi for the disappearances of the country's civil liberties and a screen behind which to hide the privatization (a.k.a. the theft) of its common property—the broadcast spectrum as well as the timber, the water, and the air, the reserves of knowledge together with the mineral deposits and the laws. Sell the suckers on the notion that their "values" are at risk (abortionists escaping the nets of the Massachusetts state police, pornographers and cosmetic surgeons busily at work in Los Angeles, farm families everywhere in the Midwest becoming chattels of the welfare state), and maybe they won't notice that their pockets have been picked.

So many saviors of the republic were raising the alarm of culture war in the mid-1980s that I now can't remember whether it was Bob Bartley writing in the *Wall Street Journal* or William Bennett speaking from his podium at the National Endowment for the Humanities who said that at Yale University the students were wallowing in the joys of sex, drugs, and Karl Marx, disporting themselves on the New Haven green in the reckless manner of nymphs and satyrs on a Grecian urn. I do remember that at one of the high-end policy institutes in Manhattan, I heard the tale told by Norman Podhoretz, then the editor at *Commentary*, the author of several contentious books (*Making It* and *Why We Were in Vietnam*), and a rabid propagandist for all things anti-liberal. What he had to say about Yale was absurd, which I happened to know because that same season I was teaching a seminar at the college. More than half the number of that year's graduating seniors had applied for work at the First Boston Corporation, and most of the students whom I'd had the chance to meet were so busy finding their way around the Monopoly board of the standard American success (figuring the angles of approach to business school, adding to the network of contacts in their Filofaxes) that they didn't have the time to waste on sexual digressions either literal or figurative. When I attempted to explain the circumstance to Podhoretz, he wouldn't hear of it. Not only was I misinformed, I was a liberal and therefore both a liar and a fool. He hadn't been in New Haven in twenty years, but he'd read William F. Buckley's book (*God and Man at Yale*, published in 1951), and he knew (because the judgment had been confirmed by something he'd been told by Donald Kagan in 1978) that the college was a sinkhole of depraved sophism. He knew it for a fact, knew it in the same way that Jerry Falwell knew that it was Satan who taught Barbra Streisand how to sing.

If Kristol was the most engaging of the agents provocateur whom I'd encountered on the conservative lecture circuit in the 1980s, Podhoretz was the dreariest—an apparatchik in the old Soviet sense of the word who believed everything he wished to prove and could prove everything he wished to believe, bringing his patrons whichever words might serve or please, anxious to secure a place near or at the boot of power. Unfortunately it was Podhoretz, not Kristol, who exemplified the character and tone of mind that edged the American conservative consensus ever further to the right during the decade of the 1990s.

The networks of reactionary opinion once again increased their rates of production, several additional foundations were recruited to the cause, and numerous activist organizations came on line, together with new and improved media outlets (most notably Rupert Murdoch's Fox News and *Weekly Standard*) broadcasting the gospels according to saints Warren Harding and William McKinley. By 1994 the Conservative Political Action Conference was attracting as many as 4,000 people, half of them college students, to its annual weekend in Arlington, Virginia, there to listen to the heroes of the hour (G. Gordon Liddy, Ralph Reed, Oliver North) speak from stages wrapped in American flags. Americans for Tax Reform under the direction of Grover Norquist declared its intention to shrink the federal government to a size small enough "to drown," like one of the long-lost hippies in Bel Air, "in a bathtub."

Although as comfortably at home on Capitol Hill as in the lobbies of the corporate law firms on K Street, and despite their having learned to suck like newborn lambs at the teats of government patronage (Kristol's son, William, serving as public relations director to Vice President Dan Quayle; Podhoretz's son-in-law, Elliot Abrams, a highly placed official within the Reagan Administration subsequently indicted for criminal misconduct), the apologists for the conservative cause continued to pose as embattled revolutionaries at odds with the "Tyranny of the Left." The pretense guaranteed a steady flow of money from their corporate sponsors, and the unexpected election of Bill Clinton in 1992 offered them yet another chance to stab the corpse of the liberal

Goliath. The smearing of the new president's name and reputation began as soon as he committed the crime of entering the White House. The *American Spectator*, a monthly journal financed by Richard Scaife, sent its scouts west into Arkansas to look for traces of Clinton's semen on the pine trees and the bar stools. It wasn't long before Special Prosecutor Kenneth Starr undertook his obsessive inspection of the president's bank records, soul, and penis. Summoning witnesses with the fury of a suburban Savonarola, Starr set forth on an exploration of the Ozark Mountains, questioning the natives about wooden Indians and painted women. For four years he camped in the wilderness, and even after he was allowed to examine Monica Lewinsky's lingerie drawer, his search for the weapon of mass destruction proved as futile as the one more recently conducted in Iraq.

Although unable to match Starr's prim self-righteousness, Newt Gingrich, the Republican congressman from Georgia elected speaker of the House in 1995, presented himself as another champion of virtue (a self-proclaimed "Teacher of the Rules of Civilization") willing to lead the American people out of the desolation of a liberal wasteland. Like Starr and Podhoretz (also like the newscasters who now decorate the right-wing television studios), Gingrich had a talent for bearing grudges. During his sixteen years in Congress he had acquired a reputation (not undeserved) for being nasty, brutish, and short, eventually coming to stand as the shared and shining symbol of resentment that bound together the several parties of the disaffected right—the Catholic conservatives with the Jewish neoconservatives, the libertarians with the authoritarians, the evangelical nationalists with the paranoid monetarists, Pat Robertson's Christian Coalition with the friends of the Ku Klux Klan. Within a few months of his elevation to the Speaker's chair, Gingrich bestowed on his fellow-plaintiffs his Contract with America, a plan for rooting out the last vestiges of liberal heresy in the mind of government. As mean-spirited in its particulars as the Mandate for Leadership handed to Ronald Reagan in 1980, the contract didn't become law, but it has since provided the terms of enlightened selfishness that shape and inspire the policies of the current Bush Administration.

During the course of the 1990s I did my best to keep up with the various lines of grievance developing within the several sects of the conservative remonstrance, but although I probably read as many as 2,000 presumably holy texts (Peggy Noonan's newspaper editorials and David Gelernter's magazine articles as well as the soliloquies of Rush Limbaugh and the sermons of Robert Bork), I never learned how to make sense of the weird and too numerous inward contradictions. How does one reconcile the demand for small government with the desire for an imperial army; apply the phrases "personal initiative" and "self-reliance" to corporation presidents utterly dependent on the federal subsidies to the banking, communications, and weapons industries; square the talk of "civility" with the strong-arm methods of Kenneth Starr and Tom DeLay; match the warmhearted currencies of "conservative compassion" with the cold cruelty of "the unfettered free market"; know that human life must be saved from abortionists in Boston but not from cruise missiles in Baghdad? In the glut of paper I could find no unifying or fundamental principle except a certain belief that money was good for rich people and bad for poor people. It was the only point on which all the authorities agreed, and no matter where the words were coming from (a report on federal housing, an essay on the payment of Social Security, articles on the sorrow of the slums or the wonder of the U.S. Navy) the authors invariably found the same abiding lesson in the tale—money ennobles rich people, making them strong as well as wise; money corrupts poor people, making them stupid as well as weak.

But if a set of coherent ideas was hard to find in all the sermons from the mount, what was not hard to find was the common tendency to believe in some form of transcendent truth. A religious as opposed to a secular way of thinking. Good versus Evil, right or wrong, saved or damned, with us or against us, and no light-minded trifling with doubt or ambiguity. Or, more plainly and as a young disciple of Ludwig Von Mises had said, long ago in the 1980s in one of the hospitality tents set up to welcome the conservative awakening to a conference on a beach at Hilton Head, "Our people deal in absolutes."

Just so, and more's the pity. In place of intelligence, which might tempt them to consort with wicked or insulting questions for which they don't already possess the answers, the parties of the right substitute ideology, which, although sometimes archaic and bizarre, is always virtuous.

Virtuous, but not necessarily the best means available to the running of a railroad or a war. The debacle in Iraq, like the deliberate impoverishment of the American middle class, bears witness to the shoddiness of the intellectual infrastructure on which a once democratic republic has come to stand. Morality deemed more precious than liberty; faith-based policies and initiatives ordained superior to common sense.

As long ago as 1964 even William F. Buckley understood that the thunder on the conservative right amounted to little else except the sound and fury of middle-aged infants banging silver spoons, demanding to know why they didn't have more—more toys, more time, more soup; when Buckley was asked that year what the country could expect if it so happened that Goldwater was elected president, he said, "That might be a serious problem." So it has proved, if not under the baton of the senator from Arizona then under the direction of his ideologically correct heirs and assigns. An opinion poll taken in 1964 showed 62 percent of the respondents trusting the government to do the right thing; by 1994 the number had dwindled to 19 percent. The measure can be taken as a tribute to the success of the Republican propaganda mill that for the last forty years has been grinding out the news that all government is bad and that the word "public," in all its uses and declensions (public service, citizenship, public health, community, public park, commonwealth, public school, etc.), connotes inefficiency and waste. The dumbing down of the public discourse follows as the day the night, and so it comes as no surprise that both candidates in this year's presidential election present themselves as embodiments of what they call "values" rather than as the proponents of an idea. Handsome images consistent with those seen in Norman Rockwell's paintings or the prints of Currier and Ives, suitable for mounting on the walls of the American Enterprise Institute or in one of the manor houses owned by Richard Mellon Scaife, maybe somewhere behind a library sofa or over the fireplace in a dining room, but certainly in a gilded frame.

2005

23. Condottieri

All who live in tyranny and hopelessness can know: The United States will not ignore your oppression or excuse your oppressors. When you stand for your liberty, we will stand with you.

—President George W. Bush

Whoever wrote the hero's boast into the president's second inaugural address at least had sense enough to omit the antecedents for the pronouns. Why spoil the effect by naming protagonists who might or might not show up for the medal ceremonies on the White House lawn? The precaution has proved the better part of valor during the months subsequent to the January speech, the "you" being seen to refer to a quorum of potentially oil-rich politicians in Iraq, the "we" to the infantry squad sent with Tom Hanks to save Private Ryan. President Bush looks to Hollywood for his lessons in geopolitics, and apparently he likes to think of himself as a military commander in the romantic tradition of Generals George A. Custer and George S. Patton. His adjutants find it hard to say anything in his presence that doesn't go well with the sound of bugles, but before he declares war on Mexico somebody ought to tell him that the American Army is best equipped to stand and serve not as an invincible combat force but as the world's largest and most heavily armed day-care center.

The several degrees of separation between the mission and the presidential mission statement furnished the national news media in February, March, and April with a steady supply of headlines from sources both foreign and domestic. No lack of "tyranny and hopelessness" abroad, almost all of it excused or ignored because where was the profit to be gained or the glory to be won by standing up for liberty in China, North Korea; Chechnya, Israel, Zimbabwe, or the Sudan? Meanwhile, at home, no end of reports about the scarcity of volunteers eager to play the game of capture the flag in the Atlas Mountains or the Khyber Pass. The latter set of dispatches brought word of the rewards currently being offered to the prospective boots on the ground—bonuses of $90,000 over three years ($20,000 in cash, $70,000 in supplemental benefits), forgiveness of college loans, the promise of citizenship to foreign nationals (currently estimated at 3 percent of the American Army), the acceptance of older recruits (now eligible to the age of thirty-nine), a general lowering of the intellectual and physical requirements (waivers granted for poor test scores, for chronic illness, in some instances for the disability of a criminal record), the chance of a generous pension, an opportunity to study the art of restaurant management.

And yet, despite the inducements and the Army's annual $300 million appropriation for a seductive advertising campaign, the ranks continue to dwindle and thin. Generals speak of "exhausted," "degenerating," "broken" force levels. Recruiting officers give way to unmanly bouts of depression when they fail to enlist more than one soldier for every 120 prospects to whom they show the promotional brochures; so do the reserve units returned, on short notice and without explanation, to another year directing traffic in Iraq and Afghanistan. The desertion rate now stands at 3.1 percent of the active service inductions; of the new recruits coming into camp, 30 percent depart within six months of their arrival.

The flow of dispiriting news provided the Harry Frank Guggenheim Foundation with a casus belli for a seminar staged in New York during the first week of April under the banner "Bearing Arms: Who Should Serve?" As a director of the foundation, I had the chance over the course of two days to hear the question answered by a number of people as strongly opinionated as they were well informed, among them Victor Davis Hanson, the military historian; Charles Moskos, the Northwestern University sociologist and adviser to the Pentagon; Josiah Bunting, president of the Foundation and former superintendent of the Virginia Military Institute; and U.S. Congressman Charles Rangel (D., N.Y.), who in 2003 proposed legislation to reestablish the military draft. The conversations encompassed a broad range of ancillary topics—America's military history, weapons both ancient and modern, the changes brought about by the enlistment of women in the armed services—but the questions that supplied the energy to the discussion were the ones touching on the reluctance of the country's privileged and well-educated youth (for the most part presumed lost in the desert of materialism) to go to war. Why had the Princeton class of 1956 sent 400 of its 900 graduates to the Army, the class of 2004 only 9 of 1,100? What had become of the homegrown courage that went ashore with "the greatest generation" on the beaches of Normandy and Iwo Jima? Where else if not in the Army was it possible to "share the burden of citizenship," learn the meaning of democracy, find a cure for the disease of selfishness that rots the country's soul?

Although admiring of the reflections derived from the works of Teddy Roosevelt ("Aggressive fighting for the right is the noblest sport the world affords"), I was struck by the fact that nobody took the trouble to consider the nature of the army that young Americans are now being invited to join. What is its purpose, and at whose pleasure does it serve? Judging by the uses to which the all-volunteer Army has been put since it was formed in 1973, the defense of the United States ranks very low on its list of priorities. So does the business of waging foreign wars. The domestic political response to the high number of American casualties in Vietnam (57,000 killed, 153,000 wounded) forced the Pentagon to the discovery that it was best to leave the world's noblest sport to well-trained machines and randomly chosen civilians. Although paid for with public money, the Army now operates for the benefit of a primarily private interest, distributing expensive gifts to venal defense contractors, rounding up goons for the oil companies doing merger and acquisition deals in hostile environments, functioning as a prop in presidential election campaigns, managing a large-scale public-works project that finds employment for the unemployable. The privatization of what was once a public service undoubtedly adds to the country's prestige as well as to the net worth of the consortiums that build planes that don't fly and tanks that sink in the sand, but it cannot be said to constitute a noble cause for which young Americans of any social-economic class—rich, poor, privileged, underachieving—sally gladly forth to fight and die.

The comparison to a day-care center serves both as metaphor and as statement of simple fact. The estimated cost of the life-long health benefits owing to retired veterans and their families over the next ten years now comes up to the sum of $150 billion, which exceeds by $50 billion the Pentagon's annual expenditure on the design of new weapons and the purchase of live ammunition. One of the panelists at the foundation's seminar told of his recent tour of an aircraft carrier in company with its chief medical officer, who pointed out the many and improbable map coordinates at which the ship's crew schedules the hasty assignations of Mars with Venus. He came away from the briefing with the impression of a floating rabbit hutch. Another of the panelists reported 40 percent of our enlisted personnel married to fellow soldiers, an arrangement he thought favorable to women otherwise at a loss to secure the health and education of their children. The recruiting posters and television commercials embody the strength and spirit of the Army as a young man outward bound in a blaze of bravery; the two figures that have come to symbolize the war in Iraq are Lynndie England and Jessica Lynch, both looking not for a way into the halls of military glory but for a way out of the hollows of Appalachian poverty.

As a matter of historical record, the experience of the two

young women from West Virginia is more nearly representative of the American attitude toward war than the handsome school-book illustrations of Andrew Jackson directing the Battle of New Orleans, Robert E. Lee astride his horse at Gettysburg. Contrary to the claims of the stern moralists who hurl sandbags of furious commentary into the pages of the *Wall Street Journal* and *National Review*, Americans never have had much liking for the heroics cherished by the ancient Romans. Given a good or necessary reason to deploy the military virtues of courage and self-sacrifice, we can rise to the occasion at Bastogne or Guadalcanal, but as a general rule we don't poke around in the cannon's mouth for the Easter eggs of fame and fortune, and if given any choice in the matter, we prefer the civilian virtues—the fast shuffle, the sharp angle, the safe bet.

The shortage of patriots during the Revolutionary War obliged the Continental Army to reward its seasonal help with a 160-acre gift of land; the troops who crossed the Delaware River with George Washington on Christmas Eve, 1776, completed their terms of service on New Year's Day, 1777, refusing to march north to the Battle of Princeton on January 3 until each of them had been paid $10 in gold for another six weeks of labor on the field of honor. President James Madison encountered similar difficulties in July 1814 when a British army arrived in Maryland, intent upon laying waste to the countryside. Madison issued a requisition for 93,500 militiamen from what were then the eighteen American states; approximately 6,000 volunteers showed up for the battle of Bladensburg, where they were promptly dispersed like a flock of birds rising on the sound of a single gunshot.

The sons of liberty were as wary of the Civil War as they had been careful to avoid enlistment in the Revolutionary War and the War of 1812. Once it was understood that the march on Richmond wasn't the holiday jaunt anticipated by the orators north of the Potomac, the federal government was hard-pressed to find soldiers willing to trample out the vintage where the grapes of wrath were stored. Between July 1863 and April 1865, the Lincoln Administration sent draft notices to a total of 776,892 men: 161,244 failed to report; 86,724 paid commutation fees ($3,750 at the current rate of exchange); 73,607 provided substitutes; and 315,509 were examined and ruled exempt. Only 46,347 were herded into uniform.

The notion of a citizen army, readily and enthusiastically assembled under the flags of honor, duty, and country, emerged from the circumstances of the Second World War. America had been attacked, by Japan at Pearl Harbor and by Germany in the Atlantic Ocean. Peace was not an option, and the American people didn't need to be reminded by a clucking of newspaper columnists that our enemies possessed weapons of mass destruction and that their objectives were murderous. The sense of a common purpose and a national identity bound together in the nucleus of war sustained the government's demand for 10 million conscripts in the years 1941–1945.

The force structure collapsed under the weight of the lies told to the American people by three American presidents trying to find a decent reason for the expedition to Vietnam. Our victory was declared inoperative in April 1975, and for the next quarter of a century when mustering the roll of the all-volunteer Army, the recruiting officers took pains to liken it to a reality-television show. Not the kind of outfit that takes casualties—a vocational school, a summer camp, a means of self-improvement for young men and women lacking the advantages (a decent education, health care, foreign travel) available to Princeton graduates. It had come to be understood that the Pentagon was in the advertising business, projecting images of supreme power in sufficiently heavy calibers to shock a French intellectual and awe an American president. Nobody on the production staff was supposed to get hurt.

Recent events in Iraq have wrecked the sales pitch, which is why the Bush Administration now seeks to carry on its crusade against all the world's evildoers with an army of robots. In Washington on March 26, an Army spokesman described the wonders of the Future Combat Systems (a.k.a. the "technological bridge" to tomorrowland), equipped, at an initial cost of $145 billion over the life expectancy of the miracle, with radio-controlled cannons, tanks, and mortars so godlike in their power and performance as to require next to nothing in the way of food, armor, water, ammunition, or sexual companionship.

The proposal is not without merit. Certainly it meets all the specifications of a government social-welfare program—no military personnel at risk, the day-care centers refurbished and enhanced, enough money lying around loose to win the heart and mind of every proud American in Congress and the weapons trade.

Even so, and not wishing to cast doubts on anybody's patriotism, I think the country might be better served if the corporations fielded their own private armies. The practice is not without precedent. The merchant princes of the Italian Renaissance had as much of a talent for collecting barbarous soldiers as they did for commissioning noble works of art and architecture. If in Michelangelo and Botticelli they could appreciate the presence of genius, so also in the mercenaries under the command of Muzio Attendolo and Sigismondo Malatesta they could recognize the high quality of men "insensible to the fear of God," who knew how to "set places on fire, to rob churches … imprison priests." Citicorp and ExxonMobil would do well to follow in the footsteps of the Medici—the military operations conceived as venture-capital deals, the soldiers promoted to the rank of shareholders and dressed in uniforms bearing the corporate insignia, the print and broadcast rights firmly under the control of the publicists, the loot divided in accordance with the rules governing the orders of battle in the National Football League.

2005

24. On Message

*But I venture the challenging statement that if American democracy
ceases to move forward as a living force, seeking day and night by peaceful means to better the lot of our citizens, then Fascism and Communism,
aided, unconsciously perhaps, by old-line Tory Republicanism, will grow
in strength in our land.*

—Franklin D. Roosevelt, November 4, 1938

In 1938 the word "fascism" hadn't yet been transferred into an
abridged metaphor for all the world's unspeakable evil and monstrous crime, and on coming across President Roosevelt's prescient
remark in one of Umberto Eco's essays, I could read it as prose
instead of poetry—a reference not to the Four Horsemen of the
Apocalypse or the pit of Hell but to the political theories that
regard individual citizens as the property of the government, happy
villagers glad to wave the flags and wage the wars, grateful for the
good fortune that placed them in the care of a sublime leader. Or,
more emphatically, as Benito Mussolini liked to say, "Everything
in the state. Nothing outside the state. Nothing against the state."

The theories were popular in Europe in the 1930s (cheering crowds, rousing band music, splendid military uniforms), and in the United States they numbered among their admirers a good many important people who believed that a somewhat modified form of fascism (power vested in the banks and business corporations instead of with the army) would lead the country out of the wilderness of the Great Depression—put an end to the Pennsylvania labor troubles, silence the voices of socialist heresy and democratic dissent.

Roosevelt appreciated the extent of fascism's popularity at the political box office; so does Eco, who takes pains in the essay "Ur-Fascism," published in *The New York Review of Books* in 1995, to suggest that it's a mistake to translate fascism into a figure of literary speech. By retrieving from our historical memory only the vivid and familiar images of fascist tyranny (Gestapo firing squads, Soviet labor camps, the chimneys at Treblinka), we lose sight of the faith-based initiatives that sustained the tyrant's rise to glory. The several experiments with fascist government, in Russia and Spain as well as in Italy and Germany, didn't depend on a single portfolio of dogma, and so Eco, in search of their common ground, doesn't look for a unifying principle or a standard text. He attempts to describe a way of thinking and a habit of mind, and on sifting through the assortment of fantastic and often contradictory notions—Nazi paganism, Franco's National Catholicism, Mussolini's corporatism—he finds a set of axioms on which all the fascisms agree. Among the most notable:

- The truth is revealed once and only once.
- Parliamentary democracy is by definition rotten because it doesn't represent the voice of the people, which is that of the sublime leader.
- Doctrine outpoints reason, and science is always suspect.
- Critical thought is the province of degenerate intellectuals, who betray the culture and subvert traditional values.
- The national identity is provided by the nation's enemies.
- Argument is tantamount to treason.

- Perpetually at war, the state must govern with the instruments of fear.
- Citizens do not act; they play the supporting role of "the people" in the grand opera that is the state.

Eco published his essay ten years ago, when it wasn't as easy as it has since become to see the hallmarks of fascist sentiment in the character of an American government. Roosevelt probably wouldn't have been surprised. He'd encountered enough opposition to both the New Deal and to his belief in such a thing as a United Nations to judge the force of America's racist passions and the ferocity of its anti-intellectual prejudice. As he may have guessed, so it happened. The American democracy won the battles for Normandy and Iwo Jima, but the victories abroad didn't stem the retreat of democracy at home, after 1968 no longer moving "forward as a living force, seeking day and night to better the lot" of its own citizens. And now, sixty years after the bomb fell on Hiroshima, it doesn't take much talent for reading a cashier's scale at Walmart to know that it is fascism, not democracy, that won the heart and mind of America's "Greatest Generation," added to its weight and strength on America's shining seas and fruited plains.

A few sorehead liberal intellectuals continue to bemoan the fact, write books about the good old days when everybody was in charge of reading his or her own mail. I hear their message and feel their pain, share their feelings of regret, also wish that Cole Porter was still writing songs, that Jean Harlow and Robert Mitchum hadn't quit making movies. But what's gone is gone, and it serves nobody's purpose to deplore the fact that we're not still riding in a coach to Philadelphia with Thomas Jefferson. The attitude is cowardly and French, symptomatic of effete aesthetes who refuse to change with the times.

As set forth in Eco's list, the fascist terms of political endearment are refreshingly straightforward and mercifully simple, many of them already accepted and understood by a gratifyingly large number of our most forward-thinking fellow citizens, multitasking and safe with Jesus. It does no good to ask the weakling's pointless question, "Is America a fascist state?" We must ask instead, in a major rather than a minor key, "Can we make America the best damned fascist state the world has ever seen," an authoritarian paradise deserving the admiration of the international capital markets, worthy of "a decent respect to the opinions of mankind"? I wish to be the first to say we can. We're Americans; we have the money and the know-how to succeed where Hitler failed, and history has favored us with advantages not given to the early pioneers.

We don't have to burn any books

The Nazis in the 1930s were forced to waste precious time and money on the inoculation of the German citizenry (too well educated for its own good) against the infections of impermissible thought. We can count it as a blessing that we don't bear the burden of an educated citizenry. The systematic destruction of the public school and library systems over the last thirty years, a program wisely carried out under administrations both Republican and Democratic, protects the market for the sale and distribution of the government's propaganda posters. The publishing companies can print as many books as will guarantee their profit (books on any and all subjects, some of them even truthful), but to people who don't know how to read or think, they do as little harm as snowflakes falling on a frozen pond.

We don't have to disturb, terrorize, or plunder the bourgeoisie

In Communist Russia as well as in Fascist Italy and Nazi Germany, the codes of social hygiene occasionally put the regime to the trouble of smashing department-store windows, beating bank managers to death, inviting opinionated merchants on complementary tours (all expenses paid, breathtaking scenery) of Siberia. The resorts to violence served as study guides for freethinking businessmen reluctant to give up on the democratic notion that the individual citizen is entitled to an owner's interest in his or her own mind.

The difficulty doesn't arise among people accustomed to regarding themselves as functions of a corporation. Thanks to the diligence of our news media and the structure of our tax laws, our affluent and suburban classes have taken to heart the lesson taught to the aspiring serial killers rising through the ranks at West Point and the Harvard Business School—think what you're told to think, and you get to keep the house in Florida or command of the Pentagon press office. And on some sunny prize day not far over the horizon the compensation committee will hand you a check for $40 million, or President George W. Bush will bestow on you the favor of a nickname as witty as the ones that on good days elevate Karl Rove to the honorific "Boy Genius," on bad days to the disappointed but no less affectionate "Turd Blossom." Who doesn't now know that the corporation is immortal, that it is the corporation that grants the privilege of an identity, confers meaning on one's life, gives the pension, a decent credit rating, and the priority standing in the community? Of course the corporation reserves the right to open one's email, test one's blood, listen to the phone calls, examine one's urine, hold the patent on the copyright to any idea generated on its premises. Why ever should it not? As surely as the loyal fascist knew that it was his duty to serve the state, the true American knows that it is his duty to protect the brand.

Having met many fine people who come up to the corporate mark—on golf courses and commuter trains, tending to their gardens in Fairfield County while cutting back the payrolls in Michigan and Mexico—I'm proud to say we're blessed with a bourgeoisie that will welcome fascism as gladly as it welcomes the rain in April and the sun in June. No need to send for the Gestapo or the Soviet Commissariat for Internal Affairs; it will not be necessary to set examples.

We don't have to gag the press or seize the radio stations

People trained to the corporate style of thought and movement have no further use for free speech, which is corrupting, overly emotional, reckless, and ill-informed, not calibrated to the time available for television talk or to the performance standards of a Super Bowl halftime show. It is to our advantage that free speech doesn't meet the criteria of the free market. We don't require the inspirational genius of a Joseph Goebbels: we can rely instead on the dictates of the Nielsen ratings and the camera angles, secure in the knowledge that the major media syndicates run the business on strictly corporatist principles—afraid of anything disruptive or inappropriate, committed to the promulgation of what is responsible, rational, and approved by experts. Their willingness to stay on message is a credit to their professionalism.

The early twentieth-century fascists had to contend with individuals who regarded their freedom of expression as a necessity —the bone and marrow of their existence, how they recognized themselves as human beings. Which was why, if sometimes they refused appointments to the state-run radio stations, they sometimes were found dead on the Italian autostrada or drowned in the Kiel Canal. The authorities looked upon their deaths as forms of self-indulgence. The same attitude governs the agreement reached between labor and management at our leading news organizations. No question that the freedom of speech is extended to every American—it says so in the Constitution—but the privilege is one that mustn't be abused. Understood in a proper and financially rewarding light, freedom of speech is more trouble than it's worth—a luxury comparable to owning a racehorse and likely to bring with it little else except the risk of being made to look ridiculous. People who learn to conduct themselves in a manner respectful of the telephone tap and the surveillance camera have no reason to fear the fist of censorship. By removing the chore of having to think for oneself, one frees up more leisure time to enjoy the convenience of the Internet services that know exactly what one likes to hear and see and wear and eat.

We don't have to murder the intelligentsia

Here again, we find ourselves in luck. The society is so glutted with easy entertainment that no writer or company of writers is troublesome enough to warrant the compliment of an arrest, or even the courtesy of a sharp blow to the head. What passes for the American school of dissent talks exclusively to itself in the pages of obscure journals, across the coffee cups in Berkeley and Park Slope, in half-deserted lecture halls in small midwestern colleges. The author on the platform or the beach towel can be relied upon to direct his angriest invective at the other members of the academy who failed to drape around the title of his latest book the garland of a rave review.

The blessings bestowed by Providence place America in the front rank of nations addressing the problems of a twenty-first century, certain to require bold geopolitical initiatives and strong ideological solutions. How can it be otherwise? More pressing demands for always scarcer resources; ever larger numbers of people who cannot be controlled except with an increasingly heavy hand of authoritarian guidance. Who better than the Americans to lead the fascist renaissance, set the paradigm, order the preemptive strikes? The existence of mankind hangs in the balance; failure is not an option. Where else but in America can the world find the visionary intelligence to lead it bravely into the future—Donald Rumsfeld our Dante, Turd Blossom our Michelangelo?

I don't say that over the last thirty years we haven't made brave strides forward. By matching Eco's list of fascist commandments against our record of achievement, we can see how well we've begun the new project for the next millennium—the notion of absolute and eternal truth embraced by the evangelical Christians and embodied in the strict constructions of the Constitution; our national identity provided by anonymous Arabs; Darwin's theory of evolution rescinded by the fiat of "intelligent design"; a state of perpetual war and a government administering, in generous and daily doses, the drug of fear; two presidential elections stolen with little or no objection on the part of a complacent populace; the nation's congressional districts gerrymandered to defend the White House for the next fifty years against the intrusion of a liberal-minded president; the news media devoted to the arts of iconography, busily minting images of corporate executives like those of the emperor heroes on the coins of ancient Rome.

An impressive beginning, in line with what the world has come to expect from the innovative Americans, but we can do better. The early twentieth-century fascisms didn't enter their golden age until the proletariat in the countries that gave them birth had been reduced to abject poverty. The music and the marching songs rose with the cry of eagles from the wreckage of the domestic economy. On the evidence of the wonderful work currently being done by the Bush Administration with respect to the trade deficit and the national debt—to say nothing of expanding the markets for global terrorism—I think we can look forward with confidence to character-building bankruptcies, picturesque bread riots, thrilling cavalcades of splendidly costumed motorcycle police.

25. Lionhearts

In the last analysis, terrorism is an idea generated by capitalism to justify better defense measures to safeguard capitalism.

—Rainer Werner Fassbinder

Although the reports from Baghdad this summer might seem to suggest that all is not well with Operation Iraqi Freedom—the city a blood-smeared ruin, the American Army hiding in holes—the impression is misleading. Understand the war on terror as free-market capitalist enterprise rather than as some sort of public or government service, and in the nightly newscasts we see before us victory, not defeat.

As is usual and to be expected, the witless liberal media get the story wrong, mistaking innovative business practice for waste and fraud, grotesquely characterizing superior sales technique as a crime against humanity. The biased commentary misconstrues both the purpose and the high quality of the work in progress. Measure the achievement by the standards that define a commercial success—maximizing the cost to the consumers of the product, minimizing the risk to the investors—and we discover in the White House and the Pentagon, also in the Congress and the Department of Homeland Security, not the crowd of incompetent fools depicted in the pages of the *New York Times* but a company of visionary entrepreneurs, worthy of comparison with the men who built the country's railroads and liberated the Western prairie from the undemocratic buffalo. Heed the message served with every Republican banquet speech—that the private interest precedes the public interest, that money is good for rich people, bad for poor people—and who can say that the war in Iraq has proved to be anything other than the transformation of a godforsaken desert into a defense contractor's Garden of Eden?

The winning numbers posted in the profit margins light the paths to glory. During the five years since the striking down of the World Trade Center towers, the U.S. Congress has appropriated well over $300 billion for the Bush Administration's never-ending war against all the world's evildoers. Now flowing eastward out of Washington at the rate of $1.5 billion a week, much of the money takes the form of no-bid contracts, cost-plus and often immune from audit—at least $12.3 billion to Halliburton; $5.3 billion for Parsons Corporation; $3.7 billion for Fluor Corporation; $3.1 billion for Washington Group International; $2.8 billion for Bechtel Corporation. The contracts specify the repair and reconstruction of Iraq's depleted infrastructure—roads, power plants, hospitals, oil fields, pipelines, schools, mosques, and sewer systems—but because so many of the project sites have been deemed unsafe for visitors, the invoices translate into art objects, intricately and lovingly decorated with surcharges for undelivered concrete and nonexistent electricity.

So also the goods and services with which private security companies supplement the American military effort in Iraq. The Pentagon furnishes 130,000 troops, many of them National Guard Reservists, poorly paid, inadequately equipped, and held against their will for extended tours of duty; the private companies field an additional 50,000 personnel, some of them earning upward of $150,000 a year for driving trucks, cleaning latrines, flying helicopters, and pitching tents. Unhampered by U.S. Army regulations or by Iraqi law, the military guest workers are most conspicuously employed as bodyguards for the cadres of American middle management requiring, in the words of one of the advertising brochures, "discreet travel companions" or a "heavily armored high profile convoy escort." For a discreet companion armed with an assault rifle and a record of prior service under the Chilean dictator General Augusto Pinochet, Blackwater USA charges $600 a day, plus a 36 percent markup for expenses—travel, weapons, insurance, hotel room, ammunition.

For the friends of the free market operating in Iraq it doesn't matter who gets killed or why; every day is payday, and if from time to time events take a turn for the worse—another twenty or thirty Arabs annihilated in a mosque, a BBC cameraman lost on the road to the airport—back home in America with the flags and the executive-compensation packages, the stock prices for our reliably patriotic corporations rise with the smoke from the car bombs exploding in Ramadi and Fallujah—Lockheed Martin up from $52 to $75 between July 2003 and July 2006; over the span of the same three years, Boeing up from $33 to $77; ExxonMobil up from $36 to $65; Chevron up from $36 to $66; Halliburton up from $22 to $74; Fluor up from $34 to $87.

In a country that recognizes no objective more worthwhile than the one incorporated in the phrase "to make a killing," I don't know why so many people insist on withholding their applause. Were it not for the vapid hypocrisy that muddles the national political debate with idle moralizing—about the withdrawal of American troops or the disappearance of Iraqi children—the Republican politicians auditioning hairstylists for their November election campaigns could afford to tell the truth, to remind the voters that our greatness as a nation stems from what Upton Sinclair knew to be "those pecuniary standards of culture which estimate the excellence of a man by the amount of other people's happiness he can possess and destroy." Unfortunately, we live in a society that no longer remembers Sinclair's name, forgets that since the days of the ancient Romans it has been on their way to war that men have found the road to wealth.

The loss of historical perspective follows from the debasement of our better universities, the once vigorously imperialist curricula softened into sentimental platitude by two generations of English professors telling their students that the arms trade is neither a gentleman's profession nor a wise career choice. The lesson is both politically and economically incorrect. The medieval age of chivalry rejoiced in the exploits of brilliantly costumed horsemen faring forth to lay waste the countryside, murder the peasantry, strip precious ornaments from the bodies of the celebrity dead, hold as captives kings and popes from whom they could extort the ransom of a fortune or a crown. The undertaking was a private venture, not a public service. The noble knight supplied his own weapons, bore his own expenses (grooms, horses, squires, armor, etc.), took his own risks, paid his own pipers. When King Richard the Lionheart joined the Third Crusade at Acre in 1191 and there failed to find the treasure promised by God, he insisted that the infidels had swallowed their jewels and gold coins in order to deny him the reward owing to his royal majesty and Christian virtue. His companions, less discreet than the ones currently for rent in Basra and Tikrit, cut open the stomachs of 3,000 Muslims in the search for truth, which, in the event, proved as determined, if eventually as disappointing, as the Bush Administration's quest for the thermonuclear genie in Saddam Hussein's magic lamp.

Unlike our latter-day writers of romantic movie scripts, the fourteenth-century poet Geoffrey Chaucer was under no illusion as to the whereabouts or meaning of the Holy Grail, and among the figures present in his *Canterbury Tales*, he draws the portrait of a perfect, gentle knight more inclined to rob a church or sodomize a nun than to retrieve the bones of a departed saint. The poet knew whereof he spoke. During the Hundred Years' War, Chaucer served in France with the English armies famous for their brutality, and of whom it was said that they went forth to war with the eager anticipation of guests invited to a wedding or a feast. The memory of the work done in the blood-soaked fields of Agincourt and Poitiers, the lords temporal dismembering one another with sword and axe, still lingers in the language of instruction learned at America's 'better business schools—asset stripping, war chest, target audience, corporate raider, downsized labor force.

The upgrading of the weapons technology in the late Middle Ages (heavier cannons, the English longbow) brought with it the appearance of private armies that in their forms of organization set the template of the modern corporation. The British historian Frances Stonor Saunders points up the similarities in a recent book, *The Devil's Broker*, in which she quotes a letter, from a fourteenth-century captain of mercenary soldiers to the papal legate in Italy, that if rendered as a procession of stately bureaucratic acronyms might as well have been sent by the president of Blackwater USA to the Senate Armed Services Committee.

> Our manner of life in Italy is well known—it is to rob, plunder and murder those who resist. Our revenues depend on ransoms levied in those provinces that we invade. Those who value their lives can buy peace and quiet by heavy tribute. Therefore, if the Lord Legate wishes to dwell at unity with us then let him do like the rest of the world—that is to say, pay! pay!

The words "merchant" and "mercenary" ultimately derive from the same root, and in Renaissance Italy Saunders finds the combined interests of the two allied professions giving rise to the entrepreneurial revolution that enriched the world with capital markets for the manufacture of fear and the sale of death. Chartered as joint stock companies known as societies of adventure or acquisition, the mercenary armies offered their services to the highest bidder (to the Duke of Milan for a raid on Siena, to a Pope at Avignon or Rome for the siege of Pisa): everybody made contracts—the soldiers with their captain (guaranteeing term of service, wage, portion of the loot): the captain with his client prince or cardinal (specifying payment in Florentine or Hungarian florins)—and in the long train of executive assistants traveling with the corporate picnic in the Tuscan countryside, none were more highly prized than the clerks who kept the accounts, named the price for a man's horse or a woman's life, supervised the cash flows, and attended to the distribution of silver goblets, fine linens, and Venetian ducats.

Made sacred by the Catholic Church and codified by Niccolò Machiavelli rediscovering the military history of ancient Rome, the notion of government-sponsored terrorism as lucrative private enterprise strengthened the advance of Western civilization for the next 400 years. The rulers of the nation-states emerging in Europe during the sixteenth and seventeenth centuries employed professional armies to extend their land holdings, replenish their finances, add luster to their bloodlines. The eighteenth and nineteenth centuries developed the business of colonial empire to regulate the trade in Asian spices, American fur, and African slaves. The cost of the increasingly expensive weapons made it impossible for individual entrepreneurs to compete with the larger corporate interests, but even when enlisted under the banners of an English king or a French dynast (among them Napoleon, who informed Austria's Prince Metternich, "You can't stop me. I spend 30,000 men a month"), an enterprising mercenary still could look forward to a fair return on his investments—a share of the prize money, the beginnings of an art collection, a chance to rape good-looking women.

Our American forefathers understood the rules of the game. The first settlers of the New England wilderness constituted themselves as a society of acquisition as well as a community of God. A seventeenth-century governor of New York bankrolled Captain William Kidd's Caribbean expeditions in exchange for a share of the pirate's takings under primitive laws of eminent domain; the old spirit of adventure manned the American privateers plundering British merchant ships during the Revolutionary War, fortified the real-estate speculation otherwise known as the Mexican War, ensured the elimination of the Indians on the trans-Mississippi frontier, backed the 1898 raid on Cuba, drummed up Wall Street's enthusiasm for America's participation in President Wilson's war to end all wars.

The twentieth century's two world wars obscured the primacy of the profit motive as the only casus belli deserving the consideration of true patriots. Over the course of the thirty-one years between 1914 and 1945, so many people were killed to no apparently remunerative purpose that the world's spiritual advisers and political theorists were put to the task of coining expensive ideal-isms to explain the lack of an owner's commercial interest on the part of the innumerable decedents. Voices of conscience on five continents contributed an impressive range of consumer choices—fascism, liberalism, nationalism, communism, capitalism, racism, Nazism, socialism, Serbian irredentism—but so great was the con-fusion in the minds of men living under the shadow of nuclear extinction that it needed another thirty-five years, thirty-five years and the coming to the White House of the blessed Ronald Reagan, before the Americans could find their way home to the meaning of warfare as it was understood in the age of chivalry.

How better to describe our reunion with the wisdom of the Renaissance than as the triumph of American conservatism, the happy return to the smile of immortal selfishness that shines forth in the face of President George W. Bush. The smile is well and truly earned. His administration has so improved the business of making war—broadening the market for the product, relocating the costs and exporting the collateral damage, coming up with innovations both technological and aesthetic—that none of the principal beneficiaries need go to the trouble of learning how to lift a sword or ride a horse. The dying is done by the hired help, by our now privatized and outsourced army, or by entire regiments of auxiliary civilians deployed as targets for the staging of Pentagon air shows. None of the combatants demand a share of the spoils, which accrue on clean well-lighted computer screens far from the fear and smell of death. More politically sophisticated than the condottieri (or mercenaries) of the Italian Renaissance, our own military industrial elites not only extract tribute from foreign legates in distant provinces but also hold to ransom the citizenry of their own country, accepting payment in the form of taxpayer contributions to the Holy Grail otherwise known as the federal military budget. Lionhearts one and all, as bold as Chaucer's knight, as generous as Napoleon, deserving of an equestrian statue and a portrait in the Louvre.

2007

26. Blowing Bubbles

Men have an indistinct notion that if they keep up this activity of joint stocks and spades long enough all will at length ride somewhere, in next to no time, and for nothing; but though a crowd rushes to the depot, and the conductor shouts "All aboard!" when the smoke is blown away and the vapor condensed, it will be perceived that a few are riding, but the rest are run over,—and it will be called, and will be, "A melancholy accident."

—Henry David Thoreau

Reading the reports from the scene of August's melancholy accident in the country's credit markets—the bursting of the home-mortgage bubble, banks sinking into the sand of subprime loans, hedge funds losing 100 percent of their imagined value in a matter of days, the Dow Jones Industrial Average dropping 250 points in the space of half an hour—I was struck by the resemblances between the speculation floated on the guarantee of easy money on Wall Street and the one puffed up on the promise of certain victory in Iraq. To buyers of highly leveraged debt the promoters of the

"All aboard!" money schemes issued PowerPoints similar to those concocted in the White House and circulated with former secretary of defense Donald Rumsfeld's proviso that "there are known unknowns ... But there are also unknown unknowns." A surplus of both commodities was found in the luggage of the travelers run over in August on the road to El Dorado. A number of them deserve to be rendered as military acronyms:

The "NINJA Loan"—Extended to borrowers possessed of no income, no job, no assets—comparable to the predatory lending of the U.S. Army to the freedom-loving sheikhs of Iraq.

The "Neutron Loan"—Designed to remove the occupants but leave the property intact. Within the next year over a million American home mortgages are due to foreclose. In August 80,000 people were "displaced by violence" from their houses and neighborhoods in Iraq; another 2.2 million Iraqis have been obliged to flee the country.

The "Teaser Loan"—An adjustable rate mortgage (ARM) sometimes requiring no money down or up front but in all variants offered at a low introductory rate that adjusts only in an upward direction. The American liberation of Iraq was originally priced at $50 billion over a span of seven months; the expenses now run to $2 billion a week. Joseph Stiglitz, the Nobel Prize-winning economist, estimates the eventual cost of the Iraqi investment at $2 trillion.

The "Liar Loan"—Requiring no documentation attesting to the borrower's net worth, annual income, or intention to repay—the same terms on which the CIA accepted the story about Saddam Hussein's weapons of mass destruction from the Iraqi defector code-named "Curveball."

SIV—"Structured investment vehicle" that "securitizes" subprime loans, thus creating credit with "access to liabilities." Soon after the invasion of Iraq the infatuation with a similar method of transforming loss into gain prompted the Pentagon to welcome terrorists arriving in Baghdad and Anbar province from everywhere in the Middle East. The bundling of America's enemies into one target supported the notion that the war on terror could be won at a single blow. Rush Limbaugh delivered the good news to his radio audience in the summer of 2003: "We don't have to go anywhere to find them! They've fielded a jihad all-star team."

"Toxic Waste"—Degraded financial material added as ballast to higher quality assets contained in a mortgage-backed bond or security.

AAA—Bond rating affixed by Moody's and Standard & Poor's to SIVs transporting "toxic waste." The certifications correspond to former CIA Director George Tenet's assuring President Bush that finding weapons of mass destruction in Iraq was a "slam dunk."

Risk Assessment Models—Systems of stock-market trading quantified as mathematical algorithms and engineered to guarantee the perpetual motion of profit. They bear comparison to the Pentagon's arsenal of high-technology weapons—the ones incapable of losing a war.

Model Misbehavior—Inexplicable displays of insubordination on the part of the algorithms, believed to account for the August loss of $5.5 trillion in the global stock markets. The Bush Administration attributes its failures in Iraq to model misbehavior on the part of the think-tank construct (computer-generated, ideologically enhanced) of a constitutional democracy in Iraq.

CDO—Collateralized debt obligation. A coalition of the willing assembled with debt instruments of a strength equivalent to the armed forces sent to Iraq from Albania.

Bubble—Employed as a verb in eighteenth-century London. "To bubble" is to cheat, swindle, perpetrate a fraud. In contemporary American military parlance, a noun—the "surge" of liquidity in the form of 30,000 troops restoring calm to the Baghdad market in civil obedience.

August's misfortunes in the credit markets produced a good deal of collateral damage elsewhere in the economy—severe losses in the construction and retail trades, to school and sewer districts, in the hotel and travel industries, to the 1.7 million families forced to flee their homes—but the proofs of Wall Street's stupefied greed didn't rouse the news media or the season's presidential candidates to exclamations of anger and disgust. Throughout the whole of its history, the American Commonwealth has been subject to the depredations of what George Washington knew to be "a corrupt squadron of paper-dealers"; a hundred or even fifty years ago the brokers of the fast shuffle might have been seen in savage cartoons like those drawn by Thomas Nast (top-hatted dancing pigs) or pilloried in the language once voiced by Walt Whitman ("canker'd, crude, superstitious and rotten ...") and E. L. Godkin ("a gaudy stream of bespangled, belaced, and beruffled barbarians").

Once upon a time in galaxies far, far away, we recognized the character of the risk in what was known to the first Dutch settlers in seventeenth-century New Amsterdam (many of them participants in land or stock-jobbing ventures) as "The Feast of Fools." It wasn't that the new arrivals on the American shore didn't believe or delight in the expectation and promise of fairy gold. Understood as the most demotic of economic activities, expressive of a yearning for freedom, the game of speculative finance aligns with the American passion for gambling and matches the spirit of the bet placed by the Declaration of Independence on the wheel of fortune set up with the slots marked "Life, Liberty and the Pursuit of Happiness." But we used to know that sometimes the numbers crap out.

The knowledge began to disappear from the American consciousness and vocabulary during the dawn of the new "Morning in America" that Ronald Reagan perceived on the horizon of the 1980s when he set up his rose-colored telescope on the White House roof. Convinced that "the difference between an American

and any other kind of person is that an American lives in anticipation of the future because he knows it will be a great place,"
Reagan brought with him the preferred attitude that the dealers
in rainbows seek to instill in the minds of the customers shopping
for financial salvation and political romance. Everybody a winner;
the flowers never die.

The attitude has been sustained over the past twenty-five years
by the corporate news media's increasingly messianic testimonies
to the wonder and wisdom of the free market (Alan Greenspan
as infallible as the Pope), by the entertainment industry's loudly
applauding the miraculous transformations of frogs into princes
(Donald Trump the hero of our time), by the government's policy
of providing the banks with infusions of cheap credit on which
to float speculative bubble baths (in 1987, 1998, 2001, again in
2007), by a steadily multiplying herd of eager buyers, their number
now estimated at one in every two Americans acting either as independent agents or as participants in mutual and pension funds,
seeking to acquire, at steadily rising prices, beachfront property
on the coast of Utopia.

Together with the promises of an always brighter tomorrow
(available on the Internet, delivered within twenty-four hours), the
widely distributed faith in the philosophers' stone (i.e., the one
with which medieval alchemists supposedly turned lead into gold)
accords with the revelation bestowed on a correspondent for the
New York Times in the autumn of 2004 by a White House sage
identified at the time as "a senior adviser to Bush" but now generally assumed to have been Karl Rove, President Bush's recently
retired man-for-all-seasons. Disdainful of the meager and obsolete
truths that informed the thinking of "the reality-based community," the sage opened a wider-angle lens on the vision beheld by
Ronald Reagan.

[Guys like you] believe that solutions emerge from your judi-
cious study of discernible reality. That's not the way the world
really works anymore. We're an empire now, and when we act, we
create our own reality. And while you're studying that reality—
judiciously, as you will—we'll act again, creating other new

realities, which you can study too, and that's how things will sort out. We're history's actors ... and you, all of you, will be left to just study what we do.

Which didn't mean that the study would be easy to pursue. The Bush Administration's obsessive hiding of its actions and motives (from itself as well as from a public audit) rules against the handing-out of brochures illustrated with the four-color posters of imperial fantasies decorating the walls at the White House, the Pentagon, the Office of the Attorney General. On Wall Street the hedge against having to tell the truth is formed with exemptions from state and federal regulation that yield the elixir of "opacity." Highly valued by the speculators in the nineteenth-century stock swindles engineered by Commodore Vanderbilt and Daniel Drew, opacity allows the private-equity operations to bubble both the government and their clients, empowering the dealers in SIVs in the same way that it serves the creators of new realities in Mesopotamia and assists the poker players in the Las Vegas casinos. Unfortunately, as with the water in the tale of the sorcerer's apprentice, too much opacity sloshing around on the trading floors makes it impossible not only to see what cards the other players hold in their hands but also to know how much money is on the table. The government in March stopped publishing the figure that measures the extent of America's money supply, possibly because by some estimates the financial risk exposure in the global markets for leveraged derivatives now stands at a sum somewhere in the vicinity of $60 trillion, four times the size of the American economy.

When the smoke was blowing away and the vapor being condensed at the scene of the August wreckage, the fear of ghosts in the Wall Street attic precluded any movement in the markets for social conscience. The headlines flowed from the springs of panic, not from the wellheads of rage, the concern expressed for the concentrations of America's wealth (its safety, comfort, and good grooming) rather than for the health and well-being of the American citizenry. Together with most everybody else in the society, the big-ticket print and electronic media are heavily invested in the virtual realities that not only sustain the opulence of the country's *rentier* classes but also shape the course of the country's politics, sponsor its shows of conspicuous consumption, control the disposition of its armies. God forbid that the emperors of ice cream should be seen standing around naked on the reefs of destruction.

The financial press rounded up expert witnesses to cite the canonical distinction between *risk* ("present when future events occur with measurable probability") and *uncertainty* ("present when the likelihood of future events is indefinite or incalculable"), to implore the Federal Reserve for a surge of more money (Jim Cramer shouting into the camera at CNBC, "We have Armageddon! ... this is not the time to be complacent!"), to say of the SIVs destroyed by the financial equivalents of improvised roadside bombs, "It is not the corpses at the surface that are scary, it is the unknown corpses below the surface that may pop up unexpectedly." "Corpse" in its Wall Street usage refers to a non-performing financial instrument, not to a dead human being.

In the context of the war in Iraq, the word refers to a nonperforming geopolitical instrument. If over the past four years Wall Street's deployment of lethal paper has increased the country's mortgage debt to $9.5 trillion, the Bush Administration's deployment of lethal weapons has outsourced or exhausted much of the country's military capacity, meanwhile reducing the credit rating of the All Aboard! American superpower scheme from an investment-grade security to that of a junk bond. By the end of August both speculations (the liberalization of America's capital markets, the liberation of the Islamic Middle East) were losing "tactical momentum" in the reality-based community. The Washington politicians faced difficulties similar to those faced by Wall Street's squadron of paper dealers—how to "securitize" the subprime loans backing the Iraqi civil war, where to find leverage in the imaginary numbers attesting to the soundness of the Anbar province ARM, what degree of protection was left in the hedge of opacity.

The preoccupation with derivatives forecloses debate about the worth of the underlying investment—the value or nonvalue of the war as a thing in itself—and shifts the discussion to the positioning of the political risk. Process, not product. Not why or to what end do we continue to kill our own soldiers (the known unknowns) as well as Iraqi civilians (the unknown unknowns), but which artful dodge stands the best chance of beguiling the voters in next year's elections while at the same time preserving the bubble floated on the belief that America's invincible military power serves as collateral for the $2.5 trillion debt to foreign central banks that America has neither the means nor the intention to repay.

Among speculators in the commodity pits trading geopolitical futures, the rumors speak, as they do among the speculators following the play in the stock markets, to the coming of "the next big thing." Soon after the Labor Day weekend the financial press was unanimous in the opinion that the Federal Reserve was bound to step up the flows of liquidity to the Wall Street banks in order to sustain the world's faith in the American dollar. Informed sources in Washington were predicting a preemptive military strike against Iran. Three Navy battle groups were known to be present in the Persian Gulf, the president was casting the Iranian Revolutionary Guard in an increasingly evil light (terrorists, enemies of civilization), and how better to replenish the credit lost in Iraq than with a weapons-grade CDO spreading the risk to investors everywhere within range of a melancholy nuclear accident. With us or against us; buy American or lose the chance of a lifetime.

2008

27. Estate Sale

> *It costs a lot of money to be rich.*
> —Peter Boyle

Not being expert at the interpretation of economic data, I'm never sure which leading indicators point in what direction, but when every morning's newspaper offers a further proof of the bankrupt American dream, I'm prepared to believe that somewhere near at hand there is a piper waiting to be paid. The voices of informed financial opinion in New York and Washington (bond salesman, stock market analyst, investment banker, currency trader, chairman of the Federal Reserve) act the part of the alarmed chorus in an ancient Greek play, bearing witness to the pride that goeth before a fall, generating the portents of doom—the American dollar sinking to record lows against the euro, the capital and credit markets reduced to a state of paralysis, hedge funds vanishing into clouds of blown-back smoke, home mortgages abandoned in the Arizona desert, banks drowned in pools of toxic debt, yet another American corporate sweetheart (department store, hotel chain, record label) sold to a syndicate of Chinese Communists or into the seraglio of an Arab emir.

When the appalled bystanders find themselves momentarily at a loss for words, they move downstage and run the numbers. The national debt pegged at $9.4 trillion (up from $6.4 trillion in 2003), running expenses of $16 billion a month for the wars in Iraq and Afghanistan (the eventual cost projected at more than $3 trillion); $4 trillion borrowed since 2002 using homes as collateral, the value of American real estate diminished by $1 trillion in a matter of months; losses of $600 billion to be incurred by investors holding debt instruments backed by specious credit, American assets in the amount of $414 billion sold to foreign buyers in 2007, the Federal Reserve on March 11, 2008, cleansing the wounds of the New York banks with $200 billion in liquidity and then, a few days later, allotting $30 billion for the salvage of Bear Stearns.

The numbers speak to the scale of the speculative bubble risen to the height of an Air Force weather balloon, but I tend to lose track of their significance in the long rows of holloweyed zeros, and so I am at least grateful for the clarification that appeared on the front page of the *New York Times* on March 1 under the headline "DRUMBEAT OF GRIM REPORTS SENDS MARKETS TUMBLING." The previous day hadn't been a happy one on the New York Stock Exchange (the Dow off 315 points in a spasm of late-afternoon panic), and the *Times* rounded up several of the usual Wall Street suspects known to have been present at or near the scene of the accident. Most of the witnesses couldn't remember how or when the tapping on the drum first came to their attention—the sound jaunty or solemn, the drum muffled or accompanied by bagpipes—and so it was left to Douglas Peta, chief investment strategist for J. & W. Seligman, to discover the moral in the tale:

> There is not any one news item that I can point to. We know that there is paper out there that we can't trust. We don't know exactly who owns it and how much. And we don't know how they are valuing it.

The observation embraced both the joys and the sorrows of an enterprise dependent upon the manufacture of something for nothing. On the summertime side of the proposition, when the fish are jumping and the cotton is high, the paperwork slows down the momentum, gets in the way of the oceanfront views. God forbid that any buyers out there (of Florida sandcastles, credit-debt obligations from JPMorgan Chase) should know exactly what they own—how much or how little of it, whether it fades in strong sunlight or washes off in the laundry. When the autumn leaves begin to fall the only intelligible paper that anybody is likely to see is the arrest warrant and the eviction notice.

Which isn't to say that the confidence game is somehow un-American or wrong. It is a national pastime as dearly beloved as baseball—appreciated as an art and enjoyed as a sport—but the rules are sometimes hard to explain to Baptist clergymen and bearded foreigners. Our creditors in Europe, Asia, and the Persian Gulf (from whom we currently borrow $2 billion a day to export the blessing of democracy to Iraq) begin to suspect that the American modus operandi doesn't lend itself to the trustworthy management of global empire. With what collateral do we secure our credit rating as the world's AAA hegemon? George Soros addressed the question at last January's meeting of the World Economic Forum in Davos, Switzerland. Speaking for what was reported as the consensus of sound judgment circulating among the assembled finance ministers, Soros referred to the break in the American housing market as "basically the end of a sixty-year period of continuing credit expansion based on the dollar as the reserve currency."

Having had occasion eleven years ago to attend the Forum's meeting at Davos, I could recall the setting—prominent businessmen, important politicians, visionary intellectuals, primetime journalists passing documents to one another across the plum tarts and the coffeepots. The remembrance of time past served to measure the life span of the American imperium billed by the Bush Administration as the deserving heir to both the glory that was Greece and the grandeur that was Rome. In 1997 the United States was flush with money and long on self-congratulation, the

Clinton Administration fat with the promise of a budget surplus and an as-yet-unexploded stock market bubble, no enemies of consequence on or below the horizon, the euro five years away from being established as a legal tender. Although for the most part unfamiliar with languages other than their own, the American participants in the Forum seldom missed a chance to preach the doctrine of enlightened globalism, awakening the representatives of less fortunate nations to the need for "transparency" in their financial dealings, to the sin of "crony capitalism" (as practiced by the Indonesians and the Turks), to the dangers of "bandit oligarchy" (as practiced by the Russians and the sub-Saharan Africans), to the subtle but necessary distinctions between a "feverish" and a "consumptive" capital market, between a "palsied" and a "suppurating" trade balance. To replay the tape is to appreciate the worth of the material as stand-up comedy.

Soros also had been present at Davos eleven years ago, which maybe was why the report of his speech brought to mind the lofty and condescending height from which, once upon a time and in a galaxy far, far away, the Liege lords of American finance looked down upon people whom they regarded as vassals, bound both by divine providence and geopolitical circumstance, to serve the new world order centered on the navel of the universe in Washington. Or possibly it was a matter of coincidence. On February 12, at the Council on Foreign Relations in New York three weeks after reading the report from Davos, I attended a roundtable discussion entitled "Sovereign Wealth Funds on the Rise: Should We Worry?" Owned and operated by foreign governments, among them Russia and China as well as Norway, Saudi Arabia, and the United Arab Emirates, the funds control a pool of capital (currently $3 trillion, expected to rise to $12 trillion in another ten years) that waters the oases of the world's credit markets. What was instructive was the attitude of the monied interest in the room—the same kind of crowd that I'd encountered at Davos, but one that had come to learn instead of teach. All present were mindful of the fact that over the past several months the sovereign wealth funds had supplied $60 billion of liquidity to a roster of favored American financial institutions, among them Citigroup and Merrill Lynch, that otherwise might have been exposed to the embarrassment of having to sell the furniture, the silver, and the CEO's daughter. The money, of course, was welcome, but was it to be accepted as an unrestricted gift from Allah, or did it come with strings attached? Did any of the attachments mean anything? If so, why, how, and to whom?

The *consiglieri* seated on the podium, among them a representative of the International Monetary Fund and a former deputy secretary of the U.S. Treasury, answered the questions with the reassuring news that, at least for the time being, geopolitical terms and conditions didn't impede the progress of the wire transfers. Nobody in Singapore was looking to acquire Donald Rumsfeld's maps or Condoleezza Rice's piano. The experienced investors, most of them Arabs, could be relied upon to do straightforward business deals unencumbered by tactical or strategic objectives; the Russians and the Chinese were learning how to behave like gentlemen. Although it was true that the international funds weren't subject to regulatory oversight, which meant that one still had to contend with the problems of both opacity and corruption, at the end of the day and all things considered, sovereign wealth money was better than private equity money—not as volatile, less eager for a quick profit, not subject to redemption. Nor was there much reason to worry about undermining the national security. Except for a few fragments of homeland defense (weapons-grade uranium, the runways at Ronald Reagan National Airport) nearly everything in the American estate sale (shopping malls, universities, telephone companies, movie studios) could be sold to almost any buyer whose name the lawyers knew how to spell. The discussion attracted the Council's equivalent of a sellout crowd—sixty or seventy high-end Wall Street lawyers and merchant bankers imbued with the wisdom of the country's ruling oligarchy—and an executive summary of both what was said and what wasn't said could have been abstracted under the headings of two PowerPoints:

1. Goodbye to the sovereignty of nation-states. The world dances to the music of money, and the only frontier that matters is the one

that separates the gardens of the rich from the deserts of the poor. The Upper East Side of Manhattan belongs to the same polity as the 8th Arrondissement in Paris and the Odintsovo district in Moscow. The yachts moored in the Bay of Naples and the lagoon at Bora Bora sail under the flags of the same admiralty that posts squadrons off the shore of Nantucket and the Costa Brava.

2. Geoeconomics trumps geopolitics. It is the value of the American dollar that imparts meaning to the principles of the American democracy; loss of confidence in the former depreciates the character of the latter. Democracy works toward an idea of equality, capitalism moves in the direction of inequality, which is the preferred travel destination.

At the end of the discussion the expressions on the faces of at least some of the gentlemen in the room registered trace elements of regret. The departing company clearly was glad to know that the foreign shills were still in the game, but there was also the humiliation of America having to cut back on the royal elephants and the pretensions to empire. One gentleman in particular looked so dispirited as he was putting on his topcoat that had I known his name or where to find his hat, I would have pointed him to the light at the end of the tunnel, assured him that the redeployment of the world's wealth wouldn't entail the giving up of his customary table at Le Cirque. Even if America were to be reclassified as a Third World country, he would discover that Third World countries are by no means as unpleasant or as dangerous as they can be made to seem by the editorial writers at the *New York Times*. The girls are good-looking, the golf courses up to the standard of those in Palm Springs, the nightclubs trendy, the secret police efficient and courteous, the income spread between the haves and have-nots in line with the one to which he was accustomed here at home.

The United States has been ridding itself of its First World status for as long as it has been privatizing its critical infrastructure (a.k.a. the common good), at the same time despoiling the natural resource embodied in the health, welfare, courage, and intelligence of its citizenry. Over the past eight years, under the absentee land-lord economic policies of the Bush Administration, the stepped-up rate of disinvestment has resulted in the Third World confusion and mismanagement for which the American guidance counselors eleven years ago at Davos rebuked their economic inferiors—bandit oligarchy, gangster capitalism, nontransparent finance, palsied capital markets, and a suppurating trade balance.

Although not touched upon at the Council on Foreign Relations, the question that remains to be discussed is the one about putting the preferred spin on the story. The going gracefully into the imperial twilight with Britain and France wouldn't sit well with the parties of the nationalist right. We do better with the production of Super Bowl halftime shows than with the staging of historical ceremony; our cathedrals don't come furnished with the tombs of museum-quality kings. As an advanced industrial nation along the lines of Holland or Germany we would run into trouble with the paperwork. From advanced industrial nations the bankers in Hong Kong and Mumbai expect sincere proofs of "accountability" as well as earnest attempts to strengthen the currency and occasional repayments of outstanding debt. The requirements aren't configured to match the irrational exuberance of the freebooting American spirit. Accountability is a concept poorly understood both in Washington and Wall Street, our economy is a faith-based initiative, we're not in the habit of honoring our debts, and we're low on creditors willing to believe that our word is as good as Barack Obama's can-do smile.

Our liabilities become assets if we can recast the United States as a developing nation that contains within its borders the excitements of an emerging market. On first looking into an emergent market for fabulous risk-free wealth, the foreign investors don't yet know what anything is really worth—how much oil is under the sand in Utah, if the chinook salmon will return to the Sacramento River, who holds the mortgage on the Brooklyn Bridge. The circumstances favor the sunny side of the American street, allow for the freedom of entrepreneurial maneuver, and encourage imaginative interpretations of what constitutes an exploitable natural resource. Together with its expression of interest in such things as the Lincoln Memorial and the Marine Corps Band, the foreign money can be counted upon to assign value to commodities that the natives believe to be worthless. The seventeenth-century princes of Europe maintained private menageries stocked with Spanish and Italian dwarves; it's conceivable that the Arab sovereign wealth funds might wish to collect, as rare specimens of an exotic breed, ornamental American CEOs prized for their capacity to turn gold into lead. Priceless objects unavailable for purchase with MasterCard, capitalist action figures embodying the treasure of the Christian West, to be as proudly displayed as the peacocks in the gardens of Doha and Riyadh.

2008

28. Elegy for a Rubber Stamp

Fulfilling your duties, where does that land you? Into jealousy, upsets, persecution. Is that the way to get on? Butter people up, good God, butter them up, watch the great, study their tastes, fall in with their whims, pander to their vices, approve of their injustices. That's the secret.
— Denis Diderot, *Rameau's Nephew*

At 3:39 P.M. on Friday, June 13, Tom Brokaw interrupted NBC's network programming with the late-breaking news that Tim Russert had died—of a heart attack earlier that afternoon while preparing his Sunday broadcast of *Meet the Press*—and by the top of the next hour the story was being wrapped up in the ribbons of a national tragedy. Maybe not as tragic as the falling of John F. Kennedy Jr.'s plane into the Atlantic Ocean but undoubtedly an historic moment, up there in lights with the death of President Ronald Reagan and the loss of Lieutenant Colonel George A. Custer on the field at the Little Bighorn.

On the off chance that a bereaved citizenry might be slow to recover from the shock and reprocess the awe, MSNBC throughout the rest of the weekend projected an election-night air of developing crisis. Brokaw and Keith Olbermann took turns reading statements incoming from the leaders of the free world—"Tim was a tough and hardworking newsman" (President George W. Bush); "He was the standard-bearer for serious journalism" (Senator Barack Obama); "The explainer-in-chief of our political life" (Senator Joe Lieberman); "Always true to his proud Buffalo roots" (joint communiqué, Bill and Hillary Clinton); "A gentleman and a giant" (Senator Edward Kennedy); "He was hard. He was fair. ... He loved the Buffalo Bills" (Senator John McCain).

During the delays between bulletins, Brokaw and Olbermann introduced a procession of Washington media celebrities arriving with rush deliveries of op-ed-page solemnity and camera-ready grief. For two days and three nights, they paid tribute to the glory that was Tim and the grandeur that is themselves. Before the red carpet was rolled up on Monday morning, America had been comforted in its sorrow by, among others, Andrea Mitchell, David Broder, Mike Barnicle, Al Hunt, Bob Woodward, Gwen Ifill, Sally Quinn, Howard Fineman, Jon Meacham, Maria Shriver, Pat Buchanan, Ben Bradlee, and Doris Kearns Goodwin. Brokaw found Russert's death so hard to imagine that his only word for it was "surreal"; Olbermann borrowed his parting word from Shakespeare's *Hamlet*, "Now cracks a noble heart. Good-night, sweet prince,/And flights of angels sing thee to thy rest!" The choir standing by in the studio supplied the doo-wop vocals.

"This is a blow to America" (Peggy Noonan)
"An unfathomable loss" (Brian Williams, from Afghanistan)
"The gold standard in everything he did" (Chris Matthews, from Paris)
"The ideal American journalist" (Dan Rather)
"He was a friend to millions of people" (Barbara Walters)

By Friday evening the rending of garments had spread, like a bloom of algae on an endangered Florida ecosystem, to all the other news organizations in town, many hours of sweet remembrance on ABC and Fox News as well as on CBS and CNN, more of it on

Saturday and Sunday, Tim's friends and fellow on-air personalities thickening the sentiment, strengthening the highlight reels, bringing the perspective. I'm pretty sure that I didn't miss any of the major talking points—Russert a "devoted father" and "a reverential son"; Russert, "Hail Mary and full of grace," certain to have been enthroned as the Pope had he chosen a career in the Catholic Church; Russert a "basic old American patriot" and a true friend of the common man; Russert likened both to Tom Sawyer and to Huck Finn, to Teddy as well as to Franklin Roosevelt; Russert born poor and humble in Buffalo, "Irish, ethnic, working-class," gone forth to become rich and famous in the capital of the universe but never losing sight of the Buffalo River; above all, Russert the tough-minded journalist, hard-hitting and relentless, unafraid to speak truth to power, so fierce in his interrogations that for a trembling public servant seated across the table from him on Meet the Press "it was like going up against an All-Star pitcher in Yankee Stadium."

On Monday I thought I'd heard the end of the sales promotion. Tim presumably had ascended to the great studio camera in the sky to ask Thomas Jefferson if he intended to run for president in 1804, and I assumed that the Washington news media would allow his soul to rest in peace. I was mistaken. For live broadcast on Wednesday, June 18, MSNBC staged a memorial service in the Kennedy Center for the Performing Arts, and if I'd thought that the bathos couldn't reach new force levels, it was because I'd failed to account for either the cynicism or the vanity of a fourth estate that regards itself as the light in the window of Western civilization. Several wire services in town shut down their operations during the ninety-minute special as a mark of respect for the departed hero, his last rites not to be disturbed with disquieting reports from Afghanistan or ugly rumors about the national economy sinking further into the quicksand of recession.

The performance attracted an opening-night crowd of the Washington carriage trade, 1,500 notables come to see themselves in the mirrors. Tom Brokaw lifted a bottle of Rolling Rock (the workingman's beer, Tim's favorite) to say that "there will be some tears, some laughs, and the occasional truth." Speeches from

Maria Shriver, Mario Cuomo, and Mike Barnicle, who was moved to blow "a kiss goodbye" to the "boy of summer," who "always, always left us smiling." An Irish tenor sang "Ave Maria"; Cardinal Theodore McCarrick presented the homily, "Pray that the beloved anchor of *Meet the Press* is now sitting at the large Table of the Lord to begin a conversation which will last forever." Via satellite from Cologne, Germany, on a large screen descending from somewhere up in the chandeliers, Bruce Springsteen appeared with his guitar to sing "Thunder Road."

The program signed off with an orchestra playing "Over the Rainbow" while the guests made their way out to the limousines to be blessed with a sign from Heaven. Lo and behold, right there in the gray twilight, swinging low over the White House and the Washington Monument, right there in plain sight, there was a real rainbow in the sky. Later that night on MSNBC's rebroadcast of the proceedings, Olbermann reported the rainbow as no coincidence. "I know that was Russert," he said. "I'd recognize him anywhere."

With Olbermann it's sometimes hard to know when or if he's attempting a joke, but if he was joking, at whom or at what was the joke directed? Certainly not at rainbows; probably not at God. Conceivably at the thought of MSNBC hunting high and low for the Easter eggs of truth, or at the idea of Tim as a knife-wielding journalist. Olbermann is an intelligent man, and how else could an intelligent man interpret the glorification of Russert if not as a joke, or as a ninety-six-hour public-service announcement paid for by General Electric, the company that owns the NBC networks but depends for its profit margins on its patriotic dealings as one of the nation's primary weapons manufacturers. Jack Welch, the company's former chairman and CEO, was among the mourners making a cameo appearance in the weekend film clips. "We all felt he was our friend. He represented us. We were proud of him. We loved him."

Many people loved Russert, and I don't doubt that they had reason to do so. I'm sure that most of what was said about him on camera was true: that he was a devoted father, a devout Catholic, and a faithful friend, generous in spirit and a joyful noise unto the Lord. I mean no disrespect to his widow or to his son, but if I have no reason to doubt his virtues as a man, neither do I have any reason to credit the miracle of Russert as a journalist eager to speak truth to power. In his professional as opposed to his personal character, his on-air persona was that of an attentive and accommodating headwaiter, as helpless as Charlie Rose in his infatuation with A-list celebrity, his modus operandi the same one that pointed Rameau's obliging nephew to the roast pheasant and the coupe aux marrons in eighteenth-century Paris: "Butter people up, good God, butter them up."

With the butter Russert was a master craftsman, his specialty the mixing of it with just the right drizzle of salt. The weekend videotapes, presumably intended to display Russert at the top of his game, deconstructed the recipe. To an important personage Russert asked one or two faintly impertinent questions, usually about a subject of little or no concern to anybody outside the rope lines around official Washington; sometimes he discovered a contradiction between a recently issued press release and one that was distributed by the same politician some months or years previously. No matter with which spoon Russert stirred the butter, the reply was of no interest to him, not worth his notice or further comment. He had sprinkled his trademark salt, his work was done. The important personage was free to choose from a menu offering three forms of response—silence, spin, rancid lie. If silence, Russert moved on to another topic; if spin, he nodded wisely; if rancid lie, he swallowed it. The highlight reels for the most part show him in the act of swallowing.

November 7, 1993: Question for President Bill Clinton, "Will you allow North Korea to build a nuclear bomb?"
A: "North Korea cannot be allowed to build a nuclear bomb."

February 25, 2001: Question for Senator John Kerry, "John Kerry, you going to run for president in 2004?"
A. "I'm running for reelection in 2002."
Q. "How about '04?"
A. "I'm not making any decisions beyond '02."

April 13, 1997: Question for Louis Farrakhan, supreme minister of the Nation of Islam, "Would you be willing to retract or apologize for some of the things you said?"

A: "If I can defend every word that I speak and every word that I speak is truth, then I have nothing to apologize for."

February 8, 2004: Question for President George W. Bush, "In light of not finding the weapons of mass destruction, do you believe the war in Iraq is a war of choice or a war of necessity?"

A: "That's an interesting question. Please elaborate on that a little bit. A war of choice or a war of necessity? It's a war of necessity."

Having seen the original broadcast of the interview with President Bush, I remember Russert's attitude as that of a trend-setting restaurateur anxious to please his best customer. The president delivered himself of his customary bombast ("Saddam Hussein was dangerous, and I'm not gonna leave him in power and trust a madman ... A free Iraq will change the world. It's historic times"); Russert was content to favor the harangue with polite suspensions of disbelief.

The attitude doesn't lead to the digging up of much news that might be of interest to the American people, but it endeared Russert to his patrons and clients. Madeleine Albright, secretary of state in the Clinton Administration, expressed her gratitude to Olbermann: "Tim was amazing because I can tell you that, as a public official, it was really, first of all, a treat to get on the show." Two days later, over at NBC, Mary Matalin (former CBS and CNN talk-show host, former counselor to Vice President Dick Cheney) seconded the motion, attributing Russert's profound knowledge of national politics to his superb qualities as a rubber stamp. "He respected politicians," Matalin said. "He knew that they got blamed for everything, got credit for nothing. He knew how much they meant. He never treated them with the cynicism that attends some of these interviews. So they had a place to be loved." Remembering Russert on ABC, Sam Donaldson explained why too much salt in the butter makes it harder to spread: "He [Russert] understood as well as anyone, maybe better than almost anyone, that the reason political reporters are there is not to speak truth to power ... but to make those who say we have the truth—politicians—explain it."

Speaking truth to power doesn't make successful Sunday-morning television, leads to "jealousy, upsets, persecution," doesn't draw a salary of $5 million a year. The notion that journalists were once in the habit of doing so we borrow from the medium of print, from writers in the tradition of Mark Twain, Upton Sinclair, H. L. Mencken, I. F. Stone, Hunter Thompson, and Walter Karp, who assumed that what was once known as "the press" received its accreditation as a fourth estate on the theory that it represented the interests of the citizenry as opposed to those of the government. Long ago in the days before journalists became celebrities, their enterprise was reviled and poorly paid, and it was understood by working newspapermen that the presence of more than two people at their funeral could be taken as a sign that they had disgraced the profession.

On television the voices of dissent can't be counted upon to match the studio drapes or serve as tasteful lead-ins to the advertisements for Pantene Pro-V and the U.S. Marine Corps. What we now know as the "news media" serve at the pleasure of the corporate sponsor, their purpose not to tell truth to the powerful but to transmit lies to the powerless. Like Russert, who served his apprenticeship as an aide-de-camp to the late Senator Daniel Patrick Moynihan, most of the prominent figures in the Washington press corps (among them George Stephanopoulos, Bob Woodward, and Karl Rove) began their careers as bagmen in the employ of a dissembling politician or a corrupt legislature. Regarding themselves as de facto members of government, enabling and codependent, their point of view is that of the country's landlords, their practice equivalent to what is known among Wall Street stock-market touts as "securitizing the junk." When requesting explanations from secretaries of defense or congressional committee chairmen, they do so with the understanding that any explanation will do. Explain to us, my captain, why the United States must go to war in Iraq, and we will relay the message to the American people in words of one or two syllables. Instruct us, Mr. Chairman, in the reasons why

K-Street lobbyists produce the paper that Congress passes into law, and we will show that the reasons are healthy, wealthy, and wise. Do not be frightened by our pretending to be suspicious or scornful. Together with the television camera that sees but doesn't think, we're here to watch, to fall in with your whims and approve your injustices. Give us this day our daily bread, and we will hide your vices in the rosebushes of salacious gossip and clothe your crimes in the aura of inspirational anecdote.

I don't doubt that Russert was as good at the game as anybody in Washington, but why the five-star goodbye? Why the scattering of incense for a journalist who so prided himself on being in the loop that off-camera he assured his informed sources that nothing they said was on the record? For a second-tier talk show host, his audience a fraction of the size of Rush Limbaugh's or Howard Stern's, whose stock in trade was the deftly pulled punch? Why a requiem mass for a pet canary?

The production values were so far out of line with the object of their affections that the memorial services collapsed into absurdity. Unless, of course, the mistake was to think of the proceedings as somehow Christian in character and intent, a variation on the singing of a Te Deum in the National Cathedral instead of as something more along the lines of Homer's Greek heroes sacrificing a milk-white bull to Apollo. Seen as pagan ritual, even the highlight reels made sense. The Washington news media worship at the altars of divine celebrity, and maybe they begin to suspect that despite the promise of their ceaseless self-promotions they are not immortal, their market share hitting new lows, their audiences drifting away to Comedy Central and the blogs. How then to regain the favor of the god in whose image they believe themselves created? With the offering of a precious gift, and what could be more precious than "the ideal American journalist," a "basic old American patriot," and the "friend to millions of people"? Before leading the animal to slaughter, the old Greeks dusted its horns with gold.

2009

29. In Broad Daylight

The Puritan ethic of hard work and saving still matters. I just hate the idea that such an ethic is more alive today in China than in America ... We need to get back to collaborating the old-fashioned way. That is, people making decisions based on business judgment, experience, prudence, clarity of communications and thinking about how—not just how much.

—Thomas Friedman, *New York Times*, October 15, 2008

I don't know what country Friedman thinks he's been living in for the past thirty years, or in which New England gift shops he searches out the treasures of the American past. I can understand why he might wish for a happy return to an imaginary state of grace, but to explain last fall's melee in the world's financial markets as a falling away from the Puritan work ethic is to misread America's economic and political history and to mistake the message encoded in the DNA of the American dream. Given any kind of choice in the matter, who among the faithful ever has preferred hard work to the fast shuffle and the artful dodge, the bird in the hand to the five in the bush? When has the thinking about the how ever been preferred to the projecting of the how much? Ask any American what money means, and the respondent is an odds-on favorite to say that it's the soul of freedom and the proof of wisdom, that if only he or she had more of it the upgraded combination of numbers must open the vault of Paradise. Add to the account the long-standing American romance with crime— the outlaw and the confidence man forever shining like the fixed stars in the Hollywood sky—and although the desire for wealth might be seen as a character trait that doesn't get along well with others, the statement "Yes, but I did it for the money" serves to explain, if not always to justify, any and all forms of conduct (tax evasion, mail fraud, a second marriage or a third divorce, the war in Iraq) that otherwise might be regarded as insensitive, stupid, self-defeating, or unjust.

The looting of the U.S. Treasury is never an easy trick, but to carry off more than $1 trillion in broad daylight while the members of Congress stand around applauding the exit strategy as one certain to guarantee the health and happiness of the American people is a wonder of entrepreneurial enterprise that surely deserves some sort of tip of the hat. When the James gang robbed the Kansas City Fair in the fall of 1872, the local paper acknowledged the achievement as "so diabolically daring and so utterly in contempt of fear that we are bound to admire it and revere its perpetra- tors," and I would have thought that our own easily awestruck news media might have found a few words of respect and esteem for the perps who knocked over the Wall Street fairgrounds last year. How not at least revere the scale of the undertaking—nine banks emptied of more than $500 billion in capital, as much as $8 trillion withdrawn from the Dow Jones Industrial Average, $2 trillion from the country's pension and retirement accounts. How not admire the "collaborating the old-fashioned way," stock- market touts working together with the Federal Reserve, invest- ment bankers with credit-rating agencies, hedge-fund managers with committees of Congress, all doing their part to gin up the numbers and shear the sheep? For the financial operatives booming the sale of worthless paper, the bonus money last year came up to the sum of $39 billion. How not at least commend so vivid a revival of the frontier American spirit and so eloquent a testimony to the powers of the unfettered free market?

Why then the sermons and no joy in Deadwood? Friedman and his associate clergy in the pulpits at *Newsweek* and the *Wall Street Journal* apparently require more edifying precedents than those to be found in Mark Twain's Nevada mining camps or in Charles and Henry Adams's *Chapters of Erie*. If they worry about straying too far from the sacred Massachusetts shore, they might wish to consult Robert Patton's *Patriot Pirates*, a history of the Revolutionary War at sea published in a timely fashion last spring soon after the prize crew from JPMorgan Chase swarmed aboard the wreck of Bear Stearns. Patton suggests, and offers a good deal of evidence to demonstrate, that our war of independence was won by the stout-hearted greed of New England ship captains licensed by the Continental Congress in the autumn of 1775 to plunder, burn, or sell at auction British vessels bringing munitions and military stores to the king's regiments quartered on the merchants of Boston. The colonists at the time had few other means of acquiring weapons with which to give voice to their rebellion, and General George Washington understood that his ill-equipped and untried troops were not likely "to do much in a land way" against the superior force of the British Army. It occurred to the general to admit the servants of Mammon to the kingdom of Heaven with the thought that a squadron of privateers steered on the compass bearings of murderous self-interest might inflict enough damage on Britain's overseas trade to persuade the British Parliament that war with its North American colonies was a losing proposition.

Opponents of the policy thought it unworthy of Christian gentlemen, one likely to encourage practices both vicious and depraved, tending to "the destruction of the morals of the people." Friedman not being present, the objections were overruled by the advocates of piracy as public service, among them John Adams, who informed his fellow representatives in Philadelphia that the innovative investment strategy securitized the criminal collateral. "It is prudent," he said, "not to put virtue to too serious a test. I would use American virtue as sparingly as possible lest we wear it out."

The voyages were rigged as venture-capital deals, the richest share of the spoils reserved to the managing partners who advanced the money to build and provision the ships, lesser amounts distributed to the officers, the subcontractors, the accomplice politicians, and the crews. The work was not without its difficulties. Great Britain in the 1770s was the world's superpower, its navy equivalent to America's twenty-first-century Air Force, and for any privateer coming within range of the broadside from a British frigate the end was as certain as foreclosure on a California mortgage armed with a subprime loan from Countrywide Financial. But for captains able to avoid unlucky shifts in the wind, the rewards were of a match with those achieved in the Civil War gold rooms, the 1920s Wall Street rise, and the Internet boom of the late 1990s—many times the cost of setting sail from Plymouth or Newburyport—and during the course of the Revolutionary War the winnowing of what came to be known as "the golden harvest" at sea developed into a big business. If in the autumn of 1775 as few as ten or twenty small schooners were cruising the Atlantic coast, by 1783 as many as 4,000 investment vehicles had been licensed to practice the art of piracy as far offshore as the West Indies and the Mediterranean.

Better yet, the costs often were defrayed by the semblance of a government in Philadelphia, the profits taken by the speculators in Boston, Providence, and Marblehead. The contracts specified a transfer of the proceeds to the Colonial war effort, but the agreements tended to go AWOL when it came time to offload the boodle, preferably gunpowder but also African slaves, tobacco, sugar, table linen, Spanish wine, and anything else the traffic happened to be bearing.

Which isn't to say that the sparing use of virtue didn't prove to be "the pivot," as Adams had foreseen and Washington had said, "on which everything else turned." The putting of country second instead of first brought with it change believed in by electorates both domestic and foreign. By 1776 the British were losing cargoes valued in the millions of dollars; by 1782 the destructive presence of American privateers in the English Channel had dis-masted the British public's enthusiasm for what was no longer a splendid little war. More importantly for the American love of liberty and pursuit of happiness, the lessons learned in the oceangoing counting houses of the Revolutionary War furnished the new republic with risk-management models that over the course of the next century settled the trans-Mississippi American West, built the steel mills and the railroads, financed numerous richly rewarding stock-market schemes, and (by 1899, the year that Thorstein Veblen published his *Theory of the Leisure Class*) advanced the country's market society to a stage in which vendible capital had replaced vendible labor as the product that turned the wheels of fortune. The pirates no longer went down to the sea in ships, but neither did they go about the getting of an honest living. Reconfigured as predatory financiers embodying the ethic of what Veblen called "the higher barbarian culture," they lived off the work of the lower industrial orders, concerning themselves only with the pleasantries of how much—never, God forbid, with the indignity of how.

Even more touching than Thomas Friedman's laying of a wreath on the grave of Cotton Mather was the sight of Alan Greenspan sitting down by the rivers of Babylon, his harp hung upon the willows, silent in a strange land. During his tenure as chairman of the Federal Reserve (1987–2006) Greenspan had believed it his duty to irrigate the fruited plain of the American economy with the flow of easy money, his policy to supply the banks with the abundant credit, at low cost and presumably risk-free, that enabled the floating of both the Internet bubble (1995–2000) and the housing bubble (2003–2006). For his efforts he was accorded the title of "maestro," his word on the country's finances trading at parity with the word of God. When it was suggested (as long ago as 1994) that the newborn market in derivatives demanded some sort of government supervision, Greenspan discounted the suggestion as insulting to the integrity of the public-spirited Wall Street gentlemen laboring on behalf of the common good; when on October 23 of last year he appeared before the House Committee on Oversight and Government Reform to explain what had gone wrong with the making of something out of nothing, his tongue cleaved to the roof of his mouth. "Those of us who have looked to the self-interest of lending institutions to protect shareholder's equity, myself included, are in a state of shocked disbelief."

To think that the Wall Street financial institutions seek to protect the equity of their customers in preference to their own is to think that at the Las Vegas poker tables the dealers seek to protect the chips stacked in front of the sweet old lady in the blue baseball cap playing a system drawn from the book of Revelation. But if Chairman Greenspan put virtue to too serious a test, so do the cupbearers of civic conscience who complain of the lack of "leadership" on the part of the government in Washington. Throughout the months of September and October the Dow was gaining or losing as many as 700 points a day (thereby enriching the speculators taking a cut of the action on both the black and the red), and from the choir lofts of the national media the news went forth that what had gone missing from both the Congress and the Bush Administration was the prudence and the clarity of communication. Avarice and incompetence at both ends of Pennsylvania Avenue, "nihilists" in the House of Representatives, corporate bagmen in the Senate, everywhere a falling away of sober business practice and the habit of self-denial—where, O Lord, was the wisdom in the shining city on the hill, where the watchers on the ramparts of freedom looking out for the safety and well-being of the American taxpayer?

As with the misreadings of the spirit of American commercial enterprise, the misinterpretings of the purpose of American government substitute the theory for the practice. Just as the stock-market speculations do what they're intended to do, which is to reward the promoters and fleece the marks, the government does what it's supposed to do, which is to enrich the creditors and plunder the debtors. The eighteenth-century New England privateers flew the American flag as a flag of convenience, not as a declaration of their allegiance to a cause but as a license to seize the wealth stored in the hulls of wooden ships. Their twenty-first-century heirs and assigns employ the semblance of a government in Washington as an investment vehicle permitting them to seize the wealth stored in the labor of the American people. The Republican and Democratic parties compete for the brokerage business, between them putting up $2.4 billion for last year's presidential campaigns—that is, for the speculative ventures that bundle junk slogans into collateralized-debt obligations, which, when it comes time to offload the boodle, transform the upside into private property, the downside into the good news that poverty replenishes the soul.

When Treasury Secretary Henry M. Paulson distributes more than $1 trillion to the country's financial overlords ($700 billion to the commercial and investment banks; $150 billion to AIG, $100 billion each to Fannie Mae and Freddie Mac, etc.), he proceeds in the time-honored manner of the governments in Washington that during the four decades after the Civil War presented the railroads with 183 million acres of subprime desert on which to set up the derivatives market in pioneer homesteads that were sold as gardens of Eden on fertile prairies "ready for the plow and spade." When the land holdings turned into fairy-tale castles of debt rising from the mists of boundless credulity, it was the farmers wondering where was the rain in western Nebraska, not the silk-hatted gentlemen rounding up the oysters in William K. Vanderbilt's palm court, who paid for the burials of the mules and the American dream. Bait-and-switch is the name of the national pastime. President Grover Cleveland confirmed the principle in 1887, explaining his veto of a bill passed by Congress to provide financial aid to the poor. "The lesson should be constantly enforced," he said, "that though the people support the government, the government should not support the people." Such has been the policy of the Bush Administration for the past eight years; so also is it the policy "alive today in China," Thomas Friedman's far-off happy land where the cheap labor relies on the Puritan work ethic to lay up its treasure in Heaven.

2009

30. Achievetrons

Few men are so disinterested as to prefer to live in discomfort under a government which they hold to be right, rather than in comfort under one which they hold to be wrong.

—C. V. Wedgwood

President Barack Obama's Christmas shopping for cabinet officers in December of last year prompted the national news media to rejoice in the glad tiding that his campaign slogan, "Change you can believe in," was only that, a slogan. Instead of showing himself partial to "closet radicals" who might pose some sort of deep downfield threat to the status quo, Obama was choosing wisely from the high-end, happy few, dispensing with "the romantic and failed notion" that individuals never before seen on the White House lawn could provide the "maturity" needed "in a time of war and economic crisis." David Brooks assured his readers in the *New York Times* that the incoming apparat, its members "twice as smart as the poor reporters who have to cover them," embodied "the best of the Washington insiders." "Achievetrons ... who got double 800s on their SATs," said Brooks, taking pains to list the schools from which they had received diplomas (Columbia, Harvard, Wellesley, Harvard Law, Stanford, Yale Law, Princeton, etc.) attesting to the worth of their wise counsel. Karl Rove, former advance man for President George W. Bush, informed the *Wall Street Journal* that Tim Geithner (Dartmouth, Johns Hopkins) as secretary of the Treasury and Larry Summers (MIT, Harvard) as director of the National Economic Council were "solid picks," both investments rated "reassuring" and "market-oriented." Max Boot, contributor to *Commentary* and visiting fellow at the Council on Foreign Relations, advised the wandering spirits in the blogosphere that "only churlish partisans of both the left and the right" could quarrel with the naming of Hillary Clinton (Wellesley, Yale Law) as secretary of state and Robert Gates (Georgetown) as secretary of defense, appointments that "could just as easily have come from a President McCain."

The mood was not as festive in the workshops of the romantic left, but even the churls who thought the appointees insufficiently progressive in their views of the American future took comfort in the remembrance of their candidate saying somewhere in a post-election speech, "Understand where the vision for change comes from. First and foremost, it comes from me." David Corn, the Washington bureau chief for *Mother Jones*, told the *Washington Post* that although the hotheads among his acquaintance were "disappointed, irritated or fit to be tied," they held fast to the belief that Obama (Columbia, Harvard Law) would set the agenda, reprogram the operatives complicit in the stupidity and cynicism of the Bush and Clinton administrations; pragmatism was the watchword, and the dawning of a bright new day was guaranteed by the installation of what Brooks proclaimed a "vale-dictocracy," postpartisan and nonideological, its shoes shined, its hair combed, its ambition neatly pressed.

The recommendation deserves to be ranked with the ones until recently in vogue at the Palm Beach Country Club among the members acquainted with the achievetron Bernie Madoff. For the past sixty years the deputies assigned to engineer the domestic and foreign policies of governments newly arriving in Washington have come outfitted with similar qualifications—first-class schools, state-of-the-art networking, apprenticeship in a legislative body or a think tank—and for sixty years they have managed to weaken rather than strengthen the American democracy, ending their terms of office as objects of ridicule if not under threat of criminal arrest.

The Harvard wunderkinds (a.k.a. "the best and the brightest") who followed President John F. Kennedy into the White House in 1961 hung around the map tables long enough to point the country in the direction of the Vietnam War. Henry Kissinger, another Harvard prodigy, imparted to American statecraft the modus operandi of a Mafia cartel. The Reagan Administration imported its book of revelation from the University of Chicago's School of Economics ("privatization" the watchword, "unfettered free market" the Christian name for Zeus) and by so doing set in motion what lately has come to be seen as a long-running Ponzi scheme. Take into account the Ivy League's contributions to the Bush Administration—Attorney General John Ashcroft (Yale), Secretary of Defense Donald Rumsfeld (Princeton), Director of Homeland Security Michael Chertoff (Harvard)—and I can imagine a doctoral thesis commissioned by the Kennedy School of Government and meant to determine which of the country's leading institutions of higher learning over the past fifty years has done the most damage to the health and happiness of the American people.

It's conceivable that the Obama Administration will prove itself the exception to the rule, but when the president says that his vision for change "comes from me" he leaves open the question as to whether he intends to generate it *ex cathedra* or *ex nihilo*. Neither method offers much chance of success if what is wanted or required is a recasting of the American democracy on a scale comparable to Franklin Roosevelt's New Deal. Socioeconomic alterations of a magnitude sufficient to be recognized as such tend to be collective enterprises, usually brought about by powers of mind and forces of circumstance outside, not inside, the circle of A-list opinion—the barbarians at the gates of fifth-century Rome, the sixteenth-century Protestant Reformation *personae non gratae* at the Vatican, the authors of the American Constitution far removed from the certain truths seated on velvet cushions in eighteenth-century London. Ulysses S. Grant, perhaps Lincoln's most effective general, was virtually unknown to the War Office in Washington before the bombardment of Fort Sumter; during the Great Depression of the 1930s, FDR composed a "Brain Trust" of individuals (some of them academics, others not, none of them rounded up from the quorum of usual suspects) as willing as the president to "take a method and try it; if it fails, admit it frankly, and try another."

The courses of undergraduate instruction at our prestigious colleges and universities no longer encourage or reward the freedoms of mind likely to disturb the country's social and political seating plan. During the early years of the twentieth century, before America fell afoul of the dream of empire, the students on the lawns of academe, most of them inheritors of wealth and social position, already were assured of their getting ahead in the world. They could afford to take chances, to read or not to read the next day's letter from Virginia Woolf or Julius Caesar, to mess up the protocols of political correctness, worship false gods, maybe go to Paris to try their luck with absinthe, their hand and eye at modern art or ancient decadence. If they strayed into the wilderness of politics, they did so in the manner of both Theodore and Franklin Roosevelt, with the enthusiasm of the amateur explorer.

The amateur spirit, which is also the democratic spirit, didn't survive the rising of the American nation-state from the ashes of Dresden and Hiroshima. The Cold War with the Russians brought with it the lesson that even the most amiable and well-intentioned of republics can't afford to leave home without a "meritocracy" so lacking in a disrespectful turn of mind as to be fit for service not only at the White House and the CIA but also with General Motors and the *New York Times*. The doctrines of egalitarianism forbid the convenience of a ruling elite present at birth. The product must be fabricated, not in the same volume as the light trucks made in Detroit, or the cattle fattened in the Omaha feed lots, but as a priority deemed equally essential to the homeland security. After some trouble with the realignment of the educational objective during the excitements of the 1960s, the universities accepted their mission as way stations on the pilgrim road to enlightened self-ishness. As opposed to the health and happiness of the American people, what is of interest is the wealth of the American corporation and the power of the American state, the syllabus geared to the arts and sciences of career management—how to brighten the test scores, assemble the résumé, clear the luggage through the checkpoints of the law and business schools. The high fees charged by the brand-name institutions include surer access to the nomenklatura that writes the nation's laws, operates its government, manages its money, and controls its news media. The catalogue also offers electives in the examined life, but the consolations of philosophy hold little value for a novitiate encouraged to believe that its acceptance into a company of the elect dispenses with the unwelcome news that there might be more things in heaven and earth than those accounted for in *Forbes* magazine's annual list of America's top 400 fortunes. Achievetrons learn to work the system, not to change it, to punch up the PowerPoints for Citigroup and Disney and figure the exchange rate between an awkward truth and a user-friendly lie. Where is the percentage in overthrowing the idols of the marketplace or the tribe? If you're not in, you're out, and when was out the better place to be?

Which isn't to say that Hillary Clinton hasn't read the letters of Abraham Lincoln, or that Tim Geithner doesn't know how to analyze (in three languages and five currencies) a Four Seasons hotel bill; that Robert Gates isn't familiar with the theory of Admiral Alfred Thayer Mahan, or that Larry Summers might make the mistake of turning to face Jerusalem instead of Mecca when begging money from a Saudi prince. What it does suggest is that President Obama's household staff, in accordance with the protocols observed by "the best of the Washington insiders," can be counted upon to place their own self-interest first and foremost and to avoid fooling around with initiatives that threaten to leave a stain on the rug. Clinton as senator from New York in 2002 voted for the invasion of Iraq not because she knew or cared why America was embarking on a mindless war but because what was wanted was a cheerful waving of the pom-poms and the flag;

Geithner as the president of the New York Federal Reserve Bank in the winter of 2007 neglected to address the impending trouble in the credit markets because to have done so would have upset the Wall Street achievetrons folding and refolding sets of imaginary numbers into paper hats and airplanes; Gates as deputy director of the CIA in the 1980s painted his portrait of the evil Soviet Empire to match the one walking around in Ronald Reagan's head, unwilling to believe that the Red Menace was mortal until the collapse of the Berlin Wall in 1989 exposed his intelligence estimates as works of science fiction; Summers in 1998 as President Bill Clinton's deputy secretary of the Treasury served as one of the principal sponsors of our current financial debacle, facilitating repeal of the Glass–Steagall Act and joining with Secretary Robert Rubin (Harvard, Yale Law) and Federal Reserve Bank Chairman Alan Greenspan (New York University) to force the resignation of Brooksley Born, chair of the Commodities Futures Trading Commission, who urged regulation of the markets in new derivatives. The motion to block the large-scale accumulation of toxic debt ran counter to the belief, then all the rage among the bankers at JPMorgan Chase and Goldman Sachs as among the members of the Palm Beach Country Club, that money, deftly cultivated by its cronies, grows on trees.

Obama, in his custom-tailored personae of U.S. senator and presidential candidate, draped himself in the same accommodating cloth—careful to avoid offending the people who count, content to leave the management of the country's finances to the discretion of the Wall Street banks, its Middle Eastern policy to the judgment of the Israeli lobby, its public-health care under the supervision of the insurance syndicates, its bankruptcy laws in the hands of the credit-card companies, its military spending to the wisdom of the Pentagon. During last year's election campaign he enjoyed the advantage of an incoherent opponent, a faltering economy, and the incumbent Bush Administration's record of failure and disgrace. His efficient acquisition of money and votes proved him to be a capable entrepreneur, his eloquence showed him to be a charismatic politician. The greater achievement—the act of electing a black man to the White House, not the image of the actor—is that of the American citizenry, a collective enterprise drawing together the energies of the democratic spirit contained in the belief that what is great about America is not the greatness of its gross domestic product but the greatness of its love of liberty.

Our leading voices of informed opinion like to say that America now finds itself in a state of unprecedented crisis, the whole of our political and economic enterprise trembling on the verge of extinction. They call upon the president to be "bold," to throw the moneychangers out of the temple, bail out the banks and the automobile industry, disgorge from the Augean stable on Capitol Hill its dungheap of cowardice and self-congratulation. I don't know anybody who questions President Obama's willingness to perform the labors of Hercules, but where does he find the lion-skin and the club? The redistributions of the society's rich and poor require the hiring of domestic help willing to move the furniture. Achievetrons don't do floors and windows. As individuals they make very good company, and at the tables down at Mory's the magic of their singing no doubt casts its spell, but if they have paid attention to their studies, they can be trusted to know, as does the valedictocracy otherwise known as the national news media, that it's a far, far better thing to live in comfort under a government they hold to be wrong than in discomfort under a government they hold to be right.

2015

31. Bombast Bursting in Air

We must make our choice. We may have democracy, or we may have wealth concentrated in the hands of a few, but we can't have both.
—Louis Brandeis

Between democracy and concentrated wealth the country throughout most of its history has preferred the latter to the former, the body politic asking only that the big money make a credible show of caring for something other than itself. For the past thirty-five years the modest requirement has been met with prolonged and costly stagings of a presidential-election campaign invariably said to be, as it was this past summer by Jeb Bush, "everybody's test, and wide open—exactly as a contest for president should be."

It is neither wide open nor, strictly speaking, a contest. It is ritual performance of the legend of democracy as fairground spectacle, this season promising the conspicuous consumption of $5.8 billion, enough money, thank God, to prove that our flag is still there. Forbidden the use of words apt to depress a Q score or disturb a Gallup poll, the candidates stand and serve as product placements meant to be seen instead of heard, their quality to be inferred from the cost of their manufacture. The sponsors of the event dress it up with star-spangled photo-ops and bombast bursting in air, the candidates so well contrived that they can be played for jokes, presented as game show contestants, mounted on selfie sticks until they come to judgment on election day before the throne of cameras by whom and for whom they are produced.

The contrivances don't come cheap. Luxury items made to the order and under the supervision of concentrated wealth, they can be counted upon, if and when elected, to stand, foursquare and true blue, for the freedom of money, moralizing and vigilant against the freedoms of movement and thought. Names of candidates inclined to think or act otherwise don't appear on the November ballot.

Why then the pretense of a democratic running for the White House roses if the race is already won? The short answer is Plato's in *The Republic*, his calling forth Socrates to explain that "noble falsehood" is the stuff that binds a society together in self-preserving myth. To the young aristocrat Glaucon preparing to become a ruler of Athens, Socrates says that the children of the city must be told that the god who made all of them mixed gold into some of them "who are adequately equipped to rule, because they are the most valuable." Whether the intel is true or false matters less than the children's remembering their duty to believe it, to know what their rulers would have them know.

In the American theater of operations the noble falsehood springs full-blown from the head of Abraham Lincoln declaring on the hallowed ground at Gettysburg in November 1863 "that government of the people, by the people, for the people, shall not perish from the earth." Nowhere in the history of mankind does the record show a government so specified lasting longer than a few brutish and chaotic months; nor was such a government what the framers of the Constitution had in mind in Philadelphia in 1787. They envisioned an enlightened oligarchy, a privileged few arranging the distribution of law and property to the less fortunate many, accommodating the private and the public good, allowing for both the motions of the heart and the movements of a market.

The balancing of the two sets of value they entrusted to a class of patrician overlords for whom, presumably, it was unnecessary to cheat and steal and lie. Men like themselves, to whom Madison ascribed "most wisdom to discern, and most virtue to pursue, the common good of the society."

But not enough wisdom and virtue to free the republic of its slaves. That task was left to men neither enlightened nor rich, giving their "last full measure of devotion" to consecrate "the proposition that all men are created equal." Lincoln's poetic framing of the high resolve that these honored dead "shall not have died in vain" established the myth that preserves the society from disunion, becomes the duty of the children to believe, of the rulers mixed with gold to teach.

Sound policy, but difficult to implement with a myth that has lost its power to enchant the populace and with presidential-election campaigns designed to be seen, not heard, the viewers invited to understand government as representative in the theatrical, not the constitutional, sense of the word. The made-for-television approach to politics installed Ronald Reagan in the White House in 1981 to represent the country's preferred image of itself, uproot the democratic style of thought and feeling that underwrote Franklin D. Roosevelt's New Deal, restore America to its rightful place where "someone can always get rich." The business at hand was show business, the message up there in lights at the welcoming ceremony produced by Frank Sinatra at the Capital Centre in Landover, Maryland, on the night before Reagan's inauguration. Seated onstage in overstuffed, thronelike armchairs, the president-elect and his wife graciously accepted the gifts of Hollywood frankincense and myrrh—Johnny Carson and Bob Hope cracking jokes, Charlton Heston standing in and up for Moses, James Stewart wearing his medals won as an Air Force general, a clown performing in blackface, Sinatra himself singing "America the Beautiful."

The evening set the tone of the incoming Republican political agenda, promising a happy return to an imaginary American past—to the amber waves of grain from sea to shining sea, the home on the range made safe from Apaches by John Wayne. The great leap backward was billed as a bright new morning in an America once again cowboy-hatted and standing tall, risen from the ashes of defeat in Vietnam, cleansed of its Watergate impurities, outspending the Russians on weapons of mass destruction. During the whole of his eight years in office Reagan was near perfect in his lines—"Mr. Gorbachev, tear down this wall!"—sure of hitting his marks on Omaha and Malibu Beach, snapping a sunny salute to a Girl Scout cookie or a nuclear submarine. The president maybe hadn't read Plato in the ancient Greek, but myth was his métier, and he had the script by heart. Facts didn't matter because, as he was apt to say, "facts are stupid things." What mattered was the warmth of Reagan's bandleader smile, his golden album of red, white, and blue sentiment instilling consumer confidence in the virtuous virtual reality of an America that wasn't there. The television cameras loved him; so did the voters. To this day he stands shoulder to shoulder with Abraham Lincoln in the annual polls asking who was America's greatest president.

The cameras also loved Bill Clinton, who modeled his presidency on *The Oprah Winfrey Show* rebooted to star himself as both big-hearted celebrity host and shamefaced celebrity guest, reaching out at the top of the hour for more love and more cheeseburgers, after the commercial break dealing bravely with the paternity of the stains on Monica Lewinsky's blue dress. He was admired not only for the ease with which he told smiling and welcome lies but also for his capacity to bear insult and humiliation with the imperturbable calm of a piñata spilling forth presidential largesse as corporate subsidy and tabloid scandal. Like Reagan, Clinton had been hired to hearten and amuse the country, not to govern it but to show that Justice Brandeis had it wrong, that the true meaning of American exceptionalism is the not having to choose between democracy and concentrated wealth.

The Arkansas prom king and the Hollywood drum major didn't make tedious distinctions between story and myth. The difference between what is and what is not was simply a matter of what was in or out of the camera shot, and during both their terms in office they were careful to preserve on camera the noble falsehood of a courageous and selfless democracy; off camera, they puffed up the pillows for a comfortable settling into place of what has become a selfish and frightened plutocracy. Their efforts were in keeping with the spirit of an age in which money was seen to be the hero with a thousand faces, greed the creative frenzy from which all blessings conspicuously flow. Credit was easy, and the cotton was high.

The restoring of America to its rightful place where "someone can always get rich" (not every someone, some of the someones connected to the right place at the right time) has resulted over the past thirty-five years in the awkward imbalancing of the values treasured by a capitalist economy and those cherished by a democratic society—more laws limiting the freedom of persons, fewer laws restraining the license of property, the letting fall into disrepair of nearly all the infrastructure that provides the country with the foundation of its common enterprise. The heavy tilt toward the reactionary right has been accompanied by the systematic juggling of the public land and light and air into the private purse; the formulation of a national-security state backed by the guarantee of never-ending foreign war and equipped with increasingly repressive police powers to still the waters of domestic discontent; the subdivision of America the Beautiful into a nation of the rich and a nation of the poor, to the point where 10 percent of the population holds 76 percent of the nation's wealth—animal and virtual, vegetable, cultural, mineral, or intellectual.

Great and good news for the dealers in high-end automotive and financial instruments, but a set of circumstances that presents a problem to the vendors of the 2016 presidential election: how to sell Lincoln's noble falsehood to the children of the city who have neither reason nor inclination to believe it? The sales pitch loses its force when the rulers of the city bend down to the electorate as if to a crowd of juvenile delinquents; deem the body politic incapable of generous impulse, selfless motive, or creative thought; deliver the insult with a headwaiter's condescending smile. How then expect the people to trust a government that invests no trust in them? Why the surprise that over the past thirty-five years the voting public has been giving ever-louder voice to its contempt for any and all politicians, no matter what their color, creed, prior arrest record, or sexual affiliation?

Proofs of government by the people, of the people, for the people are as rare upon the ground as sightings of the golden-cheeked warbler. The proposition that all men are created equal no longer wins the hearts and minds of America's downwardly mobile working classes—employed and unemployed, lower, lower-middle, middle, adjunct, and retired. Nor do the American people enjoy the privilege of direct participation in the naming of an American president. They elect a slate of unknown persons to the Electoral College, their votes ignored if unaligned with the majority assigned to one or the other of two political parties. The rigged outcome relieves the rulers of the city of the duty to address the children of the city as their fellow countrymen; they speak instead to their paymasters and advisors, to interest groups, target audiences and lobbyists, to money, not to people. They learn to say nothing offensive to sums in excess of $5,000, and the doing so puts them at the disadvantage of not knowing who their fellow countrymen are.

Which is why the 2016 Democracyland pageant is expected to cost $5 billion for the publicity and the balloons, up from $2.6 billion in 2012. The democratic turn of mind and form of self-government having gone missing in plain sight, the sponsors of the 2016 election must deploy increasingly expensive virtual realities (more plutocratic gold mixed in the democratic clay), to make credible the show of the big money caring for something other than itself.

The plutocracy is a nonpartisan equal opportunity employer of folk festival talent, and during the late winter and early spring would-be presidents of the United States parade like runway models for the buyers of political product placement. At indoor banquets and outdoor barbeques, on carpets red and blue, they stride, stare, pout (with attitude), turn, smile, pose, and wait to see who sends money and wither blows the wind that bestirreth the opinion polls. The auditions this year were particularly disappointing for the Republicans. None of the prospective Commanders-in-Chief possessed the talents of the drum major or the prom king, nor did they know how to pretend to care about anyone other than themselves. A problem, but one that the news media in the big money's petting zoos were sure of their ability to fix. The making of sow's ears into silk purses was what they were paid, and paid handsomely, to do, why the bulk of the money raised for a presidential campaign deploys as advertising that cuts and pastes a human face on a block of wood or a pillar of salt.

The self-satisfied assumption didn't survive the stepping forward onto the political stage of Donald J. Trump, real-estate mogul, star of reality-show television, self-glorifying Jack of Diamonds and Ace of Spades. Mixed with his own gold, Trump doesn't do myth; myth is for losers. Trump does deals, "big deals" like those bragged about in his 2011 book, *Time to Get Tough*, deals that he'd been doing for years in high-stakes global finance, up against "hard-driving, vicious, cutthroat financial killers, the kind of people who leave blood all over the boardroom table."

Trump declared his candidacy on June 16, a deus ex machina descending by escalator into the atrium of the Trump Tower on Manhattan's Fifth Avenue, and there to say, and say it plainly, that Justice Brandeis had it right, democracy and concentrated wealth do not a happy couple make. Money is power, and power, ladies and gentlemen, is not self-sacrificing or democratic. The big money cares for nothing other than itself, always has and always will; it is the name of the game and the nature of the beast. Trump didn't need briefing books or policy positions to front an outdated noble falsehood. He embodied—live and in person—the proof of the proposition he deemed it the duty of the children of the city to believe.

Trump established the bona fides of his claim to the White House on the simple but all-encompassing and imperishable truth that he was really, really rich, unbought and therefore unbossed, so frivolously and magnificently rich that he was free to say whatever it came into his head to say, do whatever it took to root out the corruption and stupidity in Washington, clean up the mess in the Middle East. The United States of America, the greatest show on earth, deserved the helping hand of Trump, the greatest name on earth, to make it worthy of his signature men's colognes (Empire and Success), to set it free to fulfill the destiny emblazoned on his baseball cap: MAKE AMERICA GREAT AGAIN.

Not the exact words in Trump's loud and thoughtless mouth, but the gist of the message that he shouted to the camera as June moved forward to July, Trump reminding all and sundry that the uplifting drivel about government of, by, and for the people wasn't worth a wooden nickel, even if carved in Aspen Institute scented pine or artisanal Heritage Foundation oak. The dearly deluded children of the city swallowed the sugarcoated nonsense at their peril.

The message was received with cheering and applause everywhere Trump dropped by in his helicopter to walk amidst the popular loathing for the inside-the-Beltway politics and politicians settled on the nation's capital like vultures on the liver of Prometheus. Senator Bernie Sanders of Vermont launched his campaign for the Democratic nomination on the same tide of populist anger and resentment, but he was an avowed socialist, and his muttering was summarily dismissed by the big-money media because he wasn't mixed with gold and refused to beg for it in the ante-rooms of concentrated wealth.

But Trump was rich and therefore wise, a man who knew whereof he spoke, and he was being heard not only by the usual suspects in the Fox News time zones but also, *mirabile dictu*, by women and evangelicals, by young people not yet two-and-twenty, and at the end of July the greatest name on earth was perched atop the opinion-poll leaderboards.

For the mythographers organizing the Republican 2016 election pageant the sight was not a happy one. Trump was raining on their parade floats, and their confusion so complete that they didn't know how to read, much less tell, the story unfolding before their lying eyes. Hot air blowing up the wrong balloons, platitudes going down like tenpins. Trump was worse than an embarrassment; he was a disaster, laying waste to the Republican pretensions to political and socioeconomic coherence, likely to roust out of the party any potential voters who weren't card-carrying bigots. The man was a preposterous self-promoting clown, a vulgar lout, an unscripted canary flown from its gilded cage, a braggart in boorish violation of the political-correctness codes, referring to Mexicans (some Mexicans, not all Mexicans) as "criminals" and "rapists," questioning John McCain's credentials as a war hero ("I like people who weren't captured"), telling Megyn Kelly on Fox News that if from time to time he had been heard to describe women he didn't like as "dogs, slobs, and disgusting animals," he meant "only Rosie O'Donnell."

Although often and reprovingly repeated by the oracles in residence in every sector of the news media (the *New York Times*, *National Review*, CNN, Comedy Central, the *Huffington Post*), the objections weren't sustained by the opinion polls. Trump's numbers kept moving up, no matter how gross his displays of political incorrectness, or how obvious his lack of interest in, or knowledge of, America's foreign and domestic policy. Other than the building of a wall along the Mexican border and the deportation of 11 million illegal aliens, he had little to say about how or where or when he would get tough with the Chinese or handle the situation in Syria.

Trump maybe was a brute, uncivil and unsafe, deserving to be removed at once from the sight of mother and the flag, thrown off Ronald Reagan's stagecoach four miles east of Yuma, but his hold on the popular imagination attracted 24 million viewers to the first of the Republican debates, mounted by Fox News in the Quicken Loans Arena, on August 6. The protectors of the Republican Party's virtue hoped that one of the other fifteen candidates would back Trump down the political leaderboards, if not the slow and steady Jeb Bush (self-styled "joyful tortoise") then maybe Marco Rubio, Ted Cruz, or Chris Christie, all of them rated by their touts as quick-witted, sharp-tongued, able to find Aleppo on a map. During the summer of 2015, the collective attempt at Trump removal failed because the mogul responded to the high-minded objections with a sense of humor his fellow candidates lacked both the nerve and the permission to engage.

Between the first debate and the second, on September 16 (under the wing of Ronald Reagan's Air Force One in Simi Valley, California), Trump's poll numbers continued to rise despite the fond hopes of the Republican Party's spin doctors that his star would fade, wear out its welcome, pass and be forgotten with the rest. It didn't happen as expected at the second debate despite the concerted efforts of CNN's inspectors of souls to sink it below the horizon, and as of this writing (late September), it hasn't done so yet—for reasons that Trump, schooled in the methodology of reality TV, understands, and the moralizing punditry does not.

The camera sees but doesn't think, makes no meaningful distinction between a bubble bath in Santa Monica staffed by pretty girls and a bloodbath on a beach in Libya staffed by headless corpses. The return on investment in both instances is the flow of bankable emotion, in unlimited and anonymous amounts, drawn from the dark and bottomless pools of human wish and dream. The cameras following Trump's political campaign aren't covering a set or a play of ideas; like flies to death and honey, they're attracted to the sweet, decaying smell of big-name celebrity. It doesn't matter what Trump says or doesn't say, whether he is cute and pink or headless; what matters is that Trump is a profitable return on investment in idols of the marketplace, up there in lights with Frank Sinatra and Lady Gaga.

Trump doesn't do myth because celebrity, of, in, and for itself, is noble falsehood. The camera doesn't do democracy because democracy is the holding of one's fellow citizens in respectful regard, not because they are beautiful or rich or famous but because they are one's fellow citizens, and therefore worth the knowing what they say and do. Blind to muddy boots on common ground, the camera gazes adoringly at polished boots on horseback.

Part II

Folly's Antidote

2011

32. Democracy 101

*What a king must suffer! For he knows, deep down in his heart, that he
is a poor, cheap, wormy thing like the rest of us, a sarcasm, the Creator's
prime miscarriage in inventions, the moral inferior of all the animals
… the superior of them all in one gift only, and that one not up to his
estimation of it—intellect.*

—*The Autobiography of Mark Twain*, Vol. 1

Toward the end of his life Mark Twain lost much of his liking for
what he had come to regard as "the damned human race," but he
held fast to his delight in the one gift only in which he believed
man superior to the animals. It is the mark on even the least of
the pages in the edition of his autobiography that after a century
in exile emerged last November from the University of California
Press. The happy return would have been welcome in any event,
the more so in my own particular circumstance because it excused
my absence from the winter festival of think-tank discussions
addressed to the disappearance of the American future. The losses
suffered by the Democratic Party in the midterm congressional

election prompted the springing up of symposia, like mushrooms after rain, in every barren field of liberal political thought tended by the growers of the country's conscience (blue dog, moderate, progressive), and between Thanksgiving and Christmas I was asked to work up presentations on President Obama's mishandling of the miracle of the loaves and fishes, the enslavement of a once-upon-a-time free press, the same-day deliveries of Congress to the banks. The sponsors of the programs in both the red states and the blue didn't stint on expressions of alarm. The situation was desperate, the economy in dire straits, the democracy on its deathbed.

I expressed my condolences, said that I was sorry to hear the news, but never having been sure-handed either with the assembling of Lego blocks or the numbering of PowerPoints, I was at a loss for emergency procedures. Fortunately I'd been reading Twain, keeping company with the genius of his abundant humor while exchanging emails with the Isaiahs in the void. Sometimes for the fun of it I inquired as to what it was—absent a shower of gold falling from the hand of a merciful Providence on the Continental Divide—that needed to be done, presumably at once and in a way that wouldn't cast a pall on the Academy Awards, depress television ad sales at the Super Bowl, frighten the chauffeurs at Goldman Sachs.

The messages came back with appeals for some sort of uplifting vision in a desert, the priority a watchword to reawaken the American spirit, redecorate the front parlor of the American soul. This request I took to mean that instead of bringing a polemic to Massachusetts or a piety to Texas, I could send the website link to Twain. He doesn't set much store by moral calisthenics or the laundering of soup-stained souls, but even as presented in academic grave cloths by the editors in California, his autobiography renders moot the funeral arrangements for the American idea. The man is at play with the freedom of his mind, which, unless I misread the history lesson, is what America is about.

As Twain remembers but the policy planners in our midst tend to forget, the Constitution was made for the uses of the individual, an implement on the order of a plow, an axe, a surveyor's plumb line, the institutions of government meant to support the liberties of the people as opposed to the ambitions of the state.

If America is about nothing else, it is about making it up as one goes along, the chance to build a raft of serviceable identity on which to float south to Vicksburg or the islands of the blessed. To read at will in Twain's autobiography is to be reminded that in one way or another the American is an improvisation, the character in a play of his or her own invention. Mark Twain was the name given by the young Samuel Langhorne Clemens to the figure first billed on San Francisco lecture platforms as the "Wild Humorist of The Pacific Slope." The nom de plume he requisitioned from Isaiah Sellers, a Mississippi River steamboat captain who contributed bulletins under that letterhead to the *New Orleans Picayune*. Clemens took the name after the captain's death, indebted to him for the first newspaper article he ever published, two columns of "the solid nonpareil," in which the captain had been the butt of the joke.

> Captain Sellers did me the honor to profoundly detest me from that day forth. When I say he did me the honor, I am not using empty words. It was a very real honor to be in the thoughts of so great a man as Captain Sellers, and I had wit enough to appreciate it and be proud of it. It was distinction to be loved by such a man; but it was much greater distinction to be hated by him, because he loved scores of people; but he didn't sit up nights to hate anybody but me.

America's moral code Twain understood to be political, the protection of the other fellow's liberty in exchange for the protecting of one's own, the object being to allow for the broadest range of expression and the widest room for maneuver, its emphasis on the companionable virtues—kindness, tolerance, and candor. The companionable virtues are not commandments that fall like heavy stones from heaven. They are the work of the one gift only that raises "bloody and atrocious man" to at least a modest height above the animals, Twain's judgment rendered in the absence of "respectworthy evidence that the human being has morals. He is himself the only witness. Persons who do not know him value his testimony."

Twain's faith in the uses of intellect informs the chapter of his *Life on the Mississippi* that takes up the topic of piloting steamboats:

> There is one faculty that the pilot must incessantly cultivate until he has brought it to absolute perfection … That faculty is memory. He cannot stop with merely thinking a thing is so and so, he must *know* it … One cannot easily realize what a tremendous thing it is to know every trivial detail of twelve hundred miles of river and know it with absolute exactness. If you will take the longest street in New York, and travel up and down it, conning its features patiently until you know every door and lamppost and big and little sign by heart, and know them so accurately that you could instantly name the one you are abreast of when you are set down at random in that street in the middle of an inky black night, you will then have a tolerable notion of the amount and the exactness of a pilot's knowledge who carries the Mississippi River in his head.

The exactness of Twain's intelligence was formed by the sight lines of the mid-nineteenth-century American frontier, grounded in the experience that the essayist and historian Bernard DeVoto recognized as that of a young man accustomed to scenes of human squalor and depravity, who had "observed night-riding and lynching, the flogging of slaves," was familiar with the "commonplaces of lust and corruption, violence and subornation and cruelty," "who as a printer had been little better than a tramp," had joined the surge westward to the Nevada silver mines and the California goldfields, had "conversed with murderers and harlots," had seen a sizable number of men die "in their boots under his immediate observation." A *mise en scène* in which the man who didn't see clearly didn't live long enough to hear the punch line and get the joke.

The clarity of Twain's perception presented him with difficulties when he first undertook the project of an autobiography in 1877, at the age of forty-two, already established as a famous author and confident that he could employ the approach that in 1859 had shaped his navigations of the Mississippi River. He soon encountered snags and shoals unlike those above and below Island 66, many years later admitting to a reporter from the London *Times*, "You cannot lay bare your private soul and look at it. You are too much ashamed of yourself. It's too disgusting."

Despite the hazards both apparent and submerged, he was unwilling to abandon the project. He had in mind both the story of a life and the portrait of an age, and over the course of the next twenty-five years he attempts thirty or forty further drafts, all of them unsatisfactory because "life does not consist mainly— or even largely—of facts and happenings. It consists mainly of a storm of thoughts that is forever blowing through one's head," and therefore too quickly come and gone. Together with the sheaves of misbegotten paper, his doubts accumulate during the years in which he is also writing nine other books, among them *Huckleberry Finn*. To his friend William Dean Howells, the novelist and turn-of-the-century dean of American letters, he says that maybe "between the lines some shred of the 'remorseless truth'" will show up in a manuscript that otherwise "consists mainly of extinctions of the truth, shirkings of the truth, partial revealments of the truth."

Twain doesn't intend an examination of his inner child or a confession from his cloistered id. He is by nature reserved, and although he admires the candid memoirs of both Jean-Jacques Rousseau and Giacomo Casanova, he knows himself incapable of similar indiscretions.

Eventually he takes to heart the advice from his friend John Hay, a former secretary to President Abraham Lincoln and secretary of state in the McKinley Administration, who suggests that he proceed by inference and indirection to describe the *dramatis personae* of whom he has some knowledge, and in so doing find himself reflected in the mirror of his observation, "each fact and each fiction will be a dab of paint, each will fall in its right place, and together they will paint his portrait; but not the portrait *he* thinks they are painting, but his real portrait, the inside of him, the soul of him, his character." He will, of course, tell lies, but "half-consciously" instead of "bluntly," in a way that "makes his general form comely, with his virtuous prominences discernable and his ungracious ones in shadow."

And thus it comes to pass, the result of Twain's electing to talk, not write, his autobiography. He begins the experiment in 1904 in Florence, where he has rented a handsome villa in which to care for his cherished but dying wife. Knowing that his own turn in the pilothouse is nearly up, he writes to Howells to say, "I've struck it!" a method that both suits his temperament and matches his talent for telling stories.

> You will be astonished (& charmed) to see how like *talk* it is, & how real it sounds, & how well & compactly & sequentially it constructs itself, & what a dewy & breezy & woodsy freshness it has, & what a darling & worshipful absence of the signs of starch, & flatiron, & labor & fuss & the other artificialities!

By artificialities he means his prior efforts with pen and ink, which are "too literary, too prim, too nice."

> Narrative should flow as flows the brook down through the hills and the leafy woodlands ... a brook that never goes straight for a minute, but *goes*, and goes briskly, sometimes ungrammatically, and sometimes fetching a horseshoe three-quarters of a mile around and at the end of the circuit flowing within a yard the path that it traversed an hour before; but always *going*, and always following at least one law, always loyal to that law, the law of *narrative*, which *has no law*. Nothing to do but make the trip; the how of it is not important so that the trip is made.

His wife doesn't survive her season in the Italian sun, and soon after Twain returns to America, he casts himself loose on the flood tide of his memory, giving his deposition to a series of stenographers while lying garrulously abed, "propped up against great snowy white pillows," in a Fifth Avenue town house three blocks north of Washington Square, here and there introducing into the record miscellaneous exhibits—previously published speeches, anecdotes and sketches, newspaper clippings, brief biographies, letters, philosophical digressions and theatrical asides—that he thinks might serve to mark the passage of his life. Conceiving the dictations as a "bequest to posterity," he composes his farewell address over a period of nearly four years, from the winter of 1906 until a few months before his death in the spring of 1910, imposing on his testimony the condition that it not be published before the passing of another hundred years.

His reason is twofold. He can speak freely, be "as frank and free and unembarrassed as a love letter if I knew that what I was writing would be exposed to no eye until I was dead, and unaware, and indifferent." He also can avoid the inflicting of collateral damage. As both best-selling author and for forty years a popular attraction on lecture platforms in front of literary swells in Boston, noble lords in London, and dance-hall girls in Carson City, Twain had aimed to please, to produce laughter in commercial quantity. The laughter he regarded as a blessing and a comfort, humor "the great thing, the saving thing" that makes bearable the acquaintance with grief, his own and that of everybody else in the saloon, the theater, or the drawing room. He didn't wish to hurt anybody's feelings by revealing "every private opinion I possessed relative to religion, politics, and men," and he told his literary heirs and assigns that a century's tape delay was time enough to remove from the company of his prospective readers any and all likely to take offense.

> This book is not a revenge-record. When I build a fire under a person in it, I do not do it merely because of the enjoyment I get out of seeing him fry, but because he is worth the trouble. It is then a compliment, a distinction; let him give thanks and keep quiet. I do not fry the small, the commonplace, the unworthy.

Twain's literary heirs and assigns haven't done him any favors. The book is cumbersome and heavy (736 pages, 4 pounds), the footnotes overly extensive, much of the text picked over by prior editors (among them DeVoto) and elsewhere exposed to the light of print. Twain didn't get his expected chance to amend or revise a completed manuscript eventually running to a length of 2,600 pages; the deposition taken over the last four years of his life has been reduced to the fragment given during the three months between January 9 and March 30, 1906, his instructions honored in the breach, but his editors promising to release volumes II and III sometime in the next ten years.

And yet, against all odds and expectations, the book sold upward of 300,000 copies within the first six weeks of publication. Allow for the customary deductions (a third of the copies bought as Christmas ornaments, another third as table decorations), and the country apparently still has on hand at least 100,000 citizens willing to place a $34.95 bet on the force of language and the play of mind. The number compares favorably with the populations of Periclean Athens and Elizabethan London and embodies a better hope for the American future than any anxious policy paper passed around the winter conference tables of despair.

Twain offers his autobiography as an *omnium-gatherum*, its author reserving the right to wander at will all over his life, talk only about the thing that interests him at the moment, "drop it the moment its interest threatens to pale." He leaves the reader free to adopt the same practice, which is a kindness because much of the interest in what Twain has to say is so pale that it is barely visible, sometimes as monotonous as the conversation that he reports his having suffered under the baton of the Civil War general Daniel Sickles, which reminded him of "the late Bill Nye once saying, 'I have been told that Wagner's music is better than it sounds.'" The often sluggish going of Twain's narrative around a long horseshoe bend doesn't give offense because his reader isn't obliged to be polite, isn't sitting with a one-legged general in a West 9th Street parlor festooned with "lion skins, tiger skins, leopard skins, elephant skins … gushing sprays of swords fastened in trophy form against the wall." If I come across Twain recalling a meeting of the Hartford Monday Evening Club in 1884 at which the subject of discussion is the price of cigars or the befriending of cats, I can skip over as many pages as I please to find him in Honolulu in 1866 with the survivors of forty-three days at sea in an open boat, or discover him in Calcutta in 1896 in the company of Mary Wilson, "old and gray-haired, but ... very handsome," a woman whom he had much admired in her prior incarnation as a young woman in 1849 in Hannibal, Missouri:

> We sat down and talked. We steeped our thirsty souls in the reviving wine of the past, the pathetic past, the beautiful past, the dear and lamented past; we uttered the names that had been silent upon our lips for fifty years, and it was as if they were made of music; with reverent hands we unburied our dead, the mates of our youth, and caressed them with our speech; we searched the dusty chambers of our memories and dragged forth incident after incident, episode after episode, folly after folly, and laughed such good laughs over them, with the tears running down ...

The topic of Twain's autobiography is America and the Americans, his own life the progress of an observant pilgrim carrying in his head the reviving wine of the past as if it were the Mississippi River, the flow and stream of time caught up in the net of his comprehensive and comprehending memory. No other writer of his generation had touched the life of the country in so many places, or become familiar with as many of its oddly assorted inhabitants. Born in 1835 on the frontier of what was still Indian Territory, Twain had been present not only at the wheel of the steamboat *Pennsylvania* and at the pithead of the Comstock Lode but at dinner tables with Presidents Ulysses Grant and Theodore Roosevelt, on stages with Artemus Ward, Ralph Waldo Emerson, Bret Harte, and Booker T. Washington. He also traveled forty-nine times across the Atlantic and once across the Indian Ocean and the Pacific, as a dutiful tourist surveying the sights in Rome, Paris, and the Holy Land; as an itinerant sage entertaining crowds in Australia and Ceylon; as a visitor in London in 1897 for the pageant that was Queen Victoria's Diamond Jubilee, in Vienna in 1896 for a parading of the plumes of the Hapsburg Empire, "bodies of men-at-arms in the darling velvets of the Middle Ages ... beautiful costumes not to be seen in this world now outside the opera and the picture-books."

The scenes of foreign pomp and circumstance serve Twain as occasions to prefer the unpretentiousness of things American. The turn of his mind is democratic. He holds his fellow citizens in thoughtful regard not because they are rich or beautiful or famous but because they are his fellow citizens. He finds them plying trades in Massachusetts, building roads in Illinois, murdering one another in Nevada and California, outward bound toward some optimistic future across the next stretch of mountains or around the next bend in the river where the rainbow falls into the pot of gold. He employs his dictations as "a form and method whereby the past and the present are constantly brought face-to-face resulting in contrasts which newly fire up the interest all along like contact of flint with steel." He does not favor the "showy episodes" of his life, choosing instead "the common experiences" that make up the life of the average human being, and among the great snowy pillows on lower Fifth Avenue in the last years of his life, he brings them face to face in the contrapuntal music that is his play with words, something seen in Berlin in 1891 reminding him of something else seen in San Francisco in 1864, an impression of the first time he saw Florence in 1892 sending him back to Missouri in 1847:

> The life which I led there with my cousins was full of charm, and so is the memory of it yet. I can call back the solemn twilight and mystery of the deep woods, the earthy smells, the faint odors of the wild flowers, the sheen of rainwashed foliage, the rattling clatter of drops when the wind shook the trees, the far-off hammering of woodpeckers and the muffled drumming of wood pheasants in the remotenesses of the forest, the snapshot glimpses of disturbed wild creatures scurrying through the grass,—and I can call it all back and make it as real as it ever was, and as blessed. I can call back the prairie, and its loneliness and peace, and a vast hawk hanging motionless in the sky, with his wings spread wide and the blue of the vault showing through the fringe of their end-feathers .... I can see the blue clusters of wild grapes hanging amongst the foliage of the saplings, and I remember the taste of them and the smell.

The first volume of Twain's autobiographical project is for the most part taken up with his saving humor and gregarious affections, the character of his mind revealed, as his friend John Hay had foreseen, in the dabs of paint that Twain applies to the figure in the foreground.

Here is an encounter with John Hay's wife:

That Sunday morning, twenty-five years ago, Hay and I had been chatting and laughing and carrying-on almost like our earlier selves of '67, when the door opened and Mrs. Hay, gravely clad, gloved, bonneted, and just from church, and fragrant with the odors of Presbyterian sanctity, stood in it. We rose to our feet at once, of course,—rose through a swiftly falling temperature—a temperature which at the beginning was soft and summerlike, but which was turning our breath and all other damp things to frost crystals by the time we were erect—but we got no opportunity to say the pretty and polite thing and offer the homage due: the comely young matron forestalled us. She came forward smileless, with disapproval written all over her face, said most coldly, "Good morning Mr. Clemens," and passed on and out.

There was an embarrassed pause—I may say a very embarrassed pause. If Hay was waiting for me to speak, it was a mistake; I couldn't think of a word. It was soon plain to me that the bottom had fallen out of his vocabulary, too. When I was able to walk I started toward the door, and Hay, grown gray in a single night, so to speak, limped feebly at my side, making no moan, saying no word. At the door his ancient courtesy rose and bravely flickered for a moment, then went out. That is to say, he tried to ask me to call again, but at that point his ancient sincerity rose against the fiction and squelched it. Then he tried another remark, and that one he got through with. He said pathetically, and apologetically, "She is very strict about Sunday."

In the old Music Hall in Boston, seated on the stage with Josh Billings and Petroleum V. Nasby while another of the evening's humorists meets with the catastrophe of silence:

We drew a deep sigh; it ought to have been a sigh of pity for a defeated fellow craftsman, but it was not—for we were mean and selfish, like all the human race, and it was a sigh of satisfaction to see our unoffending brother fail.

On Olivia Langdon Clemens, to whom Twain had been married for thirty-four years and who died in Florence in June 1904:

I saw her first in the form of an ivory miniature in her brother Charley's stateroom in the steamer *Quaker City* in the Bay of Smyrna, in the summer of 1867, when she was in her twenty-second year. I saw her in the flesh for the first time in New York in the following December. She was slender and beautiful and girlish—and she was both girl and woman. She remained both girl and woman to the last day of her life. Under a grave and gentle exterior burned inextinguishable fires of sympathy, energy, devotion, enthusiasm, and absolutely limitless affection.

On patriotism:

I said that no party held the privilege of dictating to me how I should vote. That if party loyalty was a form of patriotism, I was no patriot, and that I didn't think I was much of a patriot anyway, for oftener than otherwise what the general body of Americans regarded as the patriotic course was not in accordance with my views; that if there was any valuable difference between being an American and a monarchist it lay in the theory that the American could decide for himself what is patriotic and what isn't; whereas the king could dictate the monarchist's patriotism for him—a decision which was final and must be accepted by the victim; that in my belief I was the only person in the sixty millions—with Congress and the Administration back of the sixty million—who was privileged to construct my patriotism for me.

They said "Suppose the country is entering upon a war—where do you stand then? Do you arrogate to yourself the privilege of going your own way in the matter, in the face of the nation?"

"Yes," I said, "that is my position. If I thought it an unrighteous war I would say so. If I were invited to shoulder a musket in that cause and march under that flag, I would decline. I would not voluntarily march under this country's flag, nor any other, when it was my private judgment that the country was in the wrong. If the country *obliged* me to shoulder the musket I could not help myself, but I would never volunteer. To volunteer would be the act of a traitor to myself, and consequently traitor to my country. If I refused to volunteer, I should be *called* a traitor, I am well aware of that—but that would not make me a traitor. The unanimous vote of the sixty millions could not make me a traitor. I should still be a patriot, and, in my opinion, the only one in the whole country.

On receiving the news of the death of his daughter Susy Clemens:

It is one of the mysteries of our nature that a man, all unprepared, can receive a thunder-stroke like that and live. There is but one reasonable explanation of it. The intellect is stunned by the shock and but gropingly gathers the meaning of the words. The power to realize their full import is mercifully wanting. The mind has a dumb sense of vast loss—that is all. It will take mind and memory months, and possibly years, to gather together the details and thus learn and know the whole extent of the loss ... It will be years before the tale of lost essentials is complete, and not till then can he truly know the magnitude of his disaster.

The seventy-five years of Twain's life (1835–1910) ran in parallel with America's transforming an agrarian democracy into an industrial oligarchy that brought with it the feasts of conspicuous consumption to which Twain gave the name the Gilded Age. He associated the phrase with the word "citified," "that epithet which suggests the absence of all spirituality, and the presence of all kinds of paltry materialisms, and mean ideals, and mean vanities and silly cynicisms." He doesn't overlook his own paltry materialisms and mean vanities, and just as he can remember the taste and smell of the wild grapes among the foliage and saplings on the Missouri frontier, he can call back, "and make it as real as it ever was," the selfishness and hypocrisy that made both himself and America great. Thus on January 23, 1906, comfortably placed on the Fifth Avenue pillows and in the midst of talking about some harmless clergyman among the members of the Hartford Monday Evening Club, he inserts a few notes on the character of man that he thinks might go well in a properly uplifting Sunday sermon:

> There are certain sweet-smelling sugar-coated lies current in the world which all politic men have apparently tacitly conspired together to support and perpetuate. One of these is, that there is such a thing in the world as independence: independence of thought, independence of opinion, independence of action ...
>
> We are discreet sheep; we wait to see how the drove is going, and then go with the drove. We have two opinions: one private, which we are afraid to express; and another one—the one we use—which we force ourselves to wear to please Mrs. Grundy, until habit makes us comfortable in it, and the custom of defending it presently makes us love it, adore it, and forget how pitifully we came by it. Look at it in politics. Look at the candidates whom we loathe, one year, and are afraid to vote against the next; whom we cover with unimaginable filth, one year, and fall down on the public platform and worship, the next—and keep on doing it until the habitual shutting of our eyes to last year's evidences brings us presently to a sincere and stupid belief in this year's ...
>
> Let us skip the other lies, for brevity's sake. To consider them would prove nothing, except that man is what he is—loving toward his own, lovable, to his own,—his family, his friends—and otherwise the buzzing, busy trivial, enemy of his race—who tarries his little day, does his little dirt, commends himself to God, and then goes out into the darkness, to return no more, and send no messages back—selfish even in death.

On Friday, March 9, he talks about a slave woman who pulled him as a child out of Bear Creek, thereby saving his life even though she was "interfering with the intentions of a Providence wiser" than herself. When he resumes the dictation on Monday, March 12, he means to return to events in Missouri sixty years ago, but "strong as that interest is, it is for the moment pushed out of the

way by an incident of to-day, which is still stronger." He refers to
the publication in the New York papers on the preceding Friday of
a triumphant cablegram sent to the government in Washington by
General Leonard Wood, commander of America's army of occupation in the Philippines. Twain summarizes the message in a few
sarcastic paragraphs. The intrepid troops under the direction of the
heroic general have trapped a swarm of half-naked natives (600
Moros, counting women and children) in a crater fifty feet below
the rim of a defunct volcano. The Moros are armed with knives
and clubs. An equal number of American troops hoist artillery up
to the rim of the volcano and shoot all the fish in the barrel, abol-
ishing them utterly, says Twain, "leaving not even a baby alive to
cry for its dead mother." He enters into the record the congratula-
tory telegram sent to the general by President Theodore Roosevelt.

Washington, March 10
Wood, Manila:—

I congratulate you and the officers and men of your command
upon the brilliant feat of arms wherein you and they so well
upheld the honor of the American flag.

(Signed) Theodore Roosevelt

Twain is acquainted with Roosevelt, describes him elsewhere in
his dictations as a "likeable," "hearty," and "straightforward" sort
of man, who therefore is certain to know that he is lying, that it
would not have been "a brilliant feat of arms" even if Christian
America, represented by its salaried soldiers, had shot them down
with Bibles and the Golden Rule instead of bullets. He knew perfectly well that our uniformed assassins had not upheld the honor
of the American flag but had done as they had been doing con-
tinually in the Philippines—that is to say, they had dishonored it.

What saddens Twain and therefore sharpens the edge of his
satire ("The President's joy over the splendid achievement of
his fragrant pet, General Wood") is the laying waste of Roosevelt's
humanity, his devolution into "a poor, cheap, wormy thing, like
the rest of us, a sarcasm."

Twain is too intelligent not to see, as he noted in his interview with the London *Times*, the shameful and disgusting contents of his own private soul, among them his lack of candor, his wearing a suit of words to please Mrs. Grundy when it comes to the villainy of Roosevelt. He doesn't doubt the sincerity of the president's boyish enthusiasms, but the splendid little war with Spain he regards as the work of a criminal. It is an opinion he has expressed privately but not one that he has voiced in print, and he regrets his failure to do so in a letter to his daughter Clara, written two months before he died and appended to the autobiography in a footnote:

> Roosevelt closed my mouth years ago with a deeply valued, gratefully received, unasked favor; & with all my bitter detestation of him I have never been able to say a venomous thing about him in print since—that benignant deed always steps in the way & lays its consecrated hand upon my lips. I ought not to allow it to do this; & I am ashamed of allowing it, but I cannot help it, since I am made in that way, & did not make myself.

Made, like all other men, as one of the Creator's prime miscarriages in invention and therefore apt to bury the light of intellect in the dung heap of moralizing cowardice. Twain again touches on the point in one of his further reflections on the Creator's gifts to man and beast.

> The gods value morals alone; they have paid no compliments to intellect, nor offered it a single reward. If intellect is welcome anywhere in the other world, it is in hell, not heaven.

In hell's holiday resorts on earth, Twain's intellect is the weapon that he brings to the defense of what he construes as the American idea. He began the project of his autobiography in 1877, a year that the historian Allan Nevins ranked as "one of the blackest in the nation's annals." Then as now, the situation was desperate, the economy in dire straits, democracy on its deathbed. The country was in severe depression, the rates of unemployment, bankruptcy, and business failure pegged to unprecedented levels of violence, poverty, and despair. The presidential election of 1876 had been thoroughly corrupted by fraudulent vote counts in favor of each candidate (the Republican Rutherford B. Hayes, the Democrat Samuel J. Tilden, both of them held captive by the banks). A number of Republican politicians had been murdered in the Southern states for their disagreement with the policy of lynching Negroes. The Lincoln County war in New Mexico encouraged the random shooting of Mexicans; mobs formed in the streets of San Francisco to beat to death the Yellow Peril as personified in Chinese laundrymen and shopkeepers. A railroad strike in West Virginia that began in July became the first national strike in the country's history, 500,000 workers walking away from factories and mines everywhere between New Jersey and California. Strikers in Pittsburgh set fire to the property of the Pennsylvania Railroad, destroying 39 buildings, 104 engines, 46 passenger cars, more than 1,200 freight cars. The disturbance moved Tom Scott, president of the railroad, to suggest that the strikers be given "a rifle diet for a few days and see how they liked that kind of bread." State militia and federal troops complied with the suggestion, killing more than a hundred strikers in Maryland and Pennsylvania.

Twain's view of the proceedings is a good deal clearer than that of our own latter-day viewers-with-alarm. Our reluctance to see democracy for what it is follows from the dream of perfection reflected in the department-store windows of a self-glorifying second Gilded Age. Twain had counted the cost of the imperial plumes and darling velvets. His life was coincident with the calamity that was the collision of the democratic ideal with the democratic reality, the warm promise of a generous experiment run aground on the reef of destruction that is the damned human race. Although less evident in this first volume of his autobiography than in his later books and newspaper writings—*A Connecticut Yankee in King Arthur's Court*, *Following the Equator*, *Pudd'nhead Wilson*, "An Open Letter to Commodore Vanderbilt," and *To the Person Sitting in Darkness*—the intelligence that is generous, intuitive, and sympathetic is also, in DeVoto's parsing of it, "undeluded, merciless and final." An early executor of Twain's literary estate, DeVoto had a better understanding of Twain's humor than do most of our contemporary critics, among them last winter's reviewers of the autobiography for the *New Yorker* and the *New York Times*, who chose to see him as an amiable after-dinner speaker, a man who told funny stories and smoked cigars, had worn a white suit and by some inexplicable chance had written two important books for boys, but not the sort of fellow whom one would wish to mention in the same ennobling breath with Mr. Henry James.

A similarly condescending tone infuriated DeVoto when he encountered it in New York's literary salons in the 1920s, dribbling from pursed lips onto the tea tables at the Century Club. The injustice of the faint praise moved DeVoto to publish *Mark Twain's America* in 1932, a book in which he ridicules the blind mouths of polite opinion:

> Criticism has said that [Twain] directed no humor against the abuses of his time: the fact is that research can find few elements of the age that Mark Twain did not burlesque, satirize, or deride. The whole obscene spectacle of government is passed in review— the presidency, the Congress, the basis of politics, the nature of democracy, the disintegration of power, the corruption of the electorate—bribery, depravity, subornation, the farce of the people's justice .... The Gilded Age ... is his creation, and in the wide expanse of his books, there are few social ulcers he does not probe.

A society that is the sum of its vanity and greed Twain understood to be not a society at all but a state of war. If in the volume at hand there is too little of his merciless and undeluded wit, there is enough of it to demonstrate why Twain these days is so sorely missed. Democracy is a dangerous business; it allies itself with change, which engenders movement, which induces friction, which implies unhappiness, which assumes conflict not only as the normal but also as the necessary condition of its existence.

Twain comes down on the side of the liberties of the people as opposed to the ambitions of the state, pitting the force of his intellect against the "peacock shams" of the world's "colossal humbug," believing that it is the freedoms of thought that rescue a democracy from its stupidities and crimes, the courage of its dissenting citizens that protects it against the despotism of wealth and power backed up with platitudes and billy clubs and subprime loans. His laughter turns toward the darker shores of tragedy as he grows older and moves downriver, drawing from the well of his sorrow the energy of his rage. He doesn't traffic in the mockery of the cynic or the bitterness of the misanthrope. He is a disenchanted philanthropist who retains his affection for individuals, a fierce skeptic who thinks that the Constitution is the premise for a narrative rather than the design for a monument or the plan of an invasion.

The narrative is plural, not one story but many stories, and "nothing to do but make the trip; the how of it not important so that the trip is made." If democracy is a constant making and remaking, of laws and institutions as well as jokes, the other fellow always has something to say without the prompt of a surveillance camera or a directive in the PATRIOT Act. The immortality of the whole overrules the immortality of the part, allows for the possibility that one's children might prove to be happier (or stronger or wiser or luckier) than oneself. It is the reviving wine of history that defends the future against the past, satire the arson that burns down the hospitality tents of complacent and self-righteous cant.

Our contemporary brigade of satirists doesn't play with fire. The heavy calibers of Twain's humor have gone missing from our news and entertainment media because the audiences made for television don't look with favor upon the kind of jokes that cast doubt on the guarantee of happiness and the promise of redemption. Taught to believe that democracy is something quiet, orderly, and safe, a peaceful idea supportive of think-tank viewings with alarm and the keeping of pets as fragrant as Alan Greenspan and General David Petraeus, they prefer the safer forms of satire fit for privileged and frightened children. Twain was an adult.

2014

33. Crowd Control

In case of rain, the revolution will take place in the hall.

—Erwin Chargaff

For the last several years the word "revolution" has been hanging around backstage on the national television talk-show circuit waiting for somebody, anybody—visionary poet, unemployed automobile worker, late-night comedian—to cue its appearance on camera. I picture the word sitting alone in the green room with the bottled water and a banana, armed with press clippings of its once-upon-a-time star turns in America's political theater (tie-dyed and brassiereless on the barricades of the 1960s countercultural insurrection, short-haired and seersucker smug behind the desks of the 1980s Reagan Risorgimento), asking itself why it's not being brought into the segment between the German and the Japanese car commercial. Surely even the teleprompter must know that it is the beast in the belly of the news reports, more of them every day in print and *en blog*, about income inequality, class conflict, the American police state. Why then does nobody have any use for it except in the form of the adjective, *revolutionary*, unveiling a new cell phone app or a new shade of lipstick?

I can think of several reasons, among them the cautionary tale told by the round-the-clock media footage of dead revolutionaries in Syria, Egypt, and Tunisia, also the certain knowledge that anything anybody says (on camera or off, to a hotel clerk, a Facebook friend, or an ATM) will be monitored for security purposes. Even so, the stockpiling of so much careful silence among people who like to imagine themselves on the same page with Patrick Henry— "Give me liberty, or give me death"—raises the question as to what has become of the American spirit of rebellion. Where have all the flowers gone, and what, if anything, is anybody willing to risk in the struggle for "Freedom Now," "Power to the People," "Change We Can Believe In"?

My guess is next to nothing that can't be written off as a business expense or qualified as a tax deduction. The hallowed American notion of armed rebellion as a civic duty stems from the letter that Thomas Jefferson wrote from Paris in 1787 as a further commentary on the new Constitution drawn up that year in Philadelphia, a document he thinks invests the state with an unnecessary power to declare the citizenry out of order. A mistake, said Jefferson, because no country can preserve its political liberties unless its rulers know that their people preserve the spirit of resistance, and with it ready access to gunpowder: "The tree of liberty must be refreshed from time to time with the blood of patriots and tyrants. It is its natural manure."

Jefferson conceived of liberty and despotism as alternate plantings in the soil of politics, products of human cultivation subject to changes in the weather, the difference between them not unlike that between the growing of an orchard and the draining of a cesspool, both understood as means of environmental protection. It is the turning of the seasons and the cyclical motions of the stars that Jefferson has in mind when in his letter he goes on to say, "God forbid we should ever be twenty years without such a rebellion"—that is, one conceived not as a lawless upheaval but as a lawful recovery.

The twentieth-century philosopher and political scientist Hannah Arendt suggests that the American Revolution was intended as a restoration of what its progenitors believed to be a natural order of things "disturbed and violated" by the despotism of a distant and overbearing monarchy. During the hundred years prior to the Declaration of Independence, the Americans had developed tools of political management (church congregations, village assemblies, town meetings) with which to govern themselves in accordance with what they took to be the ancient liberties possessed by their fellow Englishmen on the far side of the Atlantic Ocean. They didn't bear the grievances of a subjugated populace, and the seeds of revolt were nowhere blowing in the wind until the British crown demanded new, and therefore unlawful, tax money.

Arendt's retrieval of the historical context leads her to say of the war for independence that it was "not revolutionary except by inadvertence." To sustain the point she calls on Benjamin Franklin's memory of the years preceding the shots fired at Lexington in April 1775: "I never had heard in any conversation from any person, drunk or sober, the least expression of a wish for a separation, or hint that such a thing would be advantageous to America." The men who came to power after the Revolution were the same men who held power before the Revolution, their new government grounded in a system of thought that was, in our modern parlance, conservative.

Born thirteen years later under the fixed star of a romantic certainty, the French Revolution was advertent, a violent overthrow of what its proponents, among them Maximilien de Robespierre, perceived as an unnatural order of things. Away with the old, in with the new; kill the king, remove the statues, reset the clocks, welcome to a world that never was but soon is yet to come. The freedom-loving songs and slogans were well suited to the work of ecstatic demolition, but a guillotine is not a living tree, and although manured with the blood of aristocrats and priests, it failed to blossom with the leaves of political liberty. An armed mob of newly baptized *citoyens* stormed the Bastille in 1789; Napoleon in 1804 crowned himself emperor in the cathedral of Notre Dame.

Jefferson's thinking had been informed by his study of nature and history, Robespierre's by his reading of Rousseau's poetics. Neither set of political ideas brought forth the dream-come-true products of the nineteenth-century Industrial Revolution—new worlds being born every day of the week, the incoming tide of modern manufacture and invention (the cotton gin, gas lighting, railroads) washing away the sand castles of medieval religion and Renaissance humanism, dismantling Robespierre's reign of virtue, uprooting Jefferson's tree of liberty.

So it is left to Karl Marx, along with Friedrich Engels, to acknowledge the arrival of the new world that never was with the publication in German of the *Communist Manifesto* in 1848: "The bourgeoisie cannot exist without constantly revolutionizing the instruments of production, and thereby the relations of production, and with them the whole relations of society." Men shape their tools, their tools shape their relations with other men, and the rain it raineth every day in a perfect storm of creative destruction that is amoral and relentless. The ill wind, according to Marx, blows from any and all points of the political compass with the "single, unconscionable freedom—free trade," which resolves "personal worth into exchange value," substitutes "callous 'cash payment'" for every other form of human meaning and endeavor, devotes its all-devouring enthusiasms to "naked, shameless, direct, brutal exploitation."

Over the course of the nineteenth century, the energies of the capitalist dynamic take full and proud possession of the whole of Western society. They become, in Marx's analysis, the embodiment of "the modern representative state," armed with the wealth of its always newer and more powerful machines (electricity, photography, the telephone, the automobile) and staffed by executives (i.e., politicians, no matter how labeled) who function as "a committee for managing the common affairs of the whole bourgeoisie."

What Marx sees in theory as an insatiable abstraction, the American historian Henry Adams saw as concrete and overwhelming fact. Marx was seventeen years dead and the *Communist Manifesto* a sacred text among the left-wing intelligentsia everywhere in Europe when Adams, his habit of mind as profoundly conservative as that of his great-grandfather, stands in front of a colossal dynamo at the Paris Exposition in 1900 and knows that Prometheus, no longer chained to his ancient rock, bestrides the earth wearing J. P. Morgan's top hat and P. T. Barnum's cloak of as many colors as the traffic will bear. Adams shares with Marx the leaning toward divine revelation:

> To Adams the dynamo became a symbol of infinity. As he grew accustomed to the great gallery of machines, he began to feel the forty-foot dynamos as a moral force, much as the early Christians felt the Cross. The planet itself seemed less impressive, in its old-fashioned, deliberate, annual or daily revolution, than this huge wheel, revolving within arm's length at some vertiginous speed ... Before the end, one began to pray to it; inherited instinct taught the natural expression of man before silent and infinite force.

I inherited the instinct as a true-born American bred to the worship of both machinery and money; an appreciation of its force I acquired during a lifetime of reading newspaper reports of political uprisings in the provinces of the bourgeois world state—in China, Israel, and Greece in the 1940s; in the 1950s those in Hungary, Cuba, Guatemala, Algeria, Egypt, Bolivia, and Iran; in the 1960s in Vietnam, France, America, Ethiopia, and the Congo; in the 1970s and 1980s in El Salvador, Poland, Nicaragua, Kenya, Argentina, Chile, Indonesia, Czechoslovakia, Turkey, Jordan, Cambodia, again in Iran; over the last twenty-four years in Russia, Venezuela, Lebanon, Croatia, Bosnia, Libya, Tunisia, Syria, Ukraine, Iraq, Somalia, South Africa, Romania, Sudan, again in Algeria and Egypt. The plot line tended to repeat itself—first the new flag on the roof of the palace, rapturous crowds in the streets waving banners; then searches, requisitions, massacres, severed heads raised on pikes; soon afterward the transfer of power from one police force to another police force, the latter more repressive than the former (darker uniforms, heavier motorcycles) because more frightened of the social and economic upheavals they can neither foresee nor control.

All the shiftings of political power produced changes within the committees managing regional budgets and social contracts on behalf of the bourgeois imperium. None of them dethroned or defenestrated Adams's dynamo or threw off the chains of Marx's cash nexus. That they could possibly do so is the "romantic idea" that Albert Camus, correspondent for the French Resistance newspaper *Combat* during and after World War II, sees in 1946 as having been "consigned to fantasy by advances in the technology of weaponry."

The French philosopher Simone Weil draws a corollary lesson from her acquaintance with the Civil War in Spain and from her study of the Communist *Sturm und Drang* in Russia, Germany, and France subsequent to World War I.

> One magic word today seems capable of compensating for all sufferings, resolving all anxieties, avenging the past, curing present ills, summing up all future possibilities: that word is *revolution* … This word has aroused such pure acts of devotion, has repeatedly caused such generous blood to be shed, has constituted for so many unfortunates the only source of courage for living, that it is almost a sacrilege to investigate it; all this, however, does not prevent it from possibly being meaningless.

During the turbulent decade of the 1960s in the United States, the advancing technologies of bourgeois news production (pictures in place of print) transformed the meaningless magic word into a profitable commodity, marketing it both as deadly menace and lively fashion statement. The commercial putsch wasn't organized by the CIA or planned by a consortium of advertising agencies; it evolved in two stages as a function of the capitalist dynamic that substitutes cash payment for every other form of human meaning and endeavor.

The disorderly citizenry furnishing the television footage in the early sixties didn't wish to overthrow the government of the United States. Nobody was threatening to reset the game clock in the Rose Bowl, tear down Grand Central Terminal, or remove the Lincoln Memorial. The men, women, and children confronting racist tyranny in the American South—sitting at a lunch counter in Alabama, riding a bus into Mississippi, going to school in Arkansas—risked their lives in pure acts of devotion, refreshing the tree of liberty with the blood of patriots. The Civil Rights movement and later the anti–Vietnam War protests were reformative, not revolutionary, the expression of democratic objection and dissent in accord with the thinking of Jefferson, also with President John F. Kennedy's having said in his 1961 inaugural address, "Ask not what your country can do for you—ask what you can do for your country." Performed as a civic duty, the unarmed rebellions led to the enactment in the mid-1960s of the Economic Opportunity Act, the Voting Rights Act, the Medicare and Medicaid programs, and eventually to the shutting down of the war in Vietnam.

The television camera, however, isn't much interested in political reform (slow, tedious, and unphotogenic) and so, even in the first years of protest, the news media presented the trouble running around loose in the streets as a revolution along the lines of the one envisioned by Robespierre. Caught in the chains of the cash nexus, they couldn't do otherwise. The fantasy of armed revolt sold papers, boosted ratings, monetized the fears at all times running around loose in the heads of the propertied classes. The multiple wounds in the body politic over the course of the decade—the assassination of President Kennedy, big-city race riots, student riots at venerable universities, the assassinations of Dr. Martin Luther King Jr. and Senator Robert F. Kennedy—amplified the states of public alarm. The fantastic fears of violent revolt awakened by a news media in search of a profit stimulated the demand for repressive surveillance and heavy law enforcement that over the last fifty years has blossomed into one of the richest and most innovative of the nation's growth industries. For our own good, of course, and without forgoing our constitutional right to shop.

God forbid that the excitement of the 1960s should in any way have interfered with the constant revolutionizing of the bourgeois desire for more dream-come-true products to consume and possess. The advancing power of the media solved what might have become a problem by disarming the notion of revolution as a public good, rebranding it as a private good. Again it was impossible for the technology to do otherwise. The medium is the message, and because the camera sees but doesn't think, it substitutes the personal for the impersonal; whether in Hollywood restaurants or Washington committee rooms, the actor takes precedence over the act. What is wanted is a flow of emotion, not a train of thought, a vocabulary of images better suited to the selling of a product than to the expression of an idea. Narrative becomes montage, and as commodities acquire the property of information, the amassment of wealth follows from the naming of things rather than the making of things.

The voices of conscience in the early 1960s spoke up for a government of laws, not men, for a principle as opposed to a lifestyle. By the late 1960s the political had become personal, the personal political, and it was no longer necessary to ask what one must do for one's country. The new-and-improved question, available in a wide range of colors, flower arrangements, cosmetics, and musical accompaniments, underwrote the second-stage commodification of the troubled spirit of the times.

Writing about the socialist turbulence on the late-1930s European left, Weil lists among the acolytes of the magic word, "the bourgeois adolescent in rebellion against home surroundings and school routine, the intellectual yearning for adventure and suffering from boredom." So again in America in the late 1960s, radical debutantes wearing miniskirts and ammunition belts, Ivy League professors mounting the steps of the Pentagon, self-absorbed movie actors handing around anarchist manifestos to self-important journalists seated at the tables in Elaine's. By the autumn of 1968 the restaurant on the Upper East Side of Manhattan served as a Station of the Cross for the would-be revolutionaries briefly in town for an interview with *Time* or a photo shoot for *Vogue*, and as a frequent guest of the restaurant, I could see on nearly any night of the week the birth of a new and imaginary self soon to become a boldfaced name. Every now and then I asked one of the wandering stars what it was that he or she hoped to have and to hold once the revolution was won. Most of them were at a loss for an answer. What they knew, they did not want, what they wanted, they did not know, except, of course, more—more life, more love, more drugs, more celebrity, more happiness, more music.

As a consequence of the political becoming personal, by the time the 1960s moved on to the 1980s and President Reagan's Morning in America, it was no longer possible to know oneself as an American citizen without the further identification of at least one value-adding, consumer-privileged adjective—feminist American, black American, Native American, gay American, middle-aged white American. The costumes changed, and so did the dossier of the malcontents believing themselves entitled to more than they already had. A generation of dissatisfied bourgeois reluctant to grow up gave way to another generation of dissatisfied bourgeois unwilling to grow old. The locus of the earthly Paradise shifted from a commune in the White Mountains to a gated golf resort in Palm Springs, and the fond hope of finding oneself transformed into an artist segued into the determined effort to make oneself rich. What remained constant was the policy of enlightened selfishness and the signature bourgeois passion for more plums in the pudding.

While making a magical mystery tour of the Central American revolutionary scene in 1987, Deb Olin Unferth remarks on the work in progress: "Compared to El Salvador, Nicaragua was like Ping–Pong ... like a cheerful communist kazoo concert ... We were bringing guitars, plays adapted from Nikolai Gogol, elephants wearing tasseled hats. I saw it myself and even then I found it a bit odd. The Nicaraguans wanted land, literacy, a decent doctor. We wanted a nice singalong and a ballet. We weren't a revolution. We were an armed circus."

As a descriptive phrase for what American society has become over the course of the last five decades, *armed circus* is as good as any and better than most. The constantly revolutionizing technologies have been spinning the huge bourgeois wheel of fortune at the speed of light, remaking the means of production in every field of human meaning and endeavor—media, manufacturing, war, finance, literature, crime, medicine, art, transport, and agriculture. The storm wind of creative destruction it bloweth every day, removing steel mills, relocating labor markets, clearing the ground for cloud storage, for more microbreweries and Internet connections, more golf balls, cheeseburgers, and cruise missiles; also more unemployment, more pollution, more obesity, more dysfunctional government and criminal finance, more fear. The too much of more than anybody knows what to do with obliges the impresarios of the armed circus to match the gains of personal liberty (sexual, social, economic, if one can afford the going price) with more repressive systems of crowd control.

To look back to the early 1960s is to recall a society in many ways more open and free than it has since become, when a pair of blue jeans didn't come with a radio-frequency ID tag, when it was possible to appear for a job interview without a urine sample, to say in public what is now best said not at all. So frightened of its own citizens that it classifies them as probable enemies, the U.S. government steps up its scrutiny of what it chooses to regard as a mob. So intrusive is the surveillance that nobody leaves home without it. Tens of thousands of cameras installed in the lobbies of office and apartment buildings and in the eye sockets of the mannequins in department-store windows register the comings and goings of a citizenry deemed unfit to mind its own business.

The social contract offered by the managing agents of the bourgeois state doesn't extend the privilege of political revolt, a point remarked upon by the Czech playwright Václav Havel just prior to being imprisoned in the late 1970s by the Soviet regime then governing Czechoslovakia:

> No attempt at revolt could ever hope to set up even a minimum of resonance in the rest of society, because that society is "soporific," submerged in a consumer rat race ... Even if revolt were possible, however, it would remain the solitary gesture of a few isolated individuals, and they would be opposed not only by a gigantic apparatus of national (and supranational) power, but also by the very society in whose name they were mounting their revolt in the first place.

The observation accounts for the past sell-by date of the celebrity guest alone and palely loitering in the green room with the bottled water and the banana. Who has time to think or care about political change when it's more than enough trouble to save oneself from drowning in the flood of technological change? All is not lost, however, for the magic word that stormed the Bastille and marched on the tsar's winter palace; let it give up its career as a noun, and as an adjective it can look forward to no end of on-camera promotional appearances with an up-and-coming surgical procedure, breakfast cereal, or video game.

2015

34. Pennies From Heaven

It is easier for a camel to go through the eye of a needle, than for a rich man to enter into the kingdom of God.

—Matthew 19:24

But if the rich men are left standing around on earth with the camels, wherefrom the pennies that drop from the skies of philanthropy? Who carries up the treasure to the pay windows in heaven? At what altitude does hard coin resolve itself into dew, and so fall, gently like rain, on the sorrow and heat of the desert? How high the cloud level before greed becomes good?

These questions inform the discussion of the philanthropic largesse that in America has become a very big business over the last fifty years. Big enough to warrant the casting of suspicion on its motives, doubt on its objectives, stones at its privileges. Scolding voices in the media and Congress lobby for the adage that the mark of a good deed is its not going unpunished, and the increasingly harsh tone of the complaints—philanthropy as false front for funding a political campaign, as setup for a tax dodge, preservation of a family fortune, whiteout of a criminal rap sheet—rises to the occasion of the national economy's nonprofit sector becoming an ever larger part of the whole. The most recent numbers available from the Urban Institute speak to the presence of divinity.

Nonprofit organizations report over $4.8 trillion in total assets, $2.16 trillion in total revenues, $2.03 trillion in total expenses.

Nonprofit organizations account for 5.4 percent of the country's gross domestic product, roughly 10 percent of all wages and salaries, $887 billion in annual spending.

Total annual private giving (from individuals, foundations, and businesses) in the amount of $335 billion.

Around 1.5 million nonprofit organizations in the United States, roughly one for every 213 Americans, to which more than one in four Americans volunteered an estimated 8.1 billion hours of work valued at $163 billion.

So glorious a concentration of wealth makes a joyful noise unto the Lord; the accounting for its uses opens a Pandora's box from which swarms forth a screech of lawyers. Section 501(c)(3) of the Internal Revenue Code bestows tax exemptions on nonprofit enterprises recognized as "religious, charitable, scientific, testing for public safety, literary, or educational," but a string of handsomely abstract adjectives doesn't furnish clear definition of the noun *philanthropy*. Among the vast multitude of would-be loaves and fishes, how to distinguish those that are morally wholesome, financially sound, socially nourishing? Where is it written that all good intentions are good, and which ones escape or deserve being nailed to a cross? Does support for the Metropolitan Museum of Art require equal protection for the San Francisco Bay smelt?

The questions follow from a careless use of the term *philanthropy* ("love of humanity" in the ancient Greek) as a catch-all synonym embracing different forms of its expression in societies past and present, among them Sumerian debt forgiveness, Roman bread and circuses, Muslim almsgiving, Chinook potlatch,

Catholic charity and sin removal, Protestant good works, democratic government.

Although endowed over the centuries with many benevolent connotations (compassion, forbearance, kindness, humility), the word *philanthropy* first appears in Western thought in the fifth century B.C., in Aeschylus' play *Prometheus Bound,* to name an act of rebellion and denote the crime of treason. Alone among the deities on Mount Olympus, the Titan Prometheus takes pity on the "sad, careladen" human race living like "ants in sunless caves," their every act without hope or direction, "dayflies" lost in meaningless confusion. Zeus intends to delete the species and "grow another one more to his liking." Prometheus would have it otherwise. Disposed to the love of humanity (for reasons left unstated, but none of them to do with grace or wit or beauty), he steals the "bright and dancing fire" of the gods and gives to mortal men its "wonderworking power"— heat and light, but also freedom of thought, the stores of memory and the arts of divination, knowledge of numbers and letters, of medicine, carpentry, animal husbandry, and astronomy.

Prometheus thus defies the will and tyranny of Zeus "by granting mortals honor above their due," and the punishment is merciless—his immortal flesh bound in chains, nailed to a barren rock at the far limit of the world, condemned to endure relentless torture "through endless time."

The godlike powers transferred by Prometheus as unrestricted gift to mortal men serve their purpose at sea level, here on earth with the hummingbirds and the camels, their saving grace not deferred until the beneficiaries attain celestial cruising speed. The society that was Hellenic Athens didn't assign high real estate values to an afterlife, and the rich men within the *polis,* their formidable wealth placing them at Promethean cloud level, were expected (expected, not obliged) to provide, at their own and often ruinous expense, enhancements of the public spirit and the common good—votive offerings, sacrifices and temples, gymnasia, festivals, games, banquets, the outfitting of naval vessels, and the staging of plays.

Generosity was virtue, the value of money the having it to give away. The reward was double-edged—the pleasure inherent in the act of freely giving, the honor for doing so a gift freely bestowed by one's fellow citizens. Honor, not gratitude. As long as the haves placed a higher value in their stores of virtue than on their hoards of wealth, the have-nots could look to them in admiration instead of with envy and resentment. Pericles delivering his funeral oration in 431 B.C. (the first year of the Peloponnesian War) praises Athenians as patrons of the public good, willing to make noble expenditures (of their lives, their fortunes, and their sacred honor) to preserve the city's freedoms of thought and action.

The happy state of affairs didn't survive the war with Sparta. The government of Athens fell into the grasp of an oligarchy afflicted with the disease diagnosed by the ancient Greeks as *pleonexia*, the pathological craving for more—more property, more publicity, more bling. Athens divided into a city of the poor and a city of the rich, one at war with the other and neither inclined to temper its bitterness in the interest of the common good. Aristotle mentions a faction of especially reactionary oligarchs who swear an oath of selfishness: "I will be an adversary of the people … and in the Council I will do it all the evil that I can."

Democracy congealing into plutocracy conformed to Aristotle's theorem of governments changing form in a sequence as certain as the changing of the seasons. Regimes come and go, but the have-nots always outnumber the haves, and no matter what the political name of the game (monarchy, aristocracy, or democracy), the well-being of the less-fortunate many, says Aristotle, must always depend on the philanthropy of a privileged few who give direction to dayflies, light to ants in sunless caves.

The observation leads to a follow-up question: To what extent does the glorious concentration of wealth lovingly noted by the Urban Institute portend relief from the diseased oligarchy that for the past forty years has proclaimed itself the enemy of the American democracy and vows to do all the evil it can to a government of the people, by the people, for the people?

One would like to think the odds favor if not full recovery, at least remission of the illness. Americans in their daily dealings with one another prove themselves unfailingly open-hearted and forbearing; among the world's peoples few are more generous in the giving of money, time, and effort to the practice of philanthropy. Confronted with sudden misfortune or disastrous accident (the flooding of New Orleans, the bombing of the World Trade Center), they respond with heartfelt outpourings of voluntary assistance. Wealthy patrons of humanity furnish the country with its expensive collection of museums, orchestras, hospitals, libraries, colleges, universities, churches, and football teams—more or less the same goods and services distributed in pagan antiquity by the selfless and therefore self-ennobling rich in the form of amphitheaters, baths, aqueducts, menageries of wild beasts, sacrificial pairs of gladiators.

Add to the inventory of America's goodwill the Christian love of humanity arising among the poor and for the poor, from the presence of God within all men. The Greek and Roman patrons of the public good bestowed their gifts on citizens belonging to the city or the state, not on slaves, outcasts, beggars, immigrants. Neither Pericles nor Caesar recognized a human life form classified simply as "the poor." The grouping suited the political ambition of the Christian church rising on the ruins of the Roman Empire in the fourth century, the congregations of the faithful drawn from the vast throng of have-nots littering the shores of the Mediterranean and bound together in a commonwealth of suffering. The Christian theologian Tertullian refutes the pagan faith in wealth: "Nothing sacred is to be had for money.... . We have all drunk of one and the same Holy Spirit ... are all delivered as it were from one common womb of ignorance, and called out of darkness into his marvelous light." Lactantius, early father of the Christian church, says, "The only true and certain obligation is to feed the needy and useless ... men may have no use for them, but God has."

It is Thomas Paine, the incendiary voice of the American Revolution, who in the eighteenth century converts the Christian love of humanity (shared among equals in the lower strata of society) into the promise of democratic self-government—"The strength of government and the happiness of the governed" is the freedom of the common people to "mutually and naturally support each other." One's fellow citizens are to be held in honorable regard not because they are rich or notably generous but because they are one's fellow citizens.

Traveling in America in 1831 and 1832, the French aristocrat Alexis de Tocqueville finds democracy to be a work in progress along the lines projected by Paine, the common people mutually supporting one another by forming associations to hold fêtes, found seminaries, build inns, establish hospitals, dispatch missionaries, distribute books. "When the world was controlled by a small number of powerful and wealthy individuals," says Tocqueville, "they liked to advertise how glorious it is to forget oneself and how fitting it is to do good without self-interest just like God himself ... In the United States, the beauty of virtue is almost never promoted. It is considered useful and this is proved daily."

The fact of which Walt Whitman was daily reminded during his three years as a Civil War hospital volunteer attending to sick and wounded soldiers both Union and Confederate. He notes in his diary that he'd sat next to the cots of as many as a hundred thousand frightened young men, talking to them at length, distributing gifts of writing paper or tobacco, a stamped envelope, an apple or an orange, small pieces of money. From his experience with others like him on his hospital rounds, he learns "one thing conclusively— that beneath all the ostensible greed and heartlessness of our times there is no end to the generous benevolence of men and women in the United States, when once sure of their object. Another thing became clear to me—while *cash* is not amiss to bring up the rear, tact and magnetic sympathy and unction are, and ever will be, sovereign still." Love, not money.

Which wasn't the way things were going during America's late nineteenth-century Gilded Age, so named by Mark Twain to denote a society amounting to the sum of its vanity and greed, so seen by Andrew Carnegie as a parasitical oligarchy devouring the happiness of the many to feed the pleasures of the few. Twain is defender of the democratic motions of the heart, Carnegie the progenitor of what in the twentieth century becomes large-scale philanthropic enterprise established by wealthy patrons of the common good.

Born in poverty in Scotland, Carnegie moved with his immigrant family to Allegheny, Pennsylvania, in 1848; as a boy of twelve, he was working twelve hours a day in a cotton mill. By 1889 he is owner of dark satanic steel mills in Pittsburgh, a captain of industry, abundantly rich, fearful for the future of a country herding its working classes into the shambles of desperate, possibly Communist, revolt. That same year he brings forth "The Gospel of Wealth" as remedy for all the ills that overfed capitalist flesh is heir to. The manifesto first appeared in the *North American Review*, offered by its author as "the true antidote for the temporary unequal distribution of wealth, the reconciliation of the rich and the poor." Let the rich men throughout the land give over their great fortunes before they die for the use of the living, and "we shall have an ideal state, in which the surplus wealth of the few will become, in the best sense, the property of the many." Better yet, the rich man acts as trustee and agent for his "poorer brethren," grants the blessing of his "superior wisdom," directs the money to its best uses—to dignified public works, never in the form of alms in trifling amounts to "the drunken, the slothful, the unworthy." Like Cicero in 44 B.C., Carnegie distinguished between the deserving and undeserving poor. So did Ralph Waldo Emerson in 1841 in his essay "Self-Reliance" (*Concord, MA*, page 50), "I tell thee, thou foolish philanthropist, that I grudge the dollar, the dime, the cent I give to such men as do not belong to me." He blames himself for sometimes having given "alms to sots."

Carnegie's philanthropy was pagan, not Christian. The reward was honor, not gratitude. A rich man who dies with his wealth intact, he said, "dies disgraced." It didn't occur to him to relieve the poverty of the workers in his mills (twelve-hour shifts, paltry wages, crowded and filthy housing), but he did his best to leave no money on the table of his life. When in 1901 he sold his steel mills to J. P. Morgan for $480 million he became the richest man in America; before he died in 1919 he gave away $350 million to the building of 2,811 libraries in America's cities and towns, to the setting up of numerous institutes and foundations.

The big American foundations formed during the first half of the twentieth century—Rockefeller, Ford, Pew, Sage, Rosenwald, Kellogg—deployed Carnegie's lines of reasoning and priority. They pursued large-scale projects based on scientific research—the eradication of yellow fever and malaria, the restoration of colonial Williamsburg, the preservation of the Hudson River Palisades.

The good intentions multiplied over the course of the next hundred years, as did the number of foundations lobbying for social and political change, backing civil and human rights initiatives, funding think tanks grouped around the ideological campfires on both the left and the right.

The storylines are appropriately multicultural and diverse, not subject to equal opportunity generalization. What little I know of them I borrow from Mark Dowie's *American Foundations: An Investigative History*, published in 2001. Dowie notes that the governance of big foundations eventually passes down over generations from the Promethean figure present at the creation to staffs of foundation officials, *philanthrocrats* apt to be more concerned about the safety and well-being of the money under their care than about the uses to which it might be put. The law requires the country's 86,000 grantmaking foundations to distribute every year a minimum of 5 percent of their endowments, but if carefully managed, even that minimum need not leave the premises. The tax returns filed by the Bill, Hillary, and Chelsea Clinton Foundation in 2013 teach the self-promoting lesson. The foundation received more than $140 million in grants and contributions but squandered only $8.8 million on direct aid and research projects, reserving $30 million for payroll and employee benefits; $8.7 million for rent and office expenses; $9.2 million for conferences, conventions, and meetings; $8 million for fundraising; and nearly $8.5 million for travel.

Dowie's investigation fits with Dwight Macdonald's account of his meeting in 1955 with the "forty-odd philanthropoids, who, for all practical purposes, *are* the Ford Foundation." Assigned by *The New Yorker* to review the proceedings in what was then the foundation's new headquarters building on Madison Avenue, Macdonald found the office staff conversing in foundationese—"like Latin, a dead language … designed for ceremony rather than utility. Its function is magical and incantatory—not to give information or to communicate ideas or to express feelings." Gilded functionaries loyal to the will and tyranny of Zeus, intent upon preserving rather than overturning the status quo.

The character and intent of the early generation of philanthropy I learned to appreciate in the person of John D. Rockefeller III, grandson of the nineteenth-century oil baron, son of the early twentieth-century philanthropist, elder brother of David and Nelson Rockefeller. John III was the member of the family entrusted to carry forward its tradition of philanthropic largesse, a task he had performed with skill and determination since his graduation from Princeton in 1929, but one for which his chief publicist in 1963 thought he hadn't received proper recognition. His brother Nelson was governor of New York, his brother David the president of Chase Manhattan Bank, their names in the papers nine mornings out of ten but nowhere a mention of John, who had created the Asia Society and the Population Council and provided strong support for the International Rice Research Institute in Manila, and who was putting together the $184 million needed to complete the building of Lincoln Center on the west side of Manhattan.

I was employed that year as a writer for the *Saturday Evening Post* when the publicist called to ask if I would consider traveling with John III to Asia for three months with a view to writing an article about his various projects underway in Japan, Taiwan, the Philippines, Thailand, India, and East and West Pakistan. I would have access to any and all meetings and negotiations with government officials, bankers, scientists, and politicians, and I was to be paid a per diem, with John III reserving the right to review the completed manuscript and, if so inclined, to forestall its publication.

I had no objection. I didn't care whether the article was published or not; I was being given a chance to see the world from a high elevation of wealth and power, as it might have looked to Prometheus from the heights of Olympus. Every year for twelve years John III had been making the same journey (concentrating on the problem of birth control and the prospect for high-yield plantings of rice), and at all points on the itinerary he was met with honors befitting royalty—cars on the airport tarmac, receptions at the palace, banquets with the prime minister. His knowledge of various Asian societies was profound, as was his delight in each of the people to whom he introduced me in the hope I might catch sight of their value as singular human beings. Not once in three months did he not know the name of the person to whom he was talking—the name, the pronunciation of the name, the family story, the problem at hand, the detail of the particular circumstance. Although he was a tall and imposing figure, he was modest to a fault, shy in the company of scholars and politicians, hesitant in the expression of his emotions.

Maya Angelou once said she found that "among its other benefits, giving liberates the soul of the giver." So it was with John D. Rockefeller III. His philanthropy was his escape from the prison of his shyness, his becoming part of the larger story that is the sharing in man's love for his fellow man. The Chinese philosopher Mencius came upon the thought around 330 B.C. "Not to be benevolent when nothing stands in the way is to show a lack of wisdom. A man neither benevolent nor wise, devoid of courtesy and dutifulness, is a slave."

The article was never published. The Population Council's attempt to encourage birth control in Taiwan, India, and Pakistan went against the grain of local sentiment and politics, and John III believed it counterproductive to advertise these difficulties in print. To do so might cause trouble for his friends running the clinics in Asia. Self-glorifying publicity in New York wasn't worth the price of a doctor's loss of face in Dhaka.

The times have changed. Billionaire philanthropists these days delight in the photo ops of their giving to the public good, stepping down from helicopter or horse to baptize their new naming opportunity of a football stadium or concert hall. Their magnificence recalls the story told by the Stoic philosopher Seneca in the first century about Alexander the Great presenting the gift of an entire city to a man who didn't think himself deserving of it. "I do not ask what is becoming for you to receive," replied Alexander, "but what is becoming for me to give."

The displays of noble expenditure (on the part of movie stars and prime-time athletes as well as George Soros and the Koch brothers) derive from the far larger stores of private wealth created over the past forty years as a consequence of the systematic rigging of the nation's economic outcomes to favor the rich at the expense of the poor. The familiar story (democracy smothered by oligarchy) has often been told—long ago by Aristotle, more recently in our American context by the Nobel Prize–winning economist Joseph Stiglitz—but it is nowhere better illustrated than by the reversal over the past half century of the meaning within the words "public" and "private." In the 1950s the word "public" connoted an inherent good (public health, public school, public service, public spirit); "private" was a synonym for selfishness and greed (plutocrats in top hats, pigs at troughs). The connotations traded places in the 1980s. "Private" now implies all things bright and beautiful (private trainer, private school, private plane), "public" becomes a synonym for all things ugly and dangerous (public housing, public welfare, public toilet).

The repositioning of the words underwrites the gospel according to the Bill and Melinda Gates Foundation, which, among the current generation of big-time philanthropies, is the fairest of them all. It commands an endowment of $43.5 billion (roughly a third of that sum added to its pot by Warren Buffett), and because of its size and market share it points the direction for much of the nation's foundation giving. No week goes by without the announcement of another Gates Foundation grant meant to allay disease in Africa or to improve test scores in American public schools.

A self-made Promethean figure in the image of Carnegie, Gates also looks to avoid the disgrace of dying rich. To the small company of his fellow billionaires he wrote an email in 2010 suggesting they give, "during your lifetime or through your will," the majority of their wealth to charity. To help "improve the overall quality" of their giving he offers the superior wisdom of a man who knows that private profit and public good are mutual friends, that doing well is doing good. The thought is as tried and true as the metaphor that Cotton Mather, the seventeenth-century Puritan divine, bestowed upon the Boston faithful in 1701: "A Christian, at his two callings, is a man in a boat, rowing for heaven" with two oars, one of them glorifying God "by doing good for others," the other by "getting of good for himself."

Gates repackaged the good news as a speech delivered to the World Economic Forum at Davos, Switzerland, in 2008: "I like to call this idea creative capitalism ... Such a system would have a twin mission: making profits and also improving lives of those who don't fully benefit from today's market forces ... a market-based reward for good behavior."

The gospel was well received in the temples of the god who also is Mammon; the foundation clergy have learned to come and go speaking of metrics, time frames, benchmarks, grantmaking made "cost effective," "impact oriented," "data based." The language is designed for ceremony, "magical and incantatory" assigning virtue to having and holding wealth, not to letting it wander away, unescorted, into the sorrow and heat of the desert. *Philanthrocapitalism* opening the golden door to the best of all possible futures that money can buy, nourishing the belief (very à la mode in the media shiny sheets) that it is the big-ticket, glamorous rich who will rescue the country from ruin.

The hope springs from the publicity from whence the money cometh, not in the accounting for whither it goest. The National Committee for Responsive Philanthropy estimates that only 8 percent of foundations in the United States bestow as much as 25 percent of their largesse on "social justice purposes." In 2011 the wealthiest Americans, those with earnings in the top 20 percent, contributed an average of 1.3 percent of their income to charity. Americans in the bottom 20 percent, and therefore unable to itemize a tax deduction, donated 3.2 percent.

Dowie suggests the stores of private wealth likely to be accumulated over the next two generations could increase the total assets of organized philanthropy to $4 trillion. It's an impressive number, but small in comparison with the money likely to be furnished by individual contributions that now add hundreds of billions of dollars to most of the country's charitable enterprises set up as credit unions and health clinics, food and wind-power cooperatives, crowdfunding platforms.

The opulent foundations tend to believe that money is good for rich people, bad for poor people, best given to private institutions or public acronyms; they seek the honor of being praised, as did the wealthy suppliers of the glory that was Greece and the grandeur that was Rome, "for doing good without self-interest, just like God himself." Their philanthropy, like that of Carnegie and Gates, is the giving of direction to dayflies. The philanthropy inherent in democracy as conceived by Paine, attested by Tocqueville, practiced by Whitman, is the care of other human beings, virtue "considered useful," almost never gloriously promoted. A democratic society places a premium on equality; a capitalist economy does not. The separation of powers is the difference between the worth of a thing and the price of a thing, between the motions of the heart and the movement of a market. Plato in the Republic puts the proposition as simply as it can be put: "As wealth and the wealthy are valued more in a city, so goodness and the good are valued less ... what is valued at any particular time becomes the common practice, what is not valued is neglected."

Governments reflect the quality of the men charged with their conduct and deportment. Relief from "the ostensible greed and heartlessness of our times" (Whitman's phrase in 1864 as telling now as then) doesn't fall in a shower of gold from the heaven that is a $95 million apartment on the ninety-fifth floor of a Manhattan co-op. It collects in pennies on the ground, from people who don't confuse themselves with God, who know, as did Walt Whitman, that love, not money, is "sovereign still."

35. Open to Inspection

Even if the spy, Allen Dulles, should arrive in heaven through some-body's absentmindedness, he would begin to blow up the clouds, mine the stars, and slaughter the angels.

—Ilya Ehrenburg

I cannot think that espionage can be recommended as a technique for building an impressive civilization. It's a lout's game.

—Rebecca West

By now it goes without saying or objection in most quarters of a once freedom-loving and democratic society that our lives, liberties, and pursuits of happiness are closely monitored by a paranoid surveillance apparatus possessed of the fond hopes and great expectations embedded in the fifteenth-century Spanish Inquisition. Our local fire departments don't grant permits for burnings at the stake, but our federal intelligence agencies (seventeen at last count, staffed by more than 100,000 inquisitors petty and grand) make no secret of their missionary zeal.

Four months after the fall of the World Trade Center in 2001 and President George W. Bush's preaching of holy crusade against all the world's evil, the Pentagon established an Information Awareness Office (IAO), adopting as an emblem for its letterhead and baseball cap the all-seeing eye of God. Under orders to secure the American future against the blasphemy of terrorist attack, the IAO's director, Rear Admiral John Poindexter, presented plans for programming its hydra-headed computer screens and databanks to spot incoming slings and arrows of outrageous fortune well in advance of their ETA overhead the Washington Monument or Plymouth Rock—to conduct "truth maintenance" and deploy "market-based techniques for avoiding surprises"; to defeat and classify every once and future hound from hell on a near or far horizon; no envelope or email left unopened, no phone untapped, no suspicious beard or suitcase descending unnoticed from cruise ship or Toyota.

Thirteen years further along the roads to perdition, the dream of a risk-free future under the digital umbrellas of protective fantasy is the stuff of which our wars and movies now are made, the thousand natural shocks to which the flesh is heir, projected day and night on the hundred million screens that text and shred our collective consciousness, herd our public and private lives—the latter no longer distinguishable from the former—into the shelters of heavy law enforcement and harmless speech.

When and why did the lout's game of espionage become the saving grace that makes cowards of us all? I'm familiar with at least some of the story because I'm old enough to remember the provincial and easygoing American republic of the 1940s— wisecracking, open-hearted, not so scared of the undiscovered country from whose bourn no traveler returns. I also can remember the days when people weren't afraid of cigarette smoke and saturated fats, when it was possible to apply for a job without submitting a blood or urine test, when civil liberty was a constitutional right and not a political favor, the White House unprotected by concrete revetments, and it was possible to walk the streets of New York without making a series of cameo appearances on surveillance camera.

Espionage in the ancient world was for the most part reconnaissance of a declared or foreign enemy in the field. The ancient Chinese military sage Sun Tzu recommends the use of spies in the fifth century B.C. to "ascertain the enemy's situation and condition" because they know things beforehand that "cannot be obtained from ghosts or spirits." He doesn't regard spies as "masters of victory," but if deployed in all five of their applications ("local, inside, double, dead, and live"), they construct "a divine net" that is the "ruler's treasure."

So they served the Greeks in their wars against the Trojans and the Persians. The rulers of ancient India employed spies to watch not only thieves and desperadoes on the roads outside the city but also, inside the city, strangers "who spend lavishly ... in drinking houses without having a known source of income." The instruction is specific in the Arthashastra, a teaching on governance circa 150 B.C. that suggests the disguising of clandestine agents as blind lunatics and deaf idiots as well as minstrels, jugglers, and fortune-tellers.

The searching out of metaphysical threats to the safety of the soul is the work of the papal Inquisition established by the medieval Catholic Church "to root up from the midst of Christian people the weed of heretical wickedness." *Ad extirpanda*, the mission statement released by Pope Innocent IV in 1252, consecrates torture as an effective gardening tool, affixes the Vatican's seal of approval to the techniques recently in use by the U.S. military rooting up the weed of Islamic terrorism.

Spycraft becomes statecraft during the religious wars that afflicted Europe in the sixteenth and seventeenth centuries, the lines of physical and metaphysical investigation strenuously intertwined by Sir Francis Walsingham, the Elizabethan progenitor of England's Secret Intelligence Service, tasked with objectives both spiritual and temporal: defense of the Protestant Reformation against the Catholic Counter-Reformation, holding of the body of Queen Elizabeth harmless against assassination by papist agents. A devout Puritan and shrewd diplomat, Walsingham ensnared Mary, Queen of Scots, in a treasonous plot that warranted her beheading, subjected prisoners to renditions on the rack and interrogations that stretched their awareness of God along lines drawn and quartered by Martin Luther and John Calvin. He purportedly numbered among his agents the playwright Christopher Marlowe, possibly also his son-in-law, the poet Sir Philip Sidney. Within the networks of his informants it was said that "he waited upon men's souls with his eye, discerning their secret hearts through their transparent faces."

So did Shakespeare, who was Walsingham's contemporary. The plays wait upon the assumed and masked identities behind which move the palace intrigue that was the pith and moment of Elizabethan politics, the world known to Walsingham at the court of the virgin queen doubling for the one in which Iago plays his game against Othello and Desdemona, and who therefore cannot wear his heart upon his sleeve because "I am not what I am."

America's variant of a police state emerges from the Espionage Act of 1917, carried into law to accommodate President Woodrow Wilson's wish to cleanse the world of its impurities. The self-glorifying son of a Presbyterian minister captivated at an early age by delusions of spiritual grandeur, Wilson engineered America's late entry into World War I in order that he might play the part of savior statesman.

Wilson never doubted it was America's duty to save the world, and during his eight years as instrument of divine will in office as president of the United States, he sent American troops to Cuba, Haiti, Nicaragua, the Dominican Republic, and Mexico "to teach the South American republics to elect good men." In the immediate aftermath of the Bolshevik Revolution, Wilson dispatched troops briefly to Russia to defend its people against the communism proscribed by Robert Lansing, Wilson's secretary of state, as "the most hideous and monstrous thing that the human mind has ever conceived," refuge of "the criminal, the depraved, and the mentally unfit."

The Fourteen Points of good behavior that Wilson brought to the Paris Peace Conference pledged America to consequences foreseen by John Quincy Adams, who spoke as secretary of state in 1821 against sending the U.S. Navy to dismantle Spain's colonial empire in Colombia and Venezuela. America, he said, "goes not abroad in search of monsters to destroy." Were the country to embark on such a foolish adventure,

> she would involve herself, beyond the power of extrication, in all the wars of interest and intrigue, of individual avarice, envy, and ambition, which assume the colors and usurp the standard of freedom. The fundamental maxims of her policy would insensibly change from liberty to force. She might become the dictatress of the world; she would no longer be the ruler of her own spirit.

So it has come to pass: America, the dictatress of the world, is no longer the ruler of her own spirit, which passes out of the hands of its people and society into the safekeeping of the state. The transfer of power was set in zealously administrative motion by J. Edgar Hoover, a young Justice Department operative eager to destroy monsters wherever found—in body and mind, on land, at sea, in or on the air. Wilson in his war message to Congress in 1917 said there were "millions of men and women of German birth and native sympathy who live among us," and "if there should be disloyalty, it will be dealt with a firm hand of stern repression." Wilson's admonition was Hoover's command. On January 2, 1920, as deputy to Attorney General A. Mitchell Palmer, Hoover organized the largest mass arrest in American history, rounding up an estimated 10,000 disloyalists—immigrants of all nations, citizens of German descent, subversive liberals, and suspected anarchists as well as Communists. The Red replaced the Hun as the barbarian at the gate and in the closets, and by that same year Hoover had dossiers on 60,000 people suspected of illicit dealings with Karl Marx.

During his long and relentless term as director of the FBI (from 1924 until his death in 1972) Hoover remained convinced that communism was not a political idea but a malignant and evil way of life, akin to a disease. Often and easily enraged, fanatical in his paranoid imaginings, Hoover for fifty years harried the always larger legions of his fear and prejudice (liberals, Negroes, homosexuals, Jews, hippies) with illegal arrests and detentions, break-ins, burglaries, beatings, murders, wiretaps, blackmail, suborned evidence and testimony, coerced confessions. The bureau in the 1960s opened operations against the civil rights and antiwar movements and assembled a list of more than 26,000 individuals to be summarily detained in the event of a "national emergency." By his admirers Hoover was seen as a visionary genius, by his detractors as a "goddamn sewer," by Supreme Court Justice Louis Brandeis as an armed and dangerous enemy of the American people and Constitution.

Justice Brandeis could have as easily brought the same charges against the eminent American statesman who organized the Central Intelligence Agency to fight the Cold War with the Russians. President Harry Truman established the agency under the National Security Act of 1947, and for the next six years the government spent a great deal of money on bureaucratic organization and reorganization of the agency, separating its covert military operations from its clerical intelligence gathering, acquiring thousands of volunteers in all of the applications named by Sun Tzu—uniformed military officers, artists and poets, Ivy League academics and Wall Street stockbrokers, State Department diplomats, German agents released on waivers by the Gestapo. President Dwight D. Eisenhower, in his first inaugural address in January 1953, vouched for troop movements in the vicinity of Armageddon—"forces of good and evil are massed and armed, and opposed as rarely before in history. Freedom is pitted against slavery, lightness against the dark"—but he was concerned about the readiness of the CIA to combat the forces of darkness.

For clear definition of the agency's mission, President Eisenhower turned to Air Force General Jimmy Doolittle, friend and companion-in-arms, who had flown the heroic mission over Tokyo in 1942. Doolittle in 1954 provided Ike with his top-secret report:

It is now clear that we are facing an implacable enemy whose avowed objective is world domination by whatever means and at whatever costs. There are no rules in such a game. Hitherto acceptable norms of human conduct do not apply. If the United States is to survive, longstanding American concepts of "fair play" must be reconsidered. We must develop effective espionage and counter-espionage services and must learn to subvert, sabotage, and destroy our enemies by more clever, more sophisticated means than those used against us. It may become necessary that the American people be made acquainted with, understand, and support this fundamentally repugnant philosophy.

Doolittle didn't think the agency up to the task at hand because it had "ballooned out into a vast and sprawling organization" housing unskilled, undisciplined, and incompetent "dead wood ... at virtually all levels," overly fond of covert operations "beyond its capacity to perform." The sorry state of affairs showcased the temperament of Allen Dulles, appointed director of the CIA by Eisenhower early in 1953. Dulles was the man from whom it can be fairly said the agency acquired the character of the lawless, incompetent, and deluded enterprise that is with us still, as lost in its cloud of unknowing overhead the Syrian desert in 2015 as it was asleep under the tents of its weatherproof fantasy in the rain-forests in South Vietnam in 1968.

At the age of sixty in 1953 Allen Dulles (State Department intelligence officer in World War I, active in the Office of Strategic Services [OSS] in World War II) was five years younger than his brother, John Foster, whom Eisenhower that same year appointed secretary of state. Both brothers regarded force, not liberty, as the fundamental maxim of American policy. They had been taught by the severe Presbyterian minister who was their father that Christians are weapons in the hands of God, executors of his providential will; they saw the word made flesh in the person of Woodrow Wilson, whom they accompanied to the Paris Peace Conference in 1919 as bright young Princeton graduates helping out with the platitudes and the maps.

John Foster was puritanical and direct; Allen, like Iago, was not who he pretended to be. In his own mind a hero modeled on his reading of Ian Fleming novels, he cultivated a surface of sophis-ticated charm, affable and gregarious, good with the ladies and small sailboats on Long Island Sound. He smoked a pipe, dressed in tweed, told witty stories about his days in the OSS subverting the Nazi occupation of Europe.

Behind the mask of easy upper-class insouciance, Allen was a devout proponent of the fundamentally repugnant philosophy noted by Doolittle. Often moved to predatory fury well beyond "hitherto acceptable norms of human conduct," Allen during his eight years in charge of the CIA directed the elimination of regimes he identified as Communist in Iran, Guatemala, and the Congo. The identifications were forgeries in visibly paranoid ink. Leaders of the regimes in question were socialist and nationalist, their objective to escape the bonds of European colonial empire. But Dulles didn't let facts get in the way of his hatreds. On the strength of his lying risk assessments Eisenhower authorized the CIA to assassinate Patrice Lumumba in the Congo and Fidel Castro in Cuba, to begin covert military operations in South Vietnam.

Dulles's enthusiasm for subversion, sabotage, and destruction was boundless. So was the unskilled, undisciplined incompetence of an agency that sixty years later still hasn't discovered that the Statue of Liberty cannot be made to stand on the pedestals of criminal violence. The record is in equal parts short-term comic farce and long-form geopolitical tragedy.

The game at the beginning looked to be easy and fun. The agency played with sending an émigré army to capture the lost kingdom of Albania, but once parachuted into the Balkan darkness the advance scouts were never seen or heard from again because the CIA's head of secret ops was unwittingly coordinating the event with a Soviet double agent providing the KGB with the map coordinates of the intended drop zones. To discredit Sukarno as president of Indonesia in the mid-1950s, the CIA planned to incite popular envy and resentment of his sexual prowess, shooting a propaganda film entitled *Happy Days* showing Sukarno (played by a Mexican actor wearing a mask) in bed with a Soviet agent (played by a California actress wearing a wig). To assassinate Fidel Castro the agency drew up plans to present him with an exploding cigar and poisoned scuba gear. The bungled invasion of the Bay of Pigs in 1961 assumed a crowd of joyful Cuban peasants rising from the sugar cane and marching gloriously to Havana.

The cadre of Cuban exiles was landed on the wrong tide on the wrong boats, soon confronted by Castro at the head of a column of tanks. In what came to be known as the Iran–Contra affair (running guns to the mullahs in Iran in return for money to fund a thuggish junta in Nicaragua), the "enterprise" deposited $10 million in the wrong Swiss bank account, hired drunken aircraft mechanics in El Salvador, and dropped munitions into the wrong jungles in Nicaragua.

The geopolitical consequences of the CIA's covert derring-do have for the most part proved to be both dismal and unexpected. The overthrow of Mohammad Mosaddegh's elected government in Iran in 1953 installed the vicious and corrupt tyranny of the Shah of Shahs, which in 1979 led to an Islamist revolution and the regime that now stands as America's most formidable enemy in the Middle East. By encouraging the assassination of Ngo Dinh Diem in Saigon in 1963, the United States allied itself with a policy of realpolitik no less cynical than the one it was seeking to correct. Accepting the CIA's analysis and methodology, four American presidents defined the expedition to Southeast Asia as a prolonged covert action and systematically lied to the American people about the reason for our presence in a country with which we never declared ourselves at war. As a result our effort to rid Indochina of communism, Vietnam became a unified Communist state. As a result of our effort to teach the world the lessons of democracy, we sent 58,000 American soldiers to death under a false flag and taught a generation of American citizens to think of their own government as an oriental despotism.

The CIA's failures as an intelligence-gathering operation during the second half of the century billed as America's own have borne out Doolittle's early warning of "dead wood at virtually all levels." The agency evidently didn't foresee the Soviet explosion of an atomic bomb in 1949, the invasion of South Korea in 1950, the popular uprisings in Eastern Europe in the 1950s, the installation of Soviet missiles in Cuba in 1962, the Vietcong Tet Offensive in 1968, the Arab–Israeli war in 1973, the Soviet invasion of Afghanistan in 1979, the fall of the Berlin Wall in 1989, the collapse of the Soviet Union in 1991, Iraq's invasion of Kuwait in 1990, the explosion of an atomic bomb by India in 1998, the attacks on New York and Washington in 2001, or the absence of weapons of mass destruction in Iraq in 2003.

Reports of the CIA's blunders tend to show up on the record well after the fact. I've been reading them with interest over the past fifty years, but they don't come as a surprise. Long ago and in another country, America in 1957, I sought enlistment in the CIA and sat for an interview with a credentials committee ordained by God and country and Allen Dulles. From that day forward I've never doubted the agency's talent for making a mess of almost any operation, overt or covert, beyond its capacity to perform.

In 1957 I was recently returned from a year at Cambridge University in England, where I had come to know several students who in October 1956 went to Budapest to join the uprising against the regime holding Hungary hostage to Communist domination. Two of the young men died in the street fighting, and I didn't need to be told by General Eisenhower that the Communist hordes were at the gate of Western civilization. In my last year at Yale I had been tipped to the agency by an English professor (Shakespeare scholar, Tyrolean hat, former OSS), who passed on a phone number to call if I was prepared to take a shot in the dark. At the age of twenty-two I was willing to leave at once, preferably at night, with trench coat and code name, on the next train to Berlin.

In Washington the written, physical, and psychological examinations occupied the better part of a week before I was summoned to an interview with three operatives in their late twenties, all of them graduates of Yale and not unlike President George W. Bush in appearance and manner. The interview took place in a Quonset hut near the Lincoln Memorial. The design of the building imparted an air of urgent military purpose, as did the muted, offhand bravado of the young men asking the questions. Very pleased with themselves, they exchanged knowing nods to "that damned thing in Laos," allowed me to understand that we were talking life and death, whether I had the right stuff to play for the varsity team in the big game against the Russians.

Prepared for nothing less, I had spent the days prior to the interview reading about Lenin's train and Stalin's prisons, the width of the Fulda Gap, the depth of the Black Sea. None of the study was called for. Instead of being asked about the treaties of Brest-Litovsk or the October Revolution, I was asked three questions bearing on my social qualifications for admission into what the young men at the far end of the table clearly regarded as the best fraternity on the campus of the free world:

1. When standing on the thirteenth tee at the National Golf Links in Southampton, which club does one take from the bag?
2. On final approach under sail into Hay Harbor on Fishers Island, what is the direction (at dusk in late August) of the prevailing wind?
3. Does Muffy Hamilton wear a slip?

The first and second questions I answered correctly, but Muffy Hamilton I knew only at a distance. In the middle 1950s she was a glamorous figure on the Ivy League weekend circuit, very beautiful and very rich, much admired for the indiscriminate fervor of her sexual enthusiasms. At the Fence Club in New Haven I had handed her a glass of brandy and milk (known to be her preferred drink by college football captains in five states), but about the mysteries of her underwear my sources were unreliable, my information limited to rumors of Belgian lace.

The three questions, however, put an end to my interest in the CIA. The smug complacence of my examiners was as smooth as their matching silk handkerchiefs and ties. When I excused myself from the interview (apologizing for having misread the job description and wasted everybody's quality time), I remember being frightened by the presence of so much self-glorifying certainty and primogeniture crowded into so small a room. Here were people like Woodrow Wilson before them, after them Vice President Dick Cheney and Defense Secretary Donald Rumsfeld, who knew more about what was good for the world than the world—poor, lost, unhappy, un-American world—had managed to learn on its own. Even at the age of twenty-two I was old enough to recognize the attitude as not well positioned for intelligence gathering. It was better suited to the projection of monsters on the screens of deluded fantasy than to their destruction in a forest or a swamp.

People accustomed to knowing they know everything worth knowing resent having to turn away from the mirror. The resentment framed the Bush Administration's response to the 2001 attacks on the World Trade Center and the Pentagon. Although there had been many warnings of terrorist attacks somewhere on the horizon, the signals had been lost in the maze of a national security apparatus "ballooned out into a vast and sprawling" clutter of undisciplined incompetence many orders of magnitude beyond the one reconnoitered by General Doolittle in 1954. Not knowing who, why, or wherefrom the airplanes overhead the Hudson and Potomac rivers, the Bush Administration declared war on an unknown enemy and an abstract noun, set to work forging the shields of invincible paranoia, bringing up to combat strength the levels of fear and trembling within the American body politic. In time for Halloween, Congress passed the PATRIOT ACT, claiming the government's right to arrest without charge American citizens marked as enemy combatants; the Department of Homeland Security produced its color-coded alerts, hands in the air, off with shoes and belts when passing go at the airport. The Justice Department in May 2002 named as its "first and overriding priority" the defense of the American people against terrorist intrusion and distributed a fact sheet shifting the FBI's mission from "prosecution to prevention." The supplementary PowerPoints testified to brave, bold, and expensive shuffling of bureaucratic paper (refocusing task forces, expanding alert systems, recruiting professional criminals as informants). The bureau's director, Robert Mueller III, was careful to establish plausible deniability. As compensation for its past and future failures the bureau asked to be rewarded with more money, more police power, more flow charts—not to annihilate the threat of incoming grief but to strengthen the fear of looming apocalypse. Mueller gave a speech the week before the fact sheet was released to say "there will be another terrorist attack. We will not be able to stop it."

Several weeks later at a meeting of the NATO allies in Brussels, Defense Secretary Rumsfeld observed that one never knows who the terrorist attackers are or where they might be coming from: "The message is that there are no 'knowns.' There are things that we now know we don't know. But there are also unknown unknowns ... and each year, we discover a few more of those unknown unknowns ... There's another way to phrase that, and that is that the absence of evidence is not evidence of absence."

Which was the line of thinking and investigation—paranoid, delusional, clouded in Adams's "individual avarice, envy, and ambition"—on which the Bush administration in March 2003 mounted its chase of the monster to destroy in Iraq. No evidence of Saddam Hussein's weapons of mass destruction in Babylon (land steeped in Old Testament sin), but then again no reason to doubt their existence in the eye of God or Rear Admiral Poindexter's IAO. The admiral in the summer of 2002 was busy programming a magic mirror in which to see not only the unknown future but also to step up the scrutiny of an American citizenry classified as a prospective enemy, known unknowns maybe harboring evil intentions and therefore targeted by the admiral's wizard databanks and computer screens, cross-examining medical and bank records, website visits, and credit card transactions. The all-seeing eye of God emblazoned on the IAO's letterhead and baseball cap was perched atop an Egyptian pyramid and buttressed by the rendition in Latin of the phrase, "Knowledge is power." The phrase is open to questioning: What sort of power? Power over whom? To do what?

Knowledge positioned as espionage is not only a lout's game; it is also a sucker's game in which all present at the peepholes—spy and spied upon, informant and counterinformant, whistleblower, courier, cutout, mole—draw a losing card.

Over the past decade, the federal government has devoted $533 billion to the acquisition of what former vice president Al Gore in 2013 described as "the essential apparatus of a police state"—a police state unable to protect the American homeland, people, or idea but striving, criminally and mightily, to preserve and glorify itself. The IAO's fond hopes and great expectations have been incorporated into the vast complex of federal intelligence missions. More than 3,000 government and private organizations

are involved in intelligence activities at 17,000 locations across
the United States, and the CIA's operations have been folded
into those of the Office of the Director of National Intelligence.
The megalith at Bluffdale, Utah, houses the U.S. government's
global-information grid, but a report filed by Dana Priest, an
investigative journalist granted access to one of the Pentagon's
classified workstations, suggests that the divine net of conspiracy-
minded computers (annually spilling forth 50,000 separate seri-
alized intelligence reports under 1,500 headings) doesn't know
how to connect the dots, cannot make meaning or sense out of
a vast, sprawling sound and fury signifying who knows what.
The systems are too big to do anything else but fail. The National
Security Agency loses its files to Edward Snowden; the Office of
Personnel Management gives up to Chinese hackers the records
of 22 million Americans; a teenager claims to have invaded CIA
Director John Brennan's email account. At the higher echelons of
unquotable authority in Washington it is said that America has no
defense against the cyberwarfare destined to wreak havoc on the
country's energy and communication grids.

Ask why so poor a return on so rich an investment, and the
answer shows up in John le Carré's novel *Tinker, Tailor, Soldier,
Spy*. An old connoisseur of the world's secrets tells a fellow agent
that their best information—acquired at large expense and with
heavy loss of life—is probably false. The ancient spy poses his
judgment as a question: "Ever bought a fake picture? … The more
you pay for it, the less inclined you are to doubt it." Le Carré
understands that covert actions usually take place at the not very
important margins of not very important events, and that when
extended over a period of more than four days they hide nothing
from anybody except the people paying the bills. He elsewhere
understands that the "magic formulas and hocus-pocus of the spy
world" recommend themselves to "declining powers," to men and
institutions losing their strength and becoming fearful of shadows.
"When the king is dying, the charlatans rush in."

Knowledge as magic formulas and hocus-pocus is a power of
not much use against monsters in a foreign field, but as power
for distribution to the folks at home it is the propaganda that

makes cowards of us all, classifies democracy as behavior uncivil and unsafe, and changes—not insensibly but deliberately—the fundamental maxims of American policy from liberty to force. A cowed citizenry is the cornerstone of a police state (even an incompetent police state) and the going abroad for monsters to destroy is the making at home of a monstrous sorcerer's apprentice—rocked in the cradle of the 1917 Espionage Act, swaddled in what the American historian Richard Hofstadter defined as the paranoid style of American politics, nurtured in adolescence by J. Edgar Hoover's FBI, ripened in the repugnant psychopathology of the Cold War, developed by the war on terror into a fully adult hysteria.

John Quincy Adams, like Francis Walsingham and William Shakespeare, read the future by discerning men's "secret hearts through their transparent faces." So did Reinhold Niebuhr, the great Protestant theologian serving with John Foster Dulles at the end of World War II on the Commission on a Just and Durable Peace. Dulles held to a view of a world divided between forces of good and evil, the threat to America headquartered in Moscow's onion-domed towers of hideous strength.

Niebuhr was more clear-sighted and better informed. "If we should perish," he wrote in 1952, "the ruthlessness of the foe would be only the secondary cause of the disaster. The primary cause would be that the strength of a giant nation was directed by eyes too blind to see all the hazards of the struggle; and the blindness would be induced not by some accident of nature or history but by hatred and vainglory."

36. The World in Time

Not to know what happened before one was born is always to be a child.
—Cicero

Two months before he died, in the winter of 2007 at the age of eighty-nine, Arthur M. Schlesinger Jr. published what proved to be his last word on the reading and writing of history. The essay appeared in the *New York Times* under the heading "Folly's Antidote," and as was his custom, the author began with the bringing of the past to bear on the present:

> Many signs point to a growing historical consciousness among the American people. I trust that this is so. It is useful to remember that history is to the nation as memory is to the individual. As persons deprived of memory become disoriented and lost, not knowing where they have been and where they are going, so a nation denied a conception of the past will be disabled in dealing with its present and its future.

For proofs of his hypothesis in the winter of 2007, Schlesinger needn't have looked any further than the front pages of the morning papers. America's splendid little war in Iraq was recapitulating, forty years later, the foolishness of its war in Vietnam. The country's financial and real estate markets were bubbling steadily upward in a speculative frenzy reviving the folly of 1929. The failure to connect the then with the now Arthur attributed to "delusions of omnipotence and omniscience," an illness he thought likely to lead to the death of the American enterprise unless treated with the antidote of history.

Arthur consulted libraries in the way that sailors consult a compass or a chart, and to read his books was not only to be astonished by what had sunk below the horizon three or three hundred years ago but to become aware of what was likely to show up with the lifting of tomorrow morning's fog. He was among the most distinguished of America's twentieth-century historians because he knew, as did the financier, Sir John Templeton, that the four most expensive words in the English language are "This time it's different," and together with the novelist William Faulkner, he understood that "the past is never dead. It's not even past." For Arthur the study of history was akin to playing with a kaleidoscope, a perpetual work in progress destined never to reach a final verdict or discover the lost gold mines of imperishable truth. "Problems," he once said, "will always torment us, because all important problems are insoluble: that is why they are important. The good comes from the continuing struggle to try and solve them, not from the vain hope of their solution."

History is a constant writing and rewriting as opposed to a museum-quality sculpture in milk-white marble. To read three histories of the British Empire—one of them published in 1850, the others in 1900 and 1950—is to discover three different British Empires on which the sun eventually sets. The must-see tourist attractions remain intact—Napoleon still there on his horse at Waterloo, Queen Victoria enthroned in Buckingham Palace, the subcontinent firmly fixed to its moorings in the Indian Ocean— but as to the light in which Napoleon, the Queen, or India are to be seen, accounts differ.

Each age revises its conception of the past to fit the context of its present, and the historian will find the facts that prove the truth of an interpretation. History is not what happened two hundred or two thousand years ago; it is a story about what happened two hundred or two thousand years ago. The stories change, as do the sight lines available to the tellers of the tales. Montaigne, in one of his essays, provides, as is his custom, an apt quotation:

> See how Plato is moved and tossed about. Every man, glorying in applying him to himself, sets him on the side he wants. They trot him out and insert him into all the new opinions that the world accepts.

The observation is in line with George Orwell's dictum, "Who controls the past controls the future: who controls the present controls the past." Orwell was talking about the uses of history as propaganda bent to the service of the state. Refer the dictum to the purposes of the individual, and who is the "who" controlling the past if not one's self? Where else does one live if not in a house of straw made from the reshaping of a once-upon-a-time?[1]

It's been said that over the span of nine months in the womb, a human embryo ascends through a sequence congruent with 3 billion years of evolution, that within the first six years of life,

---

[1] When I was in college in the 1950s the teaching of America's late eighteenth-century history was reflected in the mirror of what was then the present. The wisdom in office in the 1950s and 1960s—in Congress as in the news media and the universities—was predominantly liberal, in accord with the ideals and objectives of Franklin D. Roosevelt's New Deal. The classroom discussion at Yale promoted the democratic republicanism of Thomas Paine and Thomas Jefferson and decried the federalist policies of Alexander Hamilton and John Adams, which were seen to be royalist in sentiment and reactionary in character. Times changed in the 1980s. Billed under various labels of right-wing opinion (Reaganism, Republican reawakening, neoconservatism), the old Federalist lines of argument came back into fashion. The history books topping the bestseller lists for the last thirty years stress the pragmatism of Hamilton and Adams and view with suspicion the romantic idealism of Jefferson and Paine.

a human mind recapitulates the dream of its 200,000-year existence. The figures in the dream have left the signs of their passing in what we know as the historical record, navigational lights flashing across the gulf of time on scraps of papyrus and scratchings in stone, on ships' logs and bronze coins, in confessions voluntary and coerced, in five-act plays and three-part songs.

The record is mankind's common and most precious inheritance, its value in line with the remark attributed to the German poet Johann Wolfgang von Goethe, "he who cannot draw on three thousand years is living hand to mouth." It isn't with religion that men guarantee their immortality. They do so with what they've learned on their travels across the frontiers of the millennia, salvaging from the sack of cities and the wreck of empires what they have found to be useful or beautiful or true. Exploited both as natural resource and applied technology, an acquaintance with history tells us that the story painted on the old walls and printed in the old books is also our own. Construed as a means instead of an end, the world in time is as rich in possibility as were the American forests before the arrival of Sir Walter Raleigh.

Although Arthur Schlesinger was careful to point to "a growing historical consciousness among the American people," I'm not so sure that those signs are as hopeful as he might have wished. Over the last thirty-odd years at all levels of American education (private as well as public; primary, secondary, and college), the teaching of history and the humanities has been cut back to accommodate the epistemologies of mathematics and economics. The emphasis follows from what has become, over those same thirty-odd years, a constant state of alarm about American students dropping behind their counterparts in Europe and Asia. The managers of America's money and government worry about foreign competition in the global marketplace, say that unless the local kids settle down to their lessons, America could lose it all— the ball game and the farm, the Nobel Prizes as well as the aircraft carriers, the hedge funds, the Pizza Huts, and the roof-garden real estate in Palm and Pebble Beach.

The desperate run on data banks big and small tends to trample out the vintage of historical consciousness. The surfeit of new and newer news, "prioritized" and "context-sensitive," comes so quickly to hand that we are smothered in the feathers of the stuff—on air, in print, online, in Facebook; as broadcast, podcast, Tweet, and blog. Within the wind tunnels of the hyperlinked electronic media, the time is always now; the data blow away and shred, and what gets lost is all thought of what happened yesterday, last week, three months or three years ago. Not only do we lose track of our own stories (who we are, where we've been, where we might be going), but our elected representatives forget why sovereign nations go to war, or how it comes to pass that money doesn't grow on trees. The blessed states of tabloid-induced amnesia cannot sustain either the hope of individual liberty or the practice of democratic self-government.

Children unfamiliar with the world in time make easy marks for the dealers in totalitarian politics, junk science, and quack religion. They learn by example as well as by precept, and they have only to surf the Internet or to consider the careers of Lady Gaga and President George W. Bush to know that the making of a success in this American life doesn't presuppose a prior acquaintance with Edward Gibbon's *Decline and Fall of the Roman Empire*. The society doesn't count on its statesmen or its movie stars to have read John Milton or George Eliot, and the corporations eager to hire Harvard graduates don't make distinctions between those acquainted with Shakespeare's plays and those who have mastered the complete works of Danielle Steel. If the kids know how to run the computers for Disney or Goldman Sachs, figure the exchange rates between the euro and the yen, what does it matter if they don't know who won either the Revolutionary or the Civil War? It's true that a very small percentage of high school students can point to Iraq on a map; it's also true that the State Department's ambassadors often don't speak the language of the country to which they buy passage with a political campaign contribution. If a great many college students can't write a decent paragraph, the same can be said of most members of Congress.

College degrees in history and the humanities don't open as many doors into the job market as do those acquired in the sciences, and at the frequent conferences bemoaning the failures of the nation's educational systems, it's customary to assign the difference in the cost–benefit ratios to the American character and temperament—impatient, go-ahead, fast-forwarding people content to let bygones be bygones, to view the past as a long dead letter. A crying shame, of course, but not one that can be helped as long as the football coach at Florida State receives an income equivalent to that of the university's entire Classics faculty.

I don't question the statistics, but I find them hard to square with the circumstantial evidence. The movie and television screens bloom with the projection of historical documentary and romance—the glory of the British Empire, the villainy of Nazi Germany, the decadence of ancient Rome—the bestseller lists abound with new biographies of George Washington, Abraham Lincoln, and Teddy Roosevelt. The Pennsylvania countryside blossoms every summer with the appearance of ten thousand volunteers dressed in Civil War uniform to revive the battle of Gettysburg. It isn't that Americans dismiss the past as irrelevant; it's that they regard it as straw spun into gold, camera-ready for the preferred and more profitable markets in prime-time myth.

So vivid in the popular imagination is the iconography of the American past that it's no surprise when in the course of review-ing the day's news somebody at the hotel bar or the kitchen table wonders what Cotton Mather would have thought about the por-nographic film industry, or how John Wayne might have handled the Mexicans crossing the Rio Grande. No political campaign passes in parade without one or more of the season's candidates offering to "take America back," but they don't allow time for follow-up questions. Back where, from whom, what means of conveyance? Aboard the *Mayflower*, or at the point of a gun? If back home on the range, do the deer and the antelope still play with the Teton Sioux? If from the grasp of venal politicians and vampire capitalists, does Ralph Waldo Emerson go to Washington and Commodore Vanderbilt to prison?

That soap opera dressed up in a Roman toga or Marie Antoinette's wig is still soap opera was a lesson impressed upon me during the course of my first tutorial at England's Cambridge

University in the autumn of 1956. I don't now remember the name of the tutor assigned by Magdalene College to conduct the welcoming interview, but I remember the setting—damp day, tea with crumpet, coal fire in an ancient grate, preliminary remarks in favor of Admiral Lord Nelson and Samuel Pepys.

At Yale College I'd been encouraged to attempt the career of a historian, flattered by my professors to think that I had a firm hold of what was then a trendsetting course of study admitted to the curriculum under the heading of intellectual history. Mention the name of a dead poet or an unhorsed king, and I could be counted upon to attach the wiring to the appropriate zeitgeist, connect the poet to a revolution, the king to a metaphor. My tutor was delighted to learn that wonders never ceased.

Yes, well, he said, great news, of course, but perhaps you could spare a few moments for the twelfth century? Over the distance of maybe ten minutes I managed to juggle the bookish equivalents of Indian clubs, drawing the parallel between the Ptolemaic universe and the arrangement of Amsterdam's canals, sending Eleanor of Aquitaine on the Second Crusade in company with a red cross knight and a manual of courtly love, finding in the murdered St. Thomas à Becket a sculptor's model for one of the gargoyles on the western facade of Chartres Cathedral.

When I'd run through my list of boldfaced significance, the tutor poured us both a second cup of tea, and for the next quarter of an hour, with an air of utmost courtesy, offering plum cake, or perhaps a glass of sherry, he asked questions about aspects of the twelfth century that possibly I had overlooked. The coins in circulation on the Upper and Lower Rhine? Durations of travel—by land from Paris to Milan, by sea from Marseilles to Dover? What was afoot with the heavenly host in Rome? As between the two cities of Cairo and Baghdad, which boasted the larger concentrations of wealth and religious superstition? In Byzantium, the prices bid and asked for Russian fur and Christian slaves?

My failure to hazard even so much as a Hail Mary guess moved the don to a murmur of mild regret, as if he'd been hoping to see at least one of the Indian clubs defy the law of gravity. Yes, well, he said, you Americans have this wonderful talent for simplification that hasn't been granted to your poor cousins here in England. Before reaching the noble paradigm and the grand abstraction, we like to have in hand a passing acquaintance with at least some of the facts. A tedious business, of course, and very slow, more like our game of cricket than your game of baseball.[2]

A year at Cambridge put an end to any thought of my becoming a professor of history—I was reluctant to learn medieval German, my parents reluctant to finance the time required to learn it—but it allowed me to appreciate the truth of Thomas Jefferson's observation that "a morsel of genuine history is a thing so rare as to be always valuable." Not being a scholar affiliated with a tenure track, I don't much care whether the mise en scène is Athens in the fourth century B.C., Paris in the 1740s, or Moscow in the winter of 1905. I look for an understanding of the human predicament, to discover or rediscover how it is with man, who he is and how it is between him and other men. To consult the historical record in books both ancient and modern is to come across every vice, virtue, motive, behavior, obsession, consequence, joy, and sorrow to be met with on the roads in time, to agree with the novelist Virginia Woolf that "any live mind today is of the very same stuff as Plato's & Euripides ... It is this common mind that binds the whole world together; & all the world is mind."

The news from Syria and the Persian Gulf in 2014 echoes T. E. Lawrence observing in 1922 that war among the desert Arabs is messy and slow, "like eating soup with a knife." On being told that the Pentagon is posting aircraft carriers on its maps of the South China Sea, I think of the last Ming emperor believing that he was the Son of Heaven, informed by his corps of eunuchs that he could

---

2   Many years later at the Council on Foreign Relations in New York, I saw Henry Kissinger reprise my Cambridge performance with a set of heavyweight catchphrases that his audience of corporate lawyers and contented bankers chose to regard as the wisdom of Prince Clemens von Metternich temporarily on loan from the Congress of Vienna. Kissinger was more adroit, but the technique was familiar, and so was the grotesque simplification—the nuclear option trumping the China card, lines in the Middle Eastern sand connecting the Temple of Solomon to the Pentagon, America under no circumstances to be caught holding Neville Chamberlain's umbrella.

command the oceans with a gentle scratching of his vermillion pencil or by subtle movements of his yellow parasol.

I read with a pen or pencil in hand, and in books that I've read more than once, I encounter marginalia many years out of date, most of them amended or revised to match a change in attitude or plan. In a worn copy of Ayn Rand's *The Fountainhead* in what I take to be my handwriting at age seventeen, I find a series of upbeat exclamation points subsequently crossed out and accompanied by the remark, in my handwriting circa age thirty, "Fascist fairy dust." In a biography of Aaron Burr I come across a note, "Too cynical," corrected at a later date with the further note, "Maybe not." When I complicate the proceedings with a superimposition of marginalia reaching across a distance of fifty years and written while traveling in cities as unlike one another as Chicago and Havana, I begin to guess at what the physicists regard as the continuum of space and time.

It is the ignorance of the past that invites the despairing of the present, which in turn leads to the marketing of dead-end politics with ad campaigns for a lost golden age. As often as not the nostalgic sales pitch is the contrivance of a reactionary status quo floating the speculation of a redeeming tomorrow with subprime borrowings from an imaginary yesterday. The campaign rhetoric plays to the popular suspicion that somehow something has gone inexplicably wrong with the American dream. The expressions of betrayal show up on both the disaffected right and the disillusioned left, all present taking note of America's wandering eastward out of Eden. The same disheartening message streams through the firmament of the blogosphere, the sentiment sustained by the public-opinion polls and by book publishers flooding the market with melancholy tracts likening the decline of the American republic to the fall of imperial Rome. *Foreign Affairs* in the winter of 2011 asked on its cover, *IS AMERICA OVER?* and followed up the question with an essay concluding that yes, Virginia, probably it is.[3]

---

3 The foretelling of the apocalypse never loses its appeal. The ministers preaching to the faithful in the seventeenth-century New England wilderness seldom failed to see a world in ruins, so terrible the

As with the snapshots sent home to Mom and Dad from a winter vacation in Hawaii, the postcards from an illusory American past don't mention any unpleasantness or inconvenience. The pioneers going west in the 1840s carried with them the promise of a land of milk and honey into what proved to be a desert; the two-thousand-mile length of the Oregon Trail was littered with abandoned wagons and newly furnished graves. The juvenile delinquents at play in the sandbox towns of Deadwood and Nacogdoches didn't challenge one another to heroic duels in the sun; best business practice was to shoot the scoundrel in the back, at long range with a rifle. Fortunes were to be found in three principal fields of endeavor (mining, timber, land), all of them heavily dependent—as was the building of the country's canals, railroads, telephone poles, and Internet—on government subsidy. The romance of the West so fondly embraced by President Ronald Reagan was the invention of the literary East, the early scripts drafted by nineteenth-century Ivy League swells, among them Owen Wister, Teddy Roosevelt, and Frederic Remington, the subsequent production values supplied by immigrant film merchants arriving in Hollywood in the 1910s from Warsaw and Minsk.

The political campaign postcards from somewhere over a lost horizon reproduce Norman Rockwell images of a classless society, and the candidates can be counted on to mourn the passing of America's egalitarian state of grace. They deliver the message to fundraising dinners that charge up to $40,000 for the poached salmon, but the only thing worth noting in the ballroom or the hospitality tent is the absence among the invited bank accounts (prospective donor, showcase celebrity, attending journalist) of

---

constant sight of Satan that they staged delivery of their sermons with the pretense of rubbing tears from their eyes. So also our own secular news media blowing the trumpets of doom. Ever since the crumbling of the Berlin Wall in 1989, no publishing season has been complete without at least one best-selling book announcing the end of history, the death of meaning, the end of science, the loss of nature. The woeful noise unto the Lord serves as a form of crowd control, bids up the market in surveillance cameras, restricts the freedom of thought as well as the freedoms of movement.

anybody intimately acquainted with—seriously angry about, other than rhetorically interested in—the fact of being poor. Were the A-list dignitaries to be somehow so informed, they also might be permitted to remember that America has been relying on the convenience of a class system since the good old days in Puritan Massachusetts. But even if they know of such a thing, maybe having heard tell of it in a novel by Edith Wharton or F. Scott Fitzgerald, one doesn't speak of it in polite company. The topic is in bad taste, politically incorrect.

Possibly because I was born into what in America fits the description of a privileged class, I'm hard put to pretend that it doesn't exist. So would have been the wealthy and well-educated gentlemen who gathered in Philadelphia in 1787 to frame the Constitution. From Aristotle the founding fathers borrowed the theorem that all proper government, no matter what its name or form, incorporates the means by which a favored few arrange the distribution of law and property for the less fortunate many. Recognizing in themselves the sort of people graced with the wisdom to discern, and the virtue to pursue "the common good of the society," they undertook to employ an aristocratic means to achieve a democratic end.

Unlike the Magna Carta, the Constitution doesn't contemplate the sharing of the commons inherent in a bountiful wilderness. Drafted by men of property setting up a government hospitable to the acquisition of more property, the Constitution provides the means of making manifest an unequal division of the spoils. Thomas Jefferson didn't confuse the theory ("All men are created equal") with the practice ("Money, and not morality, is the principle of commerce and commercial nations").

The news is maybe unwelcome, but it doesn't come as a surprise. Where in the record books does one look for a government of the poor, by the poor, and for the poor? How else does a society know or govern itself if not with guidelines shaped by some form of class distinction? In the United States the table of organization is for sale, made with money instead of by the grace of God or the kindness of a king. Students at Yale College in the eighteenth century were ranked in the order of their pecuniary decency; so was the protocol at the balls in colonial Philadelphia, the young ladies in the room swept up into the music in a sequence dictated by their net worth. Of the first ten presidents, eight were blessed with holdings (rents, capital, slaves) valued in today's currency at more than $1 billion. Add to their company the two Presidents Roosevelt, Herbert Hoover, John F. Kennedy, and Bush *père et fils*, and the White House during the better part of its term in office has served as a second home for money.

At no moment in its history has the country not been nailed to a cross of gold. Mark Hanna, the Ohio coal merchant managing William McKinley's presidential campaign against William Jennings Bryan in 1896, reduced the proposition to an axiom: "There are two things that are important in politics. The first is money, and I can't remember what the second one is." The Supreme Court in 2010 sustained the judgment with the *Citizens United* ruling that deregulated the market in political office and thus ratified the opinion of John Jay (a coauthor of the Federalist Papers, appointed chief justice of the Supreme Court in 1789) that those who own the country ought to govern it.

Nor at any moment in its history has America declared a lasting peace between the haves and the have-nots. Temporary cessations of hostilities, but no permanent closing of the moral and social divide between debtor and creditor. The notion of a classless society derives its credibility from the relatively few periods in the life of the nation during which circumstances encouraged social readjustment and experiment—in the 1830s, 1940s, and 1950s, again in the 1940s, 1950s, and 1960s—but for the most part the record will show the game securely rigged in favor of the rich, no matter how selfish or stupid, at the expense of the poor, no matter how innovative or entrepreneurial. Within the political arenas of the United States the haves and the have-nots have been more or less violently at odds since they provided Jefferson and Hamilton with their arguments about the formation of a national bank. During the last thirty years of the nineteenth century and the first thirty years of the twentieth, class conflict presented the newspaper mills with their best and brightest headlines—railroad company thugs quelling labor unrest in the industrial East, the

Ku Klux Klan lynching Negroes in the rural South, the U.S. Army exterminating American Indians on the Western plains.

To acknowledge the numerous flaws in the American scheme of things, in the past as well as the present tense, doesn't disavow or negate the numerous triumphs of its political and commercial enterprise, or the many and magnanimous proofs of its humanity to man. To the contrary. Democracy assumes conflict not only as the normal but also as the necessary condition of its existence, the structure of the idea resembling a suspension bridge dependent upon a balance between countervailing forces. We squander the worth of our inheritance if we don't know how or why it was accumulated, against what odds, with what force of the imagination and which powers of its expression.

Take by way of both example and precept the long and uneasy life of Roger Williams, who was born in London around 1603 within sight of Shakespeare's Globe Theatre and died bankrupt at Providence, Rhode Island in 1683, his property destroyed by Narragansett Indians. As a young man Williams studied the writings of Sir Francis Bacon and served as secretary to the jurist Sir Edward Coke, in the meantime learning to speak and write in Dutch and French as well as in Greek and Latin. In the 1620s he sided with Britain's Protestant parliament against the Catholic crown of King Charles I, and in 1631, under threat of imprisonment and debt for the crime of talking freely out of turn, he removed to the newly founded Puritan colony on Massachusetts Bay.

Becoming known for his too radical improvisations on the theme of conscience and his unorthodox pleadings from Scripture, he soon fell afoul of the authorities in Governor John Winthrop's shining city upon a hill. The settlement sought to embody the glory and the will of God, and any giving way to unsanctified expressions of feeling or thought was apt to result in the slicing off of the perp's ears.

Williams believed that man's dealings with God were not subject to government regulation, and in 1636, he was deemed to have committed both the spiritual sin of pride and a temporal act of rebellion. Condemned to deportation to a British prison,

Williams dodged the ship sent to carry out the sentence. Forced to abandon his home, wife, and two children, he departed on foot from Salem in January, overwintering in the company of Indians with whom he spoke in their own language, the only white man in America at the time capable of doing so. Making his way south to what is now the state of Rhode Island, Williams in 1636 established at Providence the first government anywhere in the world that granted its citizens the freedom of religious thought.

To read Williams's biography is to find him constantly at odds with the agents of the crown in England or the Puritan inspectors of souls in Massachusetts, to be reminded that what he called "soule liberty" doesn't fall, like pennies or a gentle rain, from heaven. To know something of Williams other than the statue on the second floor of the U.S. Senate is to understand why a morsel of genuine history is both valuable and rare, to know also that such a thing as a lost golden age is best seen as golden by nonresidents. Every age is an age of anxiety, subject to the humiliation of destabilizing change. Which is to say, as did Mark Twain, that although history doesn't repeat itself, it rhymes. Allow for the variant customs of the country as well as for the geopolitical repositionings on the map of time, and the conflicts going forward at the moment in Miami, Moscow, and Beijing, like those that enlivened the scaffolds of Jacobean London and the whipping posts of seventeenth-century Salem, are conflicts between time past and time future, between the inertia implicit in things as they are and the energy inherent in the hope of things as they might become.

Williams was the earliest of the progenitors of what now goes by the name of the American idea, and he paid a dear price for the venture. So did Thomas Paine, conceivably the greatest of America's founding spirits, about whom in the spring of 2002 I was asked to speak briefly to the Thomas Paine National Historical Association in New Rochelle, New York. The sponsors of the program assured me that the membership didn't expect anything difficult or scholarly, ten or fifteen minutes at the most, the literary equivalent of a laurel wreath to set upon the head of a statue. I ignored their advice. Aware of the fact that I would be talking to people apt to catch me up or out in any mistake with an anecdote or a date, and bearing in mind the lesson learned at Cambridge from the tutor passing the tea and the plum cake, I took the precaution of rereading Paine's pamphlets. Instead of finding myself in the presence of a marble portrait bust, I met a man writing in what he knew to be "the undisguised language of historical truth," leveling a fierce polemic against the corrupt monarchy of King George III that serves (238 years later, and with no more than a few changes of name and title) as a fair description of the self-satisfied plutocracy currently parading around Washington in the costume of a democratic republic.

To read Tom Paine is to encounter the high-minded philosophy of the eighteenth-century Enlightenment rendered in words simple enough to be readily understood. Other writers of the period, among them Hamilton, Madison, and Adams, address the rich and well-educated members of their own social class; Paine talks to ship chandlers and master mechanics, and in place of a learned treatise he substitutes the telling phrase and the memorable aphorism—"Society is produced by our wants and government by our wickedness"; "The mind once enlightened cannot again become dark"; "Those who expect to reap the blessings of freedom must, like men, undergo the fatigues of supporting it."

The abundance of Paine's writings flows from the spring of his optimism, and during the twenty years of his engagement in both the American and French revolutions, he counts himself a "friend of [the world's] happiness." No matter what question Paine takes up (the predicament of women, the practice of slavery, or the organization of governments), he approaches it with a generous impulse and benevolent purpose. Distrustful of all things "monarchical or aristocratical," invariably in favor of a new beginning and a better deal, Paine speaks to his hope for the rescue of mankind in a voice that hasn't been heard in American politics for the last forty years. By comparison with the machine-made cant pushed forth by the government now in Washington, the old words bring with them the sound of water in a desert:

> When it shall be said in any country in the world, my poor are happy; neither ignorance nor distress is to be found among them;

my jails are empty of prisoners, my streets of beggars; the aged are not in want, the taxes are not oppressive ... when these things can be said, then may that country boast its constitution and its government.

Tyranny, like hell, is not easily conquered; yet we have this consolation with us, that the harder the conflict, the more glorious the triumph. What we obtain too cheap, we esteem too lightly: it is dearness only that gives everything its value.[4]

Born a subject of the British crown, Paine first landed in America in the autumn of 1774, all but penniless at the age of thirty-seven, a proven failure as both a tradesman and an excise officer, on leave from two lost marriages, without any education other than the one he had gleaned from a rural grammar school. Finding work as a journalist, a profession as new to him as were the streets of Philadelphia, Paine soon demonstrated an impassioned talent for composing political broadsides. He wrote one of the first objections to slavery ever published in the American colonies, also one of the earliest essays protesting the denial to women of the same civil rights awarded to men. Subsequent to the skirmishes at Lexington and Concord in the spring of 1775, Benjamin Rush encouraged Paine to turn his attention to the dispute with Britain, and on January 10, 1776 (fourteen months after arriving in America on a ship that also brought with it a cargo of one hundred indentured servants), he published *Common Sense*.

The pamphlet is the founding document of the American Revolution. Taking as his premise the seditious statement that "as in absolute governments the king is law, so in free countries, the law ought to be king," Paine forced the point of his argument well

---

4 Some years ago in its editorial page, the *New York Times* handed down the ruling that "great publications magnify beyond measure the voice of any single writer." The sentence employed the wrong verb. The instruments of the media amplify a voice, serving much the same purpose as the loudspeakers in a ballpark or a prison. What magnifies a voice is the force of mind and its power of expression, which is why Shakespeare's plays still draw a crowd in Central Park.

beyond the limits of protest voiced by the propertied malcontents in Massachusetts and Virginia complaining of Parliament's trade and settlement restrictions. Not enough, said Paine, merely to reach the accommodation of an "ordered liberty" with the agents of the English crown. Better to separate completely from "the natural disease of monarchy," an unjust "form of government, which so impiously invades the prerogative of heaven." It was, said Paine, "the birthday of a new world," and the time was at hand to do away with hereditary successions, class privilege, entitled aristocracy. Received with the shock of excited recognition by readers everywhere in the colonies, *Common Sense* ran through printings of 150,000 copies in six months, its success certain proof of a national resolve that persuaded Thomas Jefferson to borrow Paine's reasoning when he came to the writing of the Declaration of Independence in July 1776.

During the course of the Revolutionary War, Paine countered the frequent news of American defeat in battle with the composition of *The Crisis Papers* which were passed from hand to hand around military campfires at Valley Forge ("These are the times that try men's souls"), but the victory at Yorktown brought him little else except the prize of unemployment. The politicians and propertied gentlemen acquiring their newfound American estate looked upon Paine as a troublesome idealist on too familiar terms with the lower orders of society, not to be trusted with the task of dividing up the spoils.

Without an audience for a rhetoric suddenly become both suspect and irrelevant, Paine sailed for Europe in 1787, still bent on his great project of political transformation and social change. In England he wrote *Rights of Man*, a treatise anticipating much of the legislation that showed up 150 years later in the United States under the rubric of Franklin Roosevelt's New Deal—government welfare payments to the poor, pensions for the elderly, public funding of education, reductions of military spending, an estate tax limiting the amount of an inheritance. The book appeared in two volumes, in 1791–92, instantly and immensely popular with the reading public not only in England but also in America and France. The sale of 500,000 copies ranked it the best-selling book of the entire eighteenth century and prompted the British government to charge its author with sedition and to declare him an outlaw. Aristocrats affixed to the heels of their boots coins struck in Paine's image so that while walking to and fro on London's cobblestone streets they might grind into dust the face and fear of anarchy.

When Paine crossed the Channel to Calais in the summer of 1792, a rejoicing crowd of newly enfranchised citizens accorded him a hero's welcome. To the makers of the French Revolution, *Rights of Man* bore the stamp of divine revelation, and as testimony of their appreciation they promptly elected Paine to the political assembly then at work in Paris on the construction of yet another new republic. He remained in France for the rest of the century, becoming, together with Voltaire and Benjamin Franklin, one of the most revered figures of the Enlightenment. Napoleon Bonaparte thought him the great contemporary apostle of liberty, fraternity, and equality, to whom there "ought to be erected," in every city in the universe, "a statue of gold."

The opinion was not shared by the Federalist Party that had come to power in America during the decade of the 1790s, and on leafing through the record of Paine's life and times before going to New Rochelle in May 2002, I didn't find it hard to guess why. John Adams's summing-up of Paine's character—"a mongrel between pig and puppy, begotten by a wild boar on a bitch wolf"; "that insolent blasphemer of things sacred, and transcendent libeler of all that is good"—strikes the preferred tone of our own 113th Congress wishing to charge Edward Snowden with treason for publicizing the extent of the NSA's gathering of intelligence both domestic and foreign.

Nor do I find it strange that Paine remains in the attic of oblivion. He's been there since 1809, the year he was buried, as unceremoniously as a dog in a ditch, in unhallowed ground on his farm in New Rochelle. Sixteen years earlier in Paris he had removed himself from the American pantheon by writing *The Age of Reason*, the pamphlet in which he ridiculed the fiction of an established church and remarked on "the unrelenting vindictiveness with which more than half the Bible is filled." On his return from France to Baltimore in 1802, the Federalist newspapers in Boston damned him as a "drunkard" and "a brutal infidel."

Throughout the whole of the nineteenth century preachers everywhere in the country brandished the name of "Old Tom" Paine as a synonym for the devil; Teddy Roosevelt characterized his writing as that of a "filthy little atheist." Over the last two hundred years only five monuments have been erected in Paine's honor on American soil, none of them in Washington, DC. Not that Paine has been without his admirers; Abraham Lincoln ("I never tire of reading Paine"); Walt Whitman ("... was among the best and truest of men"); Thomas A. Edison ("... our greatest political thinker"). All character witnesses of some distinction, of course, but Paine's plain and forthright speaking is out of tune with our own contemporary political discourse, which for the most part is the gift for saying nothing.

The discussion at the moment lacks force and meaning because it is a commodity engineered, like baby formula and Broadway musicals, to dispose of any and all unwonted risk. The forces of property occupying both the government and the news media don't rate politics as a serious enterprise, certainly not one worth the trouble to suppress. It is the wisdom of the age—shared by Democrat and Republican, by forlorn idealist and anxious realist—that money rules the world, transcends the boundaries of sovereign states, waters the tree of liberty, serves as the light unto the nations. What need of statesmen, much less politicians, when it isn't really necessary to know their names or remember what they say? The country is asked to vote in November for television commercials because only in the fanciful time-zone of a television commercial can the American democracy still be seen or said to exist.

The packaging of politics as light entertainment sells the lame-duck cynicism that serves as proof of being in on the joke, alert to the stupidity in Washington and the swindling in Wall Street, on pace with Rush Limbaugh and Stephen Colbert. Cue the laugh track, enjoy the show. History is fate; the way of the world is inevitable.

Except it isn't. Like the attributing of the catastrophe of World

War I to the forces of blind, implacable abstraction (economic, social, and political), the notions of historical inevitability propose a story with no people in it. The course of events is always contingent, as likely to turn on a shift in the weather as on the accidents of human character and personality. If a heavy fog doesn't drift into New York Harbor on the morning of August 30, 1776, George Washington's retreating army, trapped by the British in Brooklyn Heights, doesn't make good its escape in rowboats across the East River to Manhattan, and if the army doesn't survive, neither does the American Revolution. Nor does the revolution succeed without the assistance of France, which wasn't a gift from Adam Smith's invisible hand. The Treaty of Alliance followed from the particular quality of Benjamin Franklin's intelligence that allowed him to persuade an absolute monarch to bankrupt his kingdom in order to finance a democratic rebellion.[5]

None of us dies in the country in which he or she was born. George Washington's America was not the America known to Abraham Lincoln, much less the ones that elected General Dwight D. Eisenhower or Barack Obama to the White House, a fact of which I was duly reminded at my fortieth college reunion in the spring of 1996. The after-dinner speakers marveled at the ways in which things had changed since our arrival on campus in the autumn of Ike's 1952 election, when a hamburger sold for twenty cents, a field-level box at Yankee Stadium for five dollars. They spoke of invisible Negroes becoming visibly black and nice girls slipping off the silk of feminine restraint, of supersonic air travel, homosexuals popping out of closets, the assassinations of John Kennedy, Robert Kennedy, and Martin Luther King Jr., manned spaceflight, the Vietnam War, the transplanted kidney and the artificial heart, Watergate, the end of the Cold War, the Internet.

The class secretary closed down the panel discussions by saying that no generation on the college's alumni books had weathered so heavy a storm of social and technological change. He didn't

---

5 The vagaries of human character cut both ways. Had it not been for the fear and trembling in the minds of not one but all of the dysfunctional statesmen in Europe in July 1914, the catastrophe that was World War I might never have come to pass.

put the motion to a vote, none of the straw hats in the room being inclined to abridge the self-congratulatory flow of beer and sympathy, and it wasn't until somewhat later in the evening that I ran the numbers. On the day that I received my diploma in 1956, the class then celebrating its fortieth reunion had arrived on campus in 1912, the year that sank the *Titanic*. The turns of event over the next forty-four years encompassed, among other occasions worthy of note, World War I, the Russian Revolution, American women granted the right to vote, Prohibition, the stock market crash of 1929, the Great Depression, World War II, the Holocaust, the atomic bomb.

America's Founding Fathers exploited the resource of history as diligently as their descendants exploited the lands and forests of the Ohio River Valley and the Trans-Mississippi frontier. They framed their several envisionings of a republic (Jefferson's and Paine's as well as those of Hamilton and Adams) on blueprints found in their readings of Cicero and Plutarch. So in its turn the Italian Renaissance derived from the rediscovery of classical antiquity. The latter progression supplied the scholar Stephen Greenblatt with the premise for his best-selling book *The Swerve*, published in 2011 but accounting for the death and resurrection of 7,400 lines of lyric but unrhymed verse, *On the Nature of Things*, composed by the Roman poet Titus Lucretius Carus in the first century B.C. Greenblatt subtitled his book, *How the World Became Modern*, attributing the metamorphosis in large part to the recovery of Lucretius's poem in a German monastery in 1417 by Poggio Bracciolini, Italian humanist, Vatican functionary, and apostolic scribe.

Lucretius had infused his poem with the thought of Epicurus, the Greek philosopher teaching his students in Athens in the fourth century B.C. that the elementary particles of matter ("the seeds of things") are eternal and that the purpose of life is the embrace of beauty and pleasure. Everything that exists—the sun and the moon, water-flies, ziggurats, mother and the flag—is made of atoms in motion, constantly colliding and combining with one another in an inexhaustible variety of form and substance. The universe consists of "atoms and void and nothing else." No afterlife, no divine retribution or reward, nothing other than a vast turmoil of creation and destruction, a ceaseless making and remaking of despots and matinee idols, of equations and songs.

To the modern mind atomic theory is old news, as it was to the school of Epicurean thought during the reign of Augustus Caesar. Christianity dispatched it to hell, reconfiguring the pursuit of pleasure as sin, the meaning of life as pain. By recovering *De rerum natura* to the land of the living, pooling its resources with those dormant in the works of Ovid, Seneca, and Plato, the Renaissance redrafted the contract between man and nature, its embrace of truth as beauty and beauty as truth made manifest in the glory of its painting, sculpture, music, architecture, and literature. Over the course of the next six centuries Lucretius' poem finds further development and expression in Machiavelli's political theory, Montaigne's essays, Shakespeare's plays, Newton's mathematics, and what is now known as the wonder of free-market capitalism.

The circumstances at hand in the early years of the twenty-first century suggest that the time is ripe for another redrafting of the contract between man and nature, with any luck of a magnitude comparable to the one that gave birth to the Renaissance. For the past fifty years it has been apparent to the lookouts on the watchtowers of Western civilization that the finite resources of the planet cannot accommodate either the promise or the theory of infinite growth, a.k.a. the American dream. Too many people coming into the world, no miracle of loaves and fishes with which to feed the multitude. The simple arithmetic underwrites the vast sea of troubles listed under the headings of worldwide environmental degradation and economic collapse. I read the relevant policy papers—on climate change, unredeemable debt, the extinction of species, the wars of all against all—and I notice that they tend toward an increasingly insistent awareness that if left to its own devices a global consumer society must devour the earth. Not with malice aforethought, but because it knows not what else to do.

The intimations of mortality lurking in the depths of the policy papers lead in turn to the recognition of the capitalist economy as a historical construct, and therefore, like a college reunion or the heads on Mt. Rushmore, a collision of atoms en route to recombination in the void. A story with a beginning (in late sixteenth-century Holland), a middle (the eighteenth- and nineteenth-century industrial revolutions in England and America), and an end, foreshadowed by the financial convulsions of the past twenty years at all points on the compass of the international commodity markets. Sensing the approach of maybe something terrible slouching toward Wall Street to be born, the guardians at the gate look for salvation to technologies as yet undreamed of by man or machine. My guess is that they're looking in the wrong direction.

An acquaintance with history doesn't pay the rent or predict the outcome of a November election, but it is the fund of energy and hope that makes possible the revolt against what G. K. Chesterton once called "the small and arrogant oligarchy of those who merely happen to be walking about." The Roman historian Livy likened history to a collection of "fine things to take as models" and "base things, rotten through and through, to avoid." The contemporary American novelist John Crowley carries the thought another two thousand years along the road to who knows where, suggesting that the past is "the new future ... its lessons not simple or singular, a big landscape of human possibility, generative, inexhaustible."

I take him at his word. The future is nonexistent, the present come and gone too quickly to establish a mailing address. Where else does one live if not in a house of straw made from the reshaping of the once-upon-a-time? What is it possible to change if not the past?

Index